I Belong To Glasgow.

To dearest Alastair.

Hope you enjoy the read .... and our shared history.

Ian.

Also by Ron Culley:

The Kaibab Resolution (Kennedy & Boyd, 2010)

I Belong to Glasgow

Ron Culley

WITH A FOREWORD BY

SIR ALEX FERGUSON

The Grimsay Press

The Grimsay Press
an imprint of
Zeticula
57 St Vincent Crescent
Glasgow
G3 8NQ
Scotland.

http://www.thegrimsaypress.co.uk
admin@thegrimsaypress.co.uk

Copyright © Ron Culley 2011
First published 2011

ISBN-13 978-1-84530-100-2

This book celebrates the memory of my parents and grandparents and is dedicated with unending love to my marvellous wife Jean and my four wonderful boys, Ron, Campbell, Conor and Ciaran.

Foreword

I published my own biography, 'Managing My Life', in 1999 and the first sentence reads... "No matter what kind of journey we make of life, where we started out will always be part of us." I 'started out' in the shadow of the shipyard crane, in Govan, Glasgow and it's been a source of enormous pride to me ever since. It rooted me, gave me my values and my early friendships – many of which continue to this day. Geographically, Ron Culley started out next door to Govan, in the housing estate of Pollok where many Govanites moved in the fifties and sixties as housing was pulled down to deal with the slum conditions and provide new 'homes fit for heroes' after the Second World War.

However, when the city planners built these new estates, they focussed upon meeting housing needs and initially forgot all about the amenities which go to make a place a community. Few shops were built. No schools, cinemas, football pitches, swimming pools or medical facilities. So it was hardly a surprise when the 'van culture' Ron talks about where everything was sold from the back of a grocery, butchers' or fish van, didn't meet the demands of the new residents and many continued to travel to Govan to visit the cinema, watch or play football or do the week's shopping.

As I did in my own book, Ron comments upon the religious bigotry that defiled our city and talks about the gang culture that existed when he was growing up in the 50's and 60's. He recalls the music and comedy of the day as Alma Cogan gave way to The Beatles and Ted Ray surrendered to the comedy of the Goons and the Pythons. But what shines from the book is the author's love of Glasgow – something that anyone born or raised in the city will understand and share.

One of my passions is helping people achieve their ultimate potential, whether it's an international footballer or a wee kid from my old school, Govan High. Ron was brought up in a single-parent family in Pollok, was expelled from school and flirted with adolescent lawlessness before his social worker helped him buckle down, obtain a belated education and go on to spend twenty three years of his forty year period of public service in Glasgow as a Chief Executive of one key city organisation or another. I think it's fair to say that he's fought his way through adversity and achieved a hell of a lot in his sixty years in the city.

Now retired, Ron has taken to writing. A novel is already on the shelves of bookshops and a sequel is to be published next year. I'm delighted he's taken the opportunity of sharing his love of Glasgow with readers through the medium of this book. 'I belong to Glasgow' is a proud claim that millions of people over the generations have made. Ron's book will certainly bring back memories for many people and, I hope, act as an inspiration for those who feel they have yet the ability to achieve more in life.

Sir Alex Ferguson CBE.
Manager, Manchester United Football Club.

Contents

Illustrations

1. Just so we understand each other.

Life is the sum of all your choices. -
Albert Camus

This book has taken more than a decade to write; deliberately, as I wanted it to capture events which included those leading up to my 60th birthday. I started to write in the second Millennium and finished in the third. The early words were written by a still athletic man with a shock of thick, dark hair and were concluded by a barrel-chested man with somewhat lesser amounts of white. I moved from being a father, to being a father and a grandfather when young Arran was born to my son Ron and his wife Lisa in September 2008. So, it's taken a while. Deliberately.

A few years ago, I wrote a novel, first called *The New Guards*, now published as *The Kaibab Resolution*, and had enjoyed the experience immensely. I'd found my ability to find time to write to be difficult due to pressures of work and the demands of family obligations. I therefore wrote only intermittently and usually when travelling or on holiday.

My initial intention upon setting out to write what appears before you now was only to be a short-term palliative, designed to scratch a creative itch, as I'd no new story to tell and writing about a few episodes from my childhood seemed an interesting way to deal with this. However, as these few words grew to chapters, I decided to make something more of it, telling myself that the relative absence of any real oral tradition in my family might best be addressed by setting down an account of some of the experiences that shaped me. I intended that it should be reflective, well-crafted, enjoyable and should conclude at or near the point of my retirement.

Nor are these chapters of my life precisely linear. Upon re-crafting my words prior to publication, I noticed that in common with my verbal style, I am prone to taking the scenic route where I find this interesting. The author and political satirist Henry Fielding, in introducing his novel *Tom Jones*, puts it rather better than me when he alerted his readers, as I do mine, that *"I think it proper before we proceed any further together, to acquaint thee that I intend to digress through this whole history as I see occasion."*

Nor will I permit criticism of my use of grammar in these pages. Although roundly regarded as something of a pedant in these matters, I've come to realise that grammar is a tool to be used in assisting understanding. So while you won't find many sentences finishing with a preposition or many infinitives split, you *will* come across the odd sentence beginning with the words 'and' or 'but' and will find commas used to mark rhythm or emphasis. I've found a new freedom in writing, while remaining true to the essentials.

Biography and autobiography have always been the forms of reading to which I've been most drawn. That said, until I started to write, it never really occurred to me that direct speech attributed to characters in any biography must, by definition, reflect a version of what took place with the probable exception of one or two episodes. And so it is here. Certain of the dialogues that are reflected here are pretty close to the mark, especially in those years most adjacent to my writing. Others merely reflect the story as it happened in my head.

I've attempted to reflect the accurate realities of that about which I write; even where I've been more than somewhat embarrassed about my behaviour. However, I have taken the liberty of changing one or two names as I'm aware of the inappropriateness of visiting my tale upon those who might prefer their role in my various adventures to remain confidential. On occasion, despite the knowledge that my rendition of an event where I had insight would make more interesting reading, I've resisted the temptation to report it lest those more newsworthy stories take precedence over my more humdrum task of telling my story. I seek not to embarrass anyone beyond one or two eejits whose behaviour deserves an airing.

Where I cite others' work, I have acknowledged this but if there are inaccuracies or mistakes the faults are mine, as are the apologies.

Inevitably, vanity will influence my words even where there has been no overt intention to do so. I was not the white Pele as a footballer... not the most reliable friend... not the most effective public servant, but I've usually tried to be the best I could be whilst acknowledging my very obvious frailties.

I've not been the best father or husband. I've been a good provider rather than a nurturing influence within the family. A disciplinarian rather than an educator. Too often after returning home from work, I headed upstairs to my home office and my computer rather than the back garden with my kids.

Over the piece, I was pretty lousy around the house, too. I've never cooked or washed up much, ironed or swept. My occasional foray into these tasks was usually predicated upon a prelude to an apology or a request for a pass-out to meet my pals in the pub; usually a pass-out.

Fortunately, despite my idiocy, those around me seemed to have coped sufficiently. I've not lived an unexamined life and I've reflected ruefully on what difference it might have made if my familial responsibilities had been rather more... well, familial. Over the years I've found it hard to shrug off my work ethic 'off duty' and have been impossible on family holidays; at least during the earlier days of a family vacation, attacking an opportunity to move to a shorter airport queue with all the intensity of Tom chasing Gerry, frying pan in hand, legs all-a-blur. I've pounced intemperately on the kids' misdemeanours over dinner as I would were I pursuing a flawed argument with an adversary. If the family aren't punctual in leaving for a day's outing or are indecisive about where to eat lunch, my impatience knows no bounds and I become a Glaswegian version of Basil Fawlty. Relaxing hasn't been my strong point. Coping with my own, skewed, personal frustrations has been problematic. Writing this book has at least had the value of keeping me out of everyone's hair until a gradual holiday easing crept over me.

When I wrote *The Kaibab Resolution* (available, if not now from *all* good bookshops, at least via the internet from Amazon and other good web sites), I acknowledged the help given me by my two eldest sons, Ron and Campbell. *I Belong To Glasgow* was written during a period when my youngest children, Conor and Ciaran, were variously babies, toddlers, young boys and young men. I apologise to them for my early morning rises during holidays to write this and remain grateful to them and to my wife Jean for their forbearance as our holidays were eroded by my 'writing time' expanding into their day. However, it's not every child who can attest to the fact that their dad taught them to swim in the pool by shouting distracted instructions from the balcony of the holiday apartment while balancing a laptop on his knee.

I'd also like to thank my good friends, John McManus, Gordon Maclennan and his wife Mhairi who acted as guardians and editors of various elements of these contents. I'm indebted.

Almost from the commencement of the project, the book was to be called '*I Belong To Glasgow*' because of the important role the city has played in making me who I am. The words of the Will Fyfe song somehow sum up the feeling of attachment to the place of my birth. I *belong* to the city; I haven't just lived and worked there.... and Glasgow *belongs* to me...its many deficiencies are dissolved in the heady liquor of partisan loyalties. My city right or wrong!

This book is designed to inform readers of events that shaped me and to an extent therefore, the circumstances that helped mould other Glaswegians as well. It also permits those of my family and friends who are interested, to remember and to reminisce at the folly and humour that so characterised my stumbling attempts at steering a course through my life.

So let my family understand, my old friends reminisce and new readers enjoy the tale.

Ron Culley
Variously:
Glasgow, Sitges, Orlando,
Tenerife, Albufeira, Lido de Jesolo,
Palma, Salou, Benodet, Havana,
Brussels, Tavira, Stornoway,
Stockholm, Manhattan, Puerto Rico,
Grand Turk, US Virgin Islands,
Istanbul, Rome, Athens
and the West Coast Main Line.
1997 – 2010.

2. Angus McKay Doesn't Cry.

If you're gonna screw up, do it while you're young. The older you get, the harder it is to bounce back.
Forrest Gump.

My father's drunken forefinger stirred the small change in the cupped palm of his left hand and slowly assembled sufficient coin to permit him to call for one for the road.

"Have you no' had enough, Ronnie?"

"It's Friday night. It's been a long week and I'm just needin' a wee chaser before I go up the road". He proffered the change to the barman. "A whisky wi' a wee drop water, please, and a couple of pints for this pair."

Ronnie Culley, my father, took his glass and surveyed the crowded bar before turning to his two drinking companions. "I've enjoyed the chat, boys, but I'm away up the road. I'm going to get an earful when I get up the road." He glanced at his watch and grimaced. "Half nine? I'm dead!"

He lifted the whisky to his lips. "I'll see you two tomorrow. All the best, boys." The whisky slipped down in a single gulp. "I'm off."

It was 1959, and I was nine years old.

Early the following morning, my mother woke me from my sleep. She was in tears, kneeling beside my bed, unable to speak. All she could do was tousle my hair and eventually bring herself to say, "You're the man of the family now, Ronald." It was clear that something was very wrong and eventually she managed through half finished sentences and much wailing to convey to me that my father had been killed.

He was thirty four years old.

Earlier that evening, my father had been drinking with his brother Arthur and a mutual friend. He'd arrived home having taken one too many after work but with a box of chocolate Maltesers as a peace offering, he figured he'd be forgiven. He was wrong. The family door was locked and after a few shouted attempts to persuade my mother to open up, he shrugged his shoulders, left the chocolates on the doorstep and returned to 'Jeannie Gebbies', an old country pub just outside Barrhead about a mile away from our home in Craigbank, Glasgow. More drink was consumed before he left the pub on his own for the second time, took a short-cut across the railway line and was hit by the London train out-bound from the city.

My clear memory of the subsequent early morning event was of my mother being even more upset because of my refusal to cry. I didn't cry upon being told and I've never cried about it since. My two brothers, Alistair and Campbell both broke their hearts when Mum told them, but I remember her taking my stony face as an indication that I didn't love my father or didn't understand, and making a big issue of it to the crowd of adults which had by now congregated in our home. They started too. "Ronald, you're father's never coming back. Don't you understand, son? He's dead." I was devastated. Trying to take it all in but something inside me refused to let anyone see my pain or comfort me.

None of us kids attended his funeral. We were shunted off to a neighbour's for some reason, but I remember my Grandparents picking up a copy of the now defunct *Evening Citizen*, where there were both details of the funeral and a small article about a Pollok man, Ronald Frank Culley who had been killed after having been hit by a train. After they'd put it down and left the room I read the small article again and again.

Thirty-four years old. One of the earliest objectives I remember giving myself was to survive until I was older than my dad's age at his death. I later decided that

that was a bit too ambitious and took a deep breath of satisfaction when at age thirteen, I celebrated becoming a teenager. Who'd have thought I'd have achieved such a grand old age! First mission accomplished.

I never really knew my father. I was born on the second of February 1950 in Glasgow. Dad was born in 1925. He would have been fourteen when the Second World War started and twenty when it ended. He may have been called up but although there was a rich oral history within the family, this was a subject which was never discussed. He was certainly in uniform for some of the time I remember him and, following his demob, he worked as a shirt manufacturer's clerk in a business located down near the Broomielaw, but my whole recollection of Dad is very sketchy. My young brother Campbell came across some old black and white photographs which at least help me remember what he looked like. God bless us. He looks like me!

I was born into a family which would have appreciated the early impacts of a Labour administration - particularly in terms of health and housing, cheaper electricity and the phasing out of war rationing. On the 23rd of February, a few weeks after I first saw the light of day, Clement Atlee won another election, albeit on a very tight majority of five seats, and was supplanted by Winston Churchill a year later. I had to wait until I was fourteen, in 1964,when the Profumo affair saw Harold Wilson recapture the nation for the people's party.

For a few years around the time I started primary school, the Culley family were housed one floor up in a dank terraced miners' cottage at 72 Donaldson Street in Kirkintilloch, a small town to the north of Glasgow. Before and after that we were brought up in Pollok, within the city boundaries. Glasgow was recovering from the war years and was still dressed in hodden grey. The five of us,

Mum, Dad, me and my two brothers all lived with Nana and Grandpa, my Mum's parents, at 7 Glenlora Terrace. It was a great house, rented from Glasgow Corporation. Three bedrooms, livingroom, kitchen and bathroom, a back and front door, garden back and front and nice neighbours.

Across the street at number 6 was Angus McKay. For years he was used by my Gran as an exemplar. "Angus McKay doesn't cry. Angus McKay always takes his medicine. Angus McKay comes in as soon as he's called". As I got to know him I realised I could get the better of him with a ball at my feet and somehow he was never as potent again. The lesson I learned from that, however, was that in childhood, you just believed without question what your parents told you. At least *I* did. When told by my mother that the dragon under my bed had gone away and wouldn't be back, I would fall into a deep, secure sleep. I've used that reality many times myself since I've kids of my own. Parental reassurance.

Upstairs was Barclay Smith, a boy of mixed ethnicity, a couple of years older than me. An adopted child, he was very talented on the piano and attended a fee paying school. At the time we thought nothing of it. So he goes to a posh school! Later we were to wonder how the family managed to meet the cost. Years later in my late thirties I went to a hypnotherapist, to stop my then alarming propensity to swear conversationally, and it was our Barclay who had a wee office at Charing Cross into whose room I was ushered.

Well done him! He completely stopped me cursing for two years and this so impressed my pals that some of them visited him for problems with weight control and smoking. Anyway, feigned or not, he said he didn't remember me, and I suppose that was reasonable, as although he lived upstairs, I don't think once ever did we see him other than him going to and from his school. He certainly never played with us. Shame really. He seemed a nice guy. I worry that his adoptive parents were concerned that these wee ruffians down the stair would have given him a hard time over the colour of his skin, his posh school or his ability to play classical piano. She needn't have worried. The only way kids were stratified in our street was in their ability to play football with a tennis ball.

Neighbours pretty much were able to come and go as they pleased and our home always resembled a small community centre with adults sitting round the coal fire drinking never-ending cups of tea. My Gran was the most popular person in the street as our home was the first in the area to have a television, and my brothers and I held court as the three boys who could make the life and death decision over whether pals got to come in to see the early black and white flickerings of *Muffin the Mule*; *Bill and Ben, The Flowerpot Men* or later, *Dr. Who*. Sunday afternoons were special as *The Adventures of Robin Hood* were screened. I don't remember anyone ever being refused permission and I don't remember any misbehaviour requiring expulsion. Sure, we had the usual lively debates about whether the Daleks could rule the world if they couldn't even climb stairs, but by and large the then cultural imperative to obey your elders politely and unquestioningly limited the likelihood of overly robust behaviour within the house; that, and the threat of exclusion from what was pretty much the only place you could go to see the TV.

These were joyful, easy, sunny days. Street decisions were always made merely by saying 'eeny meenie miney mo', football cards in the spokes of a wheel turned any bike into a motorbike, and scrapes and bruises were all cured by means of a parental kiss. But football was everything. *En route* to our school, Gowanbank Primary some 100 yards away, we kicked around a tennis ball during playtime, lunch hours, back home after dinner (or tea, as we called it, dinner was at lunchtime) until the light faded or we were called in to prepare for bed (never homework). "Angus McKay always comes in as soon as he's called".

Although football was king, we always had a range of alternative distractions that suggested themselves from time to time. One was building bogies. Usually this was inspired by one of us coming across a discarded pram whose wheels could yet be used for other purposes. We'd set to it, searching out a sturdy plank of wood and a couple of spars as axles. A piece of wood for a seat, a rope to provide for guide-reins and we'd be off to the Red Hills; a deserted piece of land adjacent to the Levern Burn which were suitably undulating in order to provide us with the required gradients. The Red Hills were merely the result of discarded shale from the mineworkings below them. The entire area was set upon a land mass riddled with mines, rendering much of it undevelopable, fit only for greening and landscaping in later years when housing developments were considered in the peripheral environs of Pollok. A dump, but when we were young, they were the Elysian fields.

Time and again we'd return home in tears as the bogies were inevitably driven to destruction, the final collision almost always causing its driver a similar amount of damage.

When not causing actual bodily harm, we acted out the dramas experienced by the various action heroes about whom we read in the colourful DC comics of the age. *Superman, Batman and Robin, Spiderman and the Hulk* were all required reading and few rainy nights passed without the doorbell ringing and one of our pals inviting us to swap comics. It was always a great bartering experience as the skill was not only in securing a comic you hadn't read but in calculating which one your pal really wanted so you could up the ante and declare that *that* particular comic required three comics in exchange.

Personal danger came during those many moments in play when we re-enacted the comic stories of the previous evening. Most superheroes wore capes and the nearest we could get to emulating these gods was to wear our duffle coats in a manner whereby only the hood was affixed to our body, attached to our head. It passed muster as an *ersatz* Superman costume, but the peril lay in being apprehended in flight by a pal as by grabbing any part of the duffle coat; the caped crusader's head was almost torn from his shoulders. Thank goodness that whiplash injuries hadn't been invented in the 1950s.

Another place we'd visit was the Corkerhill Railway Village a couple of miles away. In December 1896, the Glasgow & South Western Railway Company opened its new Corkerhill depot on its Paisley Canal line, taking its name from the nearby Corkerhill Farm. The depot was built to relieve overcrowding in the engine sheds at St Enoch Station and provided facilities for the fuelling and servicing of locomotives. Because of the depot's then rural location, the G&SWR also built a small village of two-storey tenements for employees and their families. They closed it in 1971 and built a community of tenemental properties, that suffered from all of the deficiencies of post-war Glasgow building, and they had to be demolished and rebuilt again in 2003.

It's now difficult to comprehend, but as young children, we were able to access the engine sheds and play on these sleeping giants, these huge railway engines which awaited maintenance or fuelling. Train drivers or firemen would merely ruffle our hair and ignore the fact that we were wandering around a spaghetti junction of rail tracks with points shifting and steam locomotives belching smoke and blowing whistles. It was immensely dangerous yet I remember no one being injured. We just used the place as a playground although our youthful, emerging native cunning knew better than to admit our pastime to our parents.

We began to take an interest in train-spotting at a time when there was still a measure of romance about the hobby. What I remember as 'Mallard', the fastest steam railway engine in the world (reaching 126 miles per hour in 1938), was used on the Glasgow-London line and we could witness this muscular beast powering out of Glasgow regularly. However, our interest ebbed as the era of the diesel train and electrification was in the ascendancy and there was absolutely no joy in writing down the number of identical locomotives which had none of the noisy, smoky drama of the sleek Mallard and its contemporaries. We lost interest and went back to football.

My two brothers were one and three years younger than me respectively. Campbell was always able to rely on his being the baby of the family although as he reached his teens, he became taller and better looking than either Alistair or myself. Alistair was always a wilder boy. He received some awful beatings from Dad for his misbehaviour but they seemed only to serve to make him more determined to upset everyone. On occasion, his chastisement was quite severe, the blows from Dad being delivered in an almost adult fashion. Alistair always fought back.

I found myself the diplomat in the family. Intervening to prevent further punishment or in calling Mum if the warriors paid no heed. I guess that all of us were closer to Mum and she, in turn, was close to Gran and Grandpa, her mother and father.

Hector and Madge McLeod were simply wonderful people in their own right. My Grandfather, Hector, was the gentlest man I have ever known. The worst expletive I ever heard him utter was *damp*. Much in the way the Irish use *feckin'* to embroider their invective without actually swearing, my Grandfather deployed *damp*. Irritations were a *damp* nuisance; a missing screwdriver was a *damp* mystery. He couldn't bring himself to utter even the word, *Damn*!

Hector spent almost his entire working life as a tram driver in Glasgow. Then, when the trams were removed from the streets he was transferred to the city's Subway, its underground train service, "the clockwork orange", from which he retired with his gold watch and long service medals when he was 65. He was of his age in that when he and Madge married, she never worked another day in her life. Her job, as was the case in those days, was solely to care for the family. Until then she had worked in Filshill Sweets in Bridgeton, the district in Glasgow from which she came. Hector came from Highland stock, from the Lochgilphead and Portskerra areas, but was himself born in Anderston in Glasgow.

One of the family myths which we were invited to accept was that Grandpa had an 'unusual' war. He would have been of an age when he'd have missed conscription - having been thirteen when the First World War started and seventeen when it ended. During the Second World War, he'd have been 38 years old and would have missed conscription again. That said, he was always reticent to discuss the war years, either because he was it was horrible and not the subject of dinner room conversation or because there was truth in his story that he was inclined towards pacifism.

Every so often, individually or as a threesome, us kids would gather in Gran's kitchen and would hear stories of the various adventures and misadventures of other family members and friends of the family. Gran was a great story teller. Hector was much more reticent. He'd chip in with an observation now and again but was seldom the one to do much of the talking. His rendition of his war years was simple.

"Well now, there I was, just driving my tram and, you know, I didn't think much of the war. My own father had telt me how all war was wrong so I just kept driving my tram."

He nevertheless spoke in some detail when prompted about driving his tram during the Clydebank blitz when the German *Luftwaffe* overnight reduced the town to rubble.

Always a humble, smiling man, he drew greatest pleasure from caring for his wife Madge, his two children; May (my mother; actually named Mary but Gran took the practical view that any Glaswegian named Mary would inevitably be called *Merry*, and shortened it to May on the basis that this truncated version would be more likely to be pronounced properly) and Hughie, my uncle. However, when his grandchildren came on the scene we each invariably won the battle for his affections. Every Friday when he got paid, he brought home a bar of tablet each for the three of us. It was delicious and a highlight of our week. He then gave his 'pay poke'; his weekly wage packet paid in cash, to Gran and that was the last he saw of his money.

Being a Glasgow Corporation tram driver, wearing his green uniform with a thin red stripe down the trouser leggings made him easily recognisable as a fellow employee, and he travelled to work on the bus free. Madge made him his 'pieces'; sandwiches in cheese or egg, along with a flask of hot water. This was accompanied by a tin cylinder containing tea leaves which, when inverted, had a small compartment at the other end which contained sugar. Milk was carried in a small aspirin bottle with a screw top. He didn't smoke or drink, and Madge made sure the daily paper was there for him when he got home so he didn't need to spend any cash during his working week. Tablet for the three grandweans was it; along with the latest edition of the *Beezer*, the *Tiger*, the *Topper*, the *Beano*, the *Rover* or the *Hotspur*, each of which were eagerly consumed to find out the latest antics of comic heroes such as Alf Tupper; the Tough of the Track or the Bash Street Kids.

And if ever I am caused to reflect upon the wonder of genetics, I only have to consider my earlier embarrassment as an adolescent when the family watched a romantic comedy on TV. At moments of sadness or comic romanticism throughout the movie and inevitably at its happy ending, Hector would weep with happiness at the good fortune of the male or female lead. My Grandfather would sit with tears quietly running down his face, much to my teenage awkwardness at this open display of his emotions. Nowadays, I permit a wry smile of recognition on my lips as I too, find myself caught up in my easily aroused emotions just as was he. Whether it's a romantic comedy, a speech at the inauguration of the first black President or a Scottish lament played with feeling on fiddle and accordion or on the pipes, I'm also easily and pleasantly moved to tears. I'm certain this behaviour will cause equal consternation amongst my own progeny before they, too, succumb.

While Hector was a mild man, Madge was the energy in the household. It was she who was in charge of maintaining discipline, organising budgets, approving requests to go out and play and limiting same. She was not untypical of the Glasgow matriarch at that time.

She loved to shop and over the years the household purse was managed well, permitting her to travel by bus each weekday in life, the seven miles from Pollok to Midland Street in Glasgow where she'd leave the bus and purchase some item or another to justify her trip. Many a time she'd return in the afternoon with a only a meagre prize such as a pair of socks or some sausages. She had lots of friends, all women, who would often accompany her on these expeditions. Most had husbands who didn't earn as consistently as Hector or whose smoking, drinking or gambling habit left the household poorer in monetary terms. Nevertheless, Gran was usually able to find a travelling companion, morning or afternoon.

The spendthrift in our household was Mum who, often without asking consent, made use of the accounts my Gran had in some of the city's larger retail stores such as Goldbergs or Bremners. Arguments would ensue when the monthly bill came in and Mum was called to account. However, for all the arguing about a coat she'd bought or whatever, the account was never denied her. If Gran really lost her temper and was being particularly upset at a purchase, Hector could always be relied upon to step in and forgive the purchase, permitting Gran to leave the field murmuring imprecations about Mum's generosity to herself. But peace was restored.

Mum was never rebuked however, if she'd bought something for us three boys. Both Mum and Gran invariably took the view that a purchase for one was a purchase for all three and I now have lots of photographs of the three of us in identical jumpers, coats, shirts, even skipped caps. There was no way any of us were to be encouraged to develop our own sartorial individuality. Gran differed in one respect though; she seldom if ever bought something that was put on our back immediately. A garment was always introduced to us in the living room and if it seemed to fit, was lovingly restored to its packaging and put away with care for use at some point in the future.

From time to time, Mum or Gran would take me with them into these grand *emporia*. Back in the mid-fifties, I found the act of payment and receipt redolent of what I imagined space age would look like. Each cash desk had a series of pneumatic tubes issuing from them and a metal container into which the cash and purchase note, when completed, was placed. With a loud slurping noise, it disappeared heavenward to be returned some minutes later with the change or a receipt contained within. I could only presume that they were piloted by tiny space aliens. How else might they know their way back to my Gran's position in the store?

In 1958, Mum, Dad and we three boys moved from Glenlora Terrace to the new housing scheme of Craigbank just half a mile up the road. Nowadays, 'scheme life' is somewhat derided as a failed experiment but the houses had inside toilets (as had Glenlora Terrace, if not Donaldson Street in Kirkintilloch), they had larger rooms, more of them, and in Craigbank, central heating; the first neighbourhood to be so provided in Glasgow. Initially, all of the subsequent and well documented problems were diminished in their importance because of the more obvious advantages contained within the dwelling space.

We grew up in a 'van culture' while Pollok was being built. Everything was available only from a van in the early years. Foodstuffs, milk, fish, ice cream, even bibles from Mr Crawford who lived through the wall from Gran and Grandpa at 254 Househillwood Road, and whose job was selling religious artefacts from a van which overnight he parked in the road outside my Gran's house. It was just accepted by us that selling bibles was as natural as selling fish. We never questioned it, or indeed how he made a living at it. I mean, there couldn't have been that much repeat business and what he sold on his regular visits, to our school gates at least, couldn't have kept his wife in nylons.

Primary Schools were established and operational but the state secondary school then was merely a collection of old Nissan huts; temporary accommodation located in four different sites which each remained in use for several years before Craigbank Secondary School proudly opened its doors for business in 1964.

In our younger years, we could never understand why our pals were taken from us from nine o'clock until a quarter to four and taught in another school. Catholic primary education was provided immediately across the road from our state school, Gowanbank Primary. Nothing much was made of this until in later Primary years when our Catholic friends were enjoying their Holidays of Obligation, a set of some five individual days peppered throughout the year when they were given a day off school to observe a religious festival (those of us in the state schools were given an extra week at the end of the seven weeks' summer holidays to compensate).

I can remember quite vividly standing in the playground wondering why our pals with whom we'd played football the previous night and with whom we'd play football again that night were standing outside the gates of the school throwing stones at us. Religious bigotry is instilled at a very young age in Glasgow and a major reason for the continued successful indoctrination of young minds is unquestionably the system of educational apartheid still operational in the city and the West of Scotland today.

It was a curious phenomenon, evident in our elders' behaviour as well. My Gran was a great 'windy hinger', a term used in Glasgow to denote those people (usually, but not always women) whose afternoons were spent leaning out of an open kitchen window, engaging their world in conversation.

In later years, Gran was very friendly with Mrs Taylor, mother of my pal Ian, who lived up the road at 268. It was never Mary …. always Mrs Taylor. Anyway, the pair of them would sit, night after night, in our living room laughing away at the day's events or watching a bit of telly and drinking constant cups of tea. They were great friends. On a Sunday morning, if Mrs Taylor happened to pass by *en route* to St Robert's Roman Catholic Church which stood on the corner almost exactly opposite Gran's house, Gran would acknowledge her passing by. "Morning, Mrs Taylor. Are you coming round tonight?"

"I certainly am, Mrs McLeod. Get you the kettle on and I'll be there at the back of seven. There's snooker on the telly tonight."

"The back of seven it is then, Mrs Taylor", before muttering *sotto voce*, "Fenian *get!*" Simply astonishing.

Because of the huge St Robert's chapel located across the road from us, we were permitted a glance into elements of Roman Catholic ritual normally then denied members of other faiths. Some days we'd stand wordlessly outside the church wall observing a line of black robed and be-hooded priests walking slowly in a procession from the priests' house to the chapel, looking for all the world like a satanic Ku Klux Klan. All that was missing was the fiery cross alight in someone's front garden. It clearly had an affect on us boys, as we never joked about their stately parade towards the church nor did we throw jibes. We watched with something approaching awe before moving quietly away to play football. It was all very confusing. We found ourselves making the sign of the cross and kissing our fingers because that's what we saw our pals doing. And it seemed to work … throughout our entire pre-adolescence, none of us ever had to extinguish a fiery cross in our garden.

Over my young years I'd come to accept, if not understand, this characteristic of Glasgow life. It was just something that was there. It seemed more important to my elders and didn't really touch my life until I was fourteen and my Uncle Hughie took me into the living room one day, sat me down and said to me. "Ok, Ronald, it's time for me to get you into the Lodge [pronounced *Luudge*, in Glasgow]."

"The what?"

"The Orange Lodge. To defend our faith."

I left Hughie in no doubt that I was not interested in joining anything as corrosive (as I saw it) as the Orange Lodge. The conversation which ensued was, other than failing outwardly to grieve for my father, perhaps the first time I remember taking a position which was my own and which caused consternation in our family.

"Ronald telt Hughie he wisny interested in joining the Luudge! Telt me he didn'y believe any of that stuff and that he'd never lift a flute as long as he lived!" … Mortification ran amuck in the family.

What caused me most upset was not the comprehensive hard time I received from the elders in my family. It was when my Grandfather Hector, uninvolved until then, took me aside and in his own gentle way explained how Catholics were secretly behind every negative world event. How they caused unemployment, how they had influenced city politics in a very bad way, how they had a history of betrayal and were not to be trusted. Mostly, they were just *damp* Fenians and hanging was too good for them. I'd never heard my Grandpa so agitated before but it was the cool reasoning, the absolute certainty, the quiet confidence that he spoke the fundamental truth of the matter which I found disquieting. From such a kind and gentle man, it was, indeed, unsettling.

To this day, for whatever reason, I find myself more comfortable with the Republican side of the debate in Ireland, in condemning the activities of the forces of the crown in Ireland, in preferring Celtic to Rangers than I am with the alternative attachments despite the fact that later in life I was to spend thirteen years within the confines of Ibrox Stadium, home of Rangers Football Club and the holy of holies to my Orange relatives. Naming my two youngest sons Conor and Ciaran (and using the Irish spelling) would certainly have brought condemnation from my immediate family had any of them been left alive to witness this calumny.

Many years later when in my late fifties, I was invited to a Burns Supper which I accepted, only to find that it was to be held in the 458 St John's Masonic Lodge in Busby under the auspices of a Grand Master Mason. As my hosts were also fellow topers (and Freemasons) and I anticipated their enjoyment of a good joke, I decided to attend dressed as a priest so as to test their oft-repeated claim that people of any religion – even Catholics – could be Masons. I dressed in a black suit, wore a black shirt and fashioned a white dog-collar on top of which I wrapped a large scarf to conceal my get up. I looked in the mirror before leaving and was most impressed by my appearance as I looked every bit like Father Murphy.

Upon arrival my first thought was to get a round in but as my gaze fell upon the busy bar area, my nerve failed me and it was with some trepidation some minutes later that I responded to my host, Billy Barnes' invitation to make myself comfortable and remove my scarf. I did so, revealing myself in priest's clothing to howls of laughter from Billy, who took to going round and introducing me as 'Father Ron' and asking people for application forms so I could sign up as a Freemason. My prank was taken in good stead, but some months later in the Redhurst, a drunken Ken Winter, who had been in attendance, told me that there had been a conversation that night regarding whether or not I should be 'taught a lesson' for my irreverence. It merely served to remind me why all of the trappings, culture and belief systems that underpins the Luudge, the Orange Order, Freemasonry and all their fellow-travellers have never appealed.

I remember my younger years as being warm, loving and my father's death excepted, without much incident. I was decent at football, decent enough at lessons but excelled at field sports as indeed did all three of us brothers. In my final year of primary education at Gowanbank I was 1962 school sports champion. Campbell was to follow in my footsteps three years later but Alistair, who was more gifted than either Campbell or myself (and indeed who almost won it in my own year of success despite being a year younger) came second in 1965 because he was messing around, evincing (probably genuinely, too, in all honesty) comprehensive unconcern over this sporting challenge.

I remember that first sports day well as I was generally regarded as being unbeatable in the 100 yards sprint final and it was taken as read that I could put the three points for winning that in the bag (two points for second and one for third). I remember my complete astonishment on the day when the teacher who flagged us off in the final race permitted two boys (Alistair being one of them) to start outrageously in advance of the others and didn't call for a false start. I left my blocks well behind the field and finished third, at a stroke, putting my chances of winning my first ever real contest in real peril.

Neil Ross (Mr Ross to us boys) was the teacher who taught the year group below me. He was the school disciplinarian and the sports master. Everyone was a bit wary of him because he was not a warm-hearted man. He seldom if ever smiled but so exuded authority that he was not known to have ever belted a pupil (in these days, children were routinely belted on the palm of their hands by leather tawse for misbehaviour). He had witnessed the race and took me aside after its conclusion. He knelt down so he was in eye contact with me.

"Well now! That was a bit unfair, Culley. I thought it was a false start myself, but the race is over. Can you still win the championship? "

I knew my main chance had gone following the egregious behaviour of the teaching staff, at whom I continued to glare while Mr Ross delivered his homily. Those three points for a win would have given me some leeway in the high jump, long jump and the 400 yards race. I expected to be among the points in all three remaining events but losing my 'banker' was a real blow. Mr Ross, still on one knee spoke to me about matters I didn't really understand, aged eleven, about character and stuff. What I took from it, however, was that an adult had taken me aside, empathised with my plight, spoken of his confidence in me and told me to go out there and perform to the best of my ability.

To my own personal astonishment and delight, I won the three remaining contests and finished with a total of ten points, winning the school athletic tournament. Mr Ross approached me at the end of the day's events. "Are you free on Saturday, Culley?" I told him I was and he invited me to attend a bus run he'd organised for Glasgow athletes that day to Aberdeen. I didn't know anyone on board as they were all slightly older but Mr Ross stood at the front of the bus before we left Glasgow and informed the boys on the bus of what I'd achieved and how it represented something he'd been preaching to them for the months he'd known them; character. "Get to know Culley," he instructed them. "He's shown us all what can be achieved on that front," then sat down and read his newspaper, keeping himself to himself all the way north.

Aberdeen was bathed in sunshine that day as we played football on the *machair* but I bathed in a warmth of a different kind. It was a great day. I no longer remember the nature of the group of lads Mr Ross took to Aberdeen, and don't remember meeting them again, but the event helped me understand the impact that a caring adult can have on a young mind when he empathises with them and affirms them. It was a lesson which was to serve me well in the future when I myself was to get involved in youth work, not to mention the value it had when I was the proud father of four boys myself.

3. Spare The Rod

I never let schooling interfere with my education.
Mark Twain

When I think back to my primary schooling, I guess it's sport and mischief I remember most. My memories of attending my first school, Donaldson Street Primary, in Kirkintilloch are hazy. I can remember enjoying it though and running the fifty or so yards there every day jumping across the raised doorsteps of the dozen or so steps of the miners' cottages which protruded onto the pavement and which formed a series of hurdles between my house and my school gates.

Even then the belt was used quite liberally to induce good classroom behaviour although I have no memory of receiving a Primary School *thwack* myself. Aged five or six, you'd have thought that teachers might have been able to command the attention of the class and encourage good behaviour without the use of violence but it was just such an accepted part of school life then. It wouldn't be until I was twenty years old in 1970 and was attending Jordanhill College of Education that I became aware of a body of student teachers which first formed a political lobby to remove the tawse from classrooms. I can remember then the talk among other students of how crazy this was and how it could only lead to class chaos.

When the family moved back to Glasgow, I was sent with my two brothers to Gowanbank Primary and although I had a few teachers in the infant section, it was to be Mr McGinlay who saw me through the rest of my early schooling. One of my keenest memories is the impact made on me by the school's Latin motto, set under its coat of arms and worn proudly on the badge of my school blazer, *Non Nobus Solum*; 'Not For Ourselves

Alone'. In later years it would inspire me to view the world in a more collegiate, community sense than many of my peers who perhaps took more account of self interest in pursuing their careers. Notions of service were never far from my thoughts….but that was later.

In secondary school, as is the case today, teachers taught by subject expertise and you saw them only intermittently throughout the week. However, in Primaries, you might expect to have the same teacher for a particular year group (notwithstanding the new realities of supply teaching these days which makes for a more itinerant relationship between class and teacher). But back in the fifties your teacher pretty much stayed with you through the last few years of your primary education from eight to eleven; at least ours did.

Mr McGinlay was an old fashioned teacher. He'd fought in the war although he never spoke of his exploits. Learning was largely by rote so every day the class would sit and say in unison, "Two and two is four; three and three is six". Even in spelling, we'd be expected to copy a word from the blackboard and then write it out twenty times on the page of our jotters so as to burn it irrevocably into our young minds.

I was never much taken with classroom excellence. In our class, pupils were seated according to how they performed in the regular class tests and there was always someone pronounced 'top of the class'. Well, that was never me. Indeed I don't ever remember sitting in the first row of eight pupils. I was always comfortable sitting in the second row…bright enough to be encouraged yet never in the same lower league as the 'affable glakit' as my future friend, Professor Tom Carbery would, years later, so describe those endowed with fewer academic gifts.

Mr McGinlay had known my father Ronnie because they performed together in a local amateur dramatic society. I remember seeing them both participate in a comedy play on the Gowanbank school stage one night and finding it curious that my father and my teacher actually knew one another. Perhaps as a consequence of this, Mr McGinlay kept a more avuncular eye on my classroom performances. Certainly he was always kind, if slightly remote. Teachers were always alien beings in those days; even given that Mr McGinlay lived round the corner in Newfield Square, he was not someone you'd ever see shopping or walking the streets with a dog. He sent his kids to a fee paying school so there was no way of engaging with his family on that level or on a football pitch in the evenings. His son Alan went on to become a successful dental surgeon but we never played together as youngsters ... separated by an invisible but very real educational and social gulf.

Along with all of my classmates, I was somewhat apprehensive when it came time to move up to secondary school. As I mentioned, our housing scheme was still being built and facilities such as proper schools and shops came after the houses were erected. In consequence, Craigbank Secondary and Belarmine Secondary (the local Catholic secondary) were developed only later. In the meantime we were to be educated in a number of small campuses; two and three isolated classroom units situated up and down the ribbon of Househillwood Road which stretched from the Pollok roundabout in the north to Nitshill Road in the south about a mile away. This suited me fine as it meant less time seated on a chair in class and more time spent blethering animatedly with schoolmates walking down the road *en route* to the next period of Maths or English.

We'd all been informed that upon entering secondary school, all the new kids were taken away by the older boys as a matter of routine and had their heads put down the toilets as an induction to the big school. Of course this fear was unfounded, although it was initially a bit unnerving to be in a larger playground with play which was appreciably more rowdy, rough and ready.

Again, my early years were characterised by anonymity. I floated through the experience and soon learned that there were many ways to beat the system and avoid those classes I didn't want to attend. By the time I was in third year, I was quite a sophisticated truant.

In 1964, aged 14, I was playing street football in a wintry Lunderston Drive next to the school annex when one of my schoolmates, a dolt called Derek Smith, midst great hilarity, continually used the light covering of snow on the pavement to slide-tackle me from behind and cause me painfully to lose my footing. This escalated to rougher pushing and shoving (which he continued to think was hilarious) and despite my growls at him to desist, he continued to mess about. It was only skylarking but I lost my temper and when he threw his arms around me and bear-hugged me from behind, I jabbed my elbow in his ribs, wheeled round and punched him squarely on the jaw, sending him flying.

Playground fights promised much but rarely got beyond verbal threats and some distant, non-contact sparring. No one ever actually threw a punch which connected. Well, by sheer accident, this one did and Derek lay in a heap on the pavement rubbing his chin while my classmates gathered round saying "Wow" and exclaiming fun-filled astonishment that they'd witnessed a real fight. Just like in the movies.

That one blow brought me a sufficient reputation to allow me credibility in playground disputes throughout my school career. I should say for the record that I only lifted my hands twice in my entire school career and only had one "Right, I'll see you after the bell" fight with another boy, (which I won, by the way although it was more of a wrestling match) so I was hardly Cassius Clay, as Muhammed Ali was known in those days.

However, when I overcame my surprise at flooring Derek, I realised that I'd hurt my hand and had to report to a woman teacher for treatment as it had begun to swell like a balloon.

"What happened, Culley?"

"I slipped on the snow, Miss."

"Hmm, you've bruised your knuckles. Put your hand in this bowl."

And with great care she lowered my hand into a bowl which she'd just filled with scalding hot water she'd just poured direct from a steaming kettle. It was agonising and to this day I don't know what they taught teachers about first aid in those years. However, as could have been anticipated, my swelling didn't reduce and it was obvious that I'd damaged my hand so I was escorted by a pupil in fourth year and taken up to the Victoria Infirmary where my hand was X-rayed.

I gave the nurse the same 'slipped on the snow' story of how the injury had occurred so you can imagine my surprise when sometime later the Doctor appeared, held my X ray up to a light-box and asked, "Well, who did you punch, sonny?"

I was flabbergasted at his detective work, but he just laughed at my obvious discomfiture and explained that I had broken a bone in my hand and it was known colloquially as a 'boxer's break' because it so often occurs after a punch is thrown.

Anyway, my lower arm and hand was encased in plaster for six weeks, but when the 'stookie' came off, the hospital gave me a card indicating that I had to return for physiotherapy on Monday, Wednesday and Friday the following week. I mean, this was not the most complicated injury ever suffered but my arm muscles had weakened appreciably and this short course of treatment was designed to teach me exercises which would bring about a full recovery.

I suppose in retrospect I must have been a rather confused adolescent at this time because I took the card and with some ease amended the note to say 'Monday, Wednesday and Friday...*for twelve weeks.*' It fooled my Registration Teacher. I told no one of this manoeuvre and so began a prolonged period of truancy which, to keep up the illusion of being treated for an injury, involved my visiting Queen's Park next to the Victoria Infirmary and just walking around on my own each Monday, Wednesday and Friday. I was a sociable enough wee boy and missed the normal schoolboy interaction but at the time it seemed more important to 'dog' school and keep myself to myself. It was a lonely time.

I played this game to its conclusion and looked forward to the summer holidays. I thought little more about it and was genuinely sick and ill abed for the first couple of days of the new autumn school-term. Recovered from my ailment, I met up with my pal Jim Barnes with whom I used to walk the daily mile to school and fell into conversation with him. He broke the news to me that I might find my re-entry to school unpleasant as the class had been informed that Culley had missed so much schooling that he'd have to repeat third year. I felt like I'd been punched in the *solar plexus*. It had never occurred to me that there might be a price to pay for truanting. School had always seemed to me to be something you endured, left and later got on with your life. I never saw it as a place where achievement was to be lauded or where a score was to be kept on progress.

I'd been fortunate enough to pass my 11 Plus as it was known; an aptitude test, an IQ test, which I remember taking twice towards the end of my last year in primary school and this placed me in the academic stream in secondary school. I have to say I didn't seek it and on the day of at least one of the tests, I remember quite clearly dashing answers off as quickly as I could so as to get out of the classroom into the sunshine to play football.

There was no intention on my behalf to achieve a score of any merit. It was just another daft test at school. However, I obviously did well enough and because I was placed in the group of kids who might expect to go on to further or higher education, more attention was paid to my progress and requiring me to repeat third year was an act of educational benevolence designed to help me achieve my potential. It has to be recalled that no one was aware of my truancy. My six months' meanderings had escaped attention but now I was to pay by starting my third year education all over again, getting to know a whole bunch of new schoolmates in the process.

Well, it has to be said that it made no appreciable difference in my attitude towards education. My truancy continued if only more sporadically and like everyone else, at least everyone with whom I hung out, I wouldn't attend occasional subjects which I just didn't enjoy or understand. I really had no interest in education other than in English which I loved and in which I found it easy to excel. Music and Physical Education were also favourites.

I chose classes based upon an easy ride, those which my pals attended, and only on one occasion did I ask for tuition (more of which in a moment) which I thought I might both enjoy and find useful in a future career.

By this time, I was building a reputation as a loveable rogue. I was always ready with a quip and found a role as the class entertainer and social secretary. I got on well with almost all of the teachers and entered the school's social life with enthusiasm. I stood for the SNP in a school election and won! I helped one of our teachers to start a folk club (at a time when I was just finding my way with stringed instruments), played for the school football team and also with an amateur team started by Mr Edwards, one of our Modern Studies teachers, who based the team (with no little success) on the winning school team.

However, my behaviour was also subject to a reasonable amount of healthy scepticism by a teaching staff which could never be sure that engaging with me might leave them the butt of a joke. In third year, I asked to see the headmaster, a gaunt, intimidating and aloof man called Norval Sinclair, who always reminded me of Prime Minister, Sir Alex Douglas Home, and asked him to allow me to study shorthand and typing so I might follow my Uncle Arthur, who was then a sub-editor with *The Sunday Post*, into journalism. However, the heidy was having none of it, and I was ushered from his study with some alacrity following his assessment that he was well aware that I just wanted to spend time in classes with the girls! My protestations fell on deaf ears but I had been genuine in my request. I edited the arts section of the school magazine although my reviews of the school play or of an orchestral performance were determined by the latest book I was reading. Dorothy Parker was the acerbic reviewer I most admired and my short, critical and pithy remarks were designed more to have me admitted to the Algonquin Round Table than to impress my fellow pupils which, most assuredly, they did not.

I decided that there was little point in playing the game and my behaviour deteriorated further from that point. It came to a head when Les Carson and I decided to raise money to start a folk club in the school, and came up with the bright idea of asking all of the teachers to donate their leather punishment belts and purchase them back in a fund raising event at close of play one day. Despite some humming and hawing, our excitement and genuine sincerity was obvious and we managed to persuade most of the teaching staff to part with their straps. At this point, Les had been appointed head boy and as such we received the benefit of the doubt.

Our after-school sale was a great success. We raised a decent amount of money to buy some percussion instruments on the basis that pupils would themselves provide such guitars and other instruments as we possessed, and the school would approach the Education Department for a music teacher to take the class every Thursday evening during term time.

The only problem was that one strap looks very much like another one and after school in the staff room, Carson and I witnessed the most uncivilised disputes between teachers as they argued over whose strap was whose. But they entered into the spirit of things and coughed up some shillings a time to have their tawse returned to them. A second problem, however, was that a greater number of teachers just headed for the door when the bell rang at four o'clock, didn't attend, and we were left with about twenty belts with no owners present.

Les Carson agreed that I should take responsibility for the sack of belts which would have to be returned the following morning but as I headed towards the Prefects' Room in which we'd agreed they should be placed until the next day, I had something of a brainstorm and instead made my way to what we called the 'engine room', where all of the school plant was to be found and consigned the sack to the school incinerator. After I'd done it, it dawned on me that this wee jape might not be seen as funny by the school the following morning, and I was soon proved right.

With my brother Alistair in Borstal and my truancy, skylarking, poor educational performances and erratic behaviour becoming more evident I was given a real bollocking by the Headmaster and threatened with all sorts of punishments. I really hadn't expected the force of law to be used against me for an incident such as this but shortly thereafter I was told to report to Mrs Robertson, the school social worker, who was lovely but whose involvement in my life reflected the fact that I was wandering close to the line of legal sanction. Having said that, I'd never much experienced an adult who wanted to listen to me and help and over the next few months I spent ages in her company just talking away. The chats were sufficient in and of themselves but to add to my adolescent delight, she was also an attractive, thirty-something, good looking woman who was slim and well endowed. My wee teenage heart raced one meeting during the school day when she asked me round behind her desk to look over her shoulder at a report she was reading on her desk. I couldn't concentrate on the words as for all the world it looked as if two torpedoes were about to be launched from her chest area. As truckloads of hormones began arriving at the onset of my adolescence, I found that I always looked forward to visiting Mrs Robertson and the Pointer Sisters.

Mrs Robertson was a practising Christian and was always encouraging me to attend her after-school class where religion was explored and songs were sung. My paper round duties put paid to any participation in that but she and I got on well. Having said that, she pointed out on more than one occasion that my continued misbehaviour might result in me ending up in an Approved School but continually encouraged me to believe that I had great potential and that I could amount to something if only I wanted it enough.

Around this time I experienced my first adolescent feelings towards a girl. My first love, Margaret Ferguson, was in the same class as me and took part in Mrs Robertson's class. Although it put back my evening newspaper deliveries by an hour on those evenings, hormones and teenage angst won the day and I ended up going along to the after-school class. I also asked if I could take the art class on the school curriculum because Margaret took art even although I had no artistic aptitude whatsoever and taking it meant missing music class where increasingly my leisure hours were being devoted.

My relationship with Mrs Robertson prospered to the extent that she reckoned that rather than being sent to an Approved, or List 'D' School as a miscreant, I might like to consider a career helping others and if I was interested, she'd arrange for me to spend a year in Balrossie List 'D' School in Kilmacolm, Renfrewshire working with younger kids after my Higher exams were completed. It did occur to me that she'd obviously been giving the matter some early thought if she was able to cite the school in which I might work but I was really pleased with the notion and couldn't wait until the exam diet was completed.

It didn't occur to me until I started stepping out with Maggie, as I called her then (she much prefers to be called Margaret) that pupils actually studied of an evening and completed homework. I don't believe I ever did homework in the evenings. Ever! Because I was an early riser in order to complete my paper round in the morning and was out delivering papers again after school, any compulsory homework was completed in hurried minutes before the morning school bell rang by copying the answers prepared by my more industrious schoolmates. It just seemed a sensible way to go about life. Given my values system, it was just more efficient to finish my paper round, play football or learn guitar in the evenings and copy a classmate's work the next morning. I never imagined that the purpose of attending school was to acquire an education; it was to obey the legal requirements and avoid punishment until such time as I could take up a job as a clerk of some nature. That was the ceiling I'd imposed upon myself. Indeed, the first time I actually encountered Margaret was in the joint maths class when our teacher Mr Noble invited us both to join him at the front of the class and announced that between us we'd achieved 100% in the class test. Regrettably, our scores reflected the highest and the lowest scores; Margaret had achieved 93% and I had 7%. As you might imagine, I didn't look forward to end of term results with much hope of achieving anything at all.

It was at this point that Mrs Robertson came to my assistance after I let her down by disposing of the teacher's belts. She could easily have been forgiven for having me dealt with by the authorities but she was wonderful and my subsequent career, looking back, can be attributed to her acts of kindness following my fall from grace.

Because I had to repeat a year, most of my pals in school were now in the year above me and were prefects. This involved them accepting various responsibilities as allotted by the teaching staff, and in return they were allocated a Prefects' Room where they could congregate away from the general melee of playground activities, and which offered them somewhere to relax between classes when they had a free period. I often spent time in the Prefects' Room, either dogging a class or chatting to my pals. Whenever a teacher visited I would be ushered from the room and instructed not to visit again; an instruction I never obeyed. I'd leave and return as soon as the teacher had left. Because playtime was supervised by teachers on a rota basis, I was always able to avoid the charge of 'contempt of court', a far more serious offence, because a new teacher would be next upon the scene, unaware of my earlier removal.

One memorable day, my presence in the Prefects' Room had been drawn to the attention of Mr 'Tab' Hunter (after the American teen idol and star of the then popular movie *Damn Yankees*) who was our science teacher. Tab was a great teacher, as he organised the Duke of Edinburgh's Award Scheme in the school, which involved a lot of outdoor tasks and which, when accomplished, permitted the award of a bronze, silver or gold medal. As well as various athletic events there were camping and hillwalking opportunities. Tab would selflessly take a small group of boys to some remote point in the Trossachs or the Arrochar Alps in his small car, having talked them through the map-reading and logistics earlier, then he'd drop us off and collect us one or two days later at a pre-arranged pick-up point. He constantly instilled in us safety and respect for the countryside.

One trip involved Les Carson and I being dropped off by Tab at the top of the Rest And Be Thankful, part of the A83 which ran along the bottom of Glen Croe from Ardgarten to Inveraray before climbing steeply towards the turn off to the Argyll Forest Park. These days the road has been widened and realigned but back then it was a narrow, twisting Hielan' road.

Carson and I had camped out for a couple of days in Hell's Glen on the B839 to Lochgoilhead and had arranged that instead of being collected by Tab, we'd make our own way back on the MacBrayne's bus to Glasgow. As we walked up the road to the bus stop at the top of the Rest And Be Thankful, we noticed a large, green metal plate belonging to the Forestry Commission denoting the Argyll Forest Park. Having liberated it from its mountings, we wrapped the sign in our ground-sheet and carried to the bus where we took it back to school as a trophy.

Behind the door entry to the Students' Room was a waist-high cupboard on top of which we proudly displayed our bounty, leaning it against the wall. Somehow, after a few days, Tab Hunter heard of this calumny and stormed into the Prefects' Room bursting through the door in dramatic fashion looking for me and Carson.

To our great good fortune, his aggressive entry smashed the door back against the cupboard and dislodged the heavy metal sign which immediately dropped out of sight between the cupboard and the wall! The several pupils in the room, including Carson and I, were quite taken by the ferocity of his entry and were open-jawed at the improbable disappearance of the evidence.

"Where's Culley and Carson?" he shouted, searching through the faces in the room.

Seeing us, he quizzed us on the tale of the stolen Forestry Commission sign. Our facial astonishment at the magical removal of our spoils was misinterpreted by Tab as innocence and finding no obvious proof of the alleged theft, recovered his composure and removed himself from the room, but not before grunting, "Right. Out of here, Culley. You know fine you're not allowed in this room." I left and returned, until removed again by the next duty playground teacher.

One day as we approached the summer holidays, exams having been completed, (at least mine were given that I sat only the bare minimum required of me) I was alone in the Prefects' Room killing time instead of attending a class and sat on a wooden chair. Unknown to me, the chair had been damaged and the plywood seat had been cracked from back to front. Upon sitting down, the crack in the wooden seat opened and nipped my behind. Pained, I stood up and decided that the seat was broken beyond repair. I figured that the sensible thing to do was to throw it out before someone else was hurt but the school bins were enormous things with small, twenty-four inch square holes in the top to accommodate rubbish. Realising this, I returned to the Prefects' Room and proceeded to break the offending chair into sufficiently small pieces to fit the holes in the bin. Upon reducing the chair to matchwood, I was just about to gather it up in order to dispatch it when the door of the room opened and in strode Mr Mills, the Deputy Head Teacher and the school enforcer. To be fair, Alan Mills was usually a reasonable man, but he was known as the one guy in school you didn't want to cross. Never a man to waste a smile, he looked at the chair, now in a dozen pieces at my feet.

"Did you do this, Culley?", he asked.

"Yes sir. But ..." I began to explain.

The Deputy Head shook his head. "My office. Now!"

I trailed behind him working on the explanation of what, with every step I figured he'd find increasingly difficult in viewing as an altruistic act. When we arrived at his office, he turned the key in the lock, opened the door and nodded an instruction to enter. After we did, he locked the door from the inside....that really freaked me out! He didn't assault me as I feared but read the riot act. He spoke of how I'd failed the school. I'd failed my family. I'd failed myself. I'd fallen foul of the school authorities on numerous occasions. I'd been given over to the tender mercies of the school social worker. (That said, I somehow had the impression that Mr. Mills didn't quite see the value in the tender mercies of the school social worker). I'd been told repeatedly not to use the Prefects' Room and now what did he find? An act of wanton vandalism.

My calm and articulate response to this verbal assault was to mumble, "Yessir, Yessir, Yessir" after every occasion on which his pointing finger aggressively prodded my breastbone as he punctuated his rebuke.

At this point, Mills stopped speaking and checked that he'd locked his office door. I began to figure that I was perhaps in more serious trouble than I'd anticipated but he merely grabbed the lapels of my jacket and drew me towards him.

"Culley! You're a disruption the school can do without. I see no reason why we should persevere with you any more. You are expelled from this school and shouldn't return here unless you have written permission from either myself or the headmaster."

He looked me up and down as if I was something he'd found on the sole of his shoe. "Leave these premises immediately. Do not return. I will advise Mrs Robertson of your expulsion."

As it was, the 'expulsion' was more apparent then real as my final exams had finished and I had no real cause to return anyway. What troubled me was how Mrs Robertson would react to the news. I was certain she'd cancel the placement in Balrossie School. However, the following day she visited me at home and heard my side of the story, before telling me that she felt that I was a special person who had much to give. She told me that now that I'd left school, I was outwith her responsibility and that I was going to have to make my own way in the world. She felt sure that I would both enjoy and do well at Balrossie and that if I was still game, so was she. I agreed quickly and she left, promising to write to me with details.

Some time later I received two letters in the post. One was a letter from Mrs Robertson inviting me to turn up for a year's placement at Balrossie teaching 'social responsibility' to kids who'd been sent there for some misdemeanour or other. The second was to tell me that I'd achieved an 'O' Level Arithmetic (the markers must have been in lenient mode that day). As surprisingly, 'O' Level Art (the good fortune brought on by an adolescent determination not to be seen to fail in front

41

of my first girlfriend) and Higher English. I now had some qualifications, a girlfriend and an entry level job which might see me into a professional training course. Expulsion was now behind me. I was entering the world of work. I might even have felt more settled.

4. Newspapers And Butchermeat

*When I was a boy of twelve, my elders were so ignorant I could hardly
stand to have them around. But when I got to be nineteen, I was
astonished at how much they had learned in seven years.*
Mark Twain

Backtrack!

Before recounting my Balrossie experience, I should
speak of my introduction to the world of youthful
finance. Money was never much of a problem to us in
my younger years in that we wanted for nothing. Sweets
had eventually returned to the shops after the post-war
rationing but our Gran had decided that they were bad
for us. Even in those days she was wise in those matters
which now occupy so many column inches in health
magazines. We were limited in the amount of sweets
we could eat, were regularly fed healthy vegetables and
were forbidden all other fodder until we had 'eaten our
greens'. At school we drank a small bottle of milk a day
and Gran required that we took a capsule of cod liver oil
each day in life. Initially she had given us our daily dose
neat on a teaspoon. It tasted awful so we were delighted
when the product became available in a new capsule
format.

We were always well clad and Grandpa's consistent,
if modest, earning power rendered us one of the better
off families in the street. Add our centrally heated houses
and good, local education and we were living the kind of
life that most left-wing politicians would find acceptable
for their constituents. Health care was good. Dr. Gerber
had his surgery over on the Barrhead Road and on those
occasions I had to go there it was always packed but
the receptionist, Mrs McKean, was my Gran's upstairs'
neighbour and always saw to it that we were seen, with
one exception that I will explain later.

Mum and Gran always referred to me as the man of the house and although they put no pressure on me to earn money, were always guiding me that financial security should start as soon as possible. I'd made a less than auspicious start when aged around eight. My father had given me three sixpences to take myself and my two brothers to have our hair cut at the barbers at Nitshill. We set off and on the journey we came upon the idea that only Alistair and I would have our hair cut by the barber. It couldn't be that difficult so why should not he and I cut Campbell's hair? No one would ever know and we could each spend twopence on sweets. We fell to our plan with great enthusiasm and returned home having spent the money. Now all that was left was to obtain the scissors and fix Campbell up. After some time, we agreed that adult eyes would not be able to tell which head had been coiffeured by a barber and which by us. With our most innocent looks firmly fixed on our faces, we entered the living room to the almost immediate horror of mum and to whoops of delight from Dad who just thought this was the funniest thing he'd ever seen. We hadn't a fall-back plan lest our efforts were discovered as counterfeit and so were astonished at the speed at which our carefully contrived money-making plan had been undone. Dad found it no problem to give us another sixpence and send us back to the barber to have matters remedied. He was still giggling helplessly at our entrepreneurialism when we returned later with Campbell's hair cut now resembling something he'd have got for free had he just stepped off a military parade ground.

I had another 'brush' with calamity some years later when in my early teens. Just at the advent of the Beatles during which time hairstyles had begun to get somewhat longer and unkempt, I'd sent away for a special comb which concealed a razor within its shell so that when you combed your hair, the loose ends were removed with each stroke. I had found the description in the newspaper advert to be compelling. *How sensible*, I thought. *I buy this and don't need to shell out on any further visits to the hairdressers!* I couldn't wait to take my new fangled invention into the bathroom where I carefully drew it across my shed from left to right where, just as it said in the advert, it removed hair along the path that I'd just guided it. Unfortunately, my first attempt was rather too ambitious and in an effort to balance the look, I ended up with a large bald patch on my left side. My only solution was to change the parting in my shed and to sweep my hair unnaturally from right to left rather than the more normal left to right. I figured that no one would notice. They did and it left me with a permanent 'alternative shed' for the rest of my schooldays. Now, even in adult life, I prefer what is left of my hair to be messy rather than to conform to the normal left shed so beloved of mothers in the sixties.

When I was about eleven, about eighteen months or so after my Dad's death, Gran and Grandpa were permitted by Glasgow Corporation to move from their lovely three bedroom, semi-detached terraced home with their back and front gardens, to a ground level, two bedroom tenement property at 252 Househillwood Road, just five closes down from Mum's at 268 so she could offer more support to her and us boys.

My brother Alistair had also taken early heed of their imprecations to earn money, as I was to begin to discover. Our door was regularly pounded by police officers early in the morning when the household was abed. Mum would admit them, whereupon they would reach below Alistair's bed and pull out a gas meter that he'd stolen the previous evening. Alistair would stoutly deny any knowledge of the meter but his pockets would bulge with shilling coins, the unit of payment for the gas meter. It became an event of some monotonous regularity and Alistair was soon up before the beak on a number of escalating charges which ultimately resulted in him spending eighteen months served at Her Majesty's pleasure in Polmont Borstal when he was in his teens.

Later, when on weekend leave from Borstal, his involvement with Orangism, coupled with some primitive education derived from within his new place of learning, saw him round our back garden hammering an industrial fertiliser like Ammonium nitrate or Sodium Nitrate into a pipe, crimped at one end. It was evident that he had only been taught the very rudiments of bomb making and it was only by good luck that his watching crowd weren't all blown to smithereens.

Our grandparents' move to Househillwood Road was made in an early attempt to help deal with Alistair's wayward behaviour. I was upset but removed from Alistair's behaviour in his pre-teen and early teen years. He was always in the company of other boys who indulged in criminal behaviour and was always getting into trouble at school. For all that, he was possibly the most popular of the three of us at school and in the community as his roguish charm and reputation as a scrapper held him in good stead.

The only time I got involved personally in his antics was when, in an effort to escape the attention of the police who'd hear of a reported theft of a gas meter and just turn up at our house where they'd usually find it below Alistair's bed, Alistair hit on a clever plan to avert justice by hiding the stolen meter beneath *my* bed. I wasn't particularly pleased at being woken one morning to find the offending article pointing at my participation but fortunately for me, Alistair's record was by now so lengthy that the cops just took it as read that it was Alistair's doing and believed my protestations of innocence. The shillings jingling yet again in his pocket also helped my plea.

My only formal involvement with the law was when the three of us brothers were playing behind the now defunct garage at the top of Peat Road on Nitshill Road during the summer holidays. I must have been about ten years old. The land behind the garage was derelict and used for dumping old Ford motor cars such as were used by James Cagney and Humphrey Bogart in their gangster movies. We were playing away quite happily when a uniformed police officer approached us and accused us of being the boys who had thrown stones and broken the windows of the garage the day before. Ignoring our shocked protestations, it became evident that he just wanted the crime recorded as solved in an attempt to raise his detection rates and we were eventually duly summoned to Govan Police Station in Orkney Street with Mum to face a 'Superintendent's Warning', a formal chastisement which results in an informal admonishment but which avoids a court appearance. It was used for misdemeanours rather than overt criminal activity.

Years later in my adulthood I was to be taught a number of interpersonal and assertiveness techniques by a Jesuit priest, one of which involved the calm repetition of your point of view in order to protect your position. By intuition, I applied this technique pretty effectively in front of the Divisional Commander.

Police in those days were given genuine respect and the Superintendent was almost certainly more used to contrite parents and their errant children promising better behaviour in the future. I was, however, entirely innocent as were my brothers and the Superintendent became quite irritated by my calm repetition of our innocence at the end of every one of his sentences. Admission of guilt was part of the procedure and I suppose, by his lights, he would have been within his rights to take the case to court. But whether it wasn't worth the effort or whether he believed my monotonous repetition of "Your policeman was wrong…we were just playing and didn't throw stones". I don't know where I found the nerve but he admonished us and permitted us to walk free. Mum was furious at my 'cheek'. She'd rather I'd complied with the ritual and avoided her embarrassment as opposed to standing up for the truth.

Both Mum and Gran brought me up to be helpful to neighbours, many of whom were elderly. So much so that I took it as quite natural to be called from the window of one of Gran's friends and asked to run an errand to Galbraith's or the Co-op. To this day I can still remember my Mum's Co-op dividend number; 77555, and my Gran's, 75188. Now and again if I need a password for something that requires security, because they've been burned into my brain I use these two numbers together, so providing odds of over 100 million to one to break the code … although, now that I've revealed the numbers … hmmm.

But I seldom found these requests irksome and remember feeling happy to assist. Only one neighbour, Mrs McKinnon, would take advantage of me. She'd shout, "Ronald, could you nip down the shops and get me twenty Woodbine? Come up and I'll give you the money."

On more than on one occasion when I'd arrive at her door, she'd add another item to the request. "Thanks Ronald, can you also get me a bag of coal, son? There's a good boy." Mrs McKinnon was elderly and lived alone and the small bag of coal was not that heavy, so I didn't mind, but I'd have a laugh with my grandparents as I recounted her duplicitous behaviour. There were never any tips.

My approach to generating an income was rather more legitimate than Alistair's. I bought a paper round. Having an evening paper delivered to your home was fairly commonplace and the *entrée* to this income was to purchase a round involving a few dozen customers for a sum of money, the more customers you had, the greater the amount which could be charged. I started by buying a paper round from a friend which cost a few pounds, all I could afford at the time. There was no charge levied on the customer for having a paper delivered. Paper boys were paid a penny a paper from the publisher and also hoped for a tip from satisfied customers. I was a diligent worker and with the profits earned from my first year, bought and sold customers so as to shape a better, more efficiently grouped customer round selling the *Evening Citizen* and the *Evening Times*.

After a while, I also bought a morning round and delivered *The Daily Record* and the *Express*. In Pollok at that time there was no call for broadsheet papers such as *The Herald*, then *The Glasgow Herald*. It was an early rise but we paperboys saw ourselves as superior to those of our friends who had milk rounds. They were paid a flat rate for jumping on and off a milk float and carrying freezing cold milk bottles up and down stairs. They had no entrepreneurial flair about them. They were merely hired hands.

I was delivering papers on the morning of 15th January 1968. In those days, although there must have been weather forecasts broadcast on the radio, they would have been nothing like as sophisticated as they are today and as I rose from my bed and dressed, I remember being aware that there was a bit of a storm going on outside but wild weather was not at all uncommon in Glasgow and I thought little of it until I emerged onto the street. What devastation there was! Many chimney stacks had been blown over, some into the street and some through the roof of the house to which they had been attached; trees were lying across roads, dustbins were spinning around in the air and all sorts of debris was flying around. My memory is that it wasn't raining at that point and, young as I was, I took great delight in going out into the storm to deliver my papers. It was certainly a foolhardy thing to do as anyone in the open could have been badly injured. I could hardly stand up straight, never mind walk, but everyone received their newspaper.

When quiet came, it was evident that Glasgow had been badly hit by an incredibly fierce storm.... THE GREAT STORM... as the *Evening Times* and the *Citizen* that I delivered that evening described it. When it had gone, many people were injured and nine had died, due to its enormous destructive capacity. One and a half thousand people had been made homeless due to the 'tornadic activity' of the storm as the following morning's *Daily Record* described it.

Socially, my life revolved around the Cubs and the Scouts. Mum took me along to a Cub Pack when I was about eight. She started as a helper and worked through the ranks until she was '*Akela*', the head of the pack. Mum retained her love of the scouting movement throughout much of her adult life and I followed in her enthusiasm. I remember first being a 'Sixer', my first position of responsibility in life, when I was put in charge of six other cubs. I moved up to the Scouts, as did my pal Les Carson, and together we shouldered more and more responsibility. We would turn up early on a Friday night to get things set up, we'd be the advance party to weekend Scout camps at Auchengillan, and we would be the twosome sent to the annual ten day camp at Lochgilphead near the Mull of Kintyre to make camp prior to the arrival of the troop. It was great fun.

We stayed on Barnakill Farm, situated near the village of Cairnbaan, immediately upon the Crinan Canal which links Loch Fyne to the Sound of Jura. It was accessible only by crossing the canal via the Dunardry Locks and was perhaps a fifteen minute walk from the tow-path which was sufficient distance for us boys to view ourselves as camping in a wilderness. Every couple of days, some of the leaders would walk down to the farm then drive to the nearest shop a couple of miles down the road. In the interests of equity, everyone had to bring the same (small) amount of pocket money and any items ordered such as sweets were added to the list of provisions which would be carried back to the camp. As I grew older and featured in these expeditions, I realised that one of the advantages of making this trip was that all of the leaders went into a local pub on the banks of the canal for a couple of beers. I'm sure it was because of my father's untimely and inebriated death, but I invariably refused to go in to the pub with them and sat on my own outside until they emerged. I wouldn't take strong drink until I was well into my twenties.

When Les and I were sent to make camp a couple of days before the troop arrived, it wasn't particularly onerous, just carrying all the gear about a mile from the road-end to the camp site and pitching the tents. One year, we went about our business diligently and when work was completed, we climbed the nearby hills looking for adders, Britain's only poisonous snake, which species abounded in the Lochgilphead area. Often you'd find them sunning themselves on a rock and we'd throw a blanket over them, catch them behind their head and take them back to the camp where we'd present them as trophies before killing them by pouring boiling water over them in an attempt to make their skins into belts. Kids can be cruel, and I'm ashamed now at the way we all treated these beautiful if dangerous reptiles, but then we thought we were frontiersmen, none of whom I'm aware ever actually managed to make a belt.

However, as I say, prior to the other scouts arriving, Les and I had set everything up and had climbed the hills surrounding the camp. It was a really beautiful summer's day and all was well with the world when suddenly at the edge of a cliff, the sod gave way beneath my feet and I plummeted down the side of the rock face. In the microsecond before I dropped, Carson and I shared the glance held between two German soldiers in *Dambusters* at the point where the dam was breached and they realised their fate was sealed. I was unimaginably lucky as I looked down and saw that my legs were splayed open and I was heading for a large rock shaped like a shark's fin. If I'd hit it at that angle, I'd never have fathered children, that's for sure. Somehow I twisted my body in the air and hit the rock obliquely. I caught it with quite some velocity, catching most of the impact on my right thigh. The blow knocked me sideways into gorse. Dazed, I realised that I'd survived the fall but upon congratulating myself on a miraculous escape, noticed that although nothing appeared to be broken, my right thigh had opened up and blood was spouting like a fountain. It looked like a job for Red Adair.

Miles from anywhere, Les and I determined in the outdoor spirit of the day that we'd just fix me up ourselves and I limped back to the camp where we used such medication as was available to patch me up. A large bandage round my thigh was a sure signal to our seniors upon their arrival that I'd met with an accident but because I was shrugging it off, they weren't more curious and as a result I now have a beautiful scar running the length of my thigh although it has faded with time. I was lucky no complications set in.

Scouting could be dramatic in other ways too. One sunny Friday evening in 1963 as we were gathering for a troop meeting in Levern Primary School, one of our number vaulted the sandstone wall and pronounced, "Somebody's shot Kennedy." For the life of me, I couldn't understand why somebody would shoot our erstwhile Primary School Headmaster and it took a while for the realisation to sink in that it had been the American President, JFK, who had been assassinated. Even at thirteen years old I was upset as I'd been captivated by the promise of Camelot which just seemed so different from our own tired operation down at Westminster.

Our 168th Scout Troop was run by 'Pop' Newton, a successful businessman from Eaglesham. He was probably in his sixties but was great fun. He had around him a collection of younger guys in their twenties who helped him run the troop and the unofficial HQ of the whole arrangement was our living room in 268 as Mum was still *Akela* and there was a very close connection between her Cub Pack which was the feeder for the Scout Troop. All of the office bearers, members of both sexes, would foregather regularly to plan future scouting matters but it invariably turned into cups of tea and a night's entertainment round the piano.

It was intoxicating listening to them all convene in laughter in our house. Mum was an excellent pianist and could have played professionally. She was forever being called upon to play the piano and everyone would gather round and sing along. On Saturday afternoons, Mum would often go into town and purchase the sheet music for the latest Elvis, Sinatra or Matt Munro song. But it was the patter ... the patter! It just seemed that effortlessly they'd come away with funny line after funny line ... wise crack after hilarious wise crack. I would sit in the corner of an evening just goggle eyed and observe comedy routines which seemed to my young ears and eyes to match anything available on the box at the time. I remember being most envious of their general ability to make everyone around them laugh and any small abilities I have myself enjoyed in that department over the years could be traced back quite precisely to those evenings. It was good for my Mum as well as she seemed really happy at the lively atmosphere in the house as she was living the life of a single parent and didn't have to go out to find fun and enjoyment, she just brought it home to her house.

Something else she brought home to the house was boyfriends. Over the years, two to be exact. As a youngster I never sensed any awkwardness here as they just seemed to me to be older people than me who made me laugh and who gradually came to spend more time around the place until almost imperceptibly they were there in the morning. My mother had every right to her happiness and I don't think I would have reacted as badly as I did first time around had boyfriend number one, 'Stuzy', Stewart McKerracher, not been an alcoholic. Like all of the others who came round, Stuzy was involved with the Scouts (albeit marginally in his case) but he was the only one I saw drinking alcohol. Everyone else drank tea although some of the younger Scout leaders had developed a taste for coffee.

Stuzy was bad news as far as I was concerned. I suppose my father's death through drink affected my attitude to alcohol. (As I said, I didn't begin to take strong drink until I was about twenty five - although I've compensated for my tardy start since.) Interestingly, rather than warn me of the evils of drink, my tee-total Gran frequently guided me as a teenager that if I wanted to make my way in the world, I'd need to be able to 'pass myself in company' when it came to the consumption of alcohol (an accomplishment I consider I've now mastered on those occasions when I throw myself enthusiastically upon the tender mercies of the licensing trade).

I wasn't happy with Stuzy's behaviour towards my Mum. My grandparents didn't fancy him much either. When he was sober he was great fun, full of ideas, just a big daft laddie [he was also much younger than Mum] but drunk, he was frequently sick all over the place; over my own bed on one occasion. He could be rough and argumentative and, of course, he'd disappear for days at a time, causing Mum great distress.

When I was fourteen, I awoke in the wee sma' hours upon hearing crashing noises and investigated to find Stuzy drunk and giving my Mum a hard time. He was in her bedroom and was smashing the place up rather than hitting her but it was the last straw as far as I was concerned. As soon as I appeared, Stuzy somewhat absurdly, dove into my Mum's bed and pretended to be asleep. Mum sat sobbing on the edge of the bed. Tearfully I shouted that enough was enough and that if he didn't leave the house once and for all, then I would.

After more remonstrations during which Stuzy bizarrely remained under the covers playing dogo, I stormed back to my room. Following some muted conversation between Stuzy and my Mum, she came into my room and explained at my bedside that Stuzy had been upset about something and that he had promised that he wouldn't behave like that again. I was not to be consoled. Either he left or I did. Mum was beside herself but suffice it to say that Stuzy stayed and I moved the next day to stay with Gran and Grandpa down the road at 252 with whom subsequently I lived until I left to become a student some six years later.

I suspect in an attempt to mollify a confused adolescent, my Gran and Grandpa took me almost immediately on a holiday to Dublin. I was only fourteen and this was my first trip abroad. I could barely cope with the excitement. The River Clyde in 1964 was still a bustling, dark and brooding, lead-coloured waterway and our mode of travel to Ireland was an overnight ship to Dublin. We boarded at the Broomielaw in the centre of Glasgow and were ushered below deck to a large hold where was assembled rows of the kind of chairs that were ubiquitous in schools; the hollow steel framed chairs with green canvas back and seats. Too confining for a fourteen year old, I wandered the deck on what was a beautiful, still, moonlit night and absorbed the movements, smells and noises of the ship as it sailed downriver past Greenock and out into an Irish Sea in a flat calm. It was a glorious evening and was sufficiently warm for me to snuggle down on deck on top of a large rolled tarpaulin and sleep comfortably for a while before being awakened by Grandpa who not unreasonably had become concerned at my disappearance. In those days, Health and Safety matters weren't given the attention they are today and I guess I could have slipped between the railings on the side of the ship, even though there wasn't much of a swell that night.

Dublin was then and remains today my second favourite city after Glasgow. I loved the more bohemian and relaxed atmosphere of Dublin in 1964. I was allowed into licensed premises, not that either Gran or Grandpa would have stooped to taking strong drink, for a cup of tea and was transfixed by my first exposure to a juke box where I listened to Jim Reeves' *He'll Have To Go* and *Deck Of Cards* by Wink Martindale for as long as my shillings would play them. I also saw my first slot machines and pin ball machines and thought the place just magical.

We returned after a most enjoyable and distracting week but Stuzy was still ensconced with Mum so I stayed put at 252. Stuzy stayed with my Mum for several years until he lapsed deeper into his alcoholic illness. He disappeared one day and that was that. He died in London some ten years later. By then, Mum had met and married George Goldie, a naturalised Scot, whose antecedents were from Lithuania. His birth name was Yurgis Auksoraitis.

Mum had moved on from running Cub Scouts to being in charge of a local authority run junior youth club a couple of evenings a week as she'd realised that she could earn a pretty decent part-time salary to supplement the income from her basic grade civil servant job at the National Savings Bank located just beyond Pollok roundabout.

Before the bust up when I was fourteen, Mum decided that I was to become as musical as she was and sent me off to a piano tutor in Barrhead on Tuesday evenings to learn how to play. I know it was one of many ways she had of trying to show her love for me but I was then a pre-teen adolescent who was *deeply* disinterested in piano tuition and never, but never, practised what I'd been asked to prepare for the following week. It's barely credible now but the tutor, Mrs Hutton would whip me over the knuckles with a violin bow if her frustration at my stumbling attempts to play '*Frere Jacques*' rose beyond her [rather low] boiling point. I didn't care. I didn't practice!

What compounded the felony was that I had to travel by bus to get to and from Barrhead and almost every week I'd miss my local youth club which was divided into two evening periods of an hour each; first, indoor football (which I loved) and secondly a raffia class (which I loathed). Unfortunately, my musical petulance meant that I usually missed the football and had to suffer the raffia class during the second period. After a couple of years and following a successful examination at the most elementary level, Mum, whose influence over me was waning, agreed to my pleadings and let my musical talents such as they were evolve in my own way and in my own time.

When I was seventeen, Pop Newton indicated that he intended to retire from Scouting and brought me and Les Carson into a room to explain that he and the senior staff had given a lot of thought to how the future of the troop might best be guaranteed. They'd decided to offer me the position of Troop Leader. I was delighted but Les was really pissed off. He was *much* more of a Scout than I was. He had all of his badges where I didn't bother much with that side of scouting. I was more the guy who had the laughs, the ideas and the energy as well as the ability to provide the discipline necessary to get from the start of the evening to the end of the evening without chaos ensuing. I was loud and popular but I wasn't a typical or traditional Scout. That very definitely was Les. It was also an early lesson on the politics of networking. A form of dynasty was emerging and I more than suspect that me being a Culley and being at the heart of local scouting politics was much more significant a factor than any innate abilities I possessed as a troop leader at that time.

And so my idiosyncratic ways soon found their voice as I turned the 168th Troop into more of a football club. Badges and scouting were forgotten as I adopted a populist approach and moulded the troop in my own image. The Scouts loved it but Les would have done a far better job as troop leader. However I suspect that Pop and the others remained swayed by the fact that I was associated with the inner scouting circle which met in my living room. I resigned after a couple of years with much healthier numbers attending every Friday night but it didn't much resemble the Scout Troop I inherited. I suspect with some justification that Pop Newton would have felt that the scouting movement had been let down, even if I'd increased the numbers attending substantially.

One legacy left me by my scouting days was a pair of buggered knees. One Friday night when I was fourteen, the Scout meeting had ended and we had remained in the hall playing football whilst awaiting the janitor to come and close the school. I can still remember clearly attempting a shot on goal from a ball which arrived waist high. I swivelled and fell to the floor like a bag of hammers, clutching my right knee. It was obvious that I had damaged it badly and Les Carson took my arm over his shoulder and helped me limp round to Dr Gerber's surgery as we were aware that he had an evening surgery on a Friday night in order to cater for those who worked during the day. Upon arrival, Dr Gerber and Mrs McKean his receptionist (and Gran's upstairs' neighbour), were getting into his car, the surgery having just closed. A brief consultation on the kerbside resulted in Dr Gerber telling me to go to the Southern General Hospital to get it X-rayed before he and his receptionist drove off into the night leaving me hobbling on the pavement.

Carson took me home instead and the pain receded sufficiently for me to determine that a hospital visit was unnecessary but over the next few weeks, I found myself experiencing the same agonising pain on another couple of occasions. Each time, it felt as if my leg had been broken. Eventually a teacher drove me to hospital where my knee was X-rayed and I was told that there was nothing amiss. Over the next year, I lost confidence in my ability to stress my knee. Just as I'd decide that the condition had rectified itself, I'd find myself again on the floor in agony. This resulted in a number of repeat admissions to hospital and a couple of further X-rays. However, it wasn't until I was running (ahead of the pack) in a long distance race round the school perimeter when I was observed crashing yet again to the ground by Mr Fogo, the head of PE, that he took me to the Victoria Infirmary and managed to persuade them that it was clear that I had something wrong with my knee.

Possibly because I was taken there immediately upon being felled and because Mr Fogo had strapped my leg up, this time the X-ray showed that my knee had had a chunk of bone broken off which every so often moved and locked my knee. The doctor found this quite unusual and I became an afternoon celebrity as a queue of young doctors and nurses each pushed this piece of floating bone around my knee (painlessly, I must confess). Anyway shortly thereafter I was taken to Hairmyres Hospital just outside East Kilbride and my knee was operated on.

I woke up in a ward to find the ward sister hovering over me. In a very firm voice she told me that I must get some rest because when she came round tomorrow I would be placed immediately on an exercise regime. As the fuzziness cleared, it became apparent that I was in a ward which included a couple of injured footballers. I can't remember who they were now but I remember my excitement at being treated in the same way as sporting personalities who, in the sixties, didn't have the pampered lifestyles they do now. When the nurse came round the following morning, in the wake of the doctor who pronounced himself satisfied that the operation had been successful, she lifted my leg by the foot and told me she was about to let it go so I should prepare to take the strain. I heard this instruction with some phlegmatism; what could be more simple?... but screamed out loud in pain as my leg thumped to the bed like a dead weight, my muscles having been rendered useless after the operation. The nurse had made her point, but just to re-emphasise it she indicated that I'd be tested in similar fashion every morning, so I'd better get on with my rehabilitation.

I was in for over two weeks and it was quite enjoyable. Hairmyres Hospital was in the countryside and I was by a distance the youngest patient in the ward. Listening to the stories of my fellow patients, reading and sleeping were not unpleasant activities and quite distracting from the times when I was in the gymnasium. I had been brought a small Dansette record player which permitted only one vinyl, long playing record to be played at any one time. I listened perpetually to an album of the Spencer Davis Group playing *'Keep on Running'* and became more taken each day with the astonishingly accomplished guitar work and bluesy voice of Steve Winwood, who at that time was being heralded as a child protege. In parenthesis, I should also confess that I was also threatened with immediate discharge by the *'Ward Nurse from Hell'* after Carson visited and took me for a rather pacey spin in a wheelchair along the corridors of the hospital, scattering patients and staff in our wake.

When I was eventually discharged, I was given crutches but don't remember being given any further physiotherapy or other rehabilitative support. When I could walk unaided, I did so with a pronounced limp and had a huge bandage round my right knee for what seemed like ages. Twice I had to return to hospital as I burst my stitches playing football prematurely in the street and my left leg seemed to want to come out in sympathy as I asked too much of it in protecting my injured right knee. The result of all of this was to give me a twisted pelvis and a pair of bad knees which even today can give way at any time when I'm walking. I must look odd when perambulating down the street now and again and one of my knees goes. I usually recover before I fall but it must look to all the world as if I am stricken suddenly drunk as I lurch about on the pavement trying to regain both my balance and composure. I fully suspect that in later years my knees will cause me problems as a fall occasioned by them not working properly could have more serious future repercussions than might have been experienced in my youth.

Of course, that injury now permits me to tell anyone who'll listen that were it not for the fact of my bad knees, I could have been a contender in whatever sport; football, running, golf, swimming, squash, was being discussed.

On the evening of the 4th of September 1962, my Grandfather, Hector McLeod, was honoured to be selected to drive the last tram in Glasgow. There was a huge turnout for the people of Glasgow to say, 'Farewell to the Caurs', as the event was known and at 6.30 pm, a procession of twenty trams made their stately way from Dalmarnock Road to drive across the Clyde and up Pollokshaws Road to Albert Drive where they were put on display in the newly refurbished Transport Museum. I stood with many thousands on the side of the street to watch this and along with other kids, would run out in front of an oncoming tram, which was moving at a sedate pace it has to be said, and place an old penny on the track for the tram's wheels to bend it. We hadn't accounted for the more adventurous and entrepreneurial kids from the Gorbals' side of the road who would endanger life and limb by waiting until the last second before rushing out to collect the line of pennies and disappear before the tram moved past and permit anyone from our side to remonstrate.

Hector was awarded several medals for long service, no accidents and perfect attendance, as was the tradition in those days, and I later proudly displayed them in a picture frame along with a note signed by each of the twenty drivers of the 'caurs' that day. He was moved to the Underground where he worked as a driver until he retired. An entire career spent moving his fellow

Glaswegians safely around the city. A lovely man. Gentle, kind and a great rôle model. On the 14th of August 1984, he died in Jersey while on holiday with my Mum, Gran and George. Mum told me he just went to bed one night, didn't sleep well and passed away in the morning after a doctor had been called. I was heartbroken. He was a lovely man and I loved him dearly. I only had one decent photograph of him and, wouldn't you know it, he's scowling in it, an attitude he never struck in real life.

Through my adolescent eyes, the only value Stuzy brought to the household was that he had an elderly uncle, Uncle Bill, who lived alone in a wee 'but and ben' at the bend in the road above Bridge of Brown about five miles outside Tomintoul in the Highlands. It was a very small cottage with two bedrooms and a livingroom with a bed recess where Bill slept. He was almost in his nineties but was a spry old man. His life had been pretty hard. There was no electricity and the water came from the burn. He cut the peat and chopped wood and made porridge.

Each year for about five years when I was aged from 9 to 14, Mum and Stuzy took us up for a fortnight's holiday. Old Bill had great *craic*. He was always quick with bits of wisdom which he bestowed upon us each evening as we sat in front of a roaring fire while a paraffin lamp provided light. "Never fa' oot wi' yer meat", he'd instruct, if someone left a morsel on the plate. "Mony a mickle maks a muckle!" "Whit's fur ye'll no go by ye!" I imagine he quite enjoyed the company, chaotic as it was. We certainly did.

We had great times, playing in the rivers and streams which abounded in the glen, going for walks or kicking a ball about in the rough track outside the cottage. Every so often Mum and Stuzy would drive us to nearby Grantown-on-Spey where we'd sit in the local café and play the juke box. Sometimes we'd visit the cinema, a much less sophisticated facility than we were used to in Glasgow even then. The woman who sold the tickets also showed you to your seats, operated the projection box and sold the ice cream. Still, it was heaven. We holidayed like the Broons or Oor Willie would have done had they headed north from Dundee.

One night there was a variety evening including a ventriloquist's act that performed live and we were all seated round him. To my young eyes he was very good but when during his act he asked my brother Alastair if he could see his lips moving, he was somewhat reproachful of him when Alastair replied innocently, "Only when your dummy talks!"

One matter which blighted my enjoyment considerably was the regularity that Stuzy would take Mum out for a drink in Grantown-on-Spey at night. Mum was never a drinker but Stuzy could certainly put it away and I would lie awake each night listening intently for the noise of the car returning from the pub with a drunken Stuzy at the wheel. Despite my constant requests to stay in the cottage, Mum never conceded the point and I can see that she must have enjoyed the break, leaving the three boys with old Bill and having a night to herself with her boyfriend.

In those days, the test for drunk driving was asking the driver to attempt to walk in a straight line and touch his nose with his index finger. Frequently I was on the point of using the red public phone box, which was handily situated outside the cottage, to report Stuzy to the police at a point when I figured he'd be on his way back. Instead, I played cards with old Bill and my brothers and then in bed seethed anxiously with impotent anger, worry and frustration under the covers at the thought of Stuzy drunkenly wending his way back along narrow Highland roads in the Austin A40.

If ever I find myself anywhere near the area I make a point of visiting the abandoned and ruined cottage and look around, remembering old times. Indeed for a while I harboured thoughts of trying to buy the land and build something where currently stands the cottage but common sense and the absence of funds precluded the pursuit of that dream. I did a lot of research as both Stuzy and old Bill are both dead and my guess is that they would both have died intestate. In these circumstances, the State takes ownership and would sell only at market value. So, no deal.

In 2005, I travelled to Dornoch with my friend Gordon Maclennan. On the way up north, I told him of the cottage and, being the entrepreneur he is, he suggested we turn the wheel and take a detour so that we might visit the cottage. Imagine our surprise when we turned the corner and discovered the cottage far from the ruin as I'd described it. Instead someone had bought the plot and had redeveloped it using double glazing while yet retaining the essential essence of the cottage. I could now surrender to reality and forsake the notion that with a wee bit jiggery-pokery I could become a Highland Laird.

My first summer away from Tomintoul was in 1966 when Jim Barnes and I thought we might make a few bob by becoming 'tattie howkers' (potato pickers) over the school holidays. We took a two man tent and camped in the grounds of Culzean Castle in a copse near the cliff edge but hidden from prying eyes where at night we could see the twinkling lights of the fishing boats returning to the small port of Dunure. We got into the habit of wandering down to the harbour in the wee sma' hours and asking for 'any scraps' whereby we were always rewarded with a fish or two.

Tattie howkin' was really hard graft because of all the stooping to pick up the potatoes. The foreman told me that it was easier for the girls than for the boys because of the way they were built. I had insufficient knowledge of physiology by which to contradict him but it certainly was the case that he had a goodly number of women on the rows. They all lived on a nearby farm and we didn't see them other than during the working day. The foreman told me that this was because their association with the boys of an evening led frequently to fights between the boys during the day and he needed a reliable and contented workforce.

After a few days I was completely buggered and even today blame my bad back on my *travails* in the red, sandy earth of Ayrshire. Fortunately the foreman took pity on us and suggested that we move to the machine which sorted and graded the potatoes. This was easier as although the bags weighed a hundredweight each, at least it was work to we could become accustomed without stooping and we soon became adept at throwing around heavy bags full of the finest Ayrshire potatoes.

Our co-workers on Gilliesland Farm, near Maidens, were a crew only slightly older than us who hailed from Cowdenbeath in Fife. All boys, each of them had been in trouble with the law but we got on fine with them. They were rough, though. Many of them wore belts signifying membership of the Boys Brigade, an unlikely allegiance. I was to discover one night that the reason for their use was more violence than *vogue*.

BB belts were secured by a catch rather than the traditional pin through a hole in the belt and they had filed down the clasp so that it only caught and no more. They then wore the belts tight around their midriff so that they were taut and when called upon to fight, they would slap the palm of their hand onto the belt at their belly button, thereby depressing and releasing the catch and with a twist of their wrist and a sweep of their arm, they had a dangerous weapon which they used with great dexterity. After dinner (chip sandwiches every night) we'd repair to the barn where they all slept and where their entertainment, night after night, was to stand as if gunslingers seeing how fast they could draw, whipping their belt as close to someone's face as possible. Frequently, blood was spilled due to a miscalculation and it was always greeted with howls of laughter from everyone, including the wounded farmhand. Aye, they were rough.

It was fun, if somewhat scary, passing an hour or two after dinner in this way but I was always glad to bid them goodnight and head back to the tent. (We never rose to the gunslinging challenge). One night we returned and found that someone had discovered the tent, stolen all our stuff and covered the insides with the contents of a tin of baked beans. We stayed full time down on the farm, sleeping with the guys in the barn for about a week after that, but cheap wine was commonly produced later on in the evening and given a severe thrashing. We'd earlier been oblivious to this. It was a bit more fraught then so after a few days, we picked up our wages, were given a free bag of spuds for the house and took our leave.

5. Jaikets for Goalposts

Opportunity is missed by most people because it is dressed in overalls and looks like work.
Thomas Edison

After a couple of years of selling newspapers, I had ploughed much of my earnings back into the morning and evening paper rounds and took an extra few dozen papers to sell to bus passengers while they waited each morning at the bus stop at St. Robert's Chapel for the 48 bus into town. I was making more money than any of my friends at this point, but also working harder than them as well. The smart move would have been to begin to employ others in order to expand my business but I wasn't a natural entrepreneur, just a hard worker, and instead took on a butcher's round as well – the result of which meant that I was working during more and more of my spare time.

McGuire's the Butcher had an outlet in the row of shops on Househillwood Road where it joined Priesthill Road and the boss wanted someone to deliver boxes of (heavy) butchermeat to two convents by bus, one in Barrhead and one in Cardonald, presumably as a contribution from a Roman Catholic-run shop to their general upkeep. Certainly I saw no money ever changing hands.

Big Frankie, the guy in charge, was always very busy and usually I was last to receive any attention. He was possessed of a curious mixture of customer-fawning and customer-loathing and had a high pitched voice which I imagined only dogs could hear properly. I'd wait in the back shop while he conducted affairs out in front by smiling artificially at the customers while shouting tetchy back-shop instructions to young Sandy, an apprentice only a year or so older than me. I was astonished at the behaviour of Frankie who would routinely tip quantities of sawdust into the meat concoctions that would be minced in his machine in order to save on the cost of ingredients. Sandy was often delegated this task and one night so incensed was he at the truculent attitude of Frankie that having been instructed to make him yet another cup of tea, he duly put his finger to his lips, encouraging my silence, and promptly coaxed a brief stream of urine into the cup.

Both of us collapsed in deferred laughter when Frankie appeared a few minutes later and necked the tea in one gulp, issuing further gurgled instructions to Sandy in his squeaky whine and handing me the boxed butchermeat without the slightest recognition that his tea had been tampered with.

Anyway it paid 10/- (ten shillings; post decimalisation, fifty pence) a week and only took up time on Friday evenings and a Saturday morning. So I was a butcher boy and a paperboy morning and evenings and the money I made allowed me to buy clothes, football boots, books and sweets. However, most of my spending was on music. Gran and Grandpa had a large piece of furniture called a radiogram which was an early version of today's music systems. It comprised a radio, storage space for vinyl records and a gramophone and took up the entire length of the window in the living room. The first piece of music I can remember playing over and over again was a 78 rpm disc recording of Fats Domino's *Blueberry Hill*. It still moves me now and inspired me then, even as four guys in Liverpool were forming a band and were interpreting this new music in their own way. I can't believe how lucky I was to be part of the Beatles generation. Right from the harmonica introduction of *Love Me Do*, I was hooked. All the way through my teens. All the way through the sixties, along with the rest of the world, I was inspired by the Beatles, . That said, the first record I ever bought was *'The Hippy Hippy Shake'* by the Swinging Blue Jeans. My first album? *'With the Beatles'*. All and many others purchased from my pre and after-school earnings.

I'd spend many a happy evening in front of the black and white television indulging my musical passions by watching new programmes, the like of which would have been unimaginable only a couple of years before. Initially I watched Saturday evening fare such as Juke Box Jury where new creatures called 'disc jockeys' hosted a half hour show in which a panel of four celebrities listened to an excerpt of a new release, then ventured an opinion on whether it would make the weekly top ten records calculated on sales made over the next seven days. DJ David Jacobs would invite the panellists to express their view by scoring the record's prospects a hit or a miss before, once per programme, bringing out as a surprise the hapless singer or band whose latest offering had just been traduced. Often they got it wrong big time. One week they roundly criticised a song called *Please Release Me* by Englebert Humperdinck, only to see it rise like a rocket to the top of the charts, where it remained for an eternity, keeping the Beatles' double A classic, *Strawberry Fields* and *Penny Lane* from the number one slot it deserved.

My preferred viewing, however, was broadcast on a Friday night. *Ready, Steady Go* was a live show which became a landmark in television broadcasting. It featured live all of the acts whose tunes I whistled morning, noon and night. The Rolling Stones, The Searchers, The Hollies, Gerry and The Pacemakers; importantly, the Beatles, followed a while later by American acts when folk rock, soul music and Tamla Motown became popular in the UK. Bob Dylan, The Beachboys, and Sonny and Cher all contributed to a particularly rich musical heritage.

I was also hugely taken by the new voices of comedy which hit town at the same time as the Beatles or just thereafter. Comedy at that time was largely confined to stand up acts with Tommy Trinder and Ted Ray giving way to the more polished and sophisticated Bob Monkhouse and American stand ups like Bob Hope and Bob Newhart who always just seemed much more slick. However, the tectonic plates began to shift decisively when the traditional evening entertainment of variety and games shows like *What's My Line* or Bruce Forsyth's *Sunday Night at the London Palladium* surrendered to the new satirical news and comedy programme, *That Was The Week That Was*. Beforehand, politicians had been treated with a respect bordering on reverence until Robin Day started a trend towards more aggressive interviewing. This continued in *TW3*, as it was affectionately known, when philosopher and social commentator Bernard Levin interviewed guests in a manner that today's viewer would find pretty tame but back in the mid sixties was viewed by the establishment as insulting and by the viewing public as edge-of-the-seat exciting. However, it was the comedy of David Frost, John Clease, Ronnies Corbett and Barker and the music of Millicent Martin which was the talk among the troops the next day. It featured in the newspapers, set the news agendas for the week and contributed materially to the downfall of the Conservative government of Harold Macmillan. *TW3* pummelled them over the Profumo affair after John Profumo, the Minister of Defence admitted lying to Parliament over an affair he'd had with Christine Keeler, a call girl who was simultaneously seeing a Russian spy.

Then along came Monty Python and comedy was never the same again.

I first remember feeling very proud of myself when aged thirteen I used my paper-run earnings to take my

Gran to see *'How The West Was Won'*, a Western epic, at the Coliseum Cinema in Eglinton Street near the Gorbals. It was billed as the first *'Cinerama'* experience and showed the movie on three separate but conjoined screens. It was somewhat disconcerting as the two end panels showed their elements of the movie in rather more pallid colours but beyond that, the width of the screen rendered the experience as akin to watching a game of tennis due to the swivel-necked approach that had to be taken to capture all of the right-to-left and left-to-right excitement.

It was also at the Coliseum that I witnessed what I still believe was Glasgow's most original street entertainer. I stood with my then girlfriend, Margaret, in a long queue at the side of the cinema. Next to the queue was a large area of derelict land. Panhandlers slowly cruised the line playing the mouth organ or just asking for some spare change. A young man, clearly not the full shilling and able only to communicate using loud guttural noises, caught the attention of the crowd by his sweeping theatricality while he positioned two metal drums some yards from the queue. Having caught everyone's attention, he placed a plank atop the drums and gestured towards it as if displaying a young lady who was about to be sawn in half. Positioning a glass bottle in the centre of the plank, he proceeded to step back, counting his paces by gesturing to the crowd with his fingers.

"One… two… three," they counted in unison as he stepped out ten paces…." eight, nine, TENNN…"

Stooping and picking up a rock, and after much bowing and scraping, the teenager turned, aimed and threw the stone at the bottle, exploding it. As much, I felt, out of pity as out of the admiration it provoked, the crowd erupted in applause. After milking it for a while he repeated the exercise, each repetition doubling the distance from the target than the last. He never missed until, for what was to be his last throw, the crowd beside me were murmuring, "He'll never hit it this time…..not from that distance."

But hit it he did. He was so far away in the gloom at this stage, the queue could hardly see *him* so God only knows how he could have seen the *bottle*. He was so far away when the bottle smashed, it was as if an invisible Stealth Bomber had targeted it from aloft. Again, having retrieved his bunnet from beneath the shards of glass that marked his success, he repeated his theatricals before advancing on the crowd. He must have been popular as he collected rewards, ample enough to permit him to head directly across the road and into the pub.

One assumes that this was a performance he was able to deliver only once per night as his aim might just have been skewed by the amount of alcohol he must subsequently have consumed given the monetary rewards he collected.

His place as the queue entertainer was then taken by an old down-and-out wearing a coat, tied round the middle with a piece of chord, who played a one string guitar and tunelessly sang *'I did it my way,'* without a hint of irony.

Like many others, I was inspired to learn how to play the guitar by the musical environment that surrounded me but I had no means of learning. In my mid teens, I took a deep breath and bought a pretty decent Spanish guitar for just short of £30; a not inconsiderable sum at the time. It had gut strings which were kinder on my virgin finger pads and I started learning the rudiments of guitar work after realising that the opening notes in *'What a day for a Daydream'* by the Lovin' Spoonful merely required the open plucking of the top two strings.

I began to enjoy Scottish folk music very much and my pal Jim Barnes and I bought two tickets to see The Corries, far and away Scotland's most popular folk artists, when they appeared in Paisley Town Hall. They were fabulous.

Musically they were tremendous but their humorous one-liners broke us up. We just had to see them again and decided to travel during the week to Kilmarnock where they were playing their next gig. Before we eventually managed to hitch a lift to Kilmarnock, we had to walk half way there to buy tickets, some nine miles, but were really disappointed when we saw them as their patter was identical to the show in Paisley. It hadn't occurred to us that we'd been watching a performance. We thought these guys were just naturally witty and much of the gloss was removed when we realised they were just brilliant musicians and performers who had rehearsed well.

Roy Williamson, now sadly deceased, inspired me to learn to play jigs and reels on the instrument he played for that purpose on stage, the Spanish *banduria* which unaccountably I managed to purchase in the now long gone Columbs' Music Shop in the Saltmarket. Twelve strings in six, sympathetically tuned sets that he arranged in regular guitar fashion. I found the task of mastering some traditional tunes fairly easy and before long had set up a folk group with Robert (Rab) Houston (the only one of us then proficient on guitar), Les Carson who sang with great gusto, and me. Initially I sang harmony, then helped out on melody with my banduria and as I became more adept, joined Rab on guitar. Over these years I was influenced by various styles of guitar picking. From Big Bill Broonzy and Mississippi John Hurt, I learned how to play a rolling base with my right thumb whilst picking a tune with my first and second fingers. From Scott Joplin, I learned the rudiments of ragtime. I learned that songs could be simple by listening to such as Pete Seeger and Tom Paxton and began to appreciate what is now called 'world music'; folk music from all corners of the globe which began to make sense to me as I realised the multifarious influences that saw the emergence of popular music. It was all grist to the mill and for a while I became something of an anorak as I'd refuse to appreciate the modern interpretation of blues or even Scottish music, boring all within earshot with my view that the version we were listening to was but a poor imitation of the original. I changed my views as I grew up and began to understand and be excited by the virtuosity of rock guitarists like Eric Clapton and Tex-Mex geniuses like Ry Cooder as well as musicians such as Phil Cunningham who modernised Scottish music in a most interesting and refreshing way.

Rab's father was the manager in charge of the Gorbals Waterworks, so named because they served the household needs of communities on the south side of the city among which was numbered the Gorbals in Glasgow. The waterworks were located in the countryside almost three miles from Craigbank where Les and I lived. It was a great place to rehearse because the small workers' canteen, heated by a coal fire of a winter evening had great acoustics and the three of us spent night after night bawling away, trying to master harmonies that were almost Appalachian in their resonance, thrashing our guitars and honing our act. Most nights we had an audience of one; Johnny Anderson the night watchman. Johnny loved our singing and he'd make us tea in the workers' tin billy cans which became hotter than the surface of the sun when he poured the tea but eventually cooled down about an hour later to permit us to drink tea which was even then only marginally less hot than molten magma. However, Johnny was a big fan and, for what it was worth, encouraged us no end. One of the four lochs was called 'Ryat Lynn' (pronounced Ree-at Linn) and we decided to name our band after the reservoir beside which we met in music most evenings.

Night after night for perhaps three years Les and I trooped to and back from the waterworks; two and a half miles there and two and a half miles back each night in complete darkness, me carrying my guitar in a plastic case, often in the pissing rain and the howling winds. We didn't feel a thing as we put the world to rights, quite oblivious to our personal comfort and safety.

In those days, 1965 through 1968, Glasgow was caught up in a wave of serious gang violence which was based upon territory. Our local gang was The Bundy, so named after the Bundy Clock - a time machine used by bus drivers to validate the precise time they passed it by inserting a card on which was printed the time of their arrival in Pollok. There was also The Crew, The Tongs, The Cumbie, The Young Team and scores more. Knives and swords were the weapons of choice; in many ways the devotion we had to our music removed us from that scene. Usually the only people we met on our travels home were individuals on their way to undertake a spot of illicit night-fishing in the reservoirs. Sometimes they'd be drunk but the country road was always so dark that we'd be upon one another before we'd realise it and would pass by acknowledging each other with a Glasgow, "Aye!" often pronounced solely as an audible, sharp intake of breath.

As we approached home and were illuminated once again by streetlights we occasionally had to run the gauntlet of abuse or stone throwing from local neds, for no other reason than we happened to be passing by when they decided to have some target practice or cat calling. One night a local gang member, drunk as a lord, pulled a large knife as Les and I passed by and started to chase us. I was pretty fleet of foot and even carrying a guitar outpaced him easily. Les was a heavily built guy at the time. Fat, actually. He was making heavy weather of it and without thinking of the consequences, I stopped running, turned round and darted between Les and the drunk, drawing his attention. Somehow he discovered new energy and kept up with me, knife still in hand, screaming obscenities, until I arrived at the house of my Gran in Househillwood Road. I pounded on the door and it seemed like an eternity before it opened and I rushed in past a startled grandmother just as the drunk launched himself at the now locked front door. Internal shouts that the police were on their way persuaded him to lurch drunkenly into the night, but it served to remind us that Glasgow deserved its reputation as a violent city and we counted ourselves lucky that our musical pastime pretty much kept us away from behaviour which was more routinely part of everyday life for many of our friends.

When I left the Scouts as Troop Leader, I'd been attending a folk club in Burnbrae Primary School for a couple of years and was now playing fairly regularly in public with a fluid and ever changing line up of musical pals. My guitar playing was now pretty acceptable and my ability to play jigs and reels set me apart from most others apart from one of my classmates, Davie Closs, who had a real mastery of the mandolin. Each week he would turn up with yet another Scottish or Irish reel to entertain us, his fingers in a blur as we all sat in genuine appreciation of his talents. It certainly inspired me to improve my playing, as I suspect it did everyone else.

One week the youth worker who took our class didn't turn up, because his work had taken him to England, and without him it seemed that we wouldn't be allowed to meet as a club. I phoned the Department of Education at 129 Bath Street - now the Art House Hotel - and asked to speak with Sam Swinton, the Corporation's Education Officer with responsibility for this aspect of youth work. I told him about my musical ability, my position of Troop Leader with the 168th and my ensuing placement in Balrossie School. I asked whether or not I might be allowed to take responsibility for running the folk club. I accepted that many of those attending were older than me but felt that I could hold things together. Mr Swinton not only agreed, he paid me a princely sum of more than £7 a session to do so. I hadn't expected this and the fact of me receiving money was later to create a wedge between me and a couple of older members who felt, not unreasonably, that they contributed as much to the running of the club as I did. I, however, had had the gumption to make the phone call.

I was always grateful to Sam Swinton because I became the youngest youth leader on the books and this led me to other future opportunities that I had by no means planned. I felt sorry for him mind you because he had a speech impediment which was more than a lisp. The letter 'S' was pronounced as if it were a watery gush from his upper palate. His parents couldn't have known about this when they named him Sam Swinton but, by God, the poor fellow must have felt like changing his name by deed poll each and every day he was called on to introduce himself as *Thshaam Thshwinton*.

Flushed with the success of running the publicly financed Burnbrae Folk Club, I persuaded my pal and fellow guitarist Jim Barnes to join me in running our own commercial folk club in the Orchard Park Hotel in Giffnock. Rab Houston had followed his dad to Wales and Les had also moved from Glasgow. The Ryat Lynn were no more. Jim and I had been regular attendees and performers at clubs all over the West of Scotland and although we greatly enjoyed our nights out, we were frequently critical of the lax organisation, casual start times, the poor standard of some of the entertainers and the low numbers attending. We talked with a number of hotels, saw a gap in the market on Sunday evenings and advertised our first club meeting in the *Sunday Mail,* opening in the Orchard Park Hotel with Aly Bain and Mike Whellans in 1968. It was a big success and over a couple of years, until student life robbed me of the time to continue, Jim and I brought every folk act in Scotland to the club with the exception of The Corries, who had become huge and had outgrown the circuit by some distance. Acting as Master of Ceremonies each week (Jim was less comfortable in front of a microphone), I introduced the acts and developed a line in patter, telling crap jokes and making fawning comments about the act to follow.

I was asked to back Matt McGinn on guitar, then a great hero of working class Glasgow because of his canon of wonderful, self-penned works. I was beside myself with joy on stage with Matt and thought myself in the presence of greatness until after the gig, Matt asked for his wages in crates of beer. I was brought down to earth with a bump as I saw a man with clay feet who was struggling with alcohol but as requested, agreed a deal with the hotel to exchange his fee for beer and whisky from the hotel bar. In those days, pubs and off-licences closed early and on Sunday, pubs were shut unless you were a travelling salesman and were permitted to slake your thirst in a hotel bar before, somewhat counter-intuitively, getting back into your car and driving home.

The McCalmans, Alex Campbell, Dick Gaughan, Archie Fisher and Hamish Imlach among many others all graced our folk club. Jim and I performed ourselves one evening at the Barrhead Hotel and were immersed backstage in conversation with Johnny de Silva as he'd been on the BBC's folk programme and we were completely impressed by being on the same bill as a radio star. Our discussion was distracted, however, by gales of raucous laughter coming from the main auditorium. After a while even Johnny wanted to see what all the fuss was about and we wandered through to see two bearded guys, one quieter than the other, absolutely flaying the audience. Immediately we were caught up in the humour that was Billy Connolly. Then he was one of the two original Humblebums along with Tam *Fingers* Harvey and although the songs were themselves most enjoyable and Tam's guitar playing was excellent, it was the birth of Connolly's public appearances as a great comedian that we were witnessing. Over the years I played on the bill with them on a few occasions and was flattered to be asked to MC one of their concerts in the Fairweather Halls in Newton Mearns. I was never in any doubt that Connolly was a great talent and along with all of the other Glaswegians who saw him live, acknowledged that it was only a matter of time before he found himself on television. It never occurred to us that this would be on other than the odd folk show or maybe a wee turn on a comedy programme. No one, including Billy himself I'm sure, saw the gigantic career and world-wide fame he would achieve over the years.

After a couple of years, Billy introduced Gerry Rafferty into the band. Gerry always seemed a really shy guy but his music was absolutely beautiful; quite, quite different from the stuff that the Humblebums were presenting. Songs like *'Can I have my money back?'* and *'Steamboat Row'* stood out. It must have been a difficult time for the three of them. Gerry would, in time, carve out a brilliant musical career for himself culminating in one of his songs, *Baker Street* being voted Song of the Year in 1978 and another, *'Stuck in the middle with you'*, being selected as the theme tune for Quentin Tarantino's cult film, *Reservoir Dogs*, and giving a new lease of life to his musical career by introducing a younger listening audience to his musical canon.

At that time, however, Tam Harvey would sit at the side of the stage while Connolly did Connolly and before the next Gerry Rafferty song was introduced. Whether innocently or otherwise, Tam disinterestedly fingered the notes to 'The Third Man' quietly on his guitar. Not long afterwards The Humblebums broke up and Tam fared less well than either of the other two.

I enjoyed myself immensely in the Orchard Park and was proud that Jim and I, each aged 18, ran a most successful operation and that we each left with a pretty impressive profit of £80, an unheard of circumstance in cash-strapped clubs in those days when doubtless profits were drunk rather than invested. All it took was decent organisation and a determination not to imbibe the surplus.

Jim went on to record albums with other bands but we lost touch only to meet again in the eighties. He was working as an electrician and had settled in one of the high flats in the Gorbals. He was delighted to see me again and we met up a couple of times but we'd both moved on and again we lost touch. In our teens, Jim stayed only about one hundred yards from me in Peat Road but it may as well have been one hundred miles in terms of the condition of his house. Whereas my tenemental flat was warm and dry as a consequence of the central heating, Jim's most assuredly was not and in the evenings when we'd practise our guitar-playing in his small bedroom, you could see the damp running down the walls. Neither of us were scientists although we perhaps should have been able to understand the pretty basic science that calor gas heaters merely compound conditions of dampness.

Jim always had a cough. Always! And it was with great sadness in 2004 that I read that he'd died. I knew in my bones that it would have been caused by the early conditions in which he'd been raised.

As I write this chapter, too many Glaswegians still live under these conditions.

For as long as I can remember, football was my game. As a very young child I can remember kicking a ball around. Nothing surprising there, as everyone, at least every young boy, played football, or fitba' as we called it. It was ubiquitous. And as all of the commentators say of these times, football really *was* played in the streets and it usually *was* with a tennis ball although, when we did manage to get a 'bladder' or leather football, it was treasured beyond measure and gave substance to the probably apocryphal question often alleged to have been asked in those days,

"Is Johnny comin' out to play?"

"Naw, he's stayin' in tonight."

"Well, is his ba' comin' out to play?"

I suppose it's incontrovertible that something has been lost by today's youth in sporting terms, although progress has brought an obvious and astonishing bounty. Today my young children play computer games, watch television, do homework, play music and watch DVDs and play *organised* football; skills based and routinely for two hours on a Saturday morning. They play with a group of other kids the same age under the tutelage of the Scottish Football Association and each one of them plays with their own, SFA approved boy-sized, leather football. Back in the day, we used any ball that was available but when playing *organised* football, had to use the school-approved, terrifying 'Mouldmaster', a plasticised, rubberised, dimpled thing that struck fear into all playing the game. Anyone who had to head the thing, never mind defend a strike, was guaranteed to be writhing in agony with red and purple bruising on their body seconds after impact. You certainly had to have something of the Corinthian spirit about you if you were struck by one of these balls!

My generation, not having the distractions of today's kids, just played football in the streets. Most of us were greedy footballers. When the ball came to our feet our task was to accomplish something extraordinary with it…a thunderous shot, an astonishing piece of trickery, a wondrous piece of ball control. Seldom did we consider a slide rule pass to another team mate who was better positioned; or was that just me? Bob Wylie, then my next door neighbour and thuggish centre half would certainly agree the proposition that I was all trickery and little substance. All flash and no end result. And I suppose I was. When I look at my son Conor, presently aged nine as I write this piece - my God, he's the same!

We'd play in any grassed area large enough to accommodate the size of teams which had gathered. A small rectangle would suffice if it was just "three and in" - the logic of which always eluded me. Most boys, and I was certainly no exception, didn't want to play in goals. Goalies were either crazy (because they saw that position as their own and had the scars to prove it) or crap footballers (who would be sent to play in goals so as not to annoy us, more gifted, individuals). Accordingly, "three and in" worked on the premise that a small group of, say, three or five kids would put one of their number in the despised goal and the others would dribble and shoot to their heart's content. Great fun! Until, of course, you'd scored two goals and your next score would see you sit out five minutes or so in goal because you had amassed the score of three. All of a sudden, you'd be hitting the post (a pile of players' jackets) or permitting a last minute tackle you could have seen off easily. Even, heaven forfend, passing the ball to someone else.

Another game we played was "headies" (pronounced 'heedies'). This could be played in any area that permitted some ten yards between the goals. It comprised two or four players and took the form of a headed ball played from the hand of the player guarding goal 'A' being played towards goal 'B' and being defended by the opposition or headed goalwards by your team mate where it would be saved or headed back. Caught by an opposing player on his chest before the ball touched the ground, it could be volleyed with force back towards you.

I was always a forward. In my youth I was always one of the speediest players on the pitch and was used by the coach as an outside right - sometimes also as an outside left because I worked a lot on developing my left foot as well. My contribution to the team became straightforward. Hugging the wing, I'd wait for a pass and then tempt the full back before hitting the ball past him, running away from him and crossing the ball for the centre forward to score. At least that was the theory.

In adulthood, Big Bob Wylie sent me a Christmas card one year with the far from festive inscription "Fuck's sake Culley, get the ba' intae the box", on the inside, blank side of the card in place of the rather more customary, 'Merry Christmas'... this in memory of his then stated frustration that he'd see me take off down the wing, the full back adrift of me. He'd set off on one of his 'power-runs' into the box only to see me stop the ball and attempt to beat the full back at least one more time before attempting a cross. Like he said, 'all flash and no end product'.

Anyway, I loved my football and throughout my schooldays played for the school team. No team I ever played for achieved anything in trophy terms but I always remember my teams as being one of the contenders in any league or cup we contested. A kind of Dundee United or Aston Villa as it were. We would win more often than we lost but I was never fortunate enough to play for an all-conquering side whose players went on to achieve prominence in the game. That said, I played with some really talented players. The aforementioned 'thuggish centre half', Big Bob Wylie, was always a most dependable stopper. He was tall and well built and, supported by Robert Cumming playing sweeper, won everything in the air. He was far from a shy and retiring player. His shouted instructions punctuated every football move in the game. Nor indeed was he above the odd physical indelicacy on the pitch. He was fearsome and I was always glad he was on my team rather than with the Woodfarm or Glenwood opposition.

Another team member, John Severin, was signed as an apprentice by West Ham but unaccountably reappeared in Glasgow one Saturday night some years later where, in his local, the Househill Tavern in Nitshill, he told incredulous footballing friends, who had dined out on tales of their friend John who was about to become a world beater, that he had returned to Scotland because he was a bit homesick and had decided he wanted to be an engineer! Many years later he turned up having become a wealthy farmer in the Borders! Who'd have thought?

Robert Butchard (now a senior civil servant) went on to play for Hibs and Arsenal and Murray Brodie (a detective constable in England) played for Leicester. Although we never played in the same team because he was three years my junior and in my brother Campbell's class at school, Kenny Burns played with us in kickabouts and was the most successful footballer of our generation of Craigbank schoolboys. Initially he was signed by Rangers but they couldn't keep him on the pitch because of his temper and violent play so they sold him at quite a young age. He slipped into temporary obscurity but then resurfaced at Birmingham, Leeds and Nottingham Forest in England where, first as a free scoring centre forward and then as a commanding centre half, he dominated a talented Forest team under Brian Clough as they swept all before them in England and won the European Cup twice. He also won the Player of the Year accolade when Forest were all-conquering.

Even then he didn't lose his reputation as a talented but essentially dirty player. In one oft-repeated TV clip from a major European match, he could be seen quite clearly headbutting an opponent on the back of his head because he had had the temerity to stand in front of him when Forest were forming a wall to defend a free kick. Kenny also won several full Scotland caps.

Many other of my school pals, just as talented as those mentioned above, left the game … some to university or jobs, others to drugs. One of the most gifted contemporaries I ever played with was Robert Bennett. He was quite fabulous. A small midfield player - inside right in those days - he dominated every match in which he played. He won all sorts of honours in school football but even as a boy I sensed that he was fighting personal demons. Some many years later when I was a regular attendee at Ibrox Stadium as a corporate guest, I stepped outside of the hospitality box, within which I had been enjoying a wee refreshment at half time, and came into eye contact with Rab who was apparently employed as a match steward. Stadium barriers prevented me going over to see him but we shared a Glasgow recognition; an upward lift of the chin and an expressionless face whilst in eye contact revealed Rab still with what I thought was a terrible sadness in his eyes. A real loss to the game and a genuine personal tragedy as a consequence.

I was never encouraged to support Rangers as a youth despite my family's Loyalist ethos. My Gran was the most outspoken on the matter as she was worried about my safety if I were to attend games at Ibrox. Clyde FC was her preference for some reason. They played at Shawfield Stadium, just outside Rutherglen, and were one of the poorer performing teams of the day. In those days, drinking alcohol was permitted at matches and a large proportion of the crowd would turn up drunk, especially if it was an Old Firm game featuring Rangers and Celtic. An additional factor was that in those days, games, even mid-table games, could attract large crowds. Goals were also easier to come by, or so it seemed.

The first match attended by myself and a couple of pals, ignoring the imprecations of my Grandmother, took place at Ibrox between Rangers and Ayr United. It was a delicious feeling being part of a large crowd which must have been over forty thousand, and Rangers won 7– 3.

I'd go regularly to Rangers matches largely (and this became a feature in my football attendances in the future) to watch a special footballer. Even in my immature understanding of the finer skills of football, it was obvious that Jim Baxter was a master. He was so elegant on the ball. Never rushed or hurried. Easy on the ball. Cheeky. Unfortunately he performed on a stage and at a time just before video evidence could have provided us with ineffable proof of his genius. Today I have a couple of videos of him playing in the 3 – 2 game at Wembley, when Scotland became the first team to beat England after they won the World Cup in 1966, prompting the obvious proposition (if you were a Scot) that Scotland were now effectively the world champions. Baxter taunted the English, playing keepie-uppie with the ball in their half of the pitch. Scotland could have gone on to score more but it was obvious that Baxter, Denis Law and Billy Bremner were more interested in taking the piss out of the world champions rather then winning the game handsomely. But the video clips don't do justice to his play because they fall far below the quality of film used today where colour and playbacks provide the opportunity for repeated assessment of a match episode.

In 1973 there took place a famous FA Cup Final between lowly Sunderland and the all-conquering Leeds United at Wembley. Scotsman Ian Porterfield, one of eight on the field that day, scored to win the cup for an astonished Sunderland and in the months afterwards, sociologists began to report on a phenomenon that took place in the city's workplaces where productivity shot skywards and was put down to the higher morale of its workforce as a consequence of Sunderland's new status as a footballing powerhouse. In the sixties and seventies, even into the eighties and nineties, I was privileged to watch Scottish footballing talent that propelled my country to real sporting adventures. Our players populated all of the English teams and yet the Scottish teams would regularly beat their English counterparts due to the burgeoning abilities of our local produce. I find myself depressed as I write these reminiscences due to the present paucity of ability that now characterise Scottish national teams as well as the almost complete absence in this new millennium of Scots in English teams; Scottish Teams as well, come to that. I find myself asking myself, 'Who couldn't pick a magnificent Scotland team from the likes of Billy McNeill, Peter Lorimer, Bruce Rioch, Tommy Gemmell, Sandy Jardine, Gordon McQueen, John Greig, Frank McClintock, Gary McAllister, Bertie Auld, Andy Gray, Bobby Murdoch, Gordon Strachan and great goalkeepers like Jim Leighton and Alan Rough?'

And could even the mighty Brazil have beaten a Scottish team line up of Andy Goram in goals, Danny McGrain, Alex McLeish, Willie Miller and Eddie McCreadie in defence.... Jimmy Johnstone, Billy Bremner, Kenny Dalglish and Jim Baxter in midfield with Joe Jordan and Ally McCoist up front?...perhaps too attack-minded? Maybe so. Imbalanced? Probably. But what an entertainment!...off the pitch as well as a few of them could take a drink. Jimmy Johnstone enjoyed his rowing boats, Andy Goram proved my theory beyond peradventure about goalies being crazy (Andy having allegedly been diagnosed with a mild form of schizophrenia, fans used to take to singing, "Two Andy Gorams, there's only two Andy Gorams…") and Billy Bremner liked his Woodbine full-strength.

I also watched Rangers in my youth just because they were closer geographically. Upon moving to Pollok it became evident that we were to live once again in a 'van culture' for a few years; everything was available only from one of the many vans which plied their trade by touring the housing scheme. If you wanted to do anything; swim, go to the movies, shop, play football, watch football or walk in the park, then you had to go to Govan in a 49 or 23 bus. A 48 or a 48A took you to Midland Street in the city centre.

Ibrox Park was but a twenty minute bus journey away whereas Parkhead was at the other side of Glasgow. Having said that, over the years I have watched Celtic play at home much more than Rangers largely because of the subsequent regularity of my visits to Parkhead during the several seasons when King Kenny, Kenny Dalglish, played for the hoops. He was as magnificent as Baxter but much more explosive and a simply brilliant goal-scorer to boot! Many of his goals were 'screamers'.

In 1966, aged sixteen, I was introduced to European matches at Ibrox. Tottenham Hotspur was the all conquering English team of the mid sixties. They'd won the FA Cup the year before and had drawn Rangers in their first European round of the season. Rangers were required to play a qualifying round and had defeated Seville so they were no bad team. Spurs won 5-2 at White Hart Lane and their trip north was keenly awaited. I was excited to see the majestic Jimmy Greaves, quite the consummate centre forward, who had been scoring goals for fun in the English league.

There was a crowd of some 80,000 at Ibrox and the match took place in the evening under floodlights. It was a fantastic atmosphere. A calm night with nicotine-infused smoke billowing upwards from the crowd, many of whom had a Woodbine cigarette on their lips and liquor on their breath. Outside, policemen on horses controlled the good natured queues. I can remember the crush of the crowd, all standing except for those seated in the stand. I can recall the wit and humour of the largely Glaswegian crowd as we all awaited kick-off and can also recount the stilled silence as Jimmy Greaves scored from a Dave McKay pass after five minutes. The game ended 3-2 to Spurs so the Scots weren't entirely humiliated.

In those days the entire Rangers team was comprised of Scots. And as I say, most English teams had one or two Scots playing for them, Spurs being no exception with the aforementioned Dave McKay, John White, and keeper Bill Brown all wearing their white strip.

Another difference from today's football was that in those days, clubs would routinely put out the same players week after week. There were no substitutes permitted so anyone not playing in the first team was reduced to playing in the reserves or sitting in the stand. I can still name that regular Rangers' team without taxing my memory; Ritchie, Shearer, Caldow; Greig, McKinnon, Baxter; Scott, McMillan, Millar, Brand and Wilson. I saw this team play week in week out and pretty much the only change I was to witness was the replacement of the pacey Alex Scott, who was sold to Everton, by the Rangers version of Celtic's Jimmy 'Jinky' Johnstone, Willie Henderson. They also played with a goalkeeper, two full backs; right and left, three half backs and five forwards. It wouldn't be until Alf Ramsey's World Cup-winning English team introduced the 4-2-4 system in the mid-sixties that we saw the death of wingers. Players had to become more utilitarian, fitter and more defensive. England's (and Italy's for that matter) style of play was very effective but much more boring to watch. Aye, but they called it progress.

Several of the school football team had progressed to the Juvenile team under Mr. Edwards (no one ever knew his first name) and we were joined by Bob Wylie, John Severin, mad goalkeeper Gardner Robertson and a few others, but after a couple of seasons the team began to fray at the edges as people began to drift away. I moved on to play for a season with Harmony Row from Govan, then, as today, one of the best organised Juvenile teams in the various leagues they contest. I played up front with Alistair McLeod (not the ill-fated Scotland manager) who went on to play with Hibs and won a Scotland cap. The gulf between him and everyone else was huge but it was great fun playing off the scraps he created on the few occasions when his frequent and usually successful attempts to waltz through the opposition and score came to nought.

As my teenage years progressed, I began to play organised football less and less. My placement at rural Balrossie Approved School kept me away from the game for a year; courting Margaret and, eventually, studenthood put paid to my playing although I turned out over the years for a number of teams as a guest player and eventually played decently enough to maintain a pair of football boots until well into my forties.

But there was also a world beyond football. Our house at 268 was a three story tenement building with two flats on each floor, both with their own veranda facing on to the street. Upstairs was Mrs Taylor and her brood. I've lost count now but there must have been about a dozen weans. No one was ever permitted to enter the Taylor household, I suspect because it may have been a bit of a midden. They were a poor family. Mr Taylor, an Englishman from Nottingham worked in the Govan shipyards in an office and enjoyed a pint. One day he just upped and left home and returned to Nottingham. Ian and his siblings would go to see him on summer holidays returning with exciting stories about the River Trent and Robin Hood but other than that contact, My Gran's pal, poor Mrs Taylor had to bring the kids up on her own. There was always a lot of chaotic shouting and bawling up there but fortunately although they lived above us, it was the apartment above and *across* the landing so we were protected from the noise which must have been caused round the clock by the herd of young Taylors stampeding across the uncarpeted floor.

I was friendly with Ian Taylor who was a year older than me and he and I would organise back court games such as *'Kick the Can'*, *'Who Falls the Best?'* and stealing strawberries from a netted and fecund plot within our shared back garden; a pretty large area split six ways with a drying green in the middle and a concrete bunker towards the back within which were stored the bins for household rubbish.

Our games were pretty traditional. *Kick The Can* involved someone guarding a tin can placed openly, having been liberated from the rubbish bins, while others hid. Upon seeing one of those in hiding, the guard had to run back to the can first and thereby won the discovered party to his side. Anyone eluding the guard and kicking the can freed everyone and the game started again. It was therefore not unknown for some measure of collusion to take place whereby a captured person colluded with someone to kick the can thereby securing his or her own freedom. Like *'Three and In'* it had certain inbuilt illogicalities.

Who Falls The Best? could not be considered a traditional back court game in that it emerged solely from the diet of Cowboy-and-Indian films which populated the cinemas at that time. It involved groups of us playing the part of one or other of the combatants and upon being shot by an adversary, dying in the most dramatic way possible. The 'shooter' chose the winner and we'd start again.

The next close down lived Neil Johnstone, the only other person against whom I ever raised my hands, following a blatant and painful kick from him on the football field. Again it was an instinctive punch and blackened his eye but it also served to maintain my minor reputation as someone who could throw a right hook. Neil was a really gifted centre forward and was always a certainty to start a match due to his bulk, cultured style and ability to score at will. Neil also went with me to Harmony Row but he could not prise the centre forward's jersey (understandably) from Alistair McLeod and so moved on in pretty short order.

Next door to my Gran's close lived Big Bob Wylie. Like me, as a youth he was known by his Sunday name, Robert, within the family just as I was Ronald within mine. In the street, I became known by the diminutive Ronnie, which name I held until I became a student when a lecturer began to refer to me as Ron. I thought it made me seem more adult and encouraged its usage thereafter. However Bob was referred to at the time, it was always prefixed by the adjective 'Big'. Bob was always tall and well built and fell naturally into the role of central defender in any football team.

Bob's dad was a brickie and he died suddenly of a brain haemorrhage when Bob was young. His mother somehow managed to have him educated at Alan Glen's Grammar School which was situated in the centre of town and involved long bus journeys there and back. Being a fee paying school (Bob won a bursary) it required some small measure of attention to studying after school so Bob wasn't as involved with us in our adventures. We liked making bogies out of planks of wood and pram wheels, making dams on the White Cart, a somewhat polluted stream (or burn) which flowed about half a mile away, cycling to the gorse hills along the Barrhead Road which bounded a piece of derelict land full of hillocks and trails and which permitted all sorts of Cowboys-and-Indians games, although in our case the horses were replaced by our home-built bicycles, each cannibalised from the several chassis which we owned, although only one of which was ever serviceable.

Bob's mother died when he was nineteen; the ever-caring Glasgow Corporation supported him in his moment of grief by removing him from his community and the warmth of his three apartment tenement flat in Househillwood Road to the dangerous, derelict and desperate Red Road multi-story flats at the other end of Glasgow. Bob moved on to university, unheard of in our street, and re-emerged several years later as a social worker in Castlemilk and the top man in the Militant Tendency within Scotland, the left-wing movement which determined that *entryism* as it was called, was the most efficient way of achieving the power necessary to implement their political agenda.

So it was that Militant infiltrated the Labour Party in the UK with great success until Neil Kinnock began a process to have its followers excommunicated. At this time, I was a member of the Scottish Labour Party, following the briefest flirtation with the Scottish National Party in my teens, and should have been a mortal enemy of Bob's. But he was my erstwhile team mate and next door neighbour and I took considerable vicarious pleasure from reading in the newspapers of his political success while it lasted. Bob spent most of his twenties and beyond working for Militant, a subscription-based organisation whose members were expected to contribute any earnings they made for the benefit of the party. Bob's relationship with them came to an end when, having made a few quid from writing an article for a broadsheet, he asked the Militant General Secretary, Peter Taaffe, if he might keep the cash to buy a Christmas present for his two kids, David and Susan. Taaffe held to the party's position of seeking the money for the party and disgruntled, Bob put his family first and stepped aside from his role as Scottish organiser.

Anyway, I ended my school years with a minimum of qualifications and my luck had held. I hadn't fallen foul of the law, I had the offer of a one year position in a junior Approved School after the summer holidays, I had thoughts of becoming a social worker just like Mrs Robertson (who'd have thought I'd have ambitions beyond being an anonymous clerk somewhere?), I had a girlfriend, I had developed some musical ability, had achieved prominence in the local Scouts, was regarded as a decent football player and had built a pretty impressive ability to earn a weekly wage before and after school. I was settled with Gran and Grandpa. Now I had to face up to the world of work.

6. From Balrossie To Ferguslie Park

Do all the good you can, by all the means you can, in all the ways you can, in all the places you can, at all the times you can, as long as ever you can.
John Wesley

Painted white, Balrossie Approved School was an imposing turreted castle situated on a hill just outside Kilmacolm in Renfrewshire. It was home to about eighty young boys aged from eight years old to fourteen. In 1968, Scotland had the youngest age of criminal liability in Europe. Where other countries took the view that children couldn't fully understand the consequences of their actions until they were fifteen, Scottish legislation permitted their incarceration at half that age.

Mostly they were sent there by the courts as a result of very youthful indiscretions compounded by family circumstances which failed to convince the Sheriff that their future would be safe in their hands. However, just after I started at Balrossie, the Scots introduced legislation under the 1968 Social Work Scotland Act which rendered the country the toast of the world's liberal community with the advent of Children's Hearings. Approved Schools became List 'D' Schools. Over the years they became more caring but when I spent a year at Balrossie they still retained the discipline of the parade ground. It was ludicrous, on reflection, to see small children report on parade wearing battledress. Khaki uniforms made them all look like cut down soldiers. It was absurd but it was the culture of the day and, worryingly, I took to it like a duck to water.

The teacher who effectively ran the school was Mr Abrines, the school gym teacher. He was the disciplinarian and was similar to Mr Ross in Gowanbank School in that his personality imposed respect and no small measure of affection on behalf of the boys. The headteacher was Mr

Hand, a soft spoken and very caring man who nevertheless imposed a quiet discipline. I got on well with everyone and flourished in my year's residence, other than on one occasion when I was asked to put stamps on all of the letters written weekly by the boys to their families and thoughtlessly succumbed to my republican persuasion by drawing a beard on the Queen's face on each stamp. The next day, Mr Hand very quietly invited me in to his room and with a smile on his lips gently said, "I believe you owe me some money".

I had to pay over the equivalent of my week's allowance for defacing the stamps, but other than that incident, I developed really good relationships with staff and boys and persuaded myself that I might be able to handle myself in the area of youth work or social work.

Towards the end of my year's stay there and with the encouragement of Mr Abrines, I was put in touch with the Reverend Geoff Shaw who was pioneering a community based approach to support young people in the Gorbals area of Glasgow. I became quite excited at the prospect of participating with young clergymen, police cadets and others who flocked to join with him in the service of others. I went to see him and passed the interview with flying colours. Geoff was delighted at the prospect of having a Glaswegian in the ranks, as his other interns came from all over the UK. Imagine my disappointment then when I turned up at his small tenement flat in the Gorbals clutching my letter of appointment and ready to start work, only to be told that a letter had been received that morning rejecting an application which was to have paid for my tenure. Geoff seemed more upset than me but there was to be no room at the inn. He couldn't afford to employ me.

Geoff Shaw worked tirelessly in the service of the people of the Gorbals and was elected as the first Labour

Convenor of the new Strathclyde Regional Council. Had I taken up the internship and done well, who knows how I might have prospered in Geoff's first administration. Some years later when I worked for the Regional Council after Geoff's untimely death (through overwork at a ridiculously young age) my then boss, Iain Hill, recounted that when Geoff Shaw and his first Chief Executive, Sir Lawrence Boyle, began the process of setting up this gargantuan administration, he had been selected because of his close working relationship with Boyle rather than because of any particular abilities he had. Perhaps I'd have been favoured too.

In consequence, upon leaving Balrossie, I took the first job I saw in the employment exchange, as a dustbin-man in Paisley. Nowadays garbage is separated, bagged, collected in wheelie-bins and recycled but in back in 1968, rubbish was deposited in large, heavy metal bins. These had to be lifted on one shoulder and carried out onto the street and tipped into the back of the bin lorry (or midgie lorry as we called them) before returning the empty receptacle to the bin store at the back of the house. I was very fit but found myself running all morning in pursuit of my fellow bin-men who were on piece-work, and the sooner they finished, the sooner they could get to the pub.

These guys spent each weekday afternoon drinking ; I couldn't believe their ability to show up for work the next morning at 7.00 before undergoing five or six hours of physical exercise that would test professional sportsmen. I lasted two weeks before my shoulder bruised so badly that the doctor signed me off. I hadn't worked long enough to be entitled to sick pay, so went back and was assigned the 'box buggy', a much sought-after job that merely involved me in sitting in the cab of an open-decked lorry and touring rows of shops in Paisley collecting all of the empty cardboard boxes the shopkeepers had put outside.

Compared with my earlier task, this was easy, but after a summer stint, I figured that it would be much tougher as the weather changed and found a job as a clerical worker with British Rail.

Based in offices in Central Station, I enjoyed it as a twelve month stop gap, but was quite open with my colleagues that my future lay in social work or youth work. My main task was to calculate the money due to British Rail from the staff who sold sandwiches on the longer rail routes. On the left hand of the ledger were listed downwards the dozens of various items they sold and across the top were the respective prices. At the intersection was the number showing the quantities sold. All I had to do was to work out the sub totals of, for example seventeen pies at two shillings and fivepence, thirty four teas at elevenpence, sixty one biscuits at one shilling and a penny. Then I had to add the totals. This wasn't rocket science but I found it impossible to do it accurately. Every time I calculated the figures I came up with a different total. I bought a ready reckoner - a paper book version of a hand held calculator which listed on each page the answers to each multiplication. I still got it wrong. I *could* add up but only slowly and not without using my fingers, moving my lips and squinting my eyes as if blinded by the sun.

Eventually the manager brought me into the office and warned me that if my performance didn't improve, I'd be for the off. I wasn't particularly troubled, because it wasn't a job I saw as important to me, but what saved my bacon were the problems which ensued when even my poor calculations couldn't disguise the fact that there seemed to be a routine and major drop-off in sales of sandwiches on the Glasgow/Inverness run. I struggled with the numbers for ages before having to ask for help. I figured that this would be the last straw but after investigation, the police were called in and it transpired that the rail staff were making their own sandwiches and selling them on the trains at BR prices thereby reducing the number of BR sandwiches on sale - much, I'm sure to the great delight of the customers. They were making a pretty decent supplement to their wages and I thought them rather entrepreneurial but they were charged with fraud and fired. The legal kerfuffle this caused kept me in post until I left to advance my ambition to become a youth worker.

I'd failed my driving test three times and passed it on my fourth. If I wanted to make a career of youth work I'd have to undertake professional training, and I'd sent off an application to Jordanhill Teacher Training College. My mum allowed me to drive her car and accompanied me, along with Margaret in the back seat, to Jordanhill for my interview. I felt completely at home. Confident. Articulate. I explained away my poor schooling honestly and left pretty sure that I'd done enough to be accepted. It was a really competitive course but my confidence was well placed and some months later I was informed that I was to undertake a two year course in youth and community studies starting in October 1970. I was going to be a student. But first I had to get some experience.

Between the ages of seventeen and twenty I'd retained my (pretty lucrative) involvement in running the folk club in Burnbrae School in Priesthill and had gradually built the club up as new members replaced the old guard, many of whom found it a bit much that this young whippersnapper had flounced in and was now receiving payment for something they all figured (completely accurately) that they could have done just as well. Thssham Thshwinton obviously saw something in me and asked me to apply for a job which the Corporation of Glasgow were about to advertise, as a youth worker in a new venture in Pollok.

Gang warfare in Glasgow was still rife and the education authorities decided that a new policy of intervention at a young age was the way forward, so they built a few experimental 'Youth Huts' in those areas of the city where violence was most evident. The post I was eventually successful in obtaining was as an Assistant Youth Worker in the Househillwood Youth Hut which had been built in the grounds of Househillwood Park only a few yards from the spot under the large oak tree where each night I'd race after school to collect my bundle of newspapers for delivery.

The building was little more than a prefabricated shed. It comprised a large open area which could house any kind of event from meetings to sport and abutted a smaller area where my co-worker and I shared an office and stored gear. Outside were two toilets. A large fenced area outside provided a sports field - and that was that. The park was at the intersection of gangland territory occupied by the Bundy and the Crew. Frequent fights were fought and blood was often spilled as young, testosterone-charged males sought an outlet for their energies, in a community where the facilities available didn't meet their more adventurous expectations. Stabbings were fairly common and more than one kid died as using a blade (then as now) was almost a mark of validation in the gangland culture. A favoured wound was to stab someone in the buttock on the presumption that you couldn't do much harm down there but of course every so often someone would sever a femoral artery and another young death would be heralded in the subsequent morning's papers ... and another young male was on his way to jail.

I worked under the tutelage of youth worker Roger Smith, a mid-thirties, sour man who seemed to me to be completely cynical about his entire world. He was a mirthless person whose pleasure derived mainly from others not getting any. Sarcasm hung from his every utterance like bunting. He hadn't a good word to say about anything ... the kids, the area, the schools, professional training ... anything. Not unsurprisingly, the kids who used the club didn't find him to their taste and gave him a hell of a time – merely reinforcing his prejudice against them. I, on the other hand, became quite popular. I enjoyed their company, was well known to them as someone they'd seen around the community and although I was only a couple of years older than them I somehow managed to retain an authority that was denied Roger.

Roger was a depressive, but when he did laugh he opened his enormous gob so wide you imagined it might become unhinged. It also permitted a very good view of the omni-present and well masticated lump of chewing gum secreted about his black and silver teeth. This was often ridiculed by the kids, as he required only a bandanna to look every inch a laughing pirate. I was never the chewing gum type. This and the fact that I was pally enough with their big brothers also helped. My biggest advantage, however, was that I understood the Glasgow psyche, in that I was well aware that the answer to most problems was to get a ball out and call for a game of football on the red blaes pitch that the Corporation had established outside the Youth Hut. Most energies were duly spent in sport rather than fighting.

That's not to say we didn't have our moments. There were continual spats, arguments and blows sufficient to keep the police on their toes. The one problem with which I found myself incapable of dealing effectively was how to engage with the local girls. Very often they were more violent than the boys. A favoured weapon of choice those days was a sharpened steel comb which could be lethal when used in a fight. Most of the girls carried one of these, although many did so only to act as carriers for one or other of the boys. My problem with the female gang members was also compounded by the fact that I was only a couple of years older than them. They were maturing faster than their male counterparts and more than once I could see that my attempts at professional friendliness were being misinterpreted by young women who didn't get much in the way of affirmation at home. And attempting to avoid giving them the attention they sought was an invitation to a most distressing evening, as they would react by giving me a really hard time in order to get that attention. Every so often I could face down a boy who was carrying on, by the simple technique of growling at him or by reminding him on the football field that the tackle he had just endured was an *aide memoire*. These rudimentary methods were not in my toolbag when it came to girls. My one and only (occasionally) successful method for dealing with this behaviour was to contrive a situation where the ambitions of the boys were being thwarted or diverted because of the hassle the girls were giving me ... "Sorry guys, we'll need to hold the start of this game until I can calm these girls down"... the boys soon sorted the girls out – only to get grief from the girls themselves after the place shut. But that was normal adolescent behaviour, I told myself. Basically they were all pretty good kids, if likely to grow up to be as adults the kind of eejits who clap and cheer when the holiday plane lands.

Eighteen months securing pre-college experience passed away quite happily. I was exposed to lifestyles I'd never experienced before, as I spent a lot of time in people's homes dealing with the issues which emerged every day. One day I was in the McMurray household, one of the more chaotic families in the area. Theirs was a spontaneous family. Always boisterous and threatening. I was offered a cup of tea; in accepting it I just knew it wasn't going to be a good idea. The cup was cracked and filthy but I took a deep breath and drank. A few days later I turned a lovely shade of yellow and was signed off work for nine weeks while I recovered from hepatitis. I've always put my illness down to that cup of tea, probably because of my feeling at the time than because of the concomitant health hazard I suppose. After the first couple of weeks, I felt ok but I wasn't allowed to return until I was given the all clear. I've never donated blood since.

Studenthood was a state of bliss. I'd grown up with pretty poor self esteem on the academic front. I hadn't tried at all when at school and never got excited about exams. I don't remember ever doing an hour's homework at home … ever. My grandparents had no real experience of school, both of them leaving aged fifteen, and so there was no cultural imperative to study. My sole academic idiosyncrasy as a teenager was that I took great pleasure in reading a dictionary or a book on English grammar in bed before I fell asleep. Others might read a comic book, the sports pages or perhaps a teenage novel, but I always had my nose stuck in a book about the use of language. I took great pleasure in being able to communicate ,and saw the advantages later in life when I wasn't at all abashed by the twenty-five dollar words used by lecturers or senior people at work. Indeed I'd return them with interest, and although words are meant to reveal meaning rather than to conceal, I confess my adult affectation for the 'twenty-five dollar word' might have had more complex motivation behind it. In later years, the baffled looks on the faces of my friends and colleagues when I used words like *concatenation, bifurcate, temulence* or *capricious,* or lectured them on the difference between appraise and apprise, might have had more to do with me demonstrating my insecurities than making a clear statement or request. I'd also irritate friends, foes and family alike by remorselessly correcting their grammar, even when in the most informal of circumstances. I couldn't let a split infinitive or a prepositional ending go without murmuring the correct usage. But other than my love of the English language, I hadn't exactly been a diligent pupil … not by a long shot. Now, I decided, it would be different. I was about to become a full-time student. Who'd have thought it?

I wanted to grasp this opportunity with both hands and that meant getting myself a place to stay, so as to prepare to lead the life of a student even although the Jordanhill campus was only a couple of bus journeys away. Gran was up in arms and couldn't see the need for it, but I was now twenty years old and knew what I was about. I found a room in Ibrox, paid a week's rent in advance, took my suitcase up to the room, looked out of the window, surveyed again the basic interior of my bed-sit, and was reminded of the line from Philip Larkin's bleak poem, *Mister Bleaney…* 'Bed, upright chair, sixty-watt bulb, no hook"…and returned home without even staying one bed-night in the place. Some weeks later I started my studies at Jordanhill and after a short time there, found another room in a flat but this time in the West End, in Dowanhill Street. Now I was a proper student. However, again I reflected upon what I was doing. I repeated my earlier behaviour and fled homewards to think again. But things were looking up. On this occasion I stayed one bed-night. Perhaps I was becoming more confident.

I only got the flat thing right when, at the end of the first year, I accepted a suggestion by one of my fellow students, Alan Blackie, that we share a flat. We moved into a large room in a flatted dwelling house in what has since become One Devonshire Gardens, perhaps Glasgow's most opulent boutique hotel. It certainly had no delusions of grandeur when Alan and I stayed there. Many of the rooms were occupied by residents of the nearby Gartnavel Hospital, then a facility for patients with emotional and psychological problems who had been discharged to live in the community; a 'loony-bin' in the terminology of the day. One day I had taken my washing to the local laundromat and had returned to our room only to find Alan and a strange woman who was naked from below the waist, trousers and undergarments at her ankles, in the centre of the room. I apologised immediately and made to leave but Alan called me back. I still left but was curious as to why I'd been invited to return. Perhaps Alan was into more esoteric sex games than I'd been aware of. Subsequently, Alan's cries for my attention persuaded me that I should return to the room. I discovered him in a state of consternation as in his stumbling, coded, way he managed to apprise me of the fact that he was not in a state of *l'amour impropre*, but was in fact forcibly being shown a neighbour's scars from her recent hernia operation. I stepped back out of the room for a second time, again leaving Alan to his fate, but this time because I was beside myself with laughter. Boutique hotel it was not.

In my first year I got on famously with all of my fellow students even though I could see that one or two of them had no real aptitude for working with people. God only knows why they were selected for the course. I was the second youngest student in my year. Being invited to share a flat with Alan moved me up in the scheme of things, as he was in the second year of the course, and I began to socialise with students who had been through all that was being asked of me in first year, and in consequence I found it easier to raise my game.

I also began to flirt timidly with alcohol. I'd never enjoyed the taste of it and was, I suppose, yet fearful of its effect as a consequence of my father's death. However, in my first year at Jordanhill, the college authorities opened a bar in the main building and it became the centre of all the student gaiety. I felt very much at home in a version of my mother's living room but now I was the one cracking the jokes. Drinking was ubiquitous and although I felt I was my own man, there's no doubt that standing in the kitchen at someone's party every Saturday night refusing drink or asking for yet another coke in the Student's bar eventually told on my persistence and I began to drink what my fellow students for some reason I can't recall named *Crème de Bull!* It was effectively a very weak shandy incorporating a drop of Sweetheart Stout and seven eighths lemonade. The drink was advertised in the bar along with all the others, and for some years after I left, unaccountably, remained on the drinks list, although I'm pretty certain that I was the only person ever to have tasted its extremely weak flavour. As I moved more into my twenties I began to experiment with wine and could be found at parties drinking *Liebfraumilch*, a dull very sweet wine from Germany, to which I added spoonfuls of sugar in order to be able to drink the damn stuff. Nevertheless, I began at least to *look* more sophisticated as long as no one saw me stirring my wine.

I was also elected President of the Jordanhill Folk Club and was given a small budget each term in order to entice performers along to entertain the students. Fellow student and friend Alan Murray was Secretary. We booked Mick Broderick and the Whistlebinkies, Archie Fisher, The McCalmans and Barbara Dickson - then a folk singer but soon to become the darling of Saturday night entertainment on the BBC and a famous actress in West End musicals in London. I remember saying at the time to pals in the bar some years later that 'I had that Barbara Dickson for a tenner', permitting them to muse for a moment that she might have had an earlier and more sordid past than the one of which they were aware.

My first run in with the authorities came when I was admitted to hospital. I was home alone in the flat and began feeling really unwell and so decided to walk the few hundred yards to the Western Infirmary just off the bottom of Byres Road. To this day, I only remember staggering down the road and collapsing in a heap at the entrance to the hospital. I was rushed in and when I awoke, Alan Blackie was at my bedside telling me that I'd just had a spinal tap to get a sample of cerebrospinal fluid in order to determine whether I had meningitis. I hadn't, so Alan was then quizzed about whether I might have been misusing drugs. Alan replied honestly that I didn't even misuse lager and so that was ruled out as well. I was kept in for a week of tests and discharged with talk of a mystery virus. My self-diagnosis was *biscuititis* as my grant had by then been spent and my diet for the prior two weeks consisted entirely of digestive biscuits. I'm sure that in these days of fads I could write it up as a new diet and make millions, although I suppose ending up in hospital having your spine tapped would reduce its popularity.

I felt terribly ill during the earlier part of my stay in hospital, finding myself throwing up violently in the toilet sink on more than one occasion. I was never very good at being sick. Never for me was the ability just to warble a few easy pints of liquid down a toilet bowl and retire to bed … more it was accompanied by the guttural noise of a growling pit-bull terrier with overtones of yodelling and whimpering. I was nothing if not dramatic and would end up somewhat inevitably providing a receptacle with a technicolour torrent of desiccated vomit amidst much wailing and moaning. I really hated the whole thing and so tried everything I knew to stop or delay the inevitable and in doing so probably merely compounded the felony.

During the entire first term, I'd spent my money most unwisely. I wasn't a natural spendthrift but remember that my first purchase upon receipt of the cheque was an expensive Glasgow bunnet. I can't remember why it was such a big deal but it covered my scalp from then on and throughout the rest of my time at Jordanhill. I suspect it was to make me look more like a folk singer. Ah, the follies of youth. What a dick I must have looked. That said, it's been the headgear I've worn ever since.

My discharge from hospital could have been conducted in a more elegant fashion, mind you. Before leaving, the ward sister asked me to take a shower in the bathroom at the end of the ward and upon completion, to provide a urine sample in a container that I'd find inside. I did so and bid her farewell by handing her the aforementioned container when the gradual, toe-curling realisation came over me that I'd just used a small flower vase in which to micturate. I can still see the look of complete bewilderment on her face as I handed her a cut-glass flower vase full of piss. I mustered up all of the little dignity I had left and dealt with the situation by pretending that nothing untoward had happened, flouncing out of the ward thanking all and sundry for a week's excellent health care. She must have thought I should be admitted immediately to another hospital, but this time a lunatic asylum.

The week I was in hospital coincided with the week of the first year's exams and, of course, I missed them. I was interrogated by Terry May, the Head of Department, who clearly wanted to establish whether I was a malingerer. However, my classroom results were all good and my placement reports were excellent, so he was persuaded that I was a genuine case and gave me an overall pass without requiring that I sit the exams.

This was indeed excellent news, as Margaret and I had decided to swan over to the States on a BUNAC student internship, whereby we spent a couple of months in Maine working in a summer camp for New York kids who came from mostly rich, Jewish families. The camp setting was gorgeous. Situated on the mountainous, pine-clad shores of Echo Lake, it comprised a series of log cabins each containing perhaps half a dozen boys. The girls had a similar arrangement in an adjacent part of the forest. Interposed between them was the camp centre where the dining hall and other common facilities were located. The lake was warm, its bottom sandy, the sky was blue and there wasn't any other man-made development as far as the eye could see. It was just beautiful. Just sublime.

We each had responsibility for overseeing a group of kids in a log cabin as well as for an area of activity during the day. Margaret had been a camp counsellor at Echo Lake the year before on her own and was again deployed as an arts teacher. I was a bit apprehensive about what my specialist subject might be in my letter of introduction, but Margaret guided me accurately that the Yanks would accept my word on any claim I made regarding my abilities and experience. In addition, that she knew they were finding it hard to secure the services of someone who could supervise and teach canoeing and sailing. I'd never set foot in either a canoe or a sail-boat in my life but followed her guidance. Lo and behold! if I didn't find myself in charge of a small armada of boats. Fortunately the kids who were drawn to the water were all able to sail. I set my own rules, by declaring that if you weren't an experienced sailor you had to pass my self-designed swimming test, and so whiled away many enjoyable hours teaching kids to swim who might otherwise have required that I teach them the rudiments of sailing; something I was completely unequipped to do.

Now canoeing was a different matter. The canoes on Echo Lake were the hollow, open-topped, Red Indian, Adirondack canoes much favoured by the racoon hatted, Davy Crockett, frontiersman types in western movies. I soon learned each of the three distinct paddle strokes needed to propel the things and became an expert in manoeuvring canoes around the lake. This also permitted me to develop a hierarchy of skills, whereby in order to take a sailboat out, you had first of all to be able to pass my swimming test and then to handle a canoe to my satisfaction. I regret that not too many of the kids who weren't already accomplished moved up the rankings to sailboat proficiency that year, although I did allow a certain measure of 'crewing' whereby persistent sailboat *aficionados* were permitted to assist an experienced sailor if they could swim. In this way I managed to hold my head high as a competent and contributing player in Team Echo Lake without endangering too many kids through my own lack of abilities in sailing.

By these means, my limited sailing abilities caused me no embarrassment but another aspect of my new-found talents as a canoeist continues to embarrass me to this day.

On a few occasions I was asked to take a group of kids to the other end of the lake, about three hours' canoeing away, to visit a trading post so they could buy candy and gifts. Always a very popular event, I was in charge of a flotilla of perhaps half a dozen canoes each of which carried two people. On the way there, we always stopped at a small island about the size of a couple of tennis courts; just big enough to beach the canoes, have a rest and a comfort break in the bushes. These visits always passed off without incident until one stop-off when one of the kids ran up to me excitedly and told me that a huge snake was located below a large rock and between her and her canoe.

Being an experienced snake hunter from my scouting days on the Crinan Canal, I approached the rock quietly from behind and there, sleeping and coiled three feet below me was a snake about eight feet long and thicker than my arm. Despite the fact that it was doing no one any harm, I decided that in order to permit the kids to return to their canoe safely, I'd better render it harmless.

Giving due consideration to all the options, I retreated quietly, gesturing to the kids to stay back and keep quiet while I dealt with the snake. As they cowered together I reached into the bushes and extracted a branch which I cut into a forked stick and explained to the kids that I couldn't identify the snake as poisonous but didn't want to take chances so I intended just to immobilise it by catching it just behind the head with my forked stick until everyone had reached the safety of their canoe and had pushed off the island. The kids nodded their acceptance of this brave plan and moved in a huddle round to the edge of the copse to get a better look at my heroics.

Silently, I edged up to the top of the rock, positioning myself until I was directly above the snake. Taking care to manoeuvre the forked stick at just the right angle, I paused then stabbed downwards pinning the monster to the ground and immobilising it as I'd planned.

The children cheered wildly but unfortunately, my plan hadn't been implemented perfectly as I'd only managed to pin the snake some eighteen inches behind its head which it now was able to raise in curious anger, its fangs suggesting a gradual realisation on behalf of both of us that retribution was in the offing. I was stuck. The snake couldn't move…but neither could I.

Rather than shepherding the kids into the canoes, I now sought their assistance and held tight to the stick to buy time.

"Sorry 'bout this", I grimaced, "but could someone get me a log or something?"

A canoe paddle was brought me and I asked one of the older boys to replace my hold on the forked stick while I rather shamefully beat the snake about the head until it was as flat as a pancake. The kids, rightly, were horrified.

I affected the unconcerned air of a backwoodsman who was used to the kill and instructed my assistant to remove the fork, reassuring everybody that everything was now alright. I was about to usher the ashen-faced kids back into their canoes when the snake, whose head now resembled the shape of the paddle I'd used to beat it suddenly kicked up a flurry of sand and shot into the bushes.

The small island came alive as it vacated its population of a dozen souls who churned the calm waters of the lake into a froth as they made their panicked way to the safety of their craft.

Afterwards I was the talk of the steamy but although I was genuinely ashamed of my exploits, killing one of God's creatures for no good reason, I'd overlooked the fact that Americans, even middle class professionals from New York, view hunting and killing as a sport to be encouraged. Killing a monster snake? Well that was really something. And of course the story grew legs in the retelling. I was a hero. That said, never again did any trip to the trading post call in at *Snakehead Island*!

What saw me reach Echo Lake superstardom, however, was the gradual realisation on behalf of the camp owners that I was a comparative whiz at soccer. 1972 saw the creeping acceptance of football as a sport in the States and inter-camp rivalry was great. The soccer league they had established permitted the coach to play. At Echo Lake the guy they had running things had no skills whatsoever in football, but then neither had the kids. He routinely took them out onto the playing field and put them through a punishing callisthenics routine; just a series of exercises but no ball-work worth a damn.

I didn't ask to take over, but the camp owners saw me messing about with a ball and decided that I was the white Pele. They asked me to coach the team and play in their fixtures. Frankly, it was a dawdle. I made sure that the kids learned some rudiments of the game in training and spent my time during matches winning the ball and playing it into the feet of my forwards. It was only a matter of time before we'd score and if things got a bit tight, I'd just take the ball up the park and score; it was that easy. However, I kept my showboating for the training ground so it looked more like a team performance, but as the only non-American coach in the league, and the only one who had actually played the game, our success was assured. I became a celebrity in the camp, as success in any field was celebrated big time, and Echo Lake hadn't seen much silverware in past competitions.

After the kids were dispatched home to their parents, Margaret and I were free to go see the States but on a tight budget we kept to the Boston, New York and Cape Cod area before heading back to Scotland and a final year of study.

I had become more attracted to social work as a result of being exposed to the training that Margaret and her student friends were undertaking. Upon returning for my final year, I discussed it with Terry May and Duncan Smith, the two lecturers with whom I was most close and spoke with John Round, the Head of Department in the School of Community Studies and asked for his advice. I was now viewed as a pretty decent prospect and Round was most enthusiastic that I should remain within the fledgling profession. I was keen to spread my wings however and eventually applied to Jordanhill as well as Moray House in Edinburgh on the back of my successful venture at Jordanhill. On the application form to Moray House, I listed my preference as being the one-year conversion course for mature students even although I wasn't qualified to apply as I wasn't anything like old enough. At twenty-two, I was young even for the regular two-year course and indeed was much more like the kind of age at which the three-year course for youthful entrants should have been offered me.

My interview eventually went really well though. I turned up for the series of interviews and tests but became engrossed in a newspaper over the lunch break and raced ten minutes late to a 'psychological' test which just seemed to me to be an IQ test. Doubtless because I was late and therefore hurried, I scored really well and was complimented by the lecturer afterwards on my score. I was told that I could be confident that a place might be offered to me but that I just wasn't old enough to be considered for the one-year course for mature students. When I received simultaneous offers for a place at *both* Jordanhill and Moray House I wrote back to Moray House and rejected their offer simply on the basis that Jordanhill was closer to my home. It was only the next day that Margaret, upon re-reading the offer letter, realised that they'd offered me the *one*-year course for mature students. I couldn't get on the phone quickly enough and begged the secretary who would be first to open the mail to destroy it and permit me to re-write accepting the place. She found my foolishness hugely amusing and agreed. And so it was that again I found myself the youngest student in a class of even more mature fellow students (and was voted, towards the end of the course, as 'the person most likely to succeed'). I began to view myself in a new light as I was receiving a lot of affirmation and it was doing my confidence a lot of good.

Margaret and I had being going steady since we were in something like second year at school. Neither of us had gone out with anyone else and were each very close to one another's families. Now both 23, we married in St Christopher's Church in Pollok. It was just such a natural decision and easy to reach. At the ceremony itself, I was rather nonplussed when the Minister arrived, somewhat breathless and late with a pair of football boots laced together and hung round his neck. He'd been refereeing a Boys Brigade match, he explained, as he exchanged the boots for a white dog collar, before leading me into the church to be united with my bride-to-be in order to begin proceedings, still wiping the sweat from his brow.

The wedding reception, or purvey, as we call it in Glasgow (from 'purveyors' of goods to Her Majesty the Queen or whatever) was held in the Tinto Firs Hotel, in Giffnock, which has since been demolished and turned into flats. In the wedding photographs I looked very much the long haired hippie with my shoulder length hair.

As students, Margaret and I didn't have the capacity to save and although both of us were now salaried, Margaret as a School Social Worker in St. Gerard's School in Govan and me as a Trainee Social Worker in Paisley, we still didn't have much cash to throw around. I'd negotiated a deal whereby I studied social work in Edinburgh but was paid a salary by the Council on the basis that I'd work for Paisley for two years upon qualification.

We honeymooned for a week in St Annes, near Blackpool and spent our time playing putting and walking round the town planning our life together. Nowadays a honeymoon would be a much more luscious affair with flights to an exotic Caribbean Island more likely.

Upon completing the course I found myself, I suspect uniquely in those days, having a joint qualification in community development and social work. My first post was that of a social worker in Ferguslie Park, long regarded as the poorest, most deprived housing estate in

Scotland. It was built with good intentions. The council decided to take, not 'problem families', but 'families with problems', and locate them in a small enclave, towards the edge of the estate, called Candren Oval. Here they installed Housing Assistants whose task was to support these families and assist them with debt problems and other impediments, which precluded them securing better housing in other parts of the town. Unfortunately the sociology of poverty defeated the authorities as more and more 'good tenants' moved away from the escalating mayhem, whereby violence and crime became increasingly rife. In the fullness of time, and certainly by the time I'd arrived, the place was a byword for all the social ills that might befall a community. It was a madhouse. If ever anyone needed persuasion that Thomas Hobbes presented an accurate perception of the underclass in his seminal work, *Leviathan*, they need only have visited Ferguslie Park in those days to understand that their lot was indeed 'poor, nasty, brutish and short.'

So I started my career trying to sort out, one at a time, those problems that were being experienced by people in Ferguslie Park. I dealt with parents who found that they could not deal with their children, largely because they were children themselves. Many of my early duties centred around court work as there was a huge backlog of SERs (Social Enquiry Reports) to be completed. Invariably these were reports compiled by social workers into the background of someone who had committed an offence. It was obligatory where the offence was a first offence or jail-time was being considered but was also optional if the Sheriff felt the need to have more information in front of him before dispensing justice. We provided a few pages of background information regarding the family circumstances of the person about to be sentenced along with a note of any previous offences. We could recommend dismissal, probation, deferred sentencing, a fine, a suspended sentence or imprisonment. In this regard, as many Sheriffs took our recommendations on board, we were fairly influential. That said, it really was a Sisyphean task, pushing a boulder uphill, as time after time we'd see the same people coming up from the same families and communities. It was regularly those parents whose children we took into care, those who suffered from mental illness, those who had financial problems which saw them evicted and those who just didn't have the coping skills to manage a rowdy family or hold down a job. It was all grist to the mill but I threw myself into it with all the zeal of the new boy.

One day I was busily engaged in dealing with a family called the McFoys which were in rent arrears of some twenty-odd pounds or so. My usual imprecations were falling on deaf ears, as I tried to persuade one department in my council, the Housing Department, not to throw a family into the street only to see the cost to the council shifting to another council department (the Social Work Department) and in the process, possibly escalating wildly the prospect of their children requiring unnecessarily to be taken into care. It was, as ever, to no avail and with a heavy heart I walked down to the family's home to be of whatever use I could be when the Sheriff's Officer came down to evict them that afternoon.

In those days, Sheriff's Officers were appointed to carry out the decisions of the court where finances were at issue. If the council approached the court for an order demanding payment of rent arrears or if a court-imposed fine could not be paid, these people would come to the house, *'poind'* (old Scots' legal terminology, pronounced *pind*, whereby the property of an alleged debtor could be seized) the contents and possessions and sell them by means known as a 'warrant sale' in order to raise the cash to pay not only the initial debt but also the not insignificant fee of the Sheriff's men. The poor kept chasing an ever increasing debt burden placed upon them by the authorities which were charged with helping them.

When I arrived at the household to tell the family the bad news that I had been unable to help them, I encountered a queue of people standing all the way up the stairs to the first floor flat wherein lived the McFoy family. Somewhat bewildered, I walked past them and was admitted to the house only to see that the Sheriff's Officer had already arrived and had posted a value on all items of any value; the TV, the three piece suite, the table and chairs etc, to the value of the debt he was to collect. This rendered the price on each item relatively inexpensive. However, as I watched, the man stood and collected dispassionately the requisite amounts from the line of neighbours until the last item had been sold. Throughout the few minutes this took, Mrs McFoy wept quietly but they were tears of gratitude as the neighbours had all turned up to assist in avoiding an obvious unfairness, knowing in their hearts that it could be their turn next time. Not one stick of furniture was removed from the home.

As the burly Sheriff's Officer and his henchman turned to leave, I began to appreciate that the real power to resolve many of the issues, such as I'd being trying to deal with, lay not in council departments that were engaged in some sort of ineffective administrative dance or ritual, but in communities coming together to take action in order to help one another. That day I made a commitment that I would not only devote my life to service - I'd already made that vow - but that I'd explore other ways of achieving more productive solutions than was possible, as I remember putting it at the time, "by trying to sort people's heids one at a time".

My Area Officer was Joe Rafferty, the elder brother of Gerry Rafferty who would flit briefly into my life later on and who would be responsible for a string of musical hits including those I mentioned earlier such as *'Stuck In The Middle With You'*, the featured song of the cult movie, *Reservoir Dogs*. At that time Gerry was a member of the Humblebums with Billy Connolly and Tam 'Fingers' Harvey and was achieving great success. Joe was always a tower of strength and was totally supportive of me as was his colleague Christine McCaig. He didn't always keep the best of health but turned out manfully for the Thursday evening five-a-side football matches in the newly built Apex community facility which we social workers wasted no time in taking over on Thursday evenings in preference to the good people of Ferguslie for whom the building was intended. One night Joe brought his brother Gerry down. We were all in awe of such a huge rock star at the time. He'd just been number one in the charts with *'Stuck in the middle with you'* and would go on to even greater successes with hits such as *'Baker Street'*, *'Get it right next time'*, *'The way it always starts'* and *'Can I have my money back'*. Gerry was a great musician but not much of a footballer. Rather ungraciously, I spent the evening nutmegging him. Not for the first time, I behaved inappropriately because I figured that it would make a great story in the pub afterwards.

And so I became involved in more community development approaches and with a new way of working with young offenders, somewhat grandly and inappropriately known as 'Intermediate Treatment' as if there were specific remedies which, if prescribed and the dosage taken, would lead to some amelioration of the presenting problem. Bollocks! It was merely a method whereby, by working with groups of disaffected youth, much as I did in Househillwood it might be possible to spend more time with them, build a proper relationship and where there was a glimmer of hope, encourage their diversion away from crime. In any event, there's a lot of research which shows that most of them would have moved on of their own volition at the point where they met a girl or got a job.

It was an area of work I enjoyed enormously. Regularly, other social workers and I would take groups of kids away for days where we attempted to get to know them better. These camps - usually in outdoor centres where we had the place to ourselves - could be rough but mostly they worked in terms of building relationships and the kids enjoyed them. Discipline could be a problem, as really the only sanction we had available to us was to withdraw a minor privilege or take miscreants back home early. I had to do this on a few occasions but the most memorable took place after a particularly rowdy evening. The staff agreed that it would be best for the majority of kids if three trouble-making ringleaders were escorted home the following morning.

Unfortunately, the minibus that had taken everyone from Ferguslie Park to the hutted encampment just outside the Ayrshire fishing village of Dunure was needed first thing to take the rest of the kids on a pre-booked canoeing trip so we decided that myself and fellow social worker Mike Brannigan would just walk the kids to Ayr some miles up the road where we'd catch a bus back to Glasgow then on to Paisley.

Tempers had long cooled and the kids had accepted their sanction. However, as we crested a hill below which lay the town of Ayr, I was to witness one of the shortest, most accurate but most indecipherable four word sentences ever uttered in a Glaswegian accent. As Ayr hove into view, its presence was acknowledged by one of our terrible trio. "Err Err err err" ....or "There's Ayr over there" in the Queen's English. Pure poetry!

Anyway, the upshot of all this was that I worked long and arduous hours, and acquired an early and solid reputation as one of a number of younger colleagues who was prepared to innovate. In 1975, a vacancy for a Senior Social Work post occurred to lead a team of social workers that looked after half of Paisley. There were some seriously able people there at the time. Jim Cameron, later to play a leading role in Militant with Bob Wylie, was the most talented by a distance. Rab Gowans, Mike Brannigan and a Canadian, Allan Thomson were also both very able and committed. Bill Spalding was a very experienced Mental Health Officer and taught me a lot in his own idiosyncratic way about the issues associated with mental illness. Any of them (with the possible exception of Bill ... actually, with the certain exception of Bill) would have been a great appointment. But, only eighteen months into the job and with the insouciance of youth, I applied and at the age of twenty five, was appointed to the post of Senior Social Worker, and given a team of around eighteen social workers to deploy in support of the council's raft of social care obligations across the eastern half of Paisley. Typically, most social workers back then would expect to serve for ten or more years before preferment. Looking back, it was a completely absurd appointment. I had precisely nil life experience. I was not yet at all rounded in my professional skills and I was a comparative child. The notion that I was now responsible for decisions whereby a wean could be taken from its parents was patent nonsense. The idea that I was in any way experienced enough to deal with some of the Hogarthian grotesques that populated some of the desperately poor areas of Paisley was plain daft. I had taken over a team of grizzly, experienced staff who were not impressed by my youthful zeal and had no time for my new fangled ways, which, I suppose was why I had been appointed by a department gradually coming to an appreciation that things had to change.

Over the next three years, I eventually managed to mould some of the staff into my way of thinking. Although I enjoyed increasingly productive personal relationships with older and more experienced colleagues, all I really managed to do was to change their outlook from one of outright personal hostility to one of kind indifference as they shook their head and smiled a smile which read, 'He'll learn.' Still, I introduced new ways of working despite their reluctance and I would hold to the view that my 'innovations' (hardly rocket science), which involved building deeper relationships with those we sought to serve, and engaging collaboratively with community representatives, other professionals and other organisations must have been welcomed by those on our caseloads, if not every other single member of staff.

7. Honest Men And Bonnie Lassies

Look after yer heid…it's where ye live!
John Keast.

The Area Manager when I was at Ferguslie Park was George Irving. George, now *Professor* George, was a stickler for detail and was a workaholic but he and I got on well with one another, until he left to become the Deputy Director of Social Work in the newly established Ayrshire Department of Social Work, which was ensconced within the now gigantic bureaucracy of Strathclyde Regional Council.

Within the previous Paisley Town Council, I had been required under my terms and conditions of employment to undertake 'Stand By' duties: an out of hours service whereby I had to answer each and every call for social work assistance throughout Paisley one week in twelve. It made for a gruelling week, as I was frequently called at some ungodly hour of the night and asked to drive to Stirling or Blackpool where the cops had apprehended some kid who had absconded from a List 'D' School. I would be called if someone required to be 'sectioned' (taken compulsorily into the care of a lunatic asylum) or if someone was arrested and there was, as a consequence, no one to care for the kids, and I had to take them to a Care Home.

Sometimes I'd get back home completely knackered at pre-dawn only for Margaret to tell me that the police had been on and I had to set off on another mission. That said, it was a well paid week, and that was very much welcomed, but an appointments freeze was announced and as staff left and vacancies occurred, posts were not replaced and the numbers on Stand By reduced to eight staff.

In addition to those out-of-hours tasks, during the week of Stand By, I was also expected to turn up at 9.00

the next morning and undertake a day's work as if I'd spend the previous eight hours abed. It was crazy; it was brought to a head one night in the wee small hours, as I returned home after dropping a boy off at a List 'D' School called Kerelaw just outside of Stevenston in Ayrshire. I was driving through Kilwinning and fell asleep at the wheel, coming to my senses only nanoseconds before I'd have ploughed into a steel bridge in my Mini Cooper. If I'd collided with the bridge, I'd have had no chance of surviving serious injury or perhaps even death.

Next morning I went into work and told them that they could stick their Stand By service, and that they should do whatever they chose to do in terms of discipline but there was no way I was putting my life on the line for a system which was just plain daft.

My resignation from the rota meant that it would now drop to one week in seven for the remaining staff and unknown to me, this threshold triggered trades union intervention. All hell broke loose as the out-of-hours service was suspended, and a special committee was set up by Fred Edwards, then Regional Director of Social Work, and tasked with the responsibility of fixing this thing urgently. George Irving, my old boss, was asked to head it up; as the miscreant who had inadvertently brought this crisis about, I was asked to join the group, which I did enthusiastically.

I was somewhat in awe of the rest of the group as they were all senior staff who spoke so eloquently and were so comfortable in each other's company. They were all trying to find a way of reinstalling a version of the previous service but I was having none of it. To George's credit, he began to realise that we might have to be a bit more radical and encouraged me when in a moment of frustration, I took a pencil and a round ashtray which was on the table and drew a circle around its circumference on a map of Strathclyde. It was a complete fluke but the circle centred upon Glasgow and at its southern point cut through the southern outskirts of Ayr.

"There", I said. "Outwith that circle, the *status quo* pertains because the volume of night work is negligible. Within the circle, the Department establishes a new, dedicated out-of-hours service and appoints a team of social workers to staff it. If the biggest Social Work Department in Europe can't manage this, who can?" It was as uncluttered as that. Hours of blethering and we were saved by the fortunate circumference of an ashtray. Thank God that smoking was as prevalent in those days.

Anyway, George appeared to see something in me and asked me to apply for a new post he was creating as an Adviser to the department on matters to do with innovative ways of working; Intermediate Treatment, Community Development, Group Work and Training. I was flattered and went home to consult Margaret. The job was to be based in Ayr, so we'd have to move if I was successful … and I was!

When Margaret and I had married in 1973, we lived initially in the top flat at 13 Crossflat Crescent in Paisley, a handsome red sandstone property costing us £4,000. It was only a one bedroom arrangement but it was most convenient for both of us. I would take a train to Glasgow from Paisley, thence onwards to Moray House College of Education in Edinburgh, and make the return journey at night. Margaret would head off to Govan by bus. Neither of us had a car, nor would we until Jimmy Ferguson, my new father-in-law, who was a mechanical genius and a Foreman at the Rolls Royce Engineering plant in East Kilbride advised us on selecting an inexpensive wee green Austin A40 car, whose potential he recognised and on which he worked night after night until it roared into life and he had pronounced it fit for purpose.

The original purpose was getting us to and fro from work as I'd collect Margaret from school most nights, and to use it during Stand By week. However, our first decision was to plan a holiday in France, entirely predicated upon us being able to drive there. Jimmy was appalled as he was convinced the car didn't have the legs for the journey but we were more confident. Our assessment of Jimmy's talents were well founded, as it was a blistering hot summer and we saw many a car sitting at the side of the road in Brittany with steam coming out of its radiator while ours sailed past effortlessly. What a mechanic was wee Jimmy.

In 1975 we paid around £12,000 and moved to 4 Crofthouse Road, a Meikle McTaggart, four-in-a-block property ubiquitous in Glasgow at that time in the Hillington and Cardonald areas and in Croftfoot where we stayed. We had a back and front garden and lovely neighbours. When I was unexpectedly promoted to the post of Senior Social Worker in Paisley, we figured that financial uplift permitted me to be the sole breadwinner and, on the second of June,1977, we were blessed with the birth of our firstborn, Ron junior. Ronald James Hector Culley to give him his Sunday names. James after Jimmy, Margaret's dad, and Hector, after my grandfather. As a youth he remonstrated with me over the choice of Hector as a middle name conferred upon him when he was too young to put up much of an argument but he seems to have reconciled himself to it now.

Ron was a great wee boy. Always bright and inquisitive. Both of us were completely devoted to him. It was just such unalloyed joy to have this beautiful baby in our arms. When first I held him in my arms I had a smile that went right round my face and ended at the back of my neck. I was overjoyed. It was almost overwhelming. It really is a truism that love is hard to quantify because you just keep finding more space in your heart for another person without diminishing the love you already hold for others in your life. Ron was a great kid. I don't remember any tantrums or tears although there must have been a few. Having a son and heir made me feel more responsible and also had me take more of an interest in generating an income with which to make his life materially better than mine had been. Because we lived in Croftfoot, we had easy access to my mum, my grandparents, Margaret's mum and Dad and her sister Susan and brother-in-law, Billy Harvey, who lived just down the hill so baby sitting was no problem. Not that we ventured out much. Home life tended to centre around family. One of the great unintended consequences of our marriage was that it introduced Margaret and Jimmy to Madge and Hector. Our families became great friends and over subsequent years they became very fond of one another.

Billy Harvey was a Country and Western nutcase. He introduced me to a music form that I hadn't realised until then was hugely popular in Glasgow and still is. Any evening when we'd visit Susan and Billy, there was always music from Hank Williams, Willie Nelson or Johnnie Cash as well as more esoteric artists. One of my favourite songs, *Oke from Muskogee* sung by Merle Haggard, dates from that time. To this day I still appreciate C&W and one of the most moving performances I've ever witnessed live was a rendition of *Georgia* by Willie Nelson when ex President Jimmy Carter won the Nobel Peace Award in Oslo in December 2002 and I was privileged enough to be in the audience.

For some time I struggled to define C&W music until I came upon a definition by Harlan Howard who described it memorably and succinctly as 'three chords and the truth'. Most country music isn't garlanded with complicated musical structure and invariably it tells of the day to day hardships and joys to be found in mid-west America. That said, it clearly strikes a chord worldwide because of its homespun philosophies and simple music. As someone once said, 'music is what feelings *sound* like'. And so it is with C&W.

In similar fashion to my witnessing the performance of Willie Nelson, if on a less exalted note, I've always enjoyed an evening spent at Glasgow's Grand Ole Opry, in Kinning Park in Glasgow. It's a members-run club and is devoted to the music of Country and Western artists. It really has a culture all of its own. *Aficionados* turn up on a public bus in civvies and upon entering the building (for a £2 admission fee as it was then) they would find themselves a seat, open the bag they brought with them and unselfconsciously strap on their holsters, place their Stetsons on their head and twirl their guns around their fingers before joining the queue - yes, a queue - at the bar for a drink. While they were standing waiting their turn at the bar, the tannoy would make an announcement such as..."Kid Currie to reception, Kid Currie to reception!" Everyone had their own moniker for the evening. On the occasions I've been there it has always been a great laugh and I'd leave with an immense respect for those who lived the American dream from within a converted cinema in Glasgow.

One of the highlights at the Grand Ole Opry was the interval shoot-out where two groups of Glasgow gunslingers would gather at either end of the dance floor. The M.C., Doc Holliday (as I say, everyone has their own cowboy moniker for the evening) would take the stage just as a woman in a grey knitted dress holding a microphone invited two gunslingers to step forward. The contest was to see who could draw and shoot fastest; in the Grand Ole Opry, this meant the gun clearing the holster and shooting into the floor. After the bang, the flash and the smoke had cleared, Doc Holliday would solemnly lower his head to one side as if sniffing his right armpit. After a contemplative silence, he would point to one or other of the contestants and pronounce, "Deid"!

Doc - who hailed from the American State of Drumoyne in Glasgow and is now sadly deceased - was the electronic scoreboard.

In later years I was increasingly asked to join the after-dinner speaking circuit and entertain mostly professionals who'd had a few glasses. I built one routine around my love for Country and Western music and the Grand Ole Opry and took the mickey out of contrived Glasgow versions of putative Country and Western songs which had titles like... *"They can put me in jail for lovin' you, but they can't stop my face from breakin' out;" "Tonight the malt is single, so am I;" "Get your ass off that stove there, Granny, you're too old to go ridin' the range;" and "If I'd shot her when I'd met her, I'd be out of jail by now!"*

Anyway, although Glasgow held many attractions, the prospect of living and working in Ayrshire had advantages and disadvantages. Ayrshire was undoubtedly beautiful but we'd be somewhat separated from family and friends. However, we took the plunge and moved into a newly built three bedroom semi-detached house in a new development in Riccarton, Kilmarnock. It set us back some £27,000 as I recall. The new estate was called Caprington. Our house in Darnley Drive was situated next to Caprington Golf Course and was well situated halfway between our previous connections in Glasgow and my new place of employment in the town of Ayr.

When we stayed at Croftfoot, the previous owner was a sergeant in the Mounted Police. He used to bring home dung from the stables and he and our upstairs neighbours used it to great effect in developing a superb rose garden round the back. So much so that in the missives of sale it was specifically mentioned that he would be taking his roses with him. Still, he left a fine garden and we worked away diligently bringing it back to something approaching its former glory.

Kilmarnock was very different. Here, because the house was a new build, initially access was via a wooden plank to the front door as the paths hadn't yet been laid. Back and front gardens were merely builders' rubble and clay. Not at all promising. However, for weeks we worked away at the backbreaking task of breaking up the clay using only a shovel until Rod, our next door neighbour brought home a hired rotary machine one evening which completely granulated his clay and reduced it to a fine tilth in about half an hour. When I recollect how the garden matured due to Margaret's constant attention, it is hard to remember just how barren it once was.

I loved my job in Ayr. George Irving was my line manager and the Director of Social Work for Ayrshire was Stanley Johnstone. He was a real character and took a shine to me. My office was next to his and George's and he would bring me in from time to time for a chat. He was uproarious company and had a real earthy humour, recounting to me, for instance, that the new Matron of an old folk's home was a bit prim and needed 'a guid blaw through', his dancing eyes suggesting quite clearly that he'd be the very man to help her out in that regard. He could also fly into the most uncontrollable of rages, but fortunately never at me. He'd carry a fly-fishing rod in the boot of his car. On many a summer's day he would gaze out of his window, overlooking the lovely gardens of Wellington Square, and announce that he must visit a particular old folk's home or somewhere, before winking at me and telling me he was off to see if he could catch a salmon on the River Doon or his favourite, the River Irvine. Approaching retirement, he didn't give a toss about the new regime based up at Strathclyde House in Glasgow and ran Ayrshire as much as he could almost as an autonomous region. Frequently he'd declare UDI over some policy matter he didn't agree with, and would fulminate over the incessant memos and letters which would arrive daily.

George Irving played the role of hard man to the rest of the staff across Ayrshire. But his real strength was in letting Stanley blow off steam and head for the riverbank before carefully implementing the wishes of Head Office. Increasingly he was viewed as the real power behind the throne and I was his trusted henchman. Actually, George seemed to me to harbour a very traditional approach to social work, but he had sufficient political nous to realise that the stuff I was championing was very much in favour at headquarters. Accordingly, I was allowed to make appointments, set up courses, develop area based approaches and secure resources. These were days when there were no mobile phones, computers, or e-mail so once you left the office you were free from contact. Ayrshire is a big place and my responsibilities took me regularly to all corners. My mileage occasionally brought me substantial payments, at a time when there was no need to inform the taxman of any benefit which was accrued, and a tidy supplement to my salary could pretty much be relied on each month.

Ayrshire was also the place I met John McManus and commenced a friendship that will end only when the second of us dies. I turned out as striker for the Kilmarnock social work football team, which comprised an assortment of colleagues from fieldwork and residential social work units. We played other council departments, juvenile teams, anyone who'd play us, actually. One day there appeared in our team a guy I hadn't seen before; a real terrier in midfield who scrapped away relentlessly.

Very impressive. I didn't see him after the match but was informed that he was John McManus, a trainee social worker. As such he'd be completing his course soon and would be placed somewhere in Ayrshire. Further, I was told that he and his wife Christine had recently moved into a house just round the corner from me in Caprington. Later when Margaret and I visited John and Christine, I remember leaving and declaring to Margaret that theirs must be the smallest house in the world. Little did I appreciate then that years later when John and I lived close to one another in the West End of Glasgow, John would buy a property which actually *must* have been the smallest house in the world. I didn't realise it at the time but John and I would go on to become very much the closest of friends, our lives becoming intertwined in a number of important and personal ways.

My work involved long hours. A lot of evening and weekend work. Not content with that, however, I decided that I had to make a commitment to my own community and not long after moving into the area, I went along to a meeting of the local Riccarton Community Council. It was a bit leaden. Just a few local people reading correspondence they'd received in response to correspondence they'd written. I was pretty quiet but made a contribution towards the end of the meeting. It must have made an impact as I was asked to take over as Chairman from the next meeting. I was inwardly keen to take on the responsibility, but wanted to ensure that it was the settled will of the council, so asked that we defer a decision until the next meeting, and that members be written to and advised that this would form an element of the business that night. This was duly agreed and I was unanimously elected Chairman a month later.

A further football match took place soon thereafter and afterwards John sidled up to me clearly having been briefed on my activities. "What's all this about the Community Council, then? I'm up for it too!" And so it was that John and I involved ourselves in local matters as Chair and Secretary respectively of Riccarton Community Council. The Town Council paid little or no heed to Community Councils, although they were required to finance their core costs, due to legislation imposed via the Scottish Office. John and I had a field day. We started a community newspaper called the Riccarton Rag (strapline *'Jings, crivvens, help ma Bob; the Riccarton Rag is just the job'*.) Through this medium we criticised the local councillor, waged housing campaigns and informed the community about all local matters. We took office space in the local community centre and used funds from the Manpower Services Commission to employ, eventually, some thirty-five staff. We opened a nursery for local kids, employed community handymen to undertake small tasks for elderly and disabled people in their homes, and recruited local people in doing so. One significant appointment was George Thomson. John masterminded this particular post and used funding from the Urban Programme to bring George, a qualified lawyer as well as a social worker, from Aberdeen to take on a role as Community Development Worker for Riccarton. George's specialist area was housing but we used him in a more general capacity as well. For a few years, the place was jumping - and all this in our own time.

Margaret also found part time employment there in the Nursery Project. We also had fun. When the builders of our estate were unduly tardy in completing a connecting road and after much correspondence, we just buried all their tools and invited the Sunday Post to come down and witness the subsequent 'treasure hunt'. The road was completed within days.

Perhaps the most significant work experience of my time in Ayrshire was brought about as a result of an innocuous letter the Social Work Department received one day asking for assistance. It was from the Passionist Fathers at Coodham, a Roman Catholic Retreat in a beautiful wooded country estate outside Kilmarnock. They had partially restored the old manor house in which they held their retreats and wanted us to help with a cash grant. Normally I would have written to them explaining that this was outwith our remit, but for some reason I decided to visit them and explain personally. At the meeting in Coodham I met Father Michael Carroll who, along with John McManus, would become one of the most important people in my life in terms of my personal development.

Rather than the uncomfortable meeting I'd expected, it soon became apparent that Michael was a very special person. Trained at the Jesuit Loyola University in the States, Michael was based at Coodham to offer training to those who sought his services. In a sense, he had come to the same realisation as had I that 'sorting people's heids one at a time' was not the most efficient way to intervene in troubled lives. What he was doing it transpired, was training people in interpersonal skills, assertiveness techniques and group skills to help them help others. As I began to absorb what he was about, I managed to put together a proposal which earned money for Coodham by Michael taking on contracts to run programmes for the Social Work Department. As I got to know him better he asked me if I'd be interested in working alongside him and learning the techniques myself. I jumped at the chance. It was a most improbable concatenation but I involved John so that the two of us began a journey of personal discovery and development which would have cost zillions of dollars in the States.

For five years, night after night, I worked alongside Michael and honed my skills to the point where I was running skills classes myself. Over the years John and I became pretty skilled in interpersonal communications, group skills, assertiveness techniques, managing conflict and negotiation techniques. These were skills that were never taught in school or university. They couldn't easily be picked up just anywhere in those days and John and I would agree later in life that this was perhaps the most life-changing experience each of us had had the privilege of undergoing. Certainly, they were of fundamental importance in the professional and personal successes each of us was to experience in later years. Even Michael's throwaway lines were exceptionally useful. Gems such as, 'always ask someone to give you *two* examples of an allegation they're making in conversation…most people can come up with one, but few can instantly recollect a couple of instances' …. 'when someone tells you they "don't mean to interrupt", "mean to be cheeky", "seem unkind" or whatever, they're telling you *exactly* what they're about to demonstrate' …. 'whenever someone is leaving your room after a chat and, with their hand on the door handle say, "oh, there was *one* other thing"…. that's what they came to talk to you about'.

Michael also helped me understand the importance of the bleedin' obvious. He guided me that each of us has a responsibility to achieve our potential and to help other achieve theirs. Accordingly, in order better to prepare ourselves for this life-task, we had a responsibility to surround ourselves only with the very best people … the best doctor, the best dentist, best friends, best colleagues and so on. Over the years I've worked hard to do just that and feel with no sense of immodesty that I've accomplished that task in spades!

Michael Carroll was an extraordinary guy. Each year we'd invite all of the people from the various courses to come along one night with their partner, to take part in a short ceremony where we said a few kind words and had a glass of wine. The first year Michael and I stood at the entrance and welcomed everyone. We would shake their hand and be introduced to their partner. A year would pass and when next we stood at the front door Michael would welcome everybody by their first name, *partners included*; despite only having met them once twelve months previously. Just amazing. What a memory, but it was born of his laser-like focus upon the person with whom he was speaking, the absence of any self regard and his ability to live in the present.

In 1980, Margaret and I had our second child; Campbell. As was the case with Ron, my heart was just bursting with love at the entrance of this wee baby to the world. Over the years I've considered myself so fortunate to see four beautiful sons born; each of them has engendered the same emotion of wonderment, love and concern that their future would be everything it could be. Inevitably, there was a sense of us being old hands as we'd done this before. Margaret had her bags packed and placed at the door of our Kilmarnock home and when her waters broke, we just headed nonchalantly for the car. It was night time, and we headed up the A74 to the Queen Mother's Hospital in Glasgow's west end.

Named after my younger brother, Campbell's middle name was Andrew because we'd used up all the other grandparent's names and wanted something Scottish. Campbell was eight pounds something at birth just as was his brother before him. He was another complete delight. Old photographs still confuse me when I inspect them as for the life of me I can't tell one of the boys from the other if there are no clues there to help me. I remember those early years with great affection as Campbell was just as overpowering as was Ron when he was born.

However, the early eighties were also clouded with a deep sadness, as I was overcome with a depression which saw Margaret seek intervention on my behalf from a psychiatrist to help me overcome the blackness. I had become completely exhausted and weary. I was physically and emotionally on my knees. Being a social worker, I was well aware that as many people recover spontaneously from depression as do those following a course of medication, and I stubbornly refused prescribed treatment, although Margaret had the doctor visit me a number of times at home. To this day I don't know why I resisted help but I do appreciate more personally how depression can put people beyond the reach of spouses, family and friends when it crowds out rationality.

Around this time I also became susceptible to a life-long battle against insomnia. I discovered that I just couldn't sleep. I'd have difficulty falling over and when I did, it was almost inevitable that I'd waken again in the wee small hours. My head was so full of concerns, anxieties and ideas that the only way I found to combat this was to awaken completely and physically list the agenda of issues and record in writing the resolutions to the problems with which I was wrestling before trying to get back to sleep. Over the years, this left me exhausted. It was only in 1986, when I saw an advert for a psychologist in Ayr who treated those suffering from sleep deprivation, that I took action that ultimately cured me. Even today I can slip back into periods of insomnia but now I have a toolbox of interventions which resolve matters expeditiously.

My work was now completely overwhelming me, and I was working every night and weekends, too. In addition to the very substantial responsibilities of my day job, I was working with groups in Coodham most evenings and running the Community Council. Because my workload took me to different parts of Ayrshire and had me dealing with such a variety of tasks, there was no one, except Margaret, who could see the overall effect this was having on me. Somehow, for many months, I managed to conceal my feelings of being out of control from colleagues, but soon it became evident that I was struggling. George wasn't a caring kind of guy. Not the type to put an avuncular arm round a colleague. He wore his workaholism on his sleeve like a badge of courage. He supported me by saying that we were like peas in a pod and that I should just keep plugging away.

In the weeks before I eventually left home, I found myself driving out, late at night, to park in a lay-by where I would just sit and stare into the middle distance. One evening John was driving in to the estate when I was on my way out. He had no real idea what was going on but was obviously frustrated with me, as I wasn't opening up to anyone, and he must have been puzzled. Anyway, on that evening he chose to rebuke me and told me to 'pull my socks up'. I drove on, chastened and convinced that I'd need to handle this on my own, wallowing in my own fatigue and confusion.

My work at Coodham, other training programmes I ran elsewhere in the region, community development activity, volunteer projects I'd pioneered, running residential Intermediate Treatment programmes as well as my evening obligations with the Community Council all seemed to me to be hugely important and demanded my personal, martyred participation. It couldn't be sustained but I kept pegging away. Home life became more stressful. Margaret was wonderfully supportive but I only found satisfaction and some kind of inner peace when I was out working.

The result of this and something I still can't satisfactorily explain to myself was that I decided to move out of the family home to 'find myself'. I still groan inwardly at my behaviour at that time. I took my car, my guitar and some clothes and moved back initially to stay with my Gran for a few weeks while I sorted myself out. Grandpa Hector, whom I loved dearly and who was my main adult role model, had died while on holiday in Jersey a few years previously, and both Gran and my Mum were distraught but they too were very supportive of both Margaret and me.

A terrible guilt descended on me after my move away which merely compounded the felony. In order to be near the boys, I rented a cottage in the countryside outside the village of Kilmaurs near Kilmarnock. It cost me £22 a week and was all I could afford. I entered a period of self flagellation as I had little money and what I had was spent in petrol so as to be able to get to and from work. Not unsurprisingly, I lost a couple of stones in weight.

For six weeks I made no contact with anyone. I lived a lonely and frugal existence in the cottage communicating by phone from a call box at the road end only infrequently with Margaret who was beside herself with worry. There were no mobile phones in those days. Eventually my head was sufficiently together to go back and see the boys and Margaret. It was a tearful reunion but soon thereafter I was able to take Ron and Campbell to see my wee cottage and they had a great time helping me find firewood and making toast by putting bread on the end of sticks and burning it to a crisp over the red hot coals. My main concern in all of this was, I suppose, my own confusions, but also how my departure would affect the boys. However, all the indicators, their schoolwork, sleep patterns, behaviour at home, behaviour with their friends suggested that Margaret had worked miracles in keeping them on an even keel.

I was able to see them each weekend, my sole compromise in work terms. I still worked long hours, now also because I couldn't face going home to my cold cottage and because at work and meetings, there were always cups of tea and other sustainances around and I could feed myself on scones and biscuits, but the weekends were reserved for Ron and Campbell.

Ron had become an accomplished young footballer and Campbell gave it a shot although he was never that enthusiastic. Golf was to become his sport of choice and both he and Ron would win many trophies as they learned the game together, initially under my tutelage in the public Caprington Golf Course next to their home ... or Royal Caprington as the locals called it. At weekends we'd watch Ron play up front for one or other of the teams he played for. When it came to informal kickabouts in the park, Campbell was less than interested. Now and again he'd show his displeasure at our choice of leisure activity by offering to act as one of the goalposts and would take up position some eight feet or so from a handy tree. It says something about Ron's passion for the game that he was quite happy to let Campbell play this role.

Two groups of friends helped me during this period. Christine Smith, Mary Hoy and Joan Millar were three people Michael and I had trained in Coodham and Mary and Joan were now employed in a new Volunteer Centre I'd established in Grange Street in Kilmarnock. One night after a meeting finished, they surreptitiously followed me back to the cottage by car, because they were confused about what I was up to. Very Miss Marples! The three of them would pop in to see me from time to time. They'd also ask me out for a meal sometimes and generally took an interest in my welfare. A second group was comprised of John McManus and Ian 'Fingers' McMurtrie who formed, along with me, 'The Poseurs' band, from which I found much companionship as well as friendly affection. We took on alter-egos within the band. Ian was 'Good-Rockin' Johnnie McSnotter, I was 'High-Steppin' Johnnie McSnotter and John was 'Clean-Livin' Johnnie McSnotter.

Michael was also a great support. I was working hard at Coodham during this period, and knew it could only be a matter of time before Michael heard of my separation from Margaret, with whom he was very close. One evening in Coodham he told me he had a book he wanted to give me but that it was in his room. When I entered his tiny cell-like room, he gave me the book, but sat me down and told me he'd phoned me at home and that Margaret had confided in him. I kind of half expected to be given a dressing down but he told me that he understood some of the feelings I must be experiencing, because he had made the decision to leave the church and marry a nun! You could have knocked me over with a feather. He went on to say that he'd told no one of his decision and asked me to keep it to myself, which I did.

One of the most important things Michael ever taught me was to work out what my values were, to proclaim them and to let them set my course in life. It took me some years working with him but I worked hard to figure out what drove me and settled on five values which I've tried to live up to since about 1980. In no order of importance, they are; *Respect, Service, Collaboration, No Fear of Failure* and the *Pursuit of Excellence.*

My meaning behind these is important to me. *Respect* has not been a way of avoiding conflict with others; rather it is a way of trying to behave responsibly, even in challenge. I must confess I've not always found it easy to live up to this high ideal, when I'm engaged in a struggle to achieve goals that are being thwarted by others, whose behaviour I see as selfish, self serving, short-sighted or downright stupid. I would tend to fall back on other values like *service* or *no fear of failure* to justify any action that might be construed as disrespectful. *Respect* also connotes notions of civil liberties and acceptance of others as they are.

Service is a value of mine which I've discovered can confuse people. Simply put, it is a life conviction I've made to serve others more vulnerable than me. More than once I've been engaged in conversation after a particular speech or presentation where my interlocutor has asked why I didn't take my skills into the private sector in order to earn more money and I've found it easy to explain that the mission which underpins everything I do is working to ensure that those who usually get the short end of the stick in our society get a better break because of my contribution. I've always found this ideal very easy to live with … although I must confess that it became easier as I began to earn the more remunerative salaries that might otherwise have tested my determination not to pursue a career in the private sector.

Collaboration matters more to me because I really *do* understand that few of us can make a difference on our own so the idea of working together is more of a methodology to be utilised in support of my other values. Over the years it has been this value which has tested me most, largely because I've had to engage with individuals or organisations which were populated with individuals who, now that they had the ability to operate (they thought) with less concern for the views or capacities of others, tried their hardest so to do. Operating independently of others has shallow and short term advantages. I still hear the justifications today …. focus, expeditiousness, pace, and I can see the argument sometimes. But at the end of the day we all need each other if we are to get the biggest bang for our buck; so-called conviction politicians, single minded businessmen or lazy bureaucrats all suffer from a fundamental downside …. they cannot forever ignore the need to take others with them on whatever journey they're taking. Someday they'll need the people they ignored. In addition, and more importantly, it just makes for better decision making where more rounded and better informed outcomes can be realised.

No fear of failure has always been my challenge to myself. When presented with a problem, Michael guided me to continually ask myself " *What's the worst thing that could happen?"*, to appreciate that there's little chance of things going quite so pear shaped, and then to act on my gut instinct.

"Always try to follow your heart, not your head, Ron", he'd say.

I also enjoy doing the unexpected. Make the move others wouldn't expect you to make. Michael also challenged me to answer the question, *"What would you do if you knew you just couldn't fail?"*. It's certainly a question that clears away obstacles and permits a clearer view of what you want to achieve right then in respect of a dilemma or in respect of life itself.

The *pursuit of excellence* has permitted me to ask more of myself in the service of others. Why would I wish to be second best? Why would it be appropriate for those I serve - colleagues or customers - to expect anything other than my best shot? I've had a long held interest in American politics and was impressed by President Jimmy Carter's book, *Why not the Best?* He seemed to me also to be someone who had depth to his motives although in his case they tended to be expressed in religious terms. It still gives me a kick to come top of the heap even if I have to work hard sometimes to come to terms with the inevitability of coming off second best now and again.

With these values as stars to guide me I've found Michael's advice, as ever, to be invaluable. It's made difficult decisions easy because I only have to apply the values and it's clear which road I should take. They have been ever present and unchanging and have been a real strength to me. It's funny, you know, because in all the years I worked with Michael, he never mentioned God or religion. He just spoke of values. There's a sense in which he took me along a path, which many would see as consistent with religious behaviour, and which amuses me because I am fundamentally an atheist. But I am prepared to accept that there were hidden depths and subtlety to Michael that I was light years away from appreciating.

Michael did leave the church and married the nun with whom he'd fallen in love. Years later I successfully made contact with him by letter; he was happily engaged in youth work in England. What a privilege it was to work with him and to spend five years learning at his knee.

My main support came from John and Ian *Fingers* McMurtrie. For some time we'd messed about together on guitar singing a blend of old blues and rock and roll music at which Ian excelled. We'd also sing folk songs which were more my *forte*. For fun one night we jammed a song, wrote words to it as we went along and called it *'Deprivation Blues'*. It was written as a laugh. Willie Roe for several years in the new millennium, Chairman of Highlands and Islands Enterprise and of Skills Development Scotland, but then Deputy Director of the Scottish Council for Voluntary Organisations (for whom John then worked as their Ayrshire Development Officer) - heard a version of the song and paid for us to spend a day in a recording studio recording it for a documentary he was producing. We duly recorded it in one session in a studio in Kilmarnock and found time to record another song I'd written called *'Cough Mixture'* in deference to Ian's then habit of drinking copious amounts of a particular cough mixture which produced hallucinogenic effects. It opened with the line,

' I drink cough mixture so I'm healthy when I die'

… and finished with a line which read,

'I'm smoking glue and sniffing wine and getting all mixed up.'

Ian was a particularly talented guitarist, sufficient to make us sound really professional on stage, and we found ourselves invited to play at venues all over Ayrshire and Glasgow. With our mix of music and humour we usually went down very well although one night we were asked to play at a fund-raiser at Dalmellington as the local Miners Welfare hall was under threat of closure. The audience was comprised of the blank stares of serried ranks of miners and their wives, all with their arms folded, waiting to be entertained, and we weren't exactly the most popular act that night. Up on stage I took an executive decision. "Ok, guys. Let's finish early and cut the last two songs. I don't think this is our kind of audience." We cut the set, packed away our instruments and were leaving the building mid-show when a flat cap with a wee miner inside left the main hall on the way to the toilet. Falling in step with us he asked conversationally,

"Is that you away, boys?"

"Aye."

"Thank fuck!"

So much for our altruism in helping a worthy cause.

Another tight squeak was an evening we played at the Hunting Lodge in Kilmarnock. The place was packed to the gunnels; it was all going very well when a gang of about a dozen bikers came in all dressed in leather and began shouting at us from the back. Gradually they moved forward and continued to abuse us. We were at the end of our set anyway and finished, going backstage to pack our gear. Unfortunately, the only way out of the pub was via the bar and through the crowd outside. We figured we'd be ripped to shreds and decided to make good our escape by going into a yard behind the dressing rooms and climbing a wall into the street. I was first up and couldn't believe my eyes when I scaled the wall as there on the other side were two cops having a fly puff. "What the hell are you up to?" one enquired.

I explained that the crowd were not exactly on our side. This thoroughly amused the cops, who told us to get the hell back in there and not to be so stupid. They stubbed their cigarette butts out and walked away laughing.

We took a deep collective breath and went back into the hall to engage with our critics. We pushed our way through the crowd and as we were approaching the safety of the front door, I was gripped on the shoulder by the biker who was perhaps most voluble in his abuse. I expected the worse.

"Sorry about the hard time, Jimmy. We just like bands with base players! " (We didn't have one.)"Can I buy you a drink?"

We ended up having a few sociable beers with the bikers and discussing the merits of us finding a base player so as better to meet with their approval. Appearances can be deceptive, right enough.

The Poseurs began to play quite a lot around the west of Scotland and I tended to play the role of front man where I'd try out my patter on audiences. One evening I was asked if I'd consider being the Master of Ceremonies at a series of three concerts in the recently refurbished and re-opened Palace Theatre in Kilmarnock. It was a charity event and would star the characters from the popular Scottish television soap opera 'Take The High Road'. I agreed and worked on some new routines.

At the series of concerts, which also included the Poseurs, the producer had shaped the programme around popular vaudeville shows like 'Sunday Night at the London Palladium' where between acts there would be a silly parlour game. The cast from 'Take The High Road' played charades, for example. My job was to try to make the daft bits funny and to introduce the next act before singing a few songs with the Poseurs. All went well until the last night when I was dispensing prizes to the audience. Each night was packed; in addition to paying guests, buses brought the elderly and infirm from all over Ayrshire.

Some of the prizes were impressive but others were deliberately silly ... a bag of coal ... a dozen eggs. Someone right at the back of the circle won the dozen eggs wrapped in a brown paper bag, not encased in an egg box. I was having great fun pretending that I would just throw them up to the winner and the audience was howling when, God knows why, on impulse I decided that it would be really funny if I actually threw them. With much theatricality, counting one...two... three... I hurled them to the back of the theatre as far as I could. I can still see the parabolic curve of the eggs, as if in slow motion, as they made their way to the Gods.

The woman winner had played her part in the skit by encouraging me to throw them and was standing perhaps three steps back from the railing in the top tier. As she realised I'd thrown the bloody things, she raced forwards, stumbled along the row to the right and caught the bag, to the great acclaim of the audience - who howled in subsequent disbelief as the eggs broke in her grasp covering the isle below in yellow, sticky yoke.

The house laughed and applauded and I stood astage receiving their acclaim, secure in the knowledge that I was clearly a natural at this MC lark; it was only a matter of time before some impresario whisked me off to fame and fortune in London or Las Vegas. Imagine my consternation then when I left the stage only to be confronted by a very angry Theatre Manager who, red faced, quizzed me about how the hell the cleaning of the carpet was to be paid for. I was pretty sure that these kind of questions would not be asked of someone like Bruce Forsyth, and was sure that there must be something in the MC code of conduct that permitted damages as long as the audience found it funny. That said, I was never asked back the following year despite my *bravura* performance!

Despite these forays into show business, I was still as poor as a church mouse. One of Michael's other insights was in his definition of luck ... "It's where opportunity meets good preparation," he'd tell me. For once he was out, as I'd made no advance contribution to some perverse good luck that came my way. About a year after I moved into the cottage I met with some good fortune. I'd moved back up to Househillwood Road to be with my Gran over the Christmas holidays and returned to the cottage after a few days away to discover that a break-in had occurred. A bed spread had been laid out on the floor upon which were yet more items evidently being made ready for removal. Several items had actually been taken, so I drove on up to the farm and asked to use their phone to call the police. Eventually a lone policeman called; in taking details he ventured the fact that there had been a number of burglaries in the area and on every occasion they had taken quite a lot of stuff from vacant farmhouses over the festive period. He asked me to list what had been stolen. I listed all of the goods that had been stolen, thanking my lucky stars as I had earlier decided to insure the property because the cottage was very isolated and I was always slightly anxious about how vulnerable it was to an incident like this.

The cops pursued their enquiries and delved into my own background, finding it blemish free. A couple of months later I received a cheque for four hundred pounds. At last I could see a way forward. Instead of replacing the missing items, I moved quickly to use the cash as a 5% down payment on a mortgage to buy a flat, top centre, at 698 Dumbarton Road for £4,000; the same price I paid for my first flat some ten years earlier. This flat was much less salubrious, however. A small hallway, a dining-kitchen, toilet and a living room with a bed recess. That was it. I also used a couple of quid to take Ron and Campbell on their first package holiday - to Torremolinos, in Spain. It was February but the weather was quite benevolent and we managed to spend a few days making sandcastles on the beach. We climbed the hills surrounding the resort, went to a Pirates Show and generally had a good time.

Dumbarton Road also coincided with another move. From time to time I ponder on how fate takes a hand in things and materially changes the direction in which you are travelling. Again it kind of proved Michael's dictum about good luck. I was working in the Kilmarnock Volunteer Centre one day when I took a call from *Fingers* McMurtrie, my band-mate who was also a social worker. He was also one of the least reliable friends or colleagues I had, as he just couldn't wake up in the mornings. Punctuality was not his strong hand and frequently, John and I would be standing at the side of the stage waiting for the Poseurs to be introduced when Ian would step out of the darkness, guitar in hand, apologising and just in time. Anyway, on this occasion, Ian wanted to know whether I'd act as a referee for him as he wanted to apply for a post based in the Chief Executive's Department of Strathclyde Regional Council, to help develop the Urban Programme; a funding mechanism whereby the Scottish Office part-resourced (75%) of costs associated with projects dealing with social amelioration. The post was well paid. As I listened, I realised that while Ian wouldn't have a cat-in-hell's chance of winning the appointment, my profile might fit perfectly. I told Ian that I'd be delighted but said that I'd seen the advert myself and that I intended to apply.

"Christ's sake, Ron. If you apply, I've no chance."

Armed with this lead, innocently given me by Ian, I duly applied and was subsequently appointed to a post in Glasgow in 1984, which found me more involved with policy development and the implementation of innovative projects, some of them major. It also, importantly, gave me a higher salary, so I could get back on my feet. By now Margaret was back at work herself earning a salary and the boys were settled in school and doing well, if not so outstandingly well as would have hinted at the outstanding academic success each would subsequently enjoy at university.

8. Back To The City.

This city is what it is because our citizens are what they are.
Plato.

At first I shared an office with a group of other staff who were all administrators. The unit was managed by John Scott, a meek man who stayed in his glass-fronted office all day and calculated and recalculated the spend on the Urban Programme. I was meant to be the developmental kiddo and as an early task, was asked to interview and appoint someone for the unit to be employed under the Government's Youth Opportunities Scheme. Because I was only in the door, one of my more experienced colleagues, Ryan, was asked to lead with me riding shotgun. It was perhaps the most bizarre interview session in which I've ever participated. I wasn't to know immediately but Ryan was mentally ill. The candidate we were interviewing was Gary Hamilton and over subsequent years many of us would have cause to question Gary's sanity as well!

Ryan opened up the interview by welcoming Gary and proceeding to tell him what the job might involve. So far so good. However, Ryan continued to talk; it was about 9.30 am, and talk ... and talk ... and I was getting uncomfortable that so far, Gary hadn't been invited to say a word. Then I noticed that Gary had fallen asleep in the interview chair opposite! But Ryan ignored this and kept right on talking. I was astonished. One guy was fast asleep and the other was blethering away to him like a budgie. Eventually, I had to intervene and wake Gary up and take over the interview. We appointed him but over the weeks I saw Ryan's behaviour deteriorate and drew my concerns to John Wilson, the Assistant Chief Executive who had overall responsibility for staffing matters. John promised he'd keep an eye on Ryan and asked me to maintain a watching brief, owing to my social work experience. He felt nevertheless that it might be premature to speak with Ryan about his mental health; a few days later I was called for as Ryan was sitting perched upon a window ledge in a nearby office, legs on the outside, saying he was going to jump. We worked on the fourth floor.

The Deputy Chief Executive, Ian Stuart, was alerted. Acknowledging my social work background, asked me to go in to try to talk him in, and I did. Initially they didn't think Ryan was serious, and just wanted an assessment from me before calling the authorities. Ryan was serious all right; I spent the best part of half an hour in the office just conversing with him, and eventually managed to persuade him to place both of his legs inside the office, although just by leaning back he would still fall to his death. I had just persuaded him to come inside on his proviso that he could 'hide inside a cupboard' when there was a knock on the door. Unaccountably, Ian Stuart hadn't sent for any of the uniformed services, but mouthed his new seriousness through the three inch gap in the door jamb asking me to step outside in order to 'spell' me. As I did so, I noticed with horror that the senior person replacing me was Bobby, the guy Ryan had been fulminating about for the past half hour. I managed to stop the exchange and told Iain that we needed medical help. I returned to the room and after a while, professional help arrived and Ryan was taken away to receive treatment in a hospital near to his home. John Wilson and I visited him a couple of times but he was far gone. He returned eventually but I never saw him completely healthy again.

So much for my first days in the exalted Chief Executive's department.

My Senior Executive Officer then was Keith Yates, recently retired Chief Executive of Stirling Council. Keith had been a hero since I was earlier exposed to his skills on various committees on which I served along with him in Ayrshire. He was extremely well regarded by the politicians and was capable of thinking big, bold thoughts ,like building and staffing a new college of education in the East End of the city, where there was a paucity of educational resources. He was a mad-keen long distance runner, and typically ran to and from work each day when his diary commitments allowed. He talked about it all of the time and was really fit. The only downside was that he'd take his running gear and place it to dry atop the radiator in his office, where it would stink out the entire place. Keith seemed always to be oblivious to this but more than once I left his office with my eyes streaming.

Every so often, he'd ask me into his office for a chat but sometimes it was about some minor personal issue he was dealing with at the time. For a strong, confident guy, he could yet be vulnerable on occasion. What gave further impression of this was that he had a tremor in his hands all the time, although I'd be pretty sure that this was not of an emotional genesis. Keith taught me a lot about being a caring, effective and successful bureaucrat. A smashing guy.

An intransigent and arrogant Margaret Thatcher had been elected Leader of the Conservative Party in 1975 and, like flared trousers and flower power, I had assumed she'd be of her time and would soon pass. How wrong I was. When she emerged from Tory Central Office as Leader, she famously held two fingers aloft to the camera intending the V for Victory sign but being completely unaware of social and cultural norms, managed to reverse the sign as if to say, "Up yours!", to those watching.

This was the time when Jim Callaghan had decided to 'step down for a younger man' and the Labour Party elected Michael Foot, who went on to oversee a manifesto so supremely idiotic (or principled, depending upon your political perception) that it was described as 'the longest suicide note in history'. Thatcher took Britain to war against the Argentinians; in doing so, she engendered a nationalistic fervour that swept her back into power just when she began to seem vulnerable.

Shortly afterwards, veiled from most of the electorate, without anyone recognising its significance, a 29-year-old Anthony Charles Lynton Blair was elected and began his efforts, along with Gordon Brown, to take the Labour Party back to power by making it as right-wing as Thatcher might have designed, had she been asked to create the perfect opposition party that might merely continue the work of the Tories should they lose an election. This was the young eejit who would somehow manage to accomplish what Gaitskell had failed to do and abolish Clause four of the Labour Party's constitution...."*To secure for the workers by hand or by brain the full fruits of their industry*".... It was written on the back of my membership card. Nowadays the membership card reads like a Liberal Party strapline and blethers on about how we are a democratic socialist party that seeks to have people live together in a spirit of tolerance and respect and implies that there's not much that can't be resolved with a wee cuddle. Changed days. Blair transformed the party and made it more electable but in doing so he pissed me off more than anything had done since Dylan decided his music sounded better when played on an electric guitar!

And so it was that I started to work more with a raft of politicians among whom, Tommy Graham, Ian Davidson, Tony Worthington, Jimmy Wray and Tommy McAvoy all went on to make their mark as Members of Parliament at Westminster although not all successfully. Bill Millar became a distinguished Member of the European Parliament and, over the years, a close friend.

Bill is a lovely man who doesn't have a bad bone in his body unless called upon to settle a political score. He was one of a generation of Labour Politicians in Scotland who had a visceral disregard for Scottish Nationalism and more particularly, of members of the Militant Tendency. He became renowned for his selflessness in working to assist other colleagues in elections or by-elections in order to ensure that the Nats - usually the challenging party - didn't prosper. His main reputation outside politics was his encyclopaedic knowledge of popular music and his period as European Member of Parliament, initially for Glasgow until the party changed the rules, gave him the capacity to swell his already bloated horde of acetates. Later on, another politician in Glasgow, Frank McAveety MSP, would lay claim to a greater collection than Bill's but Frank's was comprised of vinyls, CDs and tapes whereas Bill's was restricted solely to old albums - LPs, in the *lingua franca* of the day.

Ian Davidson was in many ways the most gifted of his generation of elected members. Often accused of being a 'Tankie'; a hard-line Stalinist, he was actually the most pragmatic of politicians. He had a quick wit and spoke easily and eloquently but I felt that there was a misanthropic aspect to his personality that cast a baleful shadow over his political and personal abilities. Before he went to Parliament, he would become my Chairman in a subsequent post I'd hold and I would witness his strengths up close.

In 2009 the political system at Westminster came in for substantial public admonishment when politicians of all hues were portrayed by the media as venal, spendthrift chancers when a disc containing their expense claims in detail was provided to the *Daily Telegraph* newspaper. Many resigned, many others paid back substantial sums and almost all were required to provide a quote for national or local media in explanation of their alleged misuse of public funds. All of these quotes were defensive on behalf of the politicians and all were derided by the public. Ian was different.

His receipts showed that he had attended shooting events on a corporate basis. The papers were quick to invite him to comment upon this participation given that he was always quick to take the left-wing, anti-establishment position so why was he hobnobbing with the lords and gentry at shooting parties? Ian's response was so typically Ian that it quelled any further interrogation.

"Comrade," he told the *Daily Telegraph* journalist, "when the revolution comes, riflemen will be needed!"

Tony Worthington was an academic and was perhaps the main architect behind the emphasis placed by the Council on Community Development, in some ways accepting the baton from the late lamented Geoff Shaw, Strathclyde Council's first Convenor. It was always something of a mystery to me why he never really scaled the political heights at Westminster as he seemed a perfect candidate for preferment under a Blair administration, although to be fair, he was given a Northern Ireland portfolio for a while. Tony was extremely well liked and respected but his academic background surfaced now and again. I remember once at a Community Development Committee, just before proceedings commenced, when in conversation with a few of his political colleagues who had taken their seats amidst the usual shuffling of papers, Tony evinced his concern over the absence of a formal strategy of some kind within the Council arguing, "This is just another example of disjointed incrementalism". Those of his Labour colleagues who weren't big on organisational sociology - all of them - just looked at him blankly. During the course of the rest of the meeting,

Tony was continually asked by his amused colleagues if decisions they were being asked to make on the paper before them would assist the comrades in the struggle against disjointed incrementalism.

Jimmy Wray was some act. He always had a reputation as being someone you didn't mess with. Someone with friends. A Gorbals man, Jimmy looked like one of the boxers whose sport he patronised. One day, Ian Stuart called me into his office where he was sitting with an Assistant Chief Constable. He told me that there was a committee meeting at 2.00 that afternoon where the future of a drugs counselling project housed in a Gorbals building would be reviewed. "I want you to look after that committee and make sure that the place is closed. The Chairman has been advised. This comes from the top."

I was relaxed about this duty but asked why.

"Rather than stopping the misuse of drugs, police information is that they're actually selling the bloody stuff from out the back door. I want it closed. Now!"

I can't remember which politician chaired that particular meeting, probably John Gray or Tommy McAvoy, but was surprised when, upon entering the room, I saw Jimmy Wray as the local councillor, almost certainly unaware of what was about to happen, surrounded by a phalanx of priests. Two or three on each side of him, all brought along to testify as to the efficacy of this project. I was particularly taken aback to notice that one of them was Brother Patrick, a regular visitor to Coodham and a friend of Michael Carroll's.

I went over to make myself a coffee and was approached by Brother Patrick. After some small talk he asked how I saw the decision going. I looked around to ensure that we couldn't be overheard and volunteered the suggestion that all did not appear to be well with the project. Patrick placed his arm around my shoulder and told me quietly that the Catholic Church had asked him to attend with precisely the same objective as I'd been set by Ian Stuart. Now, not for a moment would I suspect Councillor Wray to have been involved in any way with any legal inappropriateness. I'm sure he was just acting as any politician would to retain and attract resources to his ward. Nevertheless, Jimmy Wray and I became involved in a series of terse exchanges at the committee once he realised that I was out to close the place. He would have realised immediately that either I was completely stupid or that I wouldn't be doing this without the explicit authority of senior politicians as well as from the highest levels within the Chief Executive's office. This could only mean that his own Labour colleagues were acting against him without his earlier awareness. Information is power in politics and good networks are a fundamental prerequisite to obtaining that information. Jimmy seemed all at sea and we closed the project.

He was reduced to asking my name as if he'd just have this matter fixed upon leaving the room

"Ron Culley", I answered.

"How do you spell that?" he asked.

"R...O...N", I replied cheekily.

He left the room after having a quiet word with me which in summary was to the effect that he wouldn't forget this incident. I have to say, though, that many years later when I myself stood for the first Scottish Parliament, Jimmy was extremely helpful and put himself out to assist me.

Tommy McAvoy was a stalwart of the Labour Party. Out in Rutherglen his votes would be weighed rather than counted so heavily did the party dominate local politics. Tommy rose quietly and effortlessly to the senior ranks of the party under Tony Blair and became *Comptroller of Her Majesty's Household*; effectively the

Deputy Whip although Tommy told me with a laugh how many problems he had encountered explaining the niceties of this appointment to the regulars of his local pub, few of whom could be counted in the ranks of Loyalists and who not unreasonably didn't associate Tommy's title with his role in Parliament. Speaker of the House of Commons Michael Martin from Springburn excepted, in many ways Tommy was the most successful of the Strathclyde councillors who went to Westminster, as he was appointed to the post of Deputy Chief Whip in 1997, when Blair won the election, and held this office for longer than any other Whip in history.

His namesake, Tommy Graham, was unlike any politician I've ever met, then or since. I worked closely for some time with Tommy when he was Chairman of the Urban Programme Sub Committee of the Community Development Committee. It has been said that some drink copiously from the well of knowledge ... but that others merely gargle; well, many would have said that of Tommy, who was also wider than he was tall. He must have been five foot six or so and could easily have weighed twenty stones. In his mid-forties, he had a deep sonorous voice and was perpetually sweating. When he spoke, he was somehow reminiscent of Rab. C. Nesbit but with a growling *timbre* only matched by theatrical giants like Sir John Geilgud, had the thespian knight but been raised in Garthamlock in Glasgow. He was also perpetually course and enjoyed scatological humour ... at first glance, a politician with few immediately apparent redeeming features.

Tommy was not a charismatic, personable, empathic, good looking politician. Initially, I couldn't see how he could win the Westminster nomination out in Linwood near Paisley where he lived, as he was up against people like Ronald Young - then Secretary of the Labour Group and one who was possessed of all the attributes denied Tommy - but as I spent more time with him I could see why he would merit backing by the smart money. He was as shrewd as he was ruthless when it came to local politics.

One day, he talked me through the constituency nomination process for MP and forecast who would be eliminated in every round. He was completely accurate on each call. An impressive grasp of the numbers. Some years later I'd read *Master of the Senate* by Robert. A. Caro, one of a trilogy of books recounting the life and times of Lyndon Baines Johnson. I would marvel at the way in which L.B.J. would be able famously to read the voting intentions of his senatorial colleagues *en route* to the Presidency of the United States and would permit myself a wry smile as I remember Tommy's equal ability, albeit on the slightly smaller stage of Renfrewshire.

I wrote a lot of his speeches. One day he was addressing a conference on elderly care and was due to speak at 2.00 p.m. He had a number of people on whom he'd call for scripting purposes, and so it was with some surprise when at 1.30 he called on me to 'knock up a few words'. It was so late I just assumed that someone else had earlier been set the task, but I quickly set to work in a vast room within a large baronial mansion where the conference was being held. As I wrote, Tommy would walk about the room gazing at the ceiling and uttering phrases, all of which I'd studiously ignore in order to bring some semblance of cohesion to the speech. At this point Tommy had been nominated as the Labour candidate in the imminent national election, and was receiving a lot of stuff about Margaret Thatcher from the backroom boys in the Labour Party. He wanted to include a list of deceptions she had allegedly visited upon the British people but I thought this was inappropriate for a speech to a non-aligned audience who expected to hear from him on elderly care. To Tommy's credit (as far as I was concerned) he didn't challenge me when I told him not to be so daft. He just continued to walk with his thumbs jammed behind his lapels and ruminating as if he was rehearsing the speech in his head, looking for all the world like a Glaswegian version of Rumpole of the Bailey.

In the midst of our work together, an old woodsman came into the room carrying an armful of logs for the huge open fire which was situated behind us. Tommy, always a friendly and spirited man, hailed the aged handyman.

"Me and the boy here's writing a speech. Can you help us?"

The old fellah placed the logs in the hearth, leaned on the table and rubbed his grizzled chin in order to give some thought to the question. After a while he ventured, "Unaccustomed as I am to public speaking...." and looked at Tommy for some reassurance that he was on the right lines. Tommy recognised limited assistance when he saw it and instead asked the old guy, "Tell us a joke". I continued to scribble.

The old fellah told a story of a woodsman coming home for dinner one night when he heard screaming coming from his cottage. Perturbed, he ran up the stairs and witnessed his wife bathing their baby by dragging it up and down a bath by its ears.

"Woman, why are you dragging our child up and down the bath by its ears?"

"'Well, I'm certainly not putting my hands in that water", she exclaimed. "It's bloody scalding hot."

Tommy laughed, thanked him, then took my hurried scribbles, all of which had been true to the task of dealing with the expected speech.

Tommy read my bullet points on the way to the auditorium and, having been introduced, strode up to the podium and began to deliver a most impressive speech which started by him mangling my words, owing to his unaffected use of the Glasgow dialect. "I staun before yous today tae speak aboot truth and broken promises."

He then proceeded to compare the positive elements of his Committee's work on elderly issues with the let-downs he attributed to Margaret Thatcher. It was as seamless as it was effective. He finished with a story.

"And there will be some of yous in here today who will be given the job of implementing them proposals on elderly care," he bellowed, and went on to tell the story the woodsman had just told him.

"And in case any of yous are thinkin' of waashin' the baby without gettin' your hauns in the waatter, yous have another think comin'. I expect everybody to get behind them recommendations and get their hauns wet … even if the waatter's bilin', by the way!"

And he stood down to rapturous applause. He had judged the mood of his audience perfectly; even non-aligned audiences in the west of Scotland were vehemently anti-Thatcher and he got his way in the end.

Unfortunately, years later, Tommy was caught up in a bitter political battle with his next door Labour colleague, Gordon McMaster MP. All sorts of allegations surfaced including the purposeful inflation of Labour membership in Tommy's constituency by enrolling residents of old folk's homes whose postal votes would then be used to secure Tommy's re-nomination. That would have been bad enough, but quite dramatically, Gordon McMaster committed suicide, leaving behind him writings that described his inner turmoil, and Tommy was fingered by the party. In what became a sensational political scandal, Tommy had his party membership withdrawn and was deselected as an MP.

The World Socialist Web Site at the time reported the *imbroglio* as follows;

"Renfrewshire West MP Graham had been the subject of a 14-month internal Labour Party enquiry, following the suicide last year of Gordon McMaster, MP for Paisley South. Labour's National Constitutional Committee took just five minutes to reach their expulsion decision, having questioned Graham for 18 hours.

Gordon McMaster killed himself shortly after the Labour Party's election victory on May 1, 1997. A heavy drinker and ME sufferer, he had been depressed following a street attack. His suicide note, which has never been published in full, reportedly stated "I hope Don Dixon" (a former Labour official) "and Tommy Graham can live with themselves." The note also reportedly criticised Paul Mack, a political ally of Graham and former deputy leader of Renfrew District Council, and suggested that McMaster had been the target of a sexual smear campaign organised by Graham and Mack.

During the Graham investigation the *Scotsman* newspaper ran several articles on Ferguslie Park Community Business Holdings (FCBH), in Paisley. This scheme, established in the 1980s in the working class area of Ferguslie Park, was supposedly aimed at building "community" businesses as a means of tackling unemployment. The *Scotsman* reported that at least part of the FCBH, a director of which was a close associate of Graham's, had fallen under the control of Paisley's drug gangs and was being used to launder money.

Graham was cleared of any involvement in the drugs operations. However the Labour inquiry was said to have uncovered a "substantial body of evidence," pointing to the systematic attempt to gain "political and personal advantage for some individuals." Graham was accused of rigging meetings, stacking membership with his supporters and restricting access to public funds. He was also alleged to have offered Labour officials sexually compromising pictures of a leading gay Scottish trade union official in return for the personal file on Brian Oldrey, a Labour Councillor who planned to stand against Graham in his own constituency. He was found guilty on five charges including "bad mouthing" opponents, attempting to use compromising photographs, membership "irregularities", and a general "sustained course of conduct prejudicial to, and acts grossly detrimental to, the party." Graham left the hearing vowing to fight on. But the following day his lawyer announced that they would challenge only one aspect of the membership rigging charges in court.

Tommy went to ground, communicating with no one, and resurfaced only years later when I needed some help.

After about a year of my incumbency, a new senior post was created within the Council and was contested both by Keith Yates and Iain Hill. Iain had been an architect of the Regional Council and was popular amongst its politicians. He succeeded to the post although many thought that Keith was the more talented of the two. Tommy Graham told me later that he thought that Iain's openly gay demeanour would have found favour with his more politically correct colleagues who wouldn't want to view themselves as being biased against someone of a homosexual orientation. These days, Iain might have been described by a politician as 'a man who was a confirmed bachelor and who had a life-long affection for musical theatre', but back then, what Tommy *actually* said was,"It'll no' matter if Iain's a bent nail. We don't mind poofs nowadays"... said with all of the innocence of an old Labour man trying to come to terms with a new political consciousness. Nevertheless, Iain was also a man of considerable talent and he reconfigured the department, putting me into an office with three other guys as he thought that the dynamic therein would release synergistic energies.

David Asquith was an English bloke who had a background in planning. Normally quiet and unassuming, he also seemed to have a subterranean rage going on underneath his placid exterior. I never quite worked out whether it was some form of controlled passion about the work in which he was engaged or whether he was just bad tempered before he got the first morning coffee down him.

Danny Brennan was a Careers Advisor and was instrumental in helping me realise just how you could push a bureaucracy some considerable distance before resistance was experienced. He was a complete maverick in respect of the work he did in support of the unemployed. Not only did he hold the organisation in some small measure of disdain, he also parked his battered old BMW outside Council headquarters where it was inevitable that he'd collect daily parking tickets, all of which he duly peeled from his windscreen before throwing them in a corner of the office where they gathered dust. Eventually I seem to recall him coming to an agreed settlement with the Council over the amount he owed them. Even at a compromise figure it was still considerable.

Danny drove the organisation nuts by arguing that the new availability of European Structural Funds required someone to be seconded to the European Commission to take advantage of this largesse. In this assessment he was entirely right, but the organisation struggled with the notion that Danny would also be the very man to go out there and do the job. However, eventually his tenacity won the day, and he ultimately developed a very successful career in Brussels before meeting and marrying a horse-loving girl from the shires, an act which astonished Danny-watchers back home, who still cannot understand how someone so fair and fragile could stem Danny's tempestuous character.

The third person in the room was over the years to become not only one of my closest colleagues but one of my dearest friends. Laurie Russell was also a planner and was brought in to help the Council develop new approaches to youth work. Laurie, too, showed me how far it was possible to change the way a bureaucracy worked and he had great success in devising youth strategies and in seeing them incorporated within the Council's Social Strategy for the Eighties, largely penned by Keith Yates. But Laurie challenged authority in my eyes initially as a consequence of his attire. In those days every male worker in the Chief Executive's Department wore a tie. Suits were preferred although a smart jacket and trousers was also accepted. But most certainly a tie had to be worn. Laurie wore his in a way that resulted in the knot being positioned somewhere beneath his left ear, his top shirt button undone. His entire attire screamed disdain.

I was attracted to Laurie's personality in that he was a witty guy who worked hard and who was passionate about the task in hand, much the way I saw myself. He also shared my own analysis of the need for social and economic intervention and enjoyed a glass but more in keeping with my own and David's consumption. In those days, no one could keep pace with Danny. Triple spiced rums were the order of the day for our Dan where we were more pint men with maybe an occasional wee half as a chaser.

That said, we all had our moments. One winter's day there came a fierce snowstorm to our fair city and all traffic ground to a halt. The Chief Executive, Sir Robert Calderwood, sent all 135,000 staff home but Danny, Laurie and I headed to the Baby Grand Bar next door where we steadily consumed more than was wise, quite oblivious to the worsening conditions and the deepening snow outside. After annoying the bar staff one too many times with our raucous laughter, we were encouraged to make for home. Laurie and I felt that we'd be alright as Laurie stayed then in Vinicombe Street only yards from the Hillhead Underground station and I was living in Dumbarton Road, only a few hundred yards from Partick Subway Station. Danny, on the other hand stayed on the south side and had to walk. Bleary-eyed, he told us the next day how he had fallen asleep in a snowdrift and was surprisingly comfortable and warm - the first tell-tale signs of hypothermia. A stranger helped him to his feet but he still has no recollections of getting back home to the comfort of his hearth.

Laurie and I successfully managed to get on to a Subway train and I bid Laurie farewell at his Hillhead station before falling asleep. Fortunately for me, the Glasgow Subway has fifteen stations on a continuous loop which returns you to your station of choice every twenty-four minutes. Every time I arrived at Partick Station where I was to leave the train, I was fast asleep only to awaken at Govan, the next stop along the line, where I'd promptly fall asleep again. I made the circuit a few times but eventually I got it together and stepped out into the wintry blast. Glasgow had just come to a snowy standstill. It was eerie and I could well understand how Danny had managed to get himself into the predicament he had.

I also developed a good relationship with Sir Robert Calderwood. Laurie had become his PA - I noticed that he was dressed rather more smartly now - and in his new role was privy to all that was going on within the organisation. I visited Laurie a few times in the CEO's suite of offices and was much taken by the dimmed lighting and the feeling of calm it created. Sir Robert asked to see me once in connection with the proposal to close the drugs project in the Gorbals and *en passant*, asked me my views on some other matters. I forget now what these were, but I remember being quite forthright in my reply. After that, Sir Robert called me a few times and asked me up for a chat, usually about five thirty or six when most people had left the building at around five. I was always someone who came in early but was also one who stayed on for a while. Anyway, he would invite me to sit down and would chat to me about what he'd been dealing with that day and would ask my opinion. Inevitably with Sir Robert, a loquacious man, he talked more and I talked less as the conversation developed but I usually got my twopence worth. These chats were affable and interesting but I put little store by them. One evening he called me and told me that he intended financing two people to undertake a Master's Degree in the University of Strathclyde. His deputy, Ian McFarlane would make the final decision, he said, but he wanted to know if I'd be interested. I most certainly was, as although I'd obtained two professional qualifications at that point, neither had been the equal of a degree and the thought of being able to undertake a course of study leading to an even more demanding Masters degree was intoxicating. I applied and was accepted as one of only two people of the 135,000 staff who were employed by the Regional Council who was privileged enough to be sponsored in this way. I told Sir Robert that I'd work hard to justify his encouragement.

Although I was keen to undertake this study, in the evenings after work, I was rather apprehensive and was therefore completely delighted when I received great news about an amendment to the course membership. My friend John McManus had applied independently to undertake a Masters at Glasgow University. It had very similar course content if perhaps placing more emphasis on housing policy. Unfortunately, having been accepted, John learned that there was insufficient numbers to run the programme and the two faculties agreed to merge the courses. At a stroke John became one of my new classmates. Together we shared our apprehensions which were increased at the first meeting with our new colleagues. There were to be twenty-eight in the class and everyone other than John and I already had a Degree, most commonly an Honours Degree in economics or in one or other of the key academic ingredients of the course.

All of the academics who taught us had recently written books on the subject they were presenting and their lecture each week tended to consist of dealing with one or more chapters from their tome. Fair enough. And indeed, a tidy enough way to learn as long as you read round about the subject so as to be able to question the lecturer. I found this an invaluable tool as some of the lecturers, almost inconceivably as far as I was concerned, would sit in front of the class and attempt to read directly from the chapter they'd ask us to spend the previous week studying. It was designed, I'm sure, to aid those who'd been delinquent in their preparation but it put the majority of the class to sleep, my only antidote being to ask questions and argue a point of view such as was capable of keeping me awake after a long day's work.

Everyone moaned about the cramming that was necessary to accomplish all that was asked in a truncated period of two years. John and I decided together early on that it wouldn't be raw brainpower that would be the key determinant of success in the Masters - just as well for both of us - but tenacity. We decided that whatever it took, we'd meet all of the deadlines, submit everything on time, complete all of our class work and generally step up to the mark on every task the university asked of us.

It worked. Of the twenty-eight that started the class two years previously, there were only two names from our degree course in the Graduation Order of Ceremony... John McManus and Ron Culley. We had spent two years together in a foxhole and when the smoke cleared, we were the only two to have passed everything that had been asked of the class – a triumph of determination over ability!

We were mighty pleased with ourselves and that evening, having spent the previous couple of years studying quite diligently most evenings and weekends, decided to go out and celebrate. We walked up Dumbarton Road looking for a bar and spotted the Partick Tavern. Neither of us had been in before and we decided to start the evening by having a quick one in there. We noticed that there was a pub quiz on that night and flushed with our success that day, quietly remonstrated with each other that - as we were in a new pub whose culture we didn't appreciate and whose clientele we didn't know - we'd better watch we didn't win the quiz and make it look too easy.

We came thirty-second out of thirty-three entrants and realised that there was more than one area of intelligence. Had they asked questions about Lindblom's *partisan mutual adjustment* or *disjointed incrementalism*, we'd have been in clover.... but 'Who shot JR Ewing in the soap opera, Dallas?' We hadn't a clue.

This period of my life also coincided with a sharpening of my footballing activities. I was in my early thirties and had played almost continuously throughout my social work years in Paisley and Ayr and now back in Glasgow. Over the piece I'd converted from a fast right winger to a goal-scoring centre forward. I'd come to recognise, like all of us had to, that I wasn't now about to be snapped up by a professional club before my latent talents were put to good use by my country. I was, as we all were, merely journeymen footballers who enjoyed the game.

In Paisley, we had a good team, captained by Neil Graham, a brilliant guy and a sweeper of some note; another pal with whom I've remained friendly over the decades. Neil played on until he was into his fifties such was the state of his fitness and love of the game. We were a decent side and got to the final of the NALGO Cup played in Renfrew. It was a very tight game and I was indulging, as I always did, with what I called 'light-hearted banter' with the referee, but he usually called 'dissent'. I was mouthing away throughout the match despite being warned by the Ref that he was losing patience with me. "One more word out of you, number nine, and you're off!

I decided that I'd better calm down.

Five minutes to go in the cup final and it was still one-nil to the opposition. The play moved towards our goal and Neil slid in to make a saving tackle on the goal line and the ball went over. To be honest, it might have been either a corner or a bye-kick. It was fifty-fifty. The Ref gave his decision as a goal kick to us. I applauded his decision.

"Good shout, Ref!"

To my open-jawed consternation, he shook his head and marched towards me, a red card held aloft. "Right, you've been warned, number nine. You've been a pain in the arse the whole game. Yer aff!" ... and I slunk from the field back to the dressing room where I was soon to be joined by another two of my team-mates four minutes and three minutes before the end of what was now a pretty tousy affair. Skin and hair flew in all directions and eventually we lost two-nil.

I also really enjoyed playing in Ayrshire. John McManus was in midfield; and *there* was someone who didn't play at the level his talents deserved. A brilliant midfielder with a great engine… and if the goalkeeper was injured, why John would just slip on the jersey and play a stormer between the posts. I played largely on the wing then and at centre forward stood the tall, gangly presence of six foot two inch Ian McAlpine. Ian was a great guy and a smashing pal over the years. He had a mouth as big as mine on the pitch and was forever calling for the ball.

With his height, Ian was very effective in the air and on not a few occasions during the seasons we played together, I flew down the wing, crossed the ball to devastating effect and Iain nodded the ball home… at least that's how I remember it. I suspect that my pace and disinclination to take a tackle where this was avoidable had me take on the appearance of a startled deer when I got the ball, rather than a gifted and confident winger. But on one occasion I have a clear recollection of what passed in the pub later as clear evidence of my undiscovered genius. I was playing on the left wing one Sunday at Dean Park in Kilmarnock, where the pitch was a mudbath. Only the wings were really playable. I took the ball past their right-back and, looking up saw big Ian calling for it as he charged goalwards through the mire. I steadied myself and crossed with my weaker, left foot only to see it soar above Ian's head and connect with a scorching, diving header from Louis Skehal who was playing for some reason on the right wing that day as his right foot was a good as my left… which wasn't great!

Anyway it was a brilliant goal, brilliantly worked but as Ian and I both belonged to the centre-forward's union, I could understand Ian's reaction to the goal being that the cross was lousy and the goal was jammy… he was in a far better position to score!

As I moved into my forties I moved back to mid-field and was capable only of collecting the ball and playing others into the game. I enjoyed this position and raised a few eyebrows as all of my team-mates were more than aware that when playing at centre-forward, no one could expect a pass from me until I'd scored. Once I'd put the ball in the net, I was more amenable to pass and go, but until then? No chance. However, needs must and collecting and passing was all that my state of fitness would then allow.

After a game one Saturday morning against a group of community workers and politicians from Edinburgh, who were all through to watch a Rangers-Hibs match at Ibrox - to support Hibernian - we all went for a pie and a beer in the clubhouse. One of our supporters, John Kennedy, who was the MD of a local security firm, had filmed the match to play it back for our entertainment as we downed the pies. I felt that I'd played rather well, all nimble touches, cunning deceptions and artistic midfield wizardry such as would be on view later that afternoon across the road in Ibrox Stadium.

But when I saw the video of the match over lunch, I couldn't believe the hulking midfield bumbler I'd become. I was carrying too much weight, the ball was bouncing off my knee. I miss-hit and mis-read passes, I wasn't getting near tackles I'd have arrived at much earlier in previous years. I decided, upon seeing the evidence with my own eyes, that perhaps I'd better begin to reserve my footballing skills for the practice pitch and to bring on the abilities of my children. I'd certainly lost it as a player.

I was having a great time in the Chief Executive's Department. I enjoyed working with politicians, writing speeches and seeing how money invested in innovative interventions could change lives and communities, at least for a short time. Granted, I harboured nagging concerns that all I was doing was contributing to temporary palliatives and that the real prize of materially changing the circumstances in which people lived was more to do with how the really big budgets in Education, Transport, Social Work and Economic Development were permitted to bleed into one another for a greater, more sustainable good.

I was also doing quite a lot of work with Sue Angus at this time. Sue was the Area Officer for the Community Education Service in the Govanhill area of Glasgow and she and I hit it off from the start. At the time of writing, Sue, now Sue Bruce, is Chief Executive of Edinburgh City Council. She was married back then when we worked together or perhaps I'd have been tempted to ask her to step out with me. I was still a bit shy on the women front but she was lovely. We were dealing with a complex proposition involving Crossroads Youth and Community Association. They had been based for some years in railway arches on Cumberland Street in the Gorbals and had developed a strong reputation as an effective and well managed youth organisation. British Rail decided that they would develop a new 'Arches Strategy' whereby they'd upgrade old and decrepit archways underneath railway lines and modernise them in order to accrue higher levels of income.

Negotiations commenced between myself and Sue on the one hand and British Rail on the other over the compensation to be made over to Crossroads. Eventually we negotiated a deal whereby BR would isolate a couple of archways and build a new youth centre round about them in exchange for which Crossroads would give up their legal rights to inhabit the other archways which BR would then develop. The delight I was experiencing working with Sue blinded me to the obvious and embarrassing mistake I was making in not including Crossroads sufficiently in the negotiations and I was easily outmanoeuvred when they brought in the local elected member, Councillor Bill Miller, to permit them to negotiate a better deal.

I visited Sue in her converted school offices one day and was introduced to her administrative assistant, Jean Pollock with whom she was very friendly. There must have been something in the water in Govanhill because Jean struck me immediately as being absolutely beautiful. Slim and extremely pretty, she had a lovely, smiley personality. Sue warned me that Jean might be in a bit of a mood that day, as she had just fallen out with her boyfriend at the time and was simultaneously and unsuccessfully trying to ward off the advances of a prospective suitor - bizarrely, a guy who performed as Big Andrew, a giant Scottish Highland character who was often to be found on stilts at events and in street performances. He'd been leaving a single red rose underneath Jean's windscreen wipers every day and she wasn't too pleased at these unwanted advances. Still, it was nice to make her acquaintance and Sue and I continued our friendship and our work together.

One of the most enjoyable tasks I got involved in whilst serving at the pleasure of Sir Robert Calderwood was occasioned by a visit to Ibrox Stadium on the invitation of Councillor and ex-MP Helen McElhone. Helen was always on the lookout for small amounts of money for projects within her Ward and took me across the street from the stadium where a school had been burned down and a large red blaes pitch stood, potholed and unloved.

"Surely it would only take a small amount of money to fill in these holes and build a small dressing room for players," she asked. I looked round at the three acre site immediately across the road from Ibrox Stadium and asked if she appreciated what an opportunity she was sitting on. It was ripe for development and it was obvious to me that we should go big on this prospect. Of course,

Helen was delighted and over the years, it developed into a project that I committed a lot of time to. Although I started the project as an employee of the Council, it continued apace as I moved subsequently to Govan.

The Insurance claim occasioned by the fire was met and Rangers gave £70,000 after I spent only twenty minutes with David Holmes, the then Rangers Chairman, pitching the idea. My expertise with Urban Programme monies came to the fore as we built steadily towards the cost of establishing the Ibrox Community Complex, at that time the most sophisticated sports facility around. With a modern, artificial playing surface, it was the subject of great media and political attention. It did my reputation no harm either as we brought the project in within budget and on time. We formed a Trust, the Ibrox Community Trust with ex-FIFA referee Tom 'Tiny' Wharton as Chairman and ex-Convenor of the Regional Council, Councillor Bill Perry as Secretary. Helen McElhone was also a member.

Celtic expressed an interest in me developing a similar facility at Parkhead and Tom Wharton arranged lunch with members of the Celtic Board. Tom, Helen and I met at the North Rotunda restaurant on the Clyde as it had a private dining facility which was used to keep all conversation completely secret. I was asked by Tom to 'sell' them the project over lunch and to explain how the money might be amassed to finance it. I did a sterling job but I was astonished when after my informal peroration, one of the Board Members, said," All very interesting, Ron. But let me make one thing perfectly clear. If Celtic do decide to go forward with this, it'll be my idea, my vision for the club. I'll be the leader of the band. I get all the credit!"

Given that no one, to my knowledge, had ever given any thought to anything other than that being the case, I was quite disconcerted over his first reaction being all about himself, with little or no questioning about the merits of the case, available land or the Celtic contribution. After lunch, following the most polite and syrupy summary by Tom, he and I left with Helen and he excoriated the board member in his absence saying that it was little wonder that the Celtic were in the troubled condition they endured at that time, if egos such as that prevailed.

After no reaction for some years, the Celtic Board then decided instead to move their stadium out of Glasgow to a swamp near Rutherglen. That also fell through and along came Fergus McCann and Willie Haughey to rebuild the stadium to the fine footballing arena it is today.

Perhaps the most enduring legacy of that project was the friendly relationships I established with people who served on the Ibrox Trust. Alan McCreath, then the MD of ERDC Construction and, later, his lovely wife Sandy became firm friends. Bill Perry became a pal and Tom Wharton became a friend and role model in respect of the way he dealt with people.

Before the construction phase commenced, ERCD took us all to Amsterdam for a couple of days to see the kind of pitches that were being developed on the mainland. To ensure that Rangers were happy that the pitch was of a standard acceptable to their playing staff, John Greig, previously Captain and Manager of Rangers but then their Head of Public Relations accompanied us. I hadn't been to Holland before and looked forward immensely to the trip.

After a couple of days driving round a freezing Holland and into Belgium in a minibus looking at artificial pitches and trying unsuccessfully to dribble the ball around John Greig, we ended up with a free afternoon and evening in Amsterdam. I decided that I couldn't go home without seeing the famous 'Red Light'

District and as everyone paired off to go shopping that afternoon, I set out on my own.

I had never witnessed anything as brash as the Amsterdam dockland area with ladies of the night sitting in glass-fronted windows and shops openly selling marijuana but I contented myself with a visit, via a turnstile, to the extremely tame city council-run sex museum. I felt very decadent.

That night, feeling a wee bit embarrassed and contrite about visiting the area, I resolved to keep my adventure to myself and to present as if I had gone shopping as had everyone else. However, the opening remark from Helen McElhone when I went down for dinner that night was, "Don't think we didn't see you in the Red Light District". I was so taken aback that I blustered on about how I *had* been there ... admittedly ... but that I hadn't gone into any of the various emporia in the area and had only visited the sex museum ... and that was run by the city council ... and it was very tame and it had a turnstile for Pete's sake ... and ...

I could feel everyone's eyes on me when Helen admitted that she had been pulling my leg and that she had just assumed that I'd been shopping as had everyone else. I wished the ground could have opened up and swallowed me.

I had another insight into professional football during that visit. John Greig and I were occupied on an artificial surface, passing a ball to each other - with our boots on ... imagine my pride in being asked to attend with John Greig and that each of us had to bring our boots... John invariably landed the ball right on my foot from wherever he kicked it on the park; it was when we stopped that I began to realise that professional footballers really did have a level of skill denied us amateurs. John bet me a fiver that he could hit the bar of the goal frame from just outside the penalty box. Foolishly, I accepted, and then watched him hit about nine out of ten attempts. He refused the bet later saying he was only kidding. His expertise must have inspired me as I started to try the same manoeuvre and managed about forty percent of my attempts. From that distance, it wasn't too difficult. Perhaps with just a wee bit more practice, I too, could have been a footballing legend and have a statue of myself erected outside Ibrox just as had John when he was voted 'The Greatest Ever Ranger.'

Tom Wharton was the Chairman of the Ibrox Trust and took his responsibilities very seriously indeed. Perhaps the most famous ever of Scotland's referees, he was a giant of a man... six feet five inches tall and as broad as he was long hence his ironic *sobriquet* 'Tiny'. At his peak in the fifties and sixties, Tom was a legend within Scotland and across the world. His authority commanded the attention of players on either side. Many years later when he was still active in UEFA and FIFA, players would still hold him in the greatest esteem when they met off the field. He was always most gentlemanly on the pitch referring to players invariably as 'Mr Johnstone' or 'Mr Baxter' rather than by their first name. He had an almost Edwardian way about him but he could be witty as well. During one Hearts game, the story was told of how after a rather exuberant challenge, he sent off a truculent Johnnie Hamilton, who had the misfortune of having no remaining teeth of his own. Tiny beckoned to the miscreant and shaking his head wearily, informed him in his most stentorian tone, "Mr Hamilton, I regret that your illegal challenge requires that I must send you from the field of play. You may now rejoin your teeth in the dressing room."

Tom also had the reputation of not being the fittest referee ever to officiate a match in Scotland. With his huge bulk, getting up and down the pitch could be a trial, especially later on in the game. John Greig told me the story of how, again in a Rangers-Celtic match, Tom had awarded a corner to Celtic despite the fact that the ball had clearly been knocked over the line by an attacker. John protested vehemently.

"Mr. Greig," announced Tom breathlessly in that wonderfully languid, slightly posh, Newton Mearns dialect of his, "If you think for a moment that I've followed play and run all the way to the bye-line only in order to run all the way back to the centre circle again at my age... you're not on! It's a corner... *whoever* knocked the ball over the line!"

Tom was rightly regarded as a quick-witted individual. Bob Crampsey, in an obituary he later wrote about Tom, made the point that Tom always thought that common sense could save any situation. He referred to the 1962 League Cup final, in which Hearts took on Kilmarnock at Hampden. Kilmarnock, down one-nothing, appeared to have equalised in the last minute, but it appeared to Tom, wrongly, that the linesman had flagged for the use of arms. He was surrounded by protesting Kilmarnock players insisting that the linesman be consulted. Tom realised quickly that he needed a question which would be met with the answer "No!" Pushing the Killie players back, he went over to his linesman, a noted abstainer, and asked him quietly: "Ah Willie, I suppose you'll be having a wee dram this evening." His linesman, somewhat surprised, nevertheless shook his head vigorously. "Not at all, Tom," permitting Tom to turn towards the goalmouth and place the ball for a free kick, the dispute appearing to the watching crowd to have been resolved.

Tom was a complete gentleman but an arch-Conservative and every so often I had to bite my tongue as he'd lash out in his own toffee-nosed way about the Trades

Unions destroying the country or the feckless hordes that inhabited the poorer neighbourhoods of Glasgow. That said, I could forgive him a lot. He was a nice man in life and a legend in football. He was awarded the OBE by Margaret Thatcher and was appointed Deputy Chairman of the Football Trust, which helped significantly in the establishment of the Ibrox Community Complex. He died in May 2005 at the age of 77. I was upset that I couldn't attend the funeral as I was in London. The subsequent press clippings demonstrated the affection in which he was held, as great numbers turned out to pay their respects. A good man…a good man.

Sir Robert Calderwood entered my life again at this point. He had a chat with me about a new post that was about to be announced in Govan, an economic development post with which I was familiar, as a paper setting out its funding had passed before my own committee. I hadn't paid it much attention, precisely because it had to do with the economic rather than the social development of Greater Govan, and that wasn't my area of expertise. Sir Robert wondered whether this might not prove an interesting challenge and upon further reflection, I agreed and applied for the seconded post of Assistant Chief Executive of the newly formed Govan Initiative Ltd, an arms-length body tasked with improving the economy of the Greater Govan area in the south west of Glasgow. Things moved quickly and I was successful in my application. My boss, Keith Yates, had been away on a sabbatical during this process and returned to find me gone. He took it rather badly. I had the sense that Keith felt betrayed, almost as if I'd committed an act of treason by moving away from the area of activity which he attacked with such a ferocious passion. Our relationship, always good, cooled slightly after that. In hindsight, I made a mistake and should certainly have made attempts to make contact with him and advise him of my moves even although he wasn't in the country. However, I didn't and left to spend the next year and a half engaged with the task of regenerating the faltering economy of Greater Govan. Little then did I realise that my eighteen months secondment would last thirteen years.

9. Taking The Initiative.

Those things that come to those who wait might just be the things left by those who got there first!
Steven Tyler, Aerosmith.

In 1987 Margaret Thatcher was in her pomp and her Scottish Conservative Ministers, variously George Younger, Lord James Douglas Hamilton (the only human being among them) Michael Forsyth, Malcolm Rifkind, Ian Lang and the guitar-playing Michael Ancram, represented the occupying powers in the Scottish Office in Edinburgh. As usual, the Scottish electorate had returned a thumping Labour majority but the UK political set-up at the time meant that we were to be ruled by a Conservative Government. Strathclyde Regional Council was viewed by them as the enemy and it was no secret that the Tories viewed the governance of the West of Scotland much as Thatcher did the Greater London Council, which she eventually abolished. The civil service, as ever doing their job irrespective of the political colours of their masters, nevertheless seemed to take to the task of emasculating and abolishing Strathclyde as a political entity with relish.

Scotland, particularly the west, had experienced severe economic circumstances since around the end of the Second World War but they had become more pronounced as observers watched the last Hillman Imp roll off the production line of the Rootes/Chrysler car plant at Linwood in March 1976. The heavy engineering, steel and shipbuilding industries continued their decline and Scotland witnessed the slow and painful transition, from a manufacturing-based economy to one which was based upon services. One of the areas that was most badly affected was Govan.

As a child, I remembered Govan as a boisterous, smelly, noisy, wonderful place. Buses converged on the Govan

Cross from all over the city. Cinema queues bustled on the pavement, the streets were full of shipyard workers coming home from their shift or staggering home from the pub. Ibrox Stadium was where you went to watch football. The Fifty Pitches was where you went to play football. It was a lively and magical place.

The housing was almost ubiquitously red sandstone tenements, of a type which is now in such demand but then was viewed as too cramped and crumbling to meet the needs of Glasgow's population. The city fathers had begun some years earlier to demolish these beautiful buildings, and to move the population out to the more capacious and greener accommodation they'd built in the four gigantic housing estates that stood like sentries on each corner of the city: Pollok in the south-west, Castlemilk in the south-east, Drumchapel in the north-west and Easterhouse in the north-east. Initially the prospect of a family moving to one of these properties had been greeted with unalloyed joy, as Glaswegians discovered the benefits of space, of inside toilets and bathrooms and of gardens. But there were no or few community amenities. Schools hadn't been built in tandem with the houses and temporary learning accommodation abounded. The van culture reigned as shops hadn't been built in sufficient number either. Over the years, the design of the houses, based upon properties that had been built successfully on the coast of the Mediterranean Sea, proved no match for the Scottish weather. Flat roofs and poor quality materials used in order to lower both the specifications and costs provided the council with the capacity to build more but cheaper houses in order to meet demand, but also resulted in dampness and early decay.

In those communities like Govan from which the diaspora had occurred, no investment had taken place. Dogs nosed around upturned metal bins in the courtyards, great puddles appeared where demolition had taken place. Broken shop windows were boarded over, pubs were closed and an air of hopelessness pervaded the streets. The communities of Govan, Ibrox, Kinning Park, Tradeston, Kingston, Cessnock and Drumoyne - neatly hemmed in by the Clyde on the north and the M8 motorway on the south - that made up the Greater Govan area were demonstrating all of the worst characteristics of communities in terminal decline. In 1987, unemployment averaged 34.6% with many pockets experiencing 100%. Educational attainment was low as was confidence and morale. Huge tracts of land lay derelict and toxic and health indicators were very poor. The shipyards - Brown's, Connell's, Stephen's, Fairfield's and Yarrow's - were closed some years earlier in 1971 by the Heath Government but a Jimmy Reid and Jimmy Airlie led work-in had stayed their hand. They limped on until 1972 when they were nationalised and were subsequently bought by Norwegian ship owners Kvaerner, but seemed always to be one order away from closure.

A year earlier, Sir Robert Calderwood had sent down his Deputy Head of DARS, the Department of Architecture and Related Services, to scope out what might be possible in Govan and to establish the basis of what would become Govan Initiative Ltd. Sandy Forbes was a controversial, larger than life character who frequently got on the wrong side of people. He set up camp in a converted school at Govan Cross and eventually negotiated the lease of a suite of offices, about 1,000 sq ft, in Ibrox Stadium, home of Glasgow Rangers FC. In the interests of ecumenism, as I'd say later, they were located at the Celtic end.

Sandy got the legal stuff in place before retiring from public life and John Scally, previously the Deputy Director of Estates within the Regional Council, was appointed as Chief Executive. I was brought in as his assistant and together we set about building an organisation which would transform the fortunes of Govan.

Because the organisation was based upon a partnership approach, we had early secondments from the District Council, Cardonald Further Education College, and a couple of contractors who were involved in running programmes such as the Training and Employment Grants Scheme. Just four or five people, but this was the first such economic regeneration venture in Glasgow if not Scotland, so the Board which was established to oversee the initiative was more populous, owing to the widespread interest in what was taking shape. About a dozen people met monthly to drive the activities of four people. Led by the Regional Council, from which both John and I had been seconded, it was chaired by Councillor Ian Davidson, then Chair of the Education Committee, who was supported by his close friend Councillor Archie Simpson - one of the local councillors from the District Council - whose Ward was one of those embraced within Ian's Regional seat.

My first task was to sit down and utilise my pretty extensive knowledge of the Urban Programme and bring new and much needed resources to the area. In the first round, I submitted thirteen applications for funding including, *inter alia,* proposals for the establishment of pre-five Nursery provision, a Training Shop in central Govan, an Arts programme, a Secure Communities programme and a Health initiative called Braveheart. Twelve of the thirteen applications were approved and, although this took a few months, we began quickly to employ significantly increased numbers of staff.

About six months into the tenure of the company it was decided by the politicians to make a bit of a splash and to hold a formal opening in the local Bellahouston Hotel to which the press were to be invited. We were put in charge of organising it and went about our task with gusto. We arranged for the principal speaker to be Manchester United manager, Alex Ferguson, who had headed south only a few months beforehand from Aberdeen to begin what became the most illustrious football management career ever in the UK, if not the world. Dougie Donnelly, the sports broadcaster, MC'd the event and we had a number of local companies present their wares as well to provide a bit of interest around the inevitable political speeches. It was a great success as Alex spoke passionately about Govan as the greatest place in the world; and he meant it. He spoke about the closeness of the community, the school of hard knocks which had kept him grounded over the years and the incessant games of football which he'd taken part in when he was growing up.

One of the exhibitors was wee Benny Donnelly, who had manufactured a substance which was truly phenomenal. He'd invented a chemical which, when applied to material, glowed bright yellow in circumstances of complete darkness. Most pigment *reflects* light, as with the road signs we see at the side of the road, which merely have beads of glass in the mix of the paint, but Benny's stuff was interesting and much more sophisticated chemically. The French nuclear industry bought some off him as even in the daylight, the chevrons on the garments of plant operatives, when imbued with Benny's stuff, glowed brightly if they detected a nuclear leak. The Israelis painted the insides of their tanks with it so that in the case of a power failure, the interior would light up like a beacon. But Benny couldn't sell it in the UK. He had illuminated demonstrator phones which lit up during power failures, arrows which showed the way out of planes or buildings in complete darkness but he couldn't find a purchaser in Britain.

One of the other companies exhibiting their wares was a local business which made silk lingerie. We had arranged for models to parade around a catwalk set up for the purpose in order to feature the products of this company, which had emerged within an area normally associated with shipbuilding and heavy industry. Seeing an opportunity, Benny came to me before the launch and asked if he could use the models to wear some of his safety equipment – safety helmets, reflective bibs and so on. Everyone agreed.

Benny also came up with a novel idea of opening the affair, not by the usual method of unveiling a plaque but by Alex pulling back a cloth from a large yellow board on which the words 'Grow with Govan' - the initial strapline adopted by the Initiative - had been painted by Benny; also in yellow. Using his special pigment, nothing was discernable in normal light, but when the lights were cut, it would reveal the message in a bright yellow light. All was well until Alex, doing the voice over, pronounced the message using his characteristic speech articulation announced it as 'Gwo with Govan'. This confused the press as John Scally who was then still Chief Executive, hadn't nominated anyone to turn the lights off and the media were left looking at an entirely yellow board with nothing revealed and couldn't establish whether Alex had just announced the new slogan as Grow with Govan or Glow with Govan. I was dispatched to turn off the lights and to bring them back on afterwards for the lingerie show. When the pigment did its stuff, the press all went for the pun which meant it was Glow with Govan that made it into the papers the next day, much to the consternation of our PR consultants.

As for me, I had to sit by the control light at the side of the changing area and watch a parade of beautiful young women, dressed and undressed, dressing and undressing, all I must confess, completely indifferent to me and others involved with the presentation. I had to switch the lights off again when they started to wear Benny's safety gear so obviously I couldn't leave my post - not for a second!

Early on, Sandy Forbes had appointed a woman called Diane Black to deal with the admin side and, as she was one of the original members of staff, she took the view that she was as senior as John and I. I really had no problems here and was polite but clear about the lines of authority. John, however, seemed to find it difficult to give people bad news and, in his attempts to keep everybody happy, would find words which merely re-cluttered the clean lines of responsibility which maintained Diane's belief that she effectively answered to no one. Upon taking over the HR side as part of my duties, I straightened things out, moved Diane to another position and advertised her post of Administrative Officer.

A couple of days later I took a call from my pal Sue Angus who said she'd read the advert and wondered if I might consider her assistant Jean Pollock as she had all of the requirements for the post and in her view needed a move to help her develop and keep her fresh. I was keen but asked John if he'd interview her along with me to get his take on matters. John was hugely impressed by Jean's technical abilities and was much taken by her personality. He was most anxious that she be appointed and, after interviewing some more candidates to make sure that she was the best of the bunch, we agreed and Jean took up post in 1987 starting a relationship she'd have with the Initiative for more than fourteen years and, unknown to both of us at the time, a relationship she'd have with me that still lasts to this day.

Only nine months into his incumbency, John applied for and was appointed to the post of Director of Development for the Tyne and Wear Development Corporation. His interest was always upon the physical side of development, whereas I was more of a genericist if drawn more towards the social side of regeneration.

My Chairman, Ian, and I tended to circle one another. Never close, but there seemed to be a grudging respect although in truth, I had the impression that Ian never really respected many people. Archie, the Vice Chair, was adamant that Buggins' turn must apply and that the next Chief Executive would come from the ranks of the District Council so I applied for the job of Chief Executive knowing that neither of the two senior Board Members wanted me to succeed. They would be joined on the interview panel by John McDonnagh (the Managing Director of Gray Dunn, a local biscuit manufacturer), Ray Bailey (the Principal of Cardonald College) and Dr Mike Greig (Assistant Chief Executive of Strathclyde Regional Council) with whom I didn't have a great relationship either. John Scally would sit in as adviser.

There was a strong field against me as the Initiative had made a few good early headlines and was now shaping up to be quite a sizeable organisation. The salary of £35 - £40,000 was also very attractive at the time.

I figured I'd give a good account of myself because I knew the background of the work so intimately. My preparation gave me a lot of confidence and I had a superb interview. I walked out convinced that I'd given them a problem. There was no way anyone could better that performance, I figured, and I was right.

Later that morning Ian Davidson came into my office to tell me I'd been successful, but, true to his political instincts, he presented the decision as having been in the balance, but that he'd gone out on a limb for me and that he expected unswerving loyalty from me in exchange for this gesture which won me the appointment. I didn't believe him for a moment and it was later confirmed to me by both Johns that I was by far the best candidate in interview and had been appointed easily and unanimously. Later, also, Pauline told me that she'd heard Archie and Ian earlier talking about the process where Archie was arguing for a District Council appointment and she figured that the odds were being stacked against me. She also told me that the staff wanted me to get the job which was a big fillip.

At the point of my promotion, all of the projects I'd dreamt up had just been approved by the Scottish Office and the company began to move up a gear as we began to make considerable numbers of appointments. Archie, still bruised by my appointment - as he had viewed it as a done deal that the next appointee would come from the ranks of his own council - had insisted that we appoint a Deputy Chief Executive selected from the ranks of the City Council as a balance to me, and in consequence Raymond Hendry was selected. I couldn't have wished for a more loyal and caring second-in-command. He was steeped in local knowledge and, as a planner, filled the property gap left by John when he ventured south to Newcastle. I spent a lot of energy on the recruitment of staff on the basis that this task would be the single biggest determinant of the success of the organisation. Although I made some mistakes over the years in this regard, there can be no doubt that I managed to pitch the company as an exciting place to work and reaped the benefits of a keen attention to recruitment as we began to appoint really excellent people over the years.

One guy who was there as a secondee when I arrived was Jim Carruth. Over the years we'd argue playfully as to who had been with the company the longest. I argued that it was me, because I had been appointed before him but Jim argued that he was actually in the building first, if as a secondee. Jim was an intellectual gift to the company, a great strategist and a very caring person. He also worked prodigious hours and took the time to get in and around all aspects of the organisation. By the time I'd moved on, he'd occupied just about every position in the team. A great utility player as well as a great guy.

Richie Cameron also came on board as head of our Education and Skills team, and grew into one of our most effective appointments. He mastered the art of extracting money from the European Social Fund, the company prospered as a consequence and the residents of the Greater Govan area benefited disproportionately, as it became clear that Govan Initiative regularly scooped up more European money than most Councils!

Early on I appointed a cherubic young accountant as Director of Finance; Stuart Patrick. Stuart had a big brain but he was also very broad in his ambitions. Then employed by Ernst and Young, one of the big six accountancy firms, Stuart wanted to make a different kind of contribution and served with great distinction in Govan Initiative, before being headhunted by the then Glasgow Development Agency, wherein he moved on to became Senior Director of Organisational Development. He also began to invest personally in bars and restaurants after a successful quasi-commercial venture via a charity called the Four Acres Trust whose mission was to save his local Dowanhill Church, designed by Daniel Cottier. He went on to partner in the ownership of bars and restaurants all over Glasgow and managed to tie this in with his commitment to Glasgow's regeneration. Stuart was, and remains, different class, completing his rise and rise within Scottish Enterprise as Senior Commercial Director at headquarters before moving on to become the Chief Executive of Glasgow Chamber of Commerce.

One of my more risky but ultimately rewarding appointments was that of Big Jim Mullen. Jim I knew as a charismatic youth worker in Pollok. He just dominated the place with his brand of Glasgow *bonhomie* and his massive athletic frame. I spoke with him one night in his youth club and discerned a measure of 'Pollok fatigue'. Jim had been brought up there and had gone straight into youth work in his local community centre much as I had. Still in his late twenties, he hadn't moved on. I appointed him to work under our seconded Police Inspector David Christie as our Senior Community Liaison worker and he took to the task like a duck to water.

Now and again I'd want to put a pillow over my head, owing to his sense of humour. We'd decided that something had to be done to combat the increasing amount of drugs that were being sold on the streets. Our idea was to loan a telephone set to the police - it was not possible to *give* them the device lest it may have been presumed that they were surrendering a measure of independence .... absurd, but there you have it - to pay all related bills and to invite people to use its number to report dealers in Govan. Hardly rocket science. Having negotiated the deal with the local cops, I asked Jim to fashion a beer mat or something that could be distributed round pubs advertising the service. Jim took to the task with enthusiasm and returned to me a few days later with the news that he'd designed the beer mat but that on the reverse side, in order to make it more interesting, he'd posed a few football trivia questions. I took this at face value and asked him to bring the finished article through when he got it back from the printers. A week later Jim came in with David Christie, his exceptionally talented police inspector (who went on to become Divisional Commander in A Division; Glasgow City and upon retirement, the Operations Manager of SPT's Subway) and showed me the fruits of his labour. I was very pleased with the main objective having been achieved and turned the beer mat over to have a look at the football trivia. It started well. There were only five questions. Jim took the beer mat back as the answers were inscribed on its circumference and imposed himself as the quizmaster.

"Who has scored most goals against Chris Woods" [then the Rangers and English International goalkeeper] "at Ibrox?" A great question, as the answer was Terry Butcher, the Rangers centre half who'd scored more than his fair share of own goals that season. The next questions were of a similarly testing nature. Then came the last question…."Who came on at half time to score a hat trick for an English club, the last goal being scored in the last minute, overturning a two–nil deficit and winning the European Cup at Wembley?

I thought long and hard but couldn't come close to an answer. Jim sat opposite me, his face beaming. I admitted defeat. "Ok, Boss, you ready for this?" Jim - an enthusiastic footballer - always referred to me as 'Boss' despite me asking him to desist. He summoned up his most theatrical persona …. "Roy of the Rovers!"

I couldn't believe my ears. Jim was convulsed and David - ever the wise polis - stood awaiting my reaction although he obviously thought it was a great question.

I said "Jim, will people have been drinking when they ask each other these questions?"

"Sure, boss."

"Might this not lead to a wee argument down in The Black Man?"

"Och, boss, there's no harm…"

Eventually they persuaded me that the question would be taken humorously and we sent the beer mats out. They were a great success. It was a three month initiative, over £100,000 in illicit drugs were discovered as a result of information obtained via the hotline and more than 100 people pushing drugs were brought to court in consequence.

Jim and David also came into their own when, some months later, I sacked a manager summarily for gross misconduct. He'd taken off to the District Bar to drown his sorrows and had decided to phone me up to tell me what he thought of me. I was in my office dictating some mail when the call came through. Initially I merely offered understanding grunts in response to his comments but he started to tell me that he was going to get a shotgun and blow my head off. I realised I had a tape recorder in my hands and, turning it on, asked him to repeat his threats which he did. He went on at some length and when he ran out of expletives, I thanked him for phoning and called in Jim and David.

"Let him sleep it off, guys, but could you pay him a visit and play this back to him? Tell him if he behaves himself and gets another job, we'll forget it exists."

Jim and David went round to see him; they were able to report that he was suitably chastised and inspired to find new work! I suspect that David's assessment that this tape might constitute a jail sentence of some years assisted in his rehabilitation.

Jim's real ability was to be able to straddle both the legitimate and illegitimate cultures that governed Govan. One day our Head of Security, John Kennedy came in to see me.

"Ron, some wee ned's knocked a nail gun from a building site down in Broomloan Road and they're firing it at our security guards when they patrol the site. These guns arn'y hellish accurate but if a nail hits one of them it could maim or kill him. These things punch a nail into six inches of concrete... they're really dangerous."

I asked Jim Mullen and David to come in and explained the situation. David, ever the good cop, said, "I'll away down to Divisional HQ, report the crime and we'll get a notification out". They left the room and Jim returned after a couple of minutes. "Boss, I could probably fix this by close of play tonight if you want to spend £20 on it."

He asked me not to ask questions to which I didn't want to know the answers and left with £20 in his hand. About 4.30 that afternoon, Jim returned to my office and placed a nail gun on my desk. "Mission accomplished, Boss."

Jim had merely gone to the Black Man pub, the local name for Brechin's Bar, and asked at the bar if anyone knew where he could buy a nail gun. Before he'd finished his first pint he'd been approached and had done the deal for £20 although I just knew in my bones he'd done a deal for £15 and would have taken the balance as the cost of the pint and 'expenses'. For all that, no one was injured, the construction company would get their gun back and the entrepreneurial thief was happy with his lot. "Everybody wins, boss!"

My mild remonstration that this probably constituted me committing the crime of 'reset'; selling on stolen goods, was met with derision. "Naw, Boss. I thought of that. You're not selling it back to the company; you're gifting it to them. There's no way you get the jail for this." Later when I told the police of the value of more creative approaches to averting violence acts, they wholeheartedly concurred with Big Jim's view of the world.

After three very successful years at the head of Govan Initiative, I turned forty. I was both genuinely surprised and delighted when I was taken into our Board Room wherein were gathered all of my friends and colleagues from within and outwith Govan Initiative. They'd made a very professional video along the lines of *'This is your Life'* starring all of my friends and colleagues. It was hilarious, and concluded with the usual special guest flown in from the opposite side of the world at great expense; in my case, John Greig, variously Captain and Manager of Rangers who took the piss out of me big time.

Over this period I had been stepping out with a few girls but there was no serious relationship on the horizon. Typically my weekends commenced on a Friday evening with a few beers with my pals in the Ritz Bar, a relaxing Saturday watching Ron, and occasionally Campbell, playing football in the morning and then an evening with friends spent in either the Chancellor or the Exchequer bar, each of which was situated at the bottom end of Byres Road in the city's West End. Sundays were always given over to the boys who sometimes stayed over on the Saturday night although it was a tight squeeze. Often, John McManus would travel up to Glasgow to have a few beers with me. Although people moved in and out of my friendship group there was always a core group of ex-Kilmarnock people including me and John, Mary Hoy, who had moved up to a flat in Anniesland to pursue her accountancy studies, and Rose Anson, who was then employed as a Nursery Teacher in Drumchapel. Sometimes Laurie and his lovely wife Pam would join us as well.

I was always able to handle my drink and my favourite tipple at that time was whisky and a half pint of lager - a hauf an' a hauf pint. John and I would always try to get to the Chancellor first and we'd then thumb coins into the juke box in order to select most of the music for the evening. Eric Clapton, the Beatles, Mark Knopfler, Elvis and Simon and Garfunkel entertained us and we always had a great laugh but one night John complained that when I got drunk I became argumentative.

"No. I don't," I retorted … kind of proving his point. I was always a happy drunk, the life and soul of the party, and was concerned if alcohol was having this effect. I began to experiment with Bacardi and then brandy in order to replace the whisky, and my previous *bonhomie* returned. We could drink together in complete happiness again. I lived alone just along the road, in my tiny apartment on the top floor at 698 Dumbarton Road where I slept in my small bed recess off the living room, to which I returned woozy with drink after our regular Saturday carousing.

One night the doorbell rang. I seldom had visitors and expected that it was some kids fooling around as they left the newsagent's at the bottom of the stairs. When I answered the call phone, it was John. I was delighted to see him but something in his tone seemed to hint at problems.

True enough, John stepped into my hallway holding a large bag in which he told me was some clothing. He and his wife Christine had decided to go their separate ways. There were no other people involved in the decision but he now had nowhere to stay. I bid him welcome and we opened a bottle of wine.

John was distraught. I offered accommodation immediately although it was obvious that you couldn't swing a cat in the place. I had a mattress that the boys used when they stayed over and he could use that. Like me, he had ensured that his wife in Kilmarnock would have the capacity to live on in the marital home and care for their two boys whose lives and friendships would continue as earlier. In consequence, like me, he was penniless so the deal was rent free.

We actually lived easily together. Both of us were relaxed in each other's company, shared the same professional interests, had an overlapping circle of friends and about the house we were both tidy and organised. This arrangement worked pretty well for perhaps eight months and I was quite content that it continued as long as John needed it to.

Some months later when we were all having a beer in the Chancellor, John rather timidly ventured the fact that he'd started to see Rose outside of our friendship group and that they'd become sufficient of an item that Rose had decided to look for a new flat in Glasgow. I was delighted. John continued in his diffident manner.

"Actually, Rose would like to move up to Glasgow before she actually gets a flat."

Again, I was in accord with this eminently sensible suggestion.

"We were kind of wondering if she might join you and me in Dumbarton Road while she gets settled. We'd like to move in with one another as soon as possible"

I almost choked on my beer. *In the flat?* It was tiny. However, as ever, we fixed things and Rose and John moved in together in the dining kitchen. It was awful tight and Rose still reminds me of my compulsive, *'Odd Couple'* behaviour when I called a 'Flat Meeting' one evening, to remonstrate with Rose about the amount of talcum powder on the surfaces in the bathroom, and had the temerity to show her how to fold a towel the way *I* always had on the basis that my way somehow dried it quicker. The truth was it was great fun having them in the flat and I missed them both when some six months later Rose bought a flat in Maryhill and they both moved out.

I had also decided to trade up and in mentioning this in the pub, excited the interest of Mary who said that she'd like to move from her rented flat in Anniesland into her first purchased flat. She didn't have a lot of cash to spend on bid money but might I be agreeable to doing a deal? Certainly I was, and she was able to buy 698 without competition as I moved simultaneously to 35 Laurel Street in Partick, a larger two bedroom flat about 200 yards closer to the Chancellor. Life was great and it improved when John indicated that although he and Rose were getting on well, he also wanted to move into his own property. His solution was to purchase a flat that was approaching comical in terms of its size. It was micro rather than tiny. Effectively one small room with a smaller bathroom off. A kitchen that was actually just a converted twelve inch deep cupboard off the lone room and a small bed recess off. It was unbelievable ... but John had his first foot on the lowest rung of the housing market and he would go on to make shrewd investments over the years which would see him trade up consistently and live in increasingly grand properties.

Another couple of close friends I made around this time were Damien Yeates and Tadhg Dennehy. Damien was recruited as a Marketing Executive with Govan Initiative and Stuart Patrick, who interviewed him, was so taken by his personality that he interrupted me in my office and suggested I might like to have a look at this guy myself. I did and was truly impressed by his animation, his passion and his articulacy.

Too good for the likes of us, I found myself thinking. *We'll maybe get a couple of years out of him before he heads back to the private sector.* You could have knocked me over with a feather if you'd told me then that he would stay and prosper for a period of time almost longer than the 13 year shift I eventually put in myself! Eventually he moved on to become the Chief Executive of the Scottish University for Industry and then the quango, Skills Development Scotland, so our appraisal of his potential was sound!

After a period, Damien married Lesley and they moved home from Shawlands on the south side to a large semi-detached villa in Giffnock.

We became firm friends and he took me over to meet his parents, George and Mary - Moll, as Damien called her - and when in Dublin that weekend I was to meet one of the most wonderfully impressive individuals it has ever been my pleasure to meet: Tadhg Dennehy.

Tadhg was running his own business at the time designing and building small turbines that would generate power. He also ran a technology company which designed software that recognised body parts of German motor cars so they could always be tracked no matter the state of decomposition of the vehicle. Most impressive.

Tadhg was great fun, and a genuinely interesting drinking partner on all subjects, but particularly when on the subject of Irish Nationalism. A Kerry man, Tadhg was rather closer to Republican ideals than to the Reverend Ian Paisley's view of the world. We had many an enjoyable chat over a pint, and over the years I stayed with him intermittently in his house in South Circular Road in the Dolphins Barn part of Dublin.

One weekend, Damien, John McManus and I were over staying with Tadhg when Damien started teasing him about him not having a wife and having spent time the evening before chatting away to a drunken woman who had perhaps one too many to make it safely home of her own volition. As ever, Tadhg the gentleman was being nudged in the ribs for his helpful nature and allowing his motives to be misinterpreted as courtship.

"Jeezuz, Tadhg, she was an ugly oul' bitch", said Damien. "D'ye know, ye can't stay single for ever." Damien's Dublin accent became ever more pronounced when he landed back on the oul' sod.

"Aye, sure when I'm workin' all hours it's difficult to meet the wimmin 'cept when I'm out with you lads and you take me to these shit holes where there are no decent wimmin to be found"….a reference to our then preoccupation with drinking in some real dumps, or traditional Dublin pubs as they might be better known. Certainly not pick-up joints.

As the conversation progressed, the germ of an idea grew in my mind. I was aware that Tadhg, then 40 years of age, was a good Catholic boy, a very decent man, good looking, very bright - yet despite his charms, unable to find a woman who was compatible. I then thought of Mary Hoy. Living in a small studio flat, now in Newton Mearns near Glasgow, she was attractive, very bright, a great conversationalist, a good Catholic girl, the same age as Tadhg and quite unable to find the man of her dreams. I hadn't spoken to her for a couple of years.

"Hey, guys, why don't I introduce Tadhg to Mary? I bet she's still single."

Eyebrows were raised and a silence fell on the room. John was first to offer a view. "Don't be daft, Ron. Mary lives in another country."

Damien was next. "It's crazy, Ron. You said yourself that she was nuts."

I picked up a pen and paper and drew a line down the middle of the page. At the top, on either side of the line, I wrote 'Pros and Cons'.

The Pros were plentiful as Mary was indeed a lovely person. In the Cons column, I wrote a list of adjectives, pretty much all of which referenced Mary's well known inability to make a decision. She'd twist and turn, ebb and flow, decide then change her mind … then reverse it again … on whether to order a Chinese takeaway or a pizza.

I handed it to Tadhg after the other two had looked it over and added comments. Tadhg read the document with all the intensity of someone reading a legal agreement.

"She seems nice."

"Aye, she's lovely, Tadhg."

"And how would a person go about making contact with her?"

We all laughed but I found her telephone number and entered it at the bottom of the page. Within a week, Tadhg had phoned Mary out of the blue; we had been so dismissive of the idea that no one had thought it necessary to contact Mary to forewarn her. Within a fortnight, Mary had paid her first visit to Dublin. Just over a year later they were married in Kilmarnock at one of the most personal and enjoyable weddings I've attended. I figured that they would probably be too old to conceive as a couple, but a year later, when I was over in Dublin sampling their consistently generous and welcoming hospitality, I became aware that Mary must have been sampling too many pints of Guinness as she was putting on the beef around her midriff. Then I realised that she had been drinking water all night while Tadhg and I had been throwing back strong drink. Surely she couldn't be pregnant again, aged 43? Towards the end of the evening, Mary put me out of my misery.

"Are you not going to say something?" she smiled.

"And just what are you referring to?" I asked, figuring that I now knew the answer.

"We're pregnant again!" shouted Mary. She and Tadhg were deliriously happy but were anxious to keep it quiet as a consequence of their earlier experience with Theresa. I promised that the matter would never cross my lips until they made an announcement; and it didn't. Baby Anna was born in 2005, making their lives complete. Just imagine if I hadn't put that phone number on the bottom of the sheet of paper.

Back in Govan, one day I received an invitation to attend a meeting down at architects' offices in central Govan in order to discuss the possibility of redeveloping a building, now moribund, which used to house Harmony Row FC, my old football club as a juvenile. I walked in to the meeting only to find Alex Ferguson, Manager of Manchester United, at the head of the table. Alex knew me from the launch of Govan Initiative, when we had had a long and most entertaining conversation together with Dougie Donnelly and he welcomed me warmly.

"Ron, great to see you. We need your help to get this thing off the ground." He'd been aware of the work Jean and I had done with ERCD in developing the Ibrox Community Complex where we installed one of the first high quality artificial football surfaces in Scotland.

And so began my adult relationship with Harmony Row which continues to this day. Alex asked me to play a role in monitoring the finances that were being raised and myself and the Headteacher of Govan High School, Bob Lennie were the two signatories. Just as well as previous monies had allegedly been squandered by office bearers who were also local residents getting their hands on monies raised and then spending it on phones for their houses and transport, ostensibly for the players, parked outside their own homes.

Harmony Row went through a few changes in management until one day I took a call from a guy called Jim Tait, who had just been elected as Harmony Row's new Chairman. He was clearly an altogether different prospect; calm, contemplative, articulate and, as I was to discover in the many years ahead when we'd become great friends, very organised and ethical. Following a meeting with him, I was most keen that he meet Alex, whom I knew would be both interested in Jim's vision for the club, as well as being relieved that there was a new calibre of man with his hand on the tiller. New leadership that would go on with great potency to drive the club forward.

Over the years, Jim, with Alex's active support, took the club to new heights. Football teams for those under eight years old through to adulthood blossomed and money was raised for a new stadium to be built at Braehead, just on the boundary with Govan. When I was presented with a plaque from Alex on 7th October 2000, reflecting my adoption as an Honorary Member of my old club in recognition of my small and intermittent support of Harmony Row, I could not have been more proud. It hangs in my home office to this day.

I would be lying if I did not confess that a material advantage in my dealing with Harmony Row was the access it gave me to Alex Ferguson, who was always genuinely interested in matters Govan. He'd phone regularly *en route* to a reserve match in the afternoon or whatever to ask how his old place was doing.

"How's Govan?" would be barked at me over the phone and I'd talk for ten minutes on all of the latest developments, gossip and politics of his beloved Govan. Once, a journalist from 'Goal' Magazine phoned me up and asked me a lot about Alex's interest in his old community. I'd already cleared with Alex that he was content for me to respond as he was could be quite pernickety about who should be talked with and who should not. Alex was a master of the media and seemed to have a wee black book in his head and if your name appeared in it you were to be punished for a while by being denied access, so Jim Tait and I would always check first.

Anyway, Daniel Davies, the journalist, was to be indulged and I spoke at length about that part of Alex which was nothing to do with football and everything to do with what had shaped him as a man and a manager.

A couple of days later, Davies phoned me back and told me that he'd interviewed Alex personally in Old Trafford and hadn't wanted to appear stupid in front of him but had noticed two Latin sayings above Alex's head in his office.

"The first was *'Nil Sine Labore'*…" he said, puzzled.

"That's the old motto of the Burgh of Govan, still retained by the shipyards", I replied. "It means 'Nothing without work'… although sometimes we interpret it here as 'No work to be found anywhere' when the place is in the depths of a recession."

"Thanks", he said. "And what about the second *'Ahcumfigovan'*?"

Tempted as I was to render him a false account of it meaning something esoteric, I nevertheless had to explain that it wasn't Latin but a phonetic rendition in the Glasgow vernacular of Alex's pride in his home town. "It means 'I come from Govan'," I confessed.

The article which resulted was lengthy and was subsequently quoted extensively in a book by Stephen Kelly called *Fergie,* which Alex despised because it was both unsolicited and clashed with the timed release of his own autobiography 'Managing *My Life'* which he wrote himself, with sports journalist Hugh McIlvanney very much in a supporting role, unlike so many sports stars who commonly use ghost writers because they themselves don't know how to put a verb in a sentence.

Alex was one of the managers who first understood the importance of diet, insisted on plain food like pasta, and would only permit still water to be placed before the players.

"If the good Lord had wanted water to be sparkling, he'd have made it that way in the burn," he'd remonstrate if asked if he wanted a carbonated version. Having said that, he enjoyed a glass of red wine, and fulminated affectionately one night over dinner that when his then twenty-something year old boys visited him with his young grandchildren, they made straight for his *uber-*expensive collection of red wines and ignored the more humble tipple on which he himself would sip.

One Saturday, Jim Tait and I took a young Frank McAveety, then the leader of Glasgow City Council and his political adviser, Andy Kerr down to Old Trafford to meet Alex. Both Frank and Andy, along with myself, had been selected to fight the forthcoming Scottish Parliamentary election, although I was still looking for a seat and each of them had found seats in Shettleston and East Kilbride respectively.

In the dressing room before the match, Alex was at his story-telling best and recounted how he'd known Frank's younger brother, Philip, when he'd managed St Mirren.

"Good Centre Half. Couldn't jump", was Alex's positive but ultimately condemning assessment of him. He then went on to tell an astonished Frank that when Philip had played for the Scottish Youth Team at Swansea, he'd driven him and Frank's father to the game. About an hour away from the ground, Frank's father had taken what transpired to be a mild heart attack requiring Alex to take control of the car by managing to get his foot on the brake pedal and steering the car to the side of the road.

"We took him to hospital straight away and then me and another player's father went to the match. There was nothing we could do then but after the game he'd recovered sufficiently for us to drive him back up the road. He asked us not to tell his wife as she'd just worry so we all made a pact."

This was all news to Frank, who, as one of politics' more gregarious and effervescent characters, was moved almost to tears over Alex's contribution to the then continuing functioning of his family.

Towards the mid-point of Alex's time at Old Trafford, he invited Jean and I down perhaps once a season and it was great being able to take our sons Conor and Ciaran with us. Alex was great with them, posing for photographs and asking after Conor's goal scoring exploits with Harmony Row for whom he played at the time although I took him away shortly afterwards due to the incompetence and general disorganisation of his coach.

In addition, Jim Tait and I would visit Manchester from time to time in support of a Govan, Glasgow or Harmony Row task. Alex was always a most generous host and would invariably take us to dinner on the Friday evening before seeing us again the following day before and/or after the match. One such occasion was our visit where he'd arranged to collect us at our hotel but, on arrival, had realised that the restaurant he'd wanted to book was closed. Alex merely phoned the owner who promptly arranged for the restaurant to be opened just for us. Over the course of the evening it became extremely busy as it was a very popular restaurant with the footballing elite. Andy Gray and the Sky Sports presenters sat at the next table while Alex murmured imprecations to us about Richard Keys, who he felt had made inappropriate comments about his team's recent performance.

During the conversation, the talk turned to our parents and the extent to which they took a drink. Jim recounted how his father had had a wee taste for the hard stuff and I contributed by sharing the fact of my own father's demise, as he was hit by a train while drunk.

"Jesus Christ, Ron. Was he hurt?" asked Alex.

"Alex, he was hit by a train. What do you think?"

"Aye, right enough!"

Back in Govan, although I had had a few girlfriends, there was no one at all serious in my life. If ever I needed a partner for a dinner or a function, Mary was usually happy to oblige if it didn't interfere with her studies. I was content with my professional life and enjoyed the rhythm of my social life. I felt no urge to meet someone with whom to share my life. I had always had a soft spot for Jean who had become increasingly important to me at work. She had moved from heading up the company's administration via a brief spell as a business adviser before finding her feet as my personal assistant. In this role she took the major responsibility for the development of the Ibrox Community Complex and was increasingly becoming a wonderful colleague of whom I was very fond.

In 1992, following a drunken evening in a pub with some pals, arguing *inter alia* about the gullibility of those who went to see fortune readers or who asked to be connected with the spirit world so they could have a chat with their recently demised dog or whatever, I found myself saying through drink that I was going to prove the accuracy of my sceptical views and would seek out a Seer I'd heard was operating in Ibrox of all places.

I visited the woman, expecting a veiled gypsy with long fingernails to greet me at the door. In fact it was a pretty unprepossessing door, that opened to invite me into a nondescript hallway, where a room had been set aside for consultations. The equally unprepossessing woman informed me that indeed she *was* a Highland Seer and could see into the future. I held the view that these sessions were little more than Vaudeville and that the act was based upon the individual's ability to elicit information little by little before making a broad, educated guess that gave them room for manoeuvre if it didn't hit the bullseye. I had decided to say nothing other than an occasional grunt if I was called on to affirm something.

"Let's see what the cards say," said the Seer, shuffling a pack of Tarot cards.

Slowly she'd reveal the cards, explaining their significance without any reference to me but every so often she'd stop and give particular consideration to a card she'd just turned over side by side with a new card she'd just pulled from the pack. After further reflection she'd make a comment. I found myself looking at her with new eyes as she'd pronounce upon elements of my family history.

"You have two young sons"... "Your father died young"... "Your mother married twice". Observations slowly fell from her lips and I must confess I was impressed as I'd expected to be completely underwhelmed by the obvious trickery of an old fraud. She continued to turn cards and make comment, not even looking to me for confirmation. These were no wild guesses, nor were they broad generalisations.

What took the biscuit and had me running for the door to phone John was a hesitation she exhibited when turning over the Sun card, explaining its Tarot significance before saying to me, "A young woman looks after you at your place of employment." She'd have seen a startled look in my eyes had she looked up. "She's very beautiful....she has black hair." I could only imagine that she meant Jean and was now agog. She turned over the Lovers' Card. "Oh, this is interesting. This tells me that you'll marry her!"

I paid my consultation fee and phoned John with trembling hands.

John and I still spent a lot of social time together and after a few beers, I swore him to secrecy, told him what had transpired and confessed to him that I thought Jean was great. The fact that she was entirely beautiful and charming wasn't without merit but it was her personality that had me smitten.

There was a Christmas function coming up at work and John, who was attending as my guest, volunteered on my behalf to ask Jean about her personal life. Although she and I worked very closely, I had never found either the need or had the inclination to ask whether she was courting someone. Now I found myself wanting to know… badly. John was both supportive and relaxed. He told me to stop worrying. Clearly it had been written in the stars.

On the night Jean was, as ever, the life and soul of the party until the dreaded drink kicked in in the wee small hours. She ended up tearfully confessing to John that she was without a partner and that her lifestyle was such that the only time she was able to feel free was when she took her annual holiday on the Algarve in Portugal. That said, in passing, she also told John that she thought that I was just a fantastic boss and that her mother, whom she'd told all about me, thought that she was very fortunate indeed to function in such a favourable operating environment.

John's assessment was that it might be worth asking Jean out to the pictures as long as I was confident that it wouldn't ruin the excellent relationship we'd enjoyed at work, reminding me what the Seer had predicted.

I was still a bit shy. The act of just asking her out could on its own present the same problems. What if she figured I'd just crossed a line and determined that she'd better move on before things got complicated. Plus she was twelve years my junior. I fancied that I was in pretty good nick. I was trim and fit. But twelve years is a big gap. I was 42 and Jean was 30.

However, I decided that fortune favoured the brave and soon after the festive break, convinced that Jean would find her special person at some club over the holiday period, I asked her into my office and told her that I was receiving a lot of invitations to dinners and functions and that I was a bit embarrassed to go on my own. If she was free, might she accompany me on occasion … no strings attached … nothing improper … only if she wasn't doing anything else … I stumbled around in the undergrowth trying to hide my embarrassment and gave her every reason to reject my request.

Jean was absolutely super. Totally relaxed.

"Sure, I'd love to go out. Just let me know when anything crops up."

I phoned John immediately and told him of Jean's agreement to the principle of going out although I hadn't made any firm arrangements.

"Away ya eejit. Just ask her out. Never mind the fan-dancing."

Dispirited, I paced up and down the office floor rehearsing a number of different lines.

I lifted the phone. "Jean, could you pop in for a moment?"

She came in and sat down, pen and paper at the ready. I must have been a sight.

She made the whole thing easy. "Don't tell me you've got an invitation already?"

So we went to see *'The Last Of The Mohicans'* in the ABC cinema in Sauchiehall Street, had a drink, laughed like we'd known one another as pals all our lives, made a promise to go out again the following week and I was rewarded with a kiss before she drove home. I walked home on a cushion of air.

In 1997 Govan Initiative was voted Business of the Year in Scotland and the following year was voted one of the top five performing businesses in Europe. I was delighted at the results we'd achieved as if you looked at the improvements in performance we'd achieved as a company, it could have been overlaid with the improvements we could measure in the community. It wasn't rocket science but the more we focussed upon the pursuit of excellence, the more we saw improvements in the bottom line of the organisation. According to the European Commission, Govan moved from being 'an Area of Need' in 1987 through an 'Area of Need and Opportunity' in 1992 to being an 'Area of Opportunity' in 1997. The blight that blanketed the area in 1986 had been lifted and the evidence of regeneration was everywhere to be seen.

After we won the European accolade, there was loads of media attention. Although there were a few eejit councillors on the Board whom I treated badly, taking the view that they were beyond redemption, it was obvious that the Board appreciated my efforts. I was asked if I'd like to take a two week sabbatical in an American city or somewhere so as to compare and contrast approaches to local economic development. I was grateful but declined and instead asked if they'd permit me to meet 'extraordinary people'. I'd read that Royal Dutch Shell annually sent their top brass to visit with 'extraordinary people', whether they be the best juggler in the world, the best writer of science fiction, the top gardener, the best guitarist. Their view was that these people didn't achieve what they'd achieved without there being something different about them, without a spark denied others. What made them different? They were encouraged to find out.

I thought that this was an excellent idea and was given permission to do the same. I drew up a short leet and arranged to make contact with Tom Hunter (the Scottish entrepreneur), Tony Benn (the left wing MP), Anne Gloag (the multi-millionairess), Bill Robertson (Chief Constable of the Northern Constabulary), Jim Sillars (the ex-leader of the Scottish National Party, but then an adviser to the Saudi Arabian Leadership) and the Right Reverend Richard Holloway, the controversial and outspoken Bishop of Edinburgh.

Anne Gloag wrote back saying she didn't give interviews and wouldn't hear of my visiting her in her Scottish castle. The Bishop had an assistant who saw himself as a sort of Praetorian Guard. He wouldn't let me near him. I was disappointed as I'm certain the Bish would have seen me if only he knew I existed.

Other than that, they were all great. Tom Hunter spoke to me on the importance that luck had played in his rise and rise. He told me how when he was a struggling retailer, a large PLC owed him £30,000. Without this money he was dead in the water. Tom approached the Chairman of the PLC and managed to impress him, leaving the building with a cheque for the full amount; something completely against the company's procedures. One month later the company went bust but at that point they only owed Tom £126.

Jim Sillars was as eloquent and passionate as ever, advising me never to hold grudges as *'tomorrow's friends are today's enemies'* and vice versa. Jim had by that time left politics and was employed as the Assistant General Secretary to the Arab British Chamber of Commerce. My notes of the meeting reminded me that we sat in his small office and he pulled down a map to show how the British, who had dealt with the likes of Ghandi and Ian Smith, and who needed Scotland because of its strategic position relative to the Russian shipping routes north of the Shetlands, would not concede independence for Scotland. He told me that 'politics is all about power' and the Labour Party needs its regular compliment of Scottish MPs if they're ever to win a general election, so they too will not stand for independence and a consistently Conservative England. He finished by answering my question about his departure from politics by shrugging his shoulders, "I had nothing more to say, Ron. I felt I'd said all I wanted to say."

Bill Robertson was Chief Constable of the Northern Constabulary - the Highlands and Islands of Scotland, covering the largest land mass in the UK. I'd got to know him when he was Assistant Chief Constable of Strathclyde and had worked with me to deploy the first secondment of a Police Inspector at Govan Initiative. I met him again up in Inverness in September 1998. It was always refreshing dealing with Bill. He was, in my book, the first modern policeman. Tough when he needed to be but widely read and thoughtful about policing. He was an acquired taste to a police force that still hankered after an old regime where rank and power resolved all issues. Bill saw his role as that of the 'Servant Leader'. His job was to serve the front line troops, not the other way round. It was a breathtaking departure from traditional internal police relationships but it taught me a lot and I subsequently began to use that approach myself in my own leadership roles.

Tony Benn was different class. His wife was dying of cancer and he'd given up politics for a while to look after her. Years earlier he regularly held me transfixed as he'd feature on televised broadcasts from a Labour Party Conference in some coastal resort arguing the case for nuclear disarmament, saving the mining industry or abolishing the House of Lords.

I made contact with him more in hope than expectation but he must have phoned me half a dozen times at home and gave unstintingly of his time. He'd intended meeting me at the House of Commons, had he been able to get there to see me but his wife's illness precluded that. He was a simply great educationalist; a great listener as well as a great orator. He spoke of the importance of ethics, of 'not being a weather-vane but a sign post', meaning that a real politician doesn't follow the political breeze, but points to a principled position ... that politicians had to be themselves and not become caught up in the career of politics where personal benefit becomes the driving factor rather than the passion and convictions; "ishoozh", as he termed them, that brought them into politics in the first place. I was hugely impressed by Tony Benn. A simply brilliant communicator and a lovely, caring man. He watched over me when later on I stood for Parliament and would phone me at odd hours to discuss how I was getting on. God only knows why he did this. He had no need, certainly beyond a courteous reply to my initial request for a blether, if that.

Govan Initiative was going from strength to strength and my salary was increasing as the Board continued to make sure I was happy at my work. I decided one day when I was playing football with my sons, Ron and Campbell that we should go and look at the new flats they'd just developed at Spiers Wharf, a beautiful converted sandstone whisky bond on the banks of the Forth and Clyde Canal. I was much taken with them and bought a one bedroomed flat. Modern and fairly spacious, it had a good specification and had the added facility of a swimming pool, gymnasium, steam room, sauna and pool room. At night the buildings were illuminated. Close to the city centre, I thought that at last I could become the yuppie I knew must linger inside of me.

With the boys' enthusiastic connivance, I sold the flat at Laurel Street and moved to Spiers Wharf in short order. It had superb views over Glasgow and I felt much more at home there than I did in Laurel Street.

I had also experienced significant sadness at Laurel Street. My Grandmother, Madge McLeod, had suffered deterioration over the previous few years, succumbing to Alzheimer's disease. After an intermittent series of police calls telling me or my Mum that Gran had been found wandering the streets in a confused and agitated manner in the wee small hours of the morning, we decided that there was little prospect of her managing her own life independently any more. Following a period of Gran's hospitalisation, Mum and I toured a number of residential homes for the elderly, finally finding her one just off Paisley Road West. It was exceptional; I'll always appreciate the personable and caring staff that made her days there tolerable.

I visited her daily every lunchtime but it was most upsetting as she'd tell me "My big grandson Ron's visiting me later today." It was as if an alien had taken over her body. I had pinned large, blown up photographs of all the family members all round her room and written their names against each likeness but she still only had momentary flights of recognition. It really is a terrible illness. You know that this is your loving relative but they're in a world of their own and can't be the person they once were.

Mum was taking the brunt of all of the caring duties and had been hard at it over the years previously. She was also working towards her own retirement from the National Savings Bank, in which she'd worked for most of her adult life, and was still working away at youth work in the evenings. When aged 60 she put on weight dramatically and then broke her toe so badly it required an operation to have it pinned. I visited her and George at home one night and she didn't look at all great. I put it down to her illnesses and the stress of looking after Gran, even although by now she was safely tucked up in her care home.

As her general health began to falter, Gran was taken back to hospital, in the Southern General. Again, I visited her regularly but there was no real communication. It was obvious that the end was nigh. I figured that it would be a blessing. In reality, we'd lost her a couple of years back.

I'd gone to bed late one night after watching a review of the year. The cold war was over, the Berlin Wall had been torn down, Ceausescu had been dragged out and shot by a firing squad and Nelson Mandela had been released from his Island prison cell. I'd fallen asleep in an armchair in the early morning of 8th December 1989 and was awakened by a phone call from the Southern General. A nurse told me that the Doctor wanted to see me. Could I make my way down there immediately? With a heavy heart, I realised the coded significance of the message, changed and left for the hospital.

When I arrived, I made my way through the now familiar corridors and found the ward to which I'd been directed. Mum's husband, George, was standing in the anti-room in tears. He was fond of my Gran but I was surprised at his distraught reaction until he embraced me and cried, "Ron, your mother's dead. She's dead."

I peeled myself from his grasp while I took on board his message. Dead? How could this be. Surely it's my gran he's talking about?

But no, my mother had died of a cardiac infarction; a heart attack, in the early hours of Saturday morning. On the Monday evening, I received another call. Could I return to the hospital? I did, only to find that as we now pretty well expected, my Gran had also passed away. I arranged the funeral and made sure that there was a double ceremony. I've always found close personal funerals difficult but when I saw my Mum's large coffin carried down the aisle followed closely by Gran's much smaller one, as if a child's, I broke down.

Some years earlier, at my grandfather's funeral, my main feeling was one of anger as the Minister conducting the ceremony mentioned Hector's name only a couple of times. He could have been conveying anyone to the great beyond. I'm sure that biblical references bring comfort to many but that whole funeral was anonymous. I also determined that when the time comes for *me* to shuffle off this mortal coil, I'll make recompense by exiting to the tune of my favourite Scottish pipe tune, *"Hector the Hero"* as played by The Royal Scots Dragoon Guards, and leave some notes explaining its significance. It might be decades late but I'll try to share my departure with him. He was special and I loved him very much.

Well, I made sure that that didn't happen to Mum and Gran and spent ages with the Minister conducting the ceremony giving him notes and details of their accomplishments. So Mum and Gran's lives were celebrated in grand style. Now I was officially an orphan. Aged 39, I was certainly now the man of the family that my mother had always insisted I'd become when my father had died way back in 1959.

Go figure the character of some houses. I just never settled in Laurel Street. Years later, in 2005, the cost of housing had soared and as a young clinical psychologist, my son Campbell was finding it hard to make ends meet and the cost of civilised living in the West End was way beyond his means so we did a deal. I invested the capital cost of buying 15 Laurel Crescent, just off Laurel Street. Campbell paid fifty per cent of the mortgage, undertook a lot of redevelopment work on the property and enjoyed his stay there. However, following the death of my Mum and my Gran, I was glad to move out of my apartment round the corner.

Anyway, Jean and I had kept our relationship very quiet in case it became evident that it was clearly going nowhere. However, after a few months, it was obvious that the opposite was the case and I organised a grand party in my new accommodation to introduce Jean to my circle of friends, most of whom knew her already, but as my PA. Both of us were a bit anxious but the event was a great success with everyone taking her and our new relationship to their hearts immediately.

Jean's brother Ronnie had just left the house as a married man to live with his new wife, Jill. Jean still lived with her parents, Anne and Bobby, in a tenement apartment in Prospecthill Circus, an area of Glasgow developed in an attempt to re-house the people who were decanted from the Gorbals. Once an attractive suburb accommodating people like Charlie Burchill and Jim Kerr of rock band *Simple Minds,* as well as entrepreneurs like Willie Haughey, it had become a graffiti strewn, gloomy, dank place where drugs and violence were often in evidence. I was always anxious about Jean driving home late at night, as she had to park some small distance from the house, but she was always more phlegmatic than me about the risks she faced.

Jean's mother, previously my biggest fan when I was only Jean's boss, initially saw the relationship as worrying because of, among other things, the twelve year age gap. However, she was most civil and friendly when I visited her and Bobby for the first time as their daughter's suitor and over time our relationship flourished. Bobby was a great guy. He had an engineering background but the wear and tear of lying on damp ground fixing something mechanical had given him a particularly pronounced stoop and in his forties he was forced to give up work and live in receipt of Disability Allowance. This provided meagrely for the family, and Anne worked in a woman's dresswear shop in Victoria Road to supplement the family income. Bobby was a hoarder. Something always had a use, and he'd sit in his comfortable seat in the livingroom listening to his favourite Country and Western music, surrounded by all sorts of detritus for which only he could see a use. He was a great stamp collector; many nights I'd go to collect Jean only to be lectured on the characteristic of a new stamp he'd managed to obtain.

One night in my apartment in Spiers Wharf, I gave Jean a wrapped map of Paris as a gift. She opened it, puzzled and I told her I'd booked a short break in Paris for the two of us. I made sure that Jean knew it was my treat and that she need only take money if she wanted to shop. I'd pay for everything.

We were booked into a lovely city centre hotel and had a super time seeing all the sights. Because Jean had used each of her last ten annual two week holidays to meet girlfriends on the Algarve, she hadn't visited many other foreign places and I took great pleasure in showing her around. Jean had a great time.

The first morning we woke up to the Parisian sunshine, Jean told me that she intended taking me for brunch. It was the least she could do, she said. We headed up towards *l'Arc de Triomphe* and settled in a small bar where we had scrambled eggs and two brandies. When the bill came Jean had to empty the entire contents of her purse in order to pay a rather extravagant bill. I found it hilarious and Jean spent the rest of the day in astonishment at the prices in tourist Paris.

My thoughtfulness in inviting Jean to Paris, although to some extent altruistic, was also fairly obviously a ruse. We'd been seeing one another for about a year and I had determined in advance to ask her to marry me. Buoyed by the love and happiness that both of us found in each other's company, I was hopeful that she'd agree. However, at the last moment, my nerve failed me. We'd had a lovely day out dining on a boat on the River Seine and were back in our hotel room resting before going back out for a meal, this time in a less expensive part of the city.

"I tell you what, Jean, I'll nip down to the off-licence and get us a half bottle of brandy and we can have a wee drink before we go out."

"Excellent", said Jean. "I'll just rest my eyes for a few minutes." I was to discover over the remaining years of my life that 'resting her eyes' would be a constant preoccupation of Jean's.

I headed off and returned later with a half bottle. It didn't kick in immediately by any means but after I'd consumed pretty much the entire contents of an excellent wee half bottle of Remy Martin, my confidence had been sufficiently bolstered and I was eventually able drunkenly to mumble the question that resulted in Jean agreeing to be my wife.

I wanted Jean to move in with me immediately but she told me that she was an old fashioned girl and that if she was to be married, she'd be married from her parental home. We went out to celebrate and discussed the prospect of a life together, how her parents might react and how we might tell the rest of the staff that Mrs Culley was to take over from Miss Pollock.

In the event it all couldn't have been more perfect. I called a meeting of all of the staff who occupied our headquarters in Ibrox Stadium and went through some items of business before telling them that Jean and I were engaged to be married. The reaction was spontaneous. Everyone rushed to Jean's side, claiming to commiserate with her and ask if she'd taken leave of her senses. I took a lot of teasing, but I went on to say that Jean would be moving to handle the Public Relations side of the business and step back from her close involvement with me in her role as PA. People were delighted and very generous in their comments. Jean was submerged in a gaggle of women colleagues, who wanted to hear all about it, and I went back to business.

Big Jim Mullen, with whom I was pretty close, was the six-foot-something tough guy we employed on our Safe Communities Programme. After the announcement, he knocked my door.

"Hey boss, great news on the old marriage front. You and Jean were made for one another." He coughed as if calculating whether he was approaching a point of no return. "You know I hold you in the highest respect, boss, but if you don't treat Jean like the lady she is, you'll have to deal with me. I hope I make myself clear."

I reassured Big Jim that he could rest safe in the knowledge that I'd look after Jean and we laughed at his gallantry given that he had a reputation for loving and leaving a score of women within our company alone. Few weekends would pass without Jim coming in to work on the Monday and telling the guys in the staffroom that he'd 'parked the pink Cadillac' in some woman's grateful garage over the previous two days.

On the 13th May 1994, Jean and I were married in the splendour of the Buchanan Suite of the Royal Concert Hall. We'd spent many weeks negotiating with the Reverend Robert Calvert, one of John's Board Members. Initially, Robert was reluctant to conduct the ceremony because neither Jean nor I were religious and we were most anxious that the ceremony wasn't at all traditional. We wanted songs from Robert Burns, poetry readings, statements from friends … no hymns, no prayers … no God, no Jesus. We could well see Robert's point. We met three times for lunch while we negotiated this. Robert was obviously torn between his concern to be helpful and our requirement that he abandon his usual church based ceremony. At the end, the clincher was a statement I made over lunch.

I said, "Look, Robert. You and we share the same values, but Jean and I don't characterise them as religion and we don't have the same belief system. However, in plain language, if I can use an analogy … in life, you and I are currently in Glasgow and we're both just trying to get to Dumfries. The only difference is that you want to go via Moffat and we want to go via Sanquhar. Robert pondered this. "D'you know, Ron, you're perfectly right. Let's do it."

In the event, Robert cheated a bit. The ceremony was wonderful. I was much more emotional during the vows than I expected to be. When I turned to see Jean walking down the aisle, she looked absolutely radiant. This was her big day, and she certainly lived up to the part. I was lost for words whereas she was word perfect standing next to me. All of the symbolism Jean had choreographed began to strike home … each of us taking a lit candle and together lighting a fresh one to signify two becoming one. It was lovely. There was great spontaneity too. John McLaughlin had been asked to say a few words, but you don't corral John that easily and he improvised in his inimitable way and had our guests laughing and applauding our good health.

Robert had one or two tricks up his sleeve too. He spoke of how we'd negotiated an unusual ceremony but then went on to say that with our permission, perhaps we'd be prepared to treat his comments as we'd treat an advert on the television…. and said a few words of a religious nature. *Touché!* Honour was satisfied.

We had the run of the entire Concert Hall for photographs, drinks, circulation etc. Jean and I were whisked away to have some outdoor shots taken at the University of Strathclyde. Our day-guests had a few drinks and we regrouped for dinner in the Buchanan Suite before going downstairs to the Strathclyde Suite for the evening's celebrations during which our numbers swelled fourfold.

John was my best man. At the dinner, he spoke brilliantly. As might be expected, for my own contribution, I had drafted a comedy routine and was having a whale of a time showing off. John was more disciplined and spoke warmly of our adventures over the years. He even brought props and showed those gathered for dinner my specified method of folding a towel in explanation of the rather anally retentive way in which I managed the household when he and Rose had been resident.

What was even more hilarious was the fact that I'd arranged with Ian McAlpine for him to be my 'media man' and he set up the camera some way back in the hall so as to catch audience reaction to the speechifying. Innocently he'd set it up next to the table which accommodated *inter alia* my brother Campbell, Laurie and Pam Russell and Danny Brennan. Their captured hilarious one liners, delivered *sotto voce* throughout the Groom's speech was one of the highlights of the event … although I still thought my own efforts might have been treated with rather more reverence.

My one disappointment was that Ron and Campbell didn't attend. They'd have been 16 and 13 respectively and although they got on really well with Jean, their exams were on at the time and I didn't push their involvement as they must have felt confused over their role and I certainly wouldn't have wanted to complicate things with their Mother. However, over the years their relationship not only with Jean but with their two wee new brothers (of which more later) has been a revelation… one of the things of which I'm most proud in life. I've also been much taken by the way Margaret, her partner John and her mother Margaret made time for the sons that Jean and I had; Conor and Ciaran, whenever their paths crossed. There's an obvious affection there which is heartening.

Jean and I left the wedding early to catch a rather unnecessary taxi to travel the few hundred yards to our new home at Spiers Wharf as we'd to be up early to start our honeymoon in America. We'd scheduled breaks in New York, San Francisco, Las Vegas finishing in Washington DC. It was fabulous. Everything a honeymoon should be. We visited the Grand Canyon. We placed bets in the casinos. We crossed the Golden Gate Bridge and we took the elevator to the top of the Twin Towers in New York, quite oblivious to the dark place they'd have in history only eight years later.

I loved flying over America. If heading east or west, we'd see round crop circles that seem to suggest occupation by space aliens, snow capped peaks and barren deserts, arrow-straight roads and a general feeling of emptiness before confronting some urban centre, stretched over the horizon, its mirrored towers glinting in the sun. If flying south we'd overfly a deep blue sea with brilliant white edges where it met the coast, occasional cotton wool clouds and sunsets which when viewed through the effects of my glass of brandy faded into an amber wonder.

Back in Glasgow, we found life as a married couple most enjoyable. We made great friends and were able to enjoy super holidays and visit different places at will. Alex Ferguson was also most generous both to me and to Jean. He invited me to Old Trafford as his guest many times and typically he took me and Jean or other friends to dinner on the Friday evening before seeing us again on the Saturday when we'd sometimes lunch with Alex and the players before the match. Afterwards we'd repair to his own lounge area where all of his guests would gather for a bite to eat and a drink before we'd head back north.

On our first visit, Alex had called me and invited Jean and I to see his team playing Blackburn. I was excited and suggested to Jean that we make a long weekend of it, perhaps travelling by car first to Liverpool to undertake the Beatles Tour before heading for Manchester. Jean agreed but on the Thursday morning of our departure a freak snowstorm had closed roads north and south of the border. The news footage showed cars abandoned and snowdrifts causing lorries to slide into fields. Jean was very anxious and counselled that common sense suggested that we postponed the trip. "Alex would understand," she reasoned.

Well, maybe so…but I wasn't to be denied my invitation to Old Trafford and lunch with my heroes. I picked up the phone and, with Jean sitting nervously on the chair beside me, phoned the RAC.

"Hi, I was wondering what you could tell me about the road conditions on the M74 between Glasgow and Liverpool?"

"Certainly, sir. There's a general warning out because of snow drifting and cars lying abandoned. It's very difficult out there and we're advising against travel unless it's essential."

"First class, I'm so relieved."

"I don't know if you understood me sir, but the roads are very dangerous and passable only with great care. We suggest people stay at home."

"Well, that's most reassuring," I said. "Thank you for your help".

I put the phone down and turned to Jean, who had heard only my part of the conversation.

"Seems alright according to the RAC," I lied.

"Well", said Jean. "Perhaps if we're very careful".

And careful we were. It was everything the RAC man had said. Snow had been pushed to the sides of the motorway and resembled solid, chin-high, white walls for most of the journey. Every so often a car had fallen victim to the drifts, and bonnets and boots protruded from the side walls causing the newly formed snow-road to meander casually south in contrast to the more direct motorway I was used to. I actually enjoyed slaloming between frozen vehicles. It was foolhardy but we made Liverpool without too many problems and after paying homage to John, Paul, George and Ringo, headed for Manchester.

It was intoxicating, sitting at a large sprig table as the players assembled for lunch before the match. Peter Schmeichel, Roy Keene, Ryan Giggs and other footballing giants all sat around us, leaving a spare seat vacant on my right. In came David Beckham, then just coming into the public awareness as a superstar football player, and he looked every part of it. A brown leather coat as thin as tissue paper hid equally trendy and expensive netherwear. He sat next to me but didn't speak to me or anybody else while we ate. He seemed almost cripplingly shy. One by one the players rose to get more food from the cooking area. As Beckham left, I asked Alex if he'd met the famous pop singer Posh Spice to whom his right mid-fielder had recently become engaged. Alex looked around to ensure that Beckham wasn't close by and drew me a look that suggested that by some distance she wasn't the most popular member of the Manchester United family before changing the subject.

After three years of marriage, in 1997, another boy child was born to me – a first for Jean. We were most fortunate in that when I was living alone in Spiers Wharf before setting up home with Jean, I'd registered with the Woodside Health Centre in nearby Barr Street in Maryhill. The GP I was allocated was Dr. Norman (Norrie) Gaw who, it transpired, was just the most wonderful medical practitioner anyone could have wished for. He was always engaging and nothing was ever too much trouble for him. Not only was he patient in listening to my latest hypochondriacal outpourings but he was seldom too rushed not to have a blether about whatever job I was doing or how Rangers were playing … usually about how Rangers were playing. After some years in post he was also tasked with the additional responsibility of looking after GEMS, the Glasgow Emergency Medical Service, a fore-runner of NHS24. He provided excellent health care and in later years when we'd moved to the southern extremities of the south side, I asked Norrie if the family might continue to retain his services and he was delighted to do so, reflecting only that if it was urgent, he might be delayed by the traffic on the Kingston Bridge. Over the years, we took care not to trouble him in this regard as he wasn't only an excellent GP but a very hard working one and we always ensured that we went to him rather than ask him to travel.

And so it was that Jean was cared for very well during her confinement. Jean's pregnancy wasn't straightforward and my presence in the operating room reminded me of the value I'd taken from my assertiveness training at Coodham all those years earlier. Jean was in discomfort and the midwife, as ever, an angel, was in and out of the room looking after a range of responsibilities. Everything seemed alright. The midwife was content that matters were developing normally, the heart monitor at the bed side continued to give out a regular series of consistent beeps. We waited.

While we were alone in the room, the beeping became more irregular. With every change in frequency, I became more agitated and when the monitor started to issue longer *beeeeeps*, I called the only person available, an assistant, and asked her to investigate. This she did by banging the side of the monitor. I was even more concerned that she should presume, without checking, that the problem was electronic rather than medical. When the tone went flat and we could only hear a continuous *beeeeeeeeep*, I went ballistic – "Get the doctor and the midwife in here *NOW*!" I yelled. The poor assistant was scared within an inch of her life and the doctor and midwife appeared almost immediately.

The doctor took one look at the screen. "The baby's in distress. I suspect the umbilical chord is round its neck and is choking it". He disconnected some wires and personally wheeled the trolley into another operating room, shouting instructions to the battery of medical professionals who had now gathered around Jean. I was asked to sit outside but after a few minutes, a nurse invited me in. Jean was lying on an operating table, fully awake but stuffed full of analgesics and with a large green canvas screen mounted at right angles across her midriff. This permitted me the ability only to see Jean's face and upper torso while denying me a look at what was going on down below. I gave Jean all the reassurance I could but my agitation proved too much for me and I gradually got to my feet to see what was going on. Nobody stopped me as everyone was working at a hundred miles an hour to get baby Culley into the world before he was strangled.

Watching a live caesarean operation in action was impressive. It was almost cartoon-like as the doctor parted one muscle group from another, one organ from another in his attempt to reach the child. There was little of the slow, methodical surgical procedures I'd seen on TV from time to time. This was high speed stuff. This was *M*A*S*H* fast. The blood was as if something from the gory, deleted scenes from *Platoon* or some such war movie about Vietnam. Before I knew it, a bloody bundle of bawling baby was hoiked from Jean's womb and a towel wrapped around it. A midwife whisked it away to count toes and the doctor started to count swabs within Jean's now open belly.

Only then was I seen to be standing. "Hey, you. That's against the rules", said the midwife chastising me with a smile on her face. Then more conspiratorially, "Just as well you were listening to that heart monitor."

"Too right," was all I could muster in reply.

Conor, as we named him, seemed to have suffered no consequences as a result of his somewhat hurried entrance to the world. Later that day, I was sitting in the ward next to Jean and Conor when I decided that my work there was done!

"Why don't I go away and register the birth, Darling?"

Jean nodded her assent. "I suppose so. What are we going to use as his middle names? I was hoping we could continue the tradition of keeping the name Armour as one of his middle name and I was also kind of hoping that we could remember my dad in the same way." Jean's dad, Bobby had died in the Victoria Infirmary of complications after an operation a few months earlier.

"Sure", I said... and a thought occurred to me. "I've always thought that Iain was a lovely name."

"But we don't have anyone in the family called Iain."

"I know, but I've always wanted to start the trend."

On small conversations like these are children's futures founded. And so it was that I went up to the registrar's office in Eastwood Park and registered the birth of Conor Robert Armour Iain Culley... *CRAIC*, for short; the Irish Gaelic word for good times and enjoyable conversation. I thought this would be a marvellous, individualistic characteristic of our new son's name that would be available to him in the future if ever he wanted to use it for signing documents or wear it on the back of his football shirt if ever he played for Brazil.

I returned that evening to the ward. "You big eejit", said Jean having worked out what my plan was. "The sweat wasn't off my brow when you wanted to register the birth!... I knew that something was up. You'll have scarred that boy for life!"

My protestations fell on deaf ears. Nowadays in the retelling of the story, Jean claims she'd worked out immediately what the acronym was and had given her muted approval... but I know different. Over the years, Conor has become quite attached to his *sobriquet*. We'll see if it gets used as he grows into manhood.

Our next child, Ciaran, was a different matter altogether. Jean and I had planned only to have the one child until one evening, eighteen months after the birth of Conor, Jean came into the living room where I was watching television. "You're going to kill me! You're going to divorce me!"

I thought that this rather dramatic entry probably required that I turn off the football match I was watching and give Jean my full attention. Very sensible. She held up a small phial which clearly showed a distinct blue line around its circumference. "I'm pregnant again", she wailed.

Inside I was screaming. *How can we afford this? How the hell did this happen? Where can we accommodate another wean?* But fortunately my actions disguised my emotions. "Darling, what great news. A wee brother or sister for Conor!" That said, it took only the briefest period of time until I formed the view that having another child was the familial equivalent of scoring a goal in extra time. We were both completely ecstatic at the news.

Because Jean had had a Caesarean operation with Conor, no chances were taken by the staff at the Southern General Hospital in Govan, the place of both boys' birth.

Their medical advice was that Jean's birth channel was too narrow at her pelvis and that a second caesarean operation was necessary. Jean was a bit miffed at this as she wanted to experience childbirth properly and was aware that the act of cutting stomach muscles leaves a debilitating wound that takes months to heal and can completely bugger up a woman's figure due to the tonal quality of the body's musculature being ruined.

However, one advantage accruing to a caesarean operation is that it can be timed better but on the day that Jean was to be induced, Alex Ferguson was in town and wanted to lunch with Jim Tait, the estimable Bob Baldry (the retail developer who became a firm friend), and I at Braehead Retail Centre where he was opening the complex.

I managed to persuade Jean that I'd just be literally half a mile along the road from the Southern General Hospital, she could call me on my mobile phone as soon as anything happened and I'd be along like a shot. In the event, I was offered perhaps one too many glasses of wine at lunch and although my phone hadn't rung, I thought I'd better wander back along to see how Jean was doing. I have to say, Alex Ferguson, who was fond of Jean, also encouraged me on my way. "Ron, you're acting like a bloody footballer! Away and look after your wife."

I wasn't a moment too soon. Apparently no phone signal could penetrate the room we dined in and I'd missed Jean's calls. When I arrived, she was being prepared for theatre and as previously, I was admitted to the theatre but this time there was no histrionics, no panic. Everything went smoothly and again, a wee baby was produced with everything intact. What a wonderful experience for a father. The fact that I'd wet the baby's head in *advance* of the birth made it possibly a wee bit more emotional than usual but it was again just a marvellous experience of undiluted love for a small bundle of joy. I was complete. Jean, however, was completely knackered.

Again we struggled with the name for boy number four in my case, two in Jean's. Originally we'd thought of Keir after Keir Hardy and the small blue card at the end of our child's cot told the world that that was his name. However, we looked at him and thought... he's not a Keir. He doesn't look like a Keir. The card then was changed to Jamie ... then to Robbie ... and finally to Ciaran. Over the years when Ciaran's discovered himself in bad odour with his parents he lets us know that he's changing his name to Robbie when he grows up and will be moving out of the house just as soon as he starts getting pocket money. We settled on Hector McLeod as Ciaran's middle names largely because I wanted to honour my grandfather and Jean had no other male relatives she wanted to acknowledge.

Both Ciaran and Conor are developing nicely into rounded young adults as I write this. Conor is clearly going to develop his musical talents and enjoys entertaining. Ciaran has something of his father's mischief about him. On holiday in Tavira when Ciaran was nine, the family went to the Aqualand, water theme park at Albufiera to enjoy an afternoon on the slides and flumes. With us was Bob and Lida Wylie's lovely, then thirteen year old daughter, Kathryn. Taking a break from their water tobogganing, the boys sat at the bottom of their next challenge, the daunting '*Anaconda*', and assessed its difficulty for some ten minutes before deciding if they had the courage to attempt its almost vertical drop. Ciaran took an interest in a girl who seemed to be of a similar age to himself, about nine.

"Look, Conor, there's that girl again. I like her. She's a wee squealer!"

When I see him smile and converse with adults at dinner, I see a witty boy with a most engaging personality and charming smile that will be found to be very attractive by his peers in years to come. I confided to Jean, after I'd heard his assessment of the nine year old girl, that he might just be saying the same thing to his pals in a pub about another girl in ten years time.

Over the years my relationship with my wife and my four boys has brought me more joy and satisfaction than anything else in my life. Of most comfort has been the relationship they enjoy with each other. Campbell and Ron, as children, fought and tussled on a daily basis. One (rather lightweight, it has to be said) door in their erstwhile home in Kilmarnock for years still showed the repair work necessary where as teenagers, Campbell, chasing Ron, smashed his fist clean through the woodwork as the door slammed in his face … but in adulthood, they have grown together and while at university shared a flat.

They golf together, play squash and generally socialise together. Importantly, to me, Ron and Campbell have become very fond of Conor and Ciaran. Hearing the young boys' squeals of delight whenever the doorbell goes when one or other of them is expected is one of the most emotionally satisfying experiences I enjoy. Not all family relationships work out this way and I know I'm blessed in this regard.

In spring and summer 2008, Jean and I were engaged upon the business of extending *Casa Culley* for the fourth time, this time a large extension to build out Ciaran's bedroom and create office space for him as well as construct a substantial family room at the back. The place was in upheaval for some months and in an attempt to get the boys away from the place for a day, Campbell and Claire called one day to tell me that they'd hired a boat in Loch Lomond, taken an old, rusty chest with them, filled it with coins of the realm and buried it on one of the many small islands close to the edge of the loch. Campbell had then drawn a treasure map, typed directions in copperplate handwriting, burned the edges, stained it with coffee and waxed it. He handed it to me and asked me to arrange for it to be buried in the builder's debris round the back. This I did and asked Conor and Ciaran to help me clean the yard. Both complied and shortly came across the map. Well, to say they found this discovery to be exciting doesn't begin to do justice to their delight… although Ciaran did ask me why I figured it seemed to smell of coffee! "Did Pirates drink coffee in the old days?"

That aside, they each bought the idea completely although Conor was slightly more sceptical. Ciaran took the map, read the clues …

"What's the largest loch in Scotland, dad?"

"I think it's Loch Lomond, but let's check it out on the internet. I've never heard of 'Fish Island' "

As we looked at the Google Earth web site and focussed down on Loch Lomond, Ciaran jumped with glee. "Look Dad, Fish Island!"... and, emerging from the pixilated screen, sure enough was a small island shaped as if a cartoon fish. Ciaran and Conor were now convinced. "Can we go, Dad? Can we go?"

"Ask Campbell and Claire. They offered to take you."

And so a week later the four of them set out back to Loch Lomond, but this time with a metal detector. They hired a motor boat, camped upon the shore of the island, cooked sausages on a small fire and, suitably replenished, began their search by following the instructions on the map. Counting steps and finding 'the tree with no leaves', they came to the point described on the map. Starting to dig, Conor soon hit something solid and Ciaran lifted it up with his help. Opening it, they found a treasure chest sparkling with coins. Both of them yelped with joy and it was all captured on film by Campbell who edited it, put the background music of *Indiana Jones* on top of it and burned a CD showing their entire adventure. It was a great act of brotherly love, a completely wonderful adventure for the boys but it was Ciaran, the less cynical of the two who having shown me the booty upon his return asked me the one question I couldn't answer ...

"Dad, why is it if this is buried pirate's treasure, this pound coin is dated 2003?"

All I could muster was, "Now *that's* a mystery Ciaran. That's a *real* mystery!"

At Christmas 2006, I sat as if detached from the hilarity that was going on around me and took the time to appreciate the relationship the four boys had one with another. Conor and Ciaran had had a number of presents from Santa which included items from the Star Wars movies. Campbell, Ron and Lisa came up from Kilmarnock in the evening and had exchanged presents with the boys. They played some board games and fell into a spontaneous quiz on scenes from Star Wars. I was completely taken by the wealth of knowledge that my then 8- and 9-year-old boys possessed in respect of Star Wars and they each held their own in competition with their older brothers. I sat on the outside of the conversation and a wonderful feeling of love and deep satisfaction possessed me. I could see that although they might have their ups and downs in the future, we'd managed to fashion a pretty strong bond between the four boys. Life doesn't get much better when families work as they should.

In September 2009, Ciaran became very ill and was admitted to Yorkhill Children's Hospital where he was diagnosed with insulin-dependent diabetes. Although he stabilised over the weekend, the alacrity with which his three brothers responded to his now lifelong condition was overwhelming. As I say, life doesn't get much better when families work as they should.

10. There Shall Be A Scottish Parliament.

When you come to a fork in the road, take it!
Yogi Berra.

Ever since we'd shared an office in the Council Buildings in India Street, Laurie and I had met up for a pint with colleagues in the Ritz Bar in North Street, Charing Cross, most Fridays after work. The Ritz was an unpretentious place with a good selection of beers and was handy for most people. Usually there was about eight or ten of us although this number ebbed and flowed but as the evening wore on these numbers were usually reduced to a hardy few.

On one such occasion, Laurie and I were the only two remaining and by this time had consumed more than was wise. We got round to discussing the new arrangements that Donald Dewar, as Secretary of State for Scotland, was busily putting in place for the creation of a devolved Scottish Parliament. Famously, the opening words of the Scotland Act 1998 were "There shall be a Scottish Parliament." These are also the words which are today inscribed upon the Mace of the Scottish Parliament - the symbol of political authority in Scotland - as well as around the feet of Donald Dewar's statue in Buchanan Street in Glasgow. Like most Labour members, Laurie and I were totally supportive of devolution as we'd lived through the early 1980s which were barren times for supporters of Scottish devolution after the 1979 Referendum defeat.

The news media covered the muscular political debate intensely and the BBC regularly reported on the formation of the Campaign for a Scottish Assembly, comprising clergymen, pro-Home Rule politicians, intellectuals and other activist,s although the Scottish National Party continued its fight for complete independence.

Following the Tories' victory in the 1987 General Election, the idea of all party support for a devolved Scottish Assembly began to seem attractive. Scotland had rejected Thatcherism and the number of Tory MPs was cut to a then all-time low of ten. Labour could do nothing as the hated poll tax was pushed through using Scotland as a guinea pig and the factories, shipyards and steel mills, the groundswell of Scotland's earlier industrial strength, were closed down relentlessly and remorselessly.

In March 1989, the Scottish Constitutional Convention held its inaugural meeting. It was made up variously of Scotland's MPs, its MEPs, its councils and representatives of various groups such as the STUC and several church representatives.

The SNP refused to have any part in the convention which persevered with Labour and Liberal Democrat support although the Conservatives were against.

The convention met in various places across the country and in November, 1990, an agreement on the shape a Scottish assembly should take was signed. This was followed by a commitment from Labour to Proportional Representation for such a body in time for the 1992 General Election.

With the Conservatives' General Election victory in 1992, the electorate came to accept the inevitability of some form of constitutional reform which would prevent Conservative control of Scottish politics on the basis of electoral victory in England. Three times Scotland had voted against the Conservatives and three times, as a consequence of the voting patterns in *England*, we got the Conservatives anyway. The closure of the Ravenscraig steel plant and Rosyth naval dockyard in favour of respective sites in more politically marginal areas of England and Wales were seen as yet further confirmation of how the Westminster government did not have Scotland's best interests at heart. The old contests between the market and intervention, between Tory and Labour were giving way to new arguments; Scotland versus England, north versus south.

The Conservatives campaigned vigorously against devolution. They feared it would lead to eventual Scottish independence and the break-up of the United Kingdom. They argued that higher rates of taxation would result if Scotland was given its own Parliament; the "Tartan Tax". Thatcher even took to the pulpit at the General Assembly of the Church of Scotland which became known as 'the sermon on the Mound' and argued her case for there being 'no such thing as society'.

Well, these arguments were rejected by the Scots, who wiped out the elected Tory Party in Scotland. Ironically, Thatcher's legacy proved not to be the celebration of the unification of the United Kingdom but a drive towards independence for Scotland.

Immediately following its General Election win in May 1997, Labour wasted no time on moving towards devolution. A Referendums Bill for Scotland and Wales was published on 15 May followed by the White Paper on 24 July and the date for the Scottish Referendum was set for 11 September 1997. The subsequent election to the Parliament would take place on May 6th 1999 and the Labour Party had decided that they would select candidates on merit rather than by Buggins' turn.

I was buoyed by the earlier successes of Govan Initiative and Laurie too was looking for a fresh challenge. In our cups in the Ritz we were emboldened by our consumption of alcohol.

"Y'know, Ron, we could stand for Parliament. You and me. We'd be as good as any of them that are lining up as we sit here tonight."

I fell to murmuring, "Absholutely …. absholutely", as my ability to convey much else had been dissolved in brandy.

"We'd pass Dewar's tests."

"Absholutely…. absholutely."

"We're better than some of them eejit time-servers who'll just think they need to turn up to get selected."

"Absholutely… absholutely."

Donald Dewar MP, the architect of this, as with almost every aspect of the arrangements for the creation of the Parliament, had decreed that the selection of the first Labour recruits who would fight seats in their effort to become the first Members of the Scottish Parliament would be based upon a meritocracy. Application forms would have to be filled in. An account would have to be prepared explaining why you would make a fine MSP. There would be a panel interview, and a mock press interview.

Before we lurched into the darkness and home, Laurie and I had agreed that we would both seek selection and with the confidence of drunks who were confident that they were in complete possession of their faculties, also agreed with earnest, fraternal goodwill that neither of us would stand against the other if circumstances contrived to have us face each other in contest.

Sobered, we phoned one another the next day and reaffirmed our intent. We were going to give it a whirl. We applied for application forms and over the next few weeks heard stories from friends that some politicians who might have felt their seniority within local government might be sufficient to have them favoured as candidates were in trouble and were asking officers to help them complete their applications. Down in Greenock, John McManus, who was at that point the Director of Economic Development, was being asked by one councillor to complete the form because he didn't know how to answer the questions. John helped out but, for the most part, the deadwood in the party was weeded out as the system quite mercilessly separated out the chaff. The party's association with the ill-educated, the poor and downtrodden had over the years brought forth, not unreasonably, a cadre of elected politicians who had been raised in precisely the conditions they so wanted to alleviate for others. However, over subsequent years as those bright new things selected and elected by these means rather fell from grace, many of those overlooked by the hierarchy understandably felt a measure of *schadenfreude* as those earlier brought to prominence as representatives of the people made mistakes or were ousted.

Around this time a story, denied by the party, appeared in the papers that someone who wanted to be a candidate had been asked in interview to outline his convictions. Unfortunately for the poor man, he thought they meant his *criminal* convictions, not his political convictions, and asked how far back they wanted him to go.

After all of the applications had been scored, I received a phone call from Lesley Quinn, then the General Secretary of the Scottish Labour Party, informing me that I'd been successful and would now go forward to the interview stage in a couple of weeks. I wasn't sure how to prepare for this, but spent time reviewing earlier party manifestos, reading the political stories of the day and discussing it with friends within the party. I was confident, but this evaporated when I was informed that I was to be put in front of the 'Panel of Death', as the press started calling it. Ernie Ross MP chaired it. Having been a pretty far left politician over the years, he had transmogrified into one of Blair's lapdogs and, on the panel, was bookended by two other equally right-wing fundamentalist colleagues.

I turned up on the day, telling myself that I was presently enjoying a great career and that this test wouldn't affect me one bit if I lost whereas many other professional politicians would need to produce the goods. I could afford to be relaxed. I entered the lions' den at Labour Party headquarters, an old red sandstone building in Lynedoch Place, close to Park Circus in Glasgow. The Panel awaited me front and centre; behind me, out of my vision, sat an undemonstrative figure who would deal with and score the Public Relations aspect of the interview.

I was assailed straight away. Each of the panellists had a specific set of questions in the interests of fairness. Although everyone was told on pain of death to keep the questions confidential. Even acknowledging that leaking them would be most unhelpful to the leaker's own ambitions (as there were only 129 candidates being sought) rumours had commenced early on indicating the kind of questions which were being asked.

"What two political stories caught your eye in the papers recently?" "How would you spend £20 million if you held office?" "What is your assessment of the Government's current position on education?" "Name three Government policies which most appeal to you and say why." … This went on for half an hour when Ernie Ross brought proceedings to a halt by explaining that the Panel would now take the role of a press pack and would engage with me in hostile questioning. The balloon went up.

"You're nothing but a clone of Tony Blair!" one shouted at me.

"He's two years younger than I am, perhaps that makes him a clone of *me*," I responded.

"Do you really think you're better than all of the candidates we have in front of us who have long political experience?" said the disembodied voice of their media man from the rear.

"That's for others to judge. Next question."

"What would be the issue that would set you apart from the administration?"

"I am completely in line with party thinking or else I wouldn't be here today."

And so it went on for five minutes that for many must have seemed like a lifetime but I thoroughly enjoyed the scrap as I had nothing to lose. That couldn't be said for others. Denis Canavan MP was singled out for the maverick he was and still is and his application was rejected. He then stood as an independent in Falkirk and won. One in the eye for the control freaks at HQ.

An equally high profile casualty was Ian Davidson MP, my old Chairman. I had spoken with Ian a few weeks earlier and he confessed that he couldn't wait to get out of Westminster. He was tiring of the place and saw the Scottish Parliament as his best opportunity. However, on the day, newspapers subsequently revealed that he'd turned up in a football shirt saying he needed to get away sharp as he had a game on. This didn't go down well but he answered the questions he was posed with the authority that might have been expected of a seasoned pro. However, the points he allegedly dropped by his insouciance sealed his fate and he eventually withdrew his candidacy.

A week after the interview both Laurie and I received a phone call then a letter confirming that we'd passed the test and were to be two of the candidates who would represent the Labour Party in the first Scottish elections in some three hundred years. Now we had to find a seat in which to stand. I was only ever interested in Govan, that political cockpit of Scottish politics, and Laurie had his eye on a Dumbarton seat.

It was an exciting time, but I received a shock one day soon after when I was told that Laurie had been rushed to hospital. In a panic I phoned Pam, Laurie's wife.

"Pam, it's Ron. What's happening?"

"Ron", she exclaimed, obviously pleased to hear from me. "How are you doing? How's Jean?"

I couldn't believe her relaxed tone. "Never mind about us, how's Laurie?"

"Och, he's fine. He's just having the Russell Turn?"

"The what?"

"The Russell Turn. Every male in Laurie's family gets this wee turn in their forties. It's a problem with a vein in their head which gives out. They go to hospital for a week or so then they are discharged and outlive all of their friends. There's nothing to worry about."

After a week in hospital, Laurie was discharged and took some time to recover. He'd been the victim of a small palsy which effectively scuppered his chances of standing for Parliament. Frustrated, he was confined to bed for much of the campaign, although he kept a weather eye on events and tried to ready himself for a contest if his health picked up. In the immediate aftermath of his illness he had a slight squint to his smile which has now, much to everyone's relief, disappeared and he's running marathons for charity and regularly walks the West Highland Way. Pam looks like she diagnosed the situation perfectly.

I immersed myself in the campaign to win the Govan nomination. Donald Dewar had called all of the candidates together in the Mitchell Theatre to meet each other as well as members of the Labour Party Executive and to have some press shots taken.

I was glad-handing around the place and was talking to Frank McAveety whom I knew from my Springburn days when, amidst the hubbub I heard Mike Watson (Lord Watson of Invergowrie) declare, "There's Ron Culley over there".

I turned and was faced with a copper-headed lady

dressed very properly who looked me up and down as if inspecting the Guards. After a hesitation she pronounced, "Aye, you'll dae for Eastwood," and taking my hand, she led me into an ante-room where she proceeded to interrogate me.

Whatever my responses to her questions, I obviously made an impression as every so often she'd turn to a colleague who happened to be passing and say, "No' bad, eh? He's from Eastwood. This is Ron Culley. He's a coming man."

Still her curiosity wasn't satisfied. "How come I don't know about you?" More and more I had to reveal my background and my intention to stand in Govan, not Eastwood, my then domicile.

It transpired that I'd just come face to face with the redoubtable Betty Cunningham, member of the Scottish Labour Party Executive, representative of the Iron and Steel Trades Confederation, soon to be Provost of East Renfrewshire Council and general force of nature. By the time the event was over Betty had pretty much adopted me and had set up meetings with me to help plan my inroads into Scottish politics. It was evident that she approved of my ambition to secure the Govan seat and equally evident that she was also taken with Ken McIntosh, another candidate who'd been spoken of as a good candidate for Eastwood.

I had no interest in any seat but Govan and found myself quickly in the columns of the local press criticising my likely opponent if selected, Nicola Sturgeon of the SNP, who had set her own cap at the Govan seat for years. It was good knockabout stuff and the papers at the time gave me good support, referring to me as the favorite candidate and extolling my virtues.

As the campaign developed I worked hard on identifying people of influence. Cross referencing individuals who might help and negotiating Trades Union endorsements. Donald Dewar came to Govan to visit Govan High School, and his office let it be known that he'd like to meet me. I turned up to answer questions from senior pupils alongside Donald and David Murray, Chairman of Rangers. Afterward I prevailed upon his media adviser, David Whitton, to let me have a few minutes with him alone. Dewar was most encouraging but was keen to see me take an interest in seats beyond Govan as well. "You have to cast your net widely in politics sometimes," he said. "As a newcomer, I'd encourage you along those lines." It was much later when I'd realise how prescient, if coded, that statement was.

Betty was simply marvelous. She put me in touch with the ISTC - the Iron and Steel Trades Confederation. I travelled to London and was interviewed by their General Secretary, Michael Leahy. He was great. Very chatty, he made it clear that I was a perfect candidate from his perspective, as the union harboured ambitions to move from a declining union base of steel workers to those who worked in any kind of business located on sites once utilised by the steel industries. He also wanted more of a community care focus and my CV was exactly what he'd been looking for. He promised me untold financial and other support if I was selected for Govan.

Buoyed by this, I used Betty's connections to sweep up eight trades union nominations from Alan Richie at UCAT (the Union of Construction and Allied Trades Technicians), John Glass of USDAW (the Union of Shop, Distributive and Allied Workers) and Bill Tynan of the AEEU (the Amalgamated Electrical and Engineering Union). They all fell to my enthusiastic charms as did the Fire Brigade Union – even although they weren't affiliated to the Labour Party. I also won the support of APEX, MSF, UCATT and, of course, ISTC. I'd done more than anyone else to win the support of organised labour and in consequence secured the endorsement of John Foster, Professor of Economics at the University of the West of Scotland, Chairman of Govan Community Council and General Secretary of the Scottish Communist Party. John was viewed as a local hero in Govan and although he always stood against Labour at election time and always won a few hundred votes, his was the biggest political influence in the constituency as he lived in Govan Road, was heavily involved in community matters and contributed to many worthy causes. Winning his nomination brought me much local credibility and local support. I was joined enthusiastically by John Currie, a young local activist and by Councillor Stevie Dornan. John Flanagan, who sought to stand for the Govan seat as a Labour Councillor also supported me.

I met productively with Jack McConnell, then a senior partner with Beattie Media in Uddingston. My approach at the time was to ask people for the opportunity of meeting with them to ask for their 'advice' but it was a thinly veiled attempt to ask for their support. Jack was very pleasant and gave me an hour and a half instead of the half hour we'd agreed. Bruce Millan, previously the Secretary of State for Scotland and a European Commissioner, was equally helpful and gave me the advice which made me realise in retrospect that I wasn't cut out to be a politician, as he encouraged me to make haste to see Mohammad Sarwar, the Govan MP, as he would have the absolute ability to determine who was selected. Bruce pointed out that 6% of Glasgow was Asian but that 60% of the party's Govan Constituency membership was Asian. Sarwar ruled. If I wanted to win the Govan seat I'd need Sarwar's support. My notes of the meeting show Bruce encouraging me to stand as he found me a principled man who had demonstrated not only a passion for the area but also an ability to deliver. He'd back me. Although, as he pointed out, things had changed now. He'd retired and was seldom asked for his views any more. "There's nothing quite so ex- as an ex-politician", he said.

I called Big Bob Wylie who knew Sarwar through media dealings he'd had with him. Bob put in a good word but it was becoming evident that Sarwar had already decided. Donald Dewar, keen to ensure some legal experience on his prospective parliamentary team, had asked Sarwar to deliver the vote for Gordon Jackson QC, one of Scotland's top lawyers. Undeterred, I pressed on and worked away at my list of contacts.

A phone call to Tommy Graham MP brought Jimmy Wray MP to my side – largely because Tommy portrayed Jimmy as not being a huge fan of Gordon Jackson. Bob Thomson, the Chairman of the branch and ex General Secretary of Unison, also flirted with my candidacy, largely, I felt, because he was a regular maverick and just wanted to be contrary.

I also met with Jim Murphy, the MP for Eastwood who was supporting Ken McIntosh in my local contest, as was I. I sensed that Jim was rather cautious about me and hesitant to help. We met for a coffee in a bar called Pitcher and Piano just across from the then new Scottish Labour Party HQ in John Smith House in West Nile Street but after a while it seemed that Jim thawed a bit; he left, after asking me to wait for a moment. He returned with a list of the Govan constituency electorate saying that this was against party rules so I had to keep them to myself. I didn't say that they were pretty freely available in Govan and that I was already in possession of a well dog-eared copy. I left him with the impression that I was grateful.

These lists were most helpful and demonstrated the truth of Bruce Millan's assertions. The branch membership was shown as follows:

Unallocated	13
Drumoyne	61
Govan	30
Ibrox	22
Pollokshields	25
Kingston	24
Maxwell Park	47
Langside	37
Pollokshaws	24
Strathbungo	51
Total	334

Most of these votes were in Sarwar's Wards where entire families of five and seven were registered to vote. There was a sense of righteous indignation at the unfairness of this, but I knew that Sarwar's bruising battle with Mike Watson some years earlier (where Mike won by one vote only to lose after a second ballot when Sarwar accused him of cheating) would have had him make sure he'd be invulnerable to any subsequent attempt to overthrow him.

I enjoyed the hustings. I'd spoken in public countless times before but had never been called upon to make a political speech. I absolutely loved it as I could give full reign to my passion and indulge myself in the clichéd presentation so beloved of politicians when they use the *'rule of three'*...."**Not** because the Nationalists are bereft of any ideas outwith independence... **not** because the Tories have no local experience....**not** because the Liberals have different policies for one constituency and others for another constituency... but because..."

I loved it and felt I was quite at home in these surroundings. There were eventually five candidates on the ballot paper; myself, the Reverend Stuart McQuarrie, Michael Kelly (the ex Lord Provost of Glasgow credited with the Miles Better campaign), Anvari Din (a local Muslim woman whom I'd known years earlier - as a pretty and westernised young lady who worked in the

Chief Executive's Department of the Regional Council -
but who was now sporting a black Burqa and refusing to
shake the hand of any man to whom she wasn't related)
and Gordon Jackson QC.

We had to take part in hustings meetings at several of
the Wards, but not all, as amalgamations took place to
hear us all speak before the big shoot-out where the vote
would take place. Michael Kelly looked drawn and tired
and was never a threat on these occasions. In contrast, I
felt that I shone. Gordon Jackson was, by all accounts the
least effective. I had assumed that as a QC, he'd be very
comfortable on his feet but the feedback from members
was always that I'd been the best speaker and that he'd
been the poorest – perhaps because he was complacent.

Our tactic was that the only way to beat Sarwar's
army of supporters was to make them think that it was
all too easy, so I took every opportunity I could to shake
my head and pronounce the demise of my campaign to
anyone from an opposing camp.

When the big night came, I ran a bus filled with
supporters from Govan. Sarwar, also the man in charge
of managing the administration of the campaign, had
decreed that the count would take place in the community
hall in East Pollokshields, his main stronghold. His
supporters would have only to make their way out of
the front door where those who backed other candidates
would have to travel some distance.

When my bus turned the corner, it looked like a
football match had just ended and the supporters were
making their way home. The streets were crowded and
most of its inhabitants were dressed in Asian attire. They
made their way into the halls and we figured the game
was well and truly up.

Betty Cunningham had insisted upon being one of
the Labour Party invigilators at the count and many

votes were discounted as Betty wasn't satisfied as to the authenticity of the voter. Next morning the media also reported that twenty two people had been turned away. I was present with Betty at the registration desk when a group of Asian members arrived and were asked their name. They produced their membership cards and pronounced, "Gordon Jackson". The clerk repeated the question explaining that it was *their* names she wanted. "Gordon Jackson," was the reply again. It was only then we realised that these members could not speak English and had been schooled to say only, "Gordon Jackson". It was obvious, though that once everyone had registered to vote and had settled down for the candidate's speeches, Sarwar's supporters dominated the place.

I was third out and gave it everything. The *'rule of three'* was employed mercilessly. I was very well received and took the questions in my stride. One problem I knew I would encounter (via some feedback I'd received that afternoon) was that a couple of members intended having a go at me, because I misrepresented the extent of my support from the unions.

I'd learned that afternoon that Stuart McQuarrie had been telling people that he had the support of the AEEU. I'd shaken the hand of Bill Tynan on this deal some time earlier and couldn't figure out what was going on, so I phoned Bill, only to be told that he'd transferred his loyalties to McQuarrie because he needed his votes in Lanarkshire where he was fighting a personal battle to become MP. I let him know I was annoyed, not just because he'd broken a promise, but because he'd been prepared to let me go into the hustings where I'd have been excoriated for claiming support I didn't have. I insisted that he fax me an apology immediately explaining the 'misunderstanding'. Bill, to be fair, was rather embarrassed about the situation and agreed so I had the piece of paper which would allow me to defend myself that night if I needed to.

It was a boisterous meeting with a lot of good humour and I *did* need to use my get-out-of jail fax from Bill Tynan. The ambush was set but it didn't work. The last person out was Gordon Jackson. All of the candidates were cooped up in an anti-room where the actual speech from the main hall couldn't be discerned. That said, you could hear applause and cheering as when I'd returned, my colleague candidates were complimentary as they'd heard what seemed to them to have been a well received speech. As we set down to await Gordon's concluding speech before the vote, gales of laughter could be heard. Resignedly, I figured Gordon must have found his pace at last and was entertaining the crowds with his patter. Nothing could have been further from the truth. One of the questions to Gordon had been seeking his views on the 'Braehead initiative', the gigantic and controversial £300 million retail development at Braehead next door to Govan. Gordon apparently had replied that as someone who earned his corn in Edinburgh, he couldn't be expected to know 'every wee project in Govan'. Great shouts of derision and much laughter!

Gordon wasn't really on the ball but then he didn't need to be with Sarwar's backing.

After the voting took place there was pandemonium. Some were observed voting twice. It took forever but when the dust had settled, Gordon had won. Only 192 of the 334 people entitled to vote had turned up. Gordon had won 105, I came a strong second with 68 and the rest split the remainder between them. There was chaos as accusations about double voting and impersonation were being hurled at the Labour officials present. Next day, five members resigned from the party and went public claiming to have seen Asian members voting several times, one claiming that he'd witnessed a member voting for Jackson five times. The papers all carried the story the following day, with former Councillor Davie Brown, Chair of the Drumoyne Branch, resigning from the Labour Party following his comment reported in the *Daily Express* where he described the proceedings as, "the most outrageous breach of electoral practice I've ever witnessed."

However, Gordon had won and as runner up, I was eventually placed fifth on the West of Scotland list. Preferment would only have been possible if the party had gone into meltdown and didn't win any seats at the polls on the first past the post basis. Laurie was also on the West of Scotland list but was placed seventh. He hadn't been able to get involved as I had, owing to the 'Russell Turn', and had had to watch frustrated from the sidelines.

Labour won the first Scottish election and two days later I received a personally signed 'Dear Ron' letter from Gordon Brown MP, the then Chancellor commiserating with me, thanking me for my efforts and encouraging me to greater heights the next time; an impressive piece of political networking.

I dined out on my political adventures for a while as I had, with Laurie become an unusual individual in that I was a serving public sector officer locally but had also rubbed shoulders with those in the political world. Benefits and some disbenefits would accrue as a consequence of this intertwining of politics and administration in later years.

I seemed to have made a mark within the party however. Many years later Jean and I had been invited to attend a dinner party at the home of Colin McClatchie, the Managing Director (Scotland) of News International, who lived in an enormous sandstone villa in Kilmacolm.

At a charity auction, Colin had bid successfully for a well known chef and his team to cook for him at home and had taken the opportunity to invite some eight couples to dine. Included among the diners were Jack McConnell, now First Minister, and his wife Brigit. Colin had arranged the seating so that couples were separated and Jean found herself seated next to Jack. During a break in proceedings, she approached me and whispered that Jack had informed her (certainly in a spirit of great generosity) that had I been elected, I'd have been in his Cabinet.

It might have reflected the amount of alcohol I'd consumed when I responded that she should return to the table and tell Jack that had I been elected in Govan, *he'd* have been in *my* Cabinet! Ah, the deleterious effects of John Barleycorn!

The single occasion I might claim to have influenced McConnell's political agenda took place in 2004. In March of that year, I had been visiting Tadhg and Mary Dennehy in Dublin at what, serendipitously, was the first weekend of the implementation of the Irish ban on smoking in pubs. It was weird for the three of us, as we visited different bars for a refreshment, to witness the absence of fugs and fags. However, we were each (as non-smokers) impressed by the initiative, although there were many who predicted the demise of the Irish drinking classes as a consequence. Fat chance! However, the Sunday papers were full of stories about the popularity of the ban and how sales and turnover had actually risen over the evening. Hardly scientific or a longitudinal study, but nevertheless, they were promising results.

Some weeks afterwards, I attended a meeting of the Glasgow Economic Forum which was attended by the estimable Andy Kerr MSP, then Minister of Finance. It was a pretty mundane agenda in which the Scottish Government took an interest. As the agenda progressed, someone asked Andy a question about the Scottish position on a smoking ban. He answered as if a civil servant, very measured, about how they might give due consideration to a partial restriction where people were eating food or where children had access ... or ...

I found myself interrupting him intemperately.

"Jesus, Andy! How about some leadership here? Scotland has perhaps the most serious health indicators in Western Europe. We're falling over in the street and you guys are spending increasing amounts of money on ever-more sophisticated technologies and medicines to combat the effects of smoking yet given this challenge, we talk of timid, partial steps that might ameliorate but will not address the matter. The Irish take a pretty bold stance on the matter. I was over there at its inception and by God, not only did it work in terms of improving the environment within pubs but you've got to figure that there are big prizes to be won in terms of health improvement and reduced mortality."

I was as surprised as anyone at my forthrightness but Andy and I were pretty friendly and it never occurred to me that my contribution might have been considered inappropriate. Andy didn't change his stance but we spoke further after the meeting where I repeated my views of the medical, social and indeed the *political* advantages of emulating the Irish. A couple of days later, Andy had spoken to the First Minister who subsequently announced that he intended visiting Dublin on a 'fact-finding' trip in May and surprised journalists upon his return by announcing that he intended banishing smoky pubs to the history books. It took until March 2006 but Parliament approved the Act. I like to think my intervention at least accelerated a popular and efficacious improvement in the health of my fellow Scots and persuaded me that politics, if brave and imaginative, *can* make a difference. Certainly, McConnell thereafter always cited the smoking ban as his greatest achievement in office – without ever mentioning the scores of other people who brought him to the decision to act.

I have to say, however, that apart from the romance of being elected to the first Scottish Parliament in three hundred years, the life of a back-bencher doesn't really appeal. And some years later, when I subsequently realised that in political life, ultimately only the First Minister would enjoy a salary (slightly) greater than mine, I was more than consoled that I found myself serving as I did in the years following the 1999 election.

11. Crossing The Clyde.

Every man is dishonest who lives upon the labour of others, no matter if he occupies a throne.
Robert Green Ingersoll

Govan Initiative continued to thrive. We'd won the Business of the Year Award in 1996 and had been nominated for the European Award the year after. We then found out that we had been voted one of the top five performing businesses in Europe, against private sector opposition, and were to be acknowledged in the ceremony in Brussels which was to be graced by King Albert of Belgium.

It had always been my practice that I would never personally receive any team-based award, always that a regular member of the staff would undertake this task on behalf of the company. Accordingly, I asked Big Davie Coutts, our very popular caretaker, to travel to Brussels with me to accept the trophy along with Jim Carruth and Julie Reilly (who had both been a driving force behind the application) and Alastair McManus, Chair of our Finance and Resources Committee. I was astonished when I received advance word from the European Quality movement in Brussels that the King's people thought that this was a snub to the King and that I should have someone senior accept the Award. I was flustered. I wasn't going to back down and accept it myself but knowing the advantages that the award would bestow upon the company, I compromised and nominated Julie, telling them that she was more senior than she was at the time.

The event itself was the largest of its kind I'd ever attended. God knows how many thousands were in attendance and the razzmatazz which was to be found outside the main auditorium had to be seen to be believed.

Hundreds of exhibitors were busy selling new software, the best consultancy or whatever. When the ceremony commenced, I took great pleasure from the sight of a pretty, debonair, youthful Julie sitting on stage with the other grizzly, male CEOs listening to the achievements of each before the winner was announced. We didn't win but when Julie was called to receive the trophy for runner up, I pushed Big Davie up the stairs to the stage and ensured that both he and Julie were photographed by the battery of cameras which greeted everyone who stepped from the podium.

But it wasn't all hard work at Govan Initiative. I was fully aware of the virtues of good networking and in 1994 came up with the idea of 'The Govan Initiative International Golf Challenge for Diddies'. This event stemmed from the basic premise that many people enjoyed a game of golf, many people resented the time it took to play it well without playing it frequently, and many people didn't play it frequently.

In consequence, I devised an event which encouraged a day's golfing for those who were crap at the game, high handicappers whose main ambition on the day was to have a few drinks and enjoy the *craic* without getting too serious about the golf. I always found it easy to persuade a private company to sponsor the day. Each year, we hosted it at Ross Priory, Strathclyde University's club for faculty and alumni which is located on the beautiful banks of Loch Lomond. I was a member there so the cost was minimal. Nine holes in the morning; lunch and a drink; nine holes in the afternoon and then dinner and prize-giving. For those who scored well, a golf ball and our derision. For those who understood the advantage of the 'leather wedge' (kicking the ball back on to the fairway at no penalty) and who were awarded the accolade of 'Best shot from the car park' or whatever, a Pringle Sweater or somesuch. No one left without a prize. Over the years the event became extremely popular and was to continue after I left. We had to run a bus from Glasgow each year. Grudging admission but little respect was given to those such as Jim Tait, Bill Perry, Bob Wylie and others whose golf was of a high standard. They would be sent from the clubhouse early to get them out of the way so the rest of us might brutalise the ball and the fairway for the rest of the day.

The event became a standard with lots of people seeking an invitation. Certain aspirants didn't get the idea of the competition being for losers and were ignored. Over the years we managed to amass a considerable number of Glasgow's elite who were dreadful at the golf. They were welcomed with open arms.

A culture grew up around the event which saw Bill Perry give a vote of thanks each year. His first, impromptu, speech was so hilarious that he was asked to do it every year … and participants, like spectators at a rock concert, would cry out for favourite jokes and then join in the acclaim for them when the punch line was repeated. Usually we tried to have the event on a Friday as there weren't too many people ready for a day's work the following morning.

One of the ideas which Jean had developed around this time was to hold our first 'Celebration of Learning'. She reasoned that every academic establishment held graduation ceremonies for successful students but that the level of achievement attained by our own people from Govan was usually much less exalted and therefore usually ignored, even though the distance they'd travelled emotionally, intellectually and in terms of their skills acquisition was certainly the equal of a middle class twenty-something getting an expected degree from within a supportive family setting.

She booked the Royal Concert Hall and we invited Elaine C. Smith, the popular Glasgow actress, singer and comedienne to say a few words. To give substance to the event and to make the link between skills acquisition and the world of work, we invited Tom O'Neill, the MD of Pilkington Electronics, the company soon to become incorporated as part of Thales, the French defence giant, which had a large plant down on the River Clyde at Govan.

I'd come to know Tom slightly over the previous two years as a major local employer. He was always generous with his time and he and I had got on well. I recalled my earlier Jesuit teaching that *'there is no such thing as good luck... only benefits which accrue when good preparation meets opportunity'*. My meeting with Tom permitted me to see the importance of this. It transpired that the one person he'd love to meet because of the esteem in which he held her... was Elaine C. Smith. It further emerged that he wasn't comfortable doing a lot of public speaking. Would I provide him with a speech? I thought little of either request and facilitated a meeting between Tom and Elaine which went very well. I wrote him a speech which he delivered well and said a few words of my own, passionately explaining the importance of improving oneself and drawing attention to the fact that usually parents sat in the auditorium applauding the efforts of their children. but that here it was the reverse with hundreds of adults receiving awards from Govan Initiative in front of their children. because they'd returned to education and had achieved something they hadn't been able to when they were younger. I spoke of the importance of 'second chances' and the inevitability that each of us would somehow fail in life ... in work ... in marriage ... in school ... but there was always another chance. The trick was to know this and to try to make sure that we didn't need a third chance.

It went down very well and the sight of the people we'd encouraged back to education being capped and gowned for the photographer so that they, too could have a photograph under the lampshade in the front room, brought a lump to my throat and still does when I think about it.

Tom was most impressed by the event and we parted on very friendly terms. It had all worked out well.

Tom had some months earlier been appointed to the Board of the Glasgow Development Agency and it seemed to me possible that I might use my relationship with Tom to influence them as they were one of our key funders and from time to time we found ourselves in a tense relationship with them. Frequently dismissive of us as a customer, they could be arrogant and unhelpful and it would be good to have a friend at court. I was therefore more than delighted when some further months on, Tom was appointed Chairman of the GDA.

Soon thereafter, Stuart Gulliver, the Chief Executive of the GDA was announced in the press as moving on to accept a post as Professor of City Studies at the University of Glasgow. Stuart and I had gone from a really strong relationship to one which seemed mutually respectful, but we had argued bitterly over some structural changes he'd announced within the city which seemed to me to exemplify the lack of empathy and consultation which so characterised his organisation.

Following another pub conversation with Laurie, it was agreed that I should write to Tom O'Neill, raise the issues which were causing the city problems by our lights and seek a meeting with him in order that Laurie, myself, and Steve Inch, then the Assistant Director of the Department of Regeneration Services in the city council, could tell him the perceptions of his organisation held by those who represented his key partners in the city. I did so, writing a substantial and considered letter in which I also took the liberty of offering a few names of people who would bring new energy and direction to the efforts of the GDA, were they to be appointed by Tom as the new Chief Executive.

Tom graciously accepted my invitation to meet and we lunched in Ibrox Stadium, with me kidding him on that he'd get food poisoning because somehow the chef would know that he was a mad-keen Celtic fan. The lunch seemed to be successful, as the three of us spoke honestly and not a little stridently about the need for change. I repeated the names I'd mentioned in my letter to him and Laurie and Steve joined in on descant. Afterwards we walked him to his car and bid him farewell. As we went our separate ways, Laurie and Steve drove away and I bid farewell to all three. Tom lingered until they had left the car park, approached my own car and asked whether I'd given thought myself to becoming the next Chief Executive of the GDA. I blustered something about Tom misunderstanding the purpose of my intervention. It was quite genuinely about trying to help fix things for the future. Tom said, "I've been tasked by the Board to find a new Chief Executive, and we'll go through the public process all right, but I'm more likely to get the guy I want if I just encourage his application in person."

He spoke of the esteem he'd built up for my work with the Initiative and how impressed he'd been with my speech in the Royal Concert Hall. I repeated my position and told him how happy I was at Govan. Only a few weeks before, my Board had given me a much appreciated five thousand pounds bonus, asked me if I wanted to spend a couple of weeks on a study tour and had made it quite clear that they felt indebted to me. Their affection was reciprocated by me and I had intended to work with the people of Govan and the south west of Glasgow until I retired some ten or fifteen years in the future.

Tom asked me if I'd think about it and have lunch with him again the following week. I agreed on the basis that he'd permit me to advance my case for the reform of his organisation one more time but that I couldn't see me betraying the trust of my Chairman and his Board.

A long week followed. I told Jean but no one else. Jean did what I guess many others would have done; she guided me to do what I thought was right and not to take account of any financial incentives. Happiness and contentment meant more. We had a young family and she didn't want me reverting to the workaholic tendencies that were always so close to the surface.

I met Tom again as agreed and entered the restaurant in Ibrox Stadium, persuaded that I was right and determined to reject his offer. I honestly felt that others would be able to make a more effective contribution than me; Laurie and Steve to start with. I told him that, and he agreed the merits of their potential candidacy, but he'd decided he wanted me.

I felt I couldn't leave Govan Initiative at an important time in its development. I told him that too. I told him my assessment of what needed to change. Tom listened intently and when I finished my carefully rehearsed speech, responded by telling me that every time I explained why it shouldn't be my name in the frame, he was ever more convinced that it should be. He told me that I'd be able to address my socio-economic agenda much more effectively as CEO of the GDA and that he saw me as precisely the kind of guy he was looking for as the top man in the organisation. He wanted a communicator, someone who saw the need for improvements in the quality of the products it delivered and who had a proven track record in delivering change, someone who was impassioned about the broad sweep of economic development and wasn't tied to only skills, physical development or business growth; *all* of the ingredients of economic development were needed if Glasgow was to realise its potential. He also liked my sense of humour and was convinced that his Board would love me. I was very flattered, as would be anyone, I guess, but Tom was clearly well seasoned in negotiation skills and homed in on perhaps my major issue; my love of Govan Initiative and the feeling that I'd be letting down my Chairman, John McLaughlin.

"I tell you what, Ron. Why don't you let me speak with John McLaughlin and if he's prepared to let your name go forward, why don't you give it a whirl?" He went on to tell me that he couldn't guarantee the post as it was a public appointment and he'd have to work within the protocols set down. He just wanted me to know that I'd have his full support but that there would be others who would hold strong – and possibly contrary views. There would be internal candidates, some of them very strong - and other external candidates would come out of the woodwork. I felt myself being drawn into Tom's design and speculated that Gordon Kennedy would be the front runner. Gordon was effectively deputy to Stuart Gulliver, and was much better known than Stuart within the various partnerships across the city. He was urbane and witty and extremely bright. Tom agreed, but said that he wanted an external candidate to shake the place up. I suggested that if Gordon felt cheated of his rightful claim he might not support the eventual incumbent. Tom was much more upbeat about Gordon's attitude and confessed that he'd already spoken to him, guiding him that he shouldn't apply for the post.

Defeated but flattered, I agreed, with now more than a hint of excitement that I'd decided to throw my hat into the ring. If Tom squared things with John at least I was on a shot to nothing. Like my recent parliamentary adventure, if I failed I always had a job that I loved and in which role I was recognised as being strong.

Later that afternoon, John McLaughlin announced himself as usual in the outer office by the accompanying gales of laughter from everyone in his presence as he swept into my office. He closed the door and his smile faded as he told me that Tom O'Neill had just been on the phone so he'd come up straight away. He and I had a somewhat dewy-eyed conversation about Tom's approach, but John was resolute that it was best for Glasgow if I applied for the job. He also told me that he hoped that I didn't get it; half in fun but wholly in earnest, I sensed.

When I got home and told Jean she was rather surprised as I'd left that morning quite determined to resist the blandishments and cajolery I knew in advance I'd receive from Tom. She figured that my usual stubbornness would win the day!

As ever when I had a project on, I threw myself wholesale into it. One of my early difficulties was that Laurie had also determined to throw his hat into the ring. Tom had asked me to keep our conversations confidential but I was genuinely ambivalent about all of this as Laurie is a competitive individual and a great friend who would clearly merit a place on the short leet. Had I told him of my conversation with Tom, he might have taken the view (had he been cynical, which assuredly, he is not) that I was merely trying to manoeuvre him out of contention. With hindsight, I suspect he'd have believed me but I didn't want to bruise our relationship so we both set our cap at the CEO post. Laurie got through to the penultimate round of interviews, so underlining his abilities but ultimately he fell as a consequence of my earlier concordat with the Chairman.

Tom had agreed that I could speak with Gordon Kennedy as he'd counsel him in advance that I was his favoured candidate and ask if he would provide me with background information about the work involved that might help me in interview. I knew Stuart Patrick much better, as I'd worked with him in Govan and believed him to have a good relationship with Gordon so phoned him up first and he both confirmed his relationship with Gordon and his excitement at my candidature. We all three agreed to meet.

We met in the Ubiquitous Chip restaurant in Ashton Lane in the West End, the part of the city in which both Gordon and Stuart lived. Both were most helpful and friendly. Gordon pointed out that the parent organisation had been renamed Scottish Enterprise and that the Glasgow Development Agency was also now renamed Scottish Enterprise *Glasgow* following the appointment of Robert Crawford as Chief Executive of SE only a couple of weeks before. This early centralisation would, Gordon speculated, result in Crawford's intense interest in the post as it would be one of the key roles within his new responsibility. He would be aware that, as Chief Executive of the parent organisation, he had the power of veto over the appointment and Gordon speculated that a post of this significance would almost certainly attract Crawford's personal intervention. He also speculated that I could expect Robert to field the 'company candidate' and that he would doubtless lean on Tom to deliver the Scottish Enterprise man. I wouldn't have it easy.

The press took an interest in speculating who might succeed the throne and my name was cited as an interesting external candidate although initially it was dismissed on the basis that I was an external candidate and no one had ever been appointed from outwith the organisation directly to Chief Executive of an Enterprise Company before.

I took distinct pleasure over this period as Gordon and Stuart kept me up to date on the rumours which were circulating within the building. My candidacy was being rejected out of hand by those who felt that I might be a threat to their continued presence with SEG. I was viewed as a maverick and the general view was that there was no way the company would risk such an adventurous (or insane) appointment.

Jean and I took a holiday over the summer and booked a lovely apartment in a complex near Marbella in Spain. One morning, I was awoken by my mobile phone ringing. It was one of my Assistant Chief Executives, Damien Yeates.

"Hi, Ron. Are you enjoying the break?"

"I was till you woke me up."

"Your photograph is on the front page of the *Daily Record* today… large as life."

"Aye, right!"

Damien began to talk. While I genuinely thought he was taking the mick, the fact that his sentences were well constructed (as far as the *Daily Record* would allow) began to make me feel uncomfortable.

" 'Two council managers have pocketed almost £100,000 in redundancy payments while still working full time for public bodies in Glasgow … it has also emerged that Ron Culley could be set for another new job' "….

"What the … !"

"Big article, Ron. Front page. Full story page five!"

Damien then read the story to me. Some months earlier, the cash-strapped city council had decided to lay off staff and having undertaken due process, had decided that a number of staff who had been seconded to other organisations at arms-length from the Council as Laurie and I had been should be made redundant. Both Laurie and I resisted this fiercely, as we calculated that this would materially affect our pension, and we had a number of meetings with the Chief Executive of the Council as well as the Leader of the Council, Frank McAveety, in order to argue for our retention.

Tempers had flared at the meeting with Frank in the imposing office of the Leader of the Council as he sat Laurie and I down and listened as his Deputy Head of HR explained why the decision would not be rescinded. I caught Frank disinterestedly reading his mail during this exchange and rebuked him intemperately, saying he should be 'taking this fucking seriously'. However, it was no use and a few weeks later, Laurie and I were summoned to the office of the then Director of Regeneration Services, Roger McConnell where I was handed my redundancy notice along with a cheque for £36,000. Roger was civil enough and expressed the expectation that we'd find ourselves continuing our relationship in some capacity or other.

Govan Initiative, as an independent company continued me in employment with immediate effect, even arranging that I start on the Saturday as opposed to the Monday in order to ensure no problems with pensions (Govan Initiative was also an 'admitted body' to the Strathclyde Pension Fund which allowed me to continue my pension arrangements.) Effectively, there was no change in my conditions of employment other than the fact that the supposedly cash-strapped council had had to shell out thirty-six grand to me and a similar amount to Laurie despite us pointing out to them over a series of meetings that in practical terms their redundancies changed nothing other than them getting our names off their books.

The article was therefore accurate other than they ascribed a selfish motivation to Laurie and I (initially Laurie was a 'mystery employee' until he outed himself to the Herald the next day in a show of solidarity) and got the figures wrong. I hired a media lawyer and eventually managed to get a small paragraph in the *Record* apologising for the various inaccuracies in the article. Small comfort, however, as it was completely dwarfed by the original article which also had had the effect of prompting similar articles in all of the other papers.

I later discovered when I returned from holiday that the media had been camped on my front door for a couple of days but had given up when they eventually believed Damien's protestations that I was indeed on a pre-planned family holiday. Later again when in post at SEG, I read a personal note in my file from Robert Crawford to the effect that 'Ron must have some real enemies out there!

Scottish Enterprise undertook their duties regarding the appointment of a successor Chief Executive with a clandestine secrecy that would have done justice to MI5. I was written to and asked to keep matters confidential and invited to meet Debbie Mackie, then Deputy Head of HR, in Waterstone's Bookshop in Sauchiehall Street for a coffee, whereupon I'd be delivered of a folder containing a battery of psychometric tests which I'd have to take home and complete. I didn't know Debbie and phoned Stuart Patrick for a description so I could identify her.

"Eh …. she's trim ..." Given that that was usually the description that Para Handy offered of his Clyde puffer, the 'Vital Spark', I wasn't confident that I'd recognise her but we met and Debbie conducted herself like the professional she was. And trim she was too.

Having returned the psychometric tests, I attended for interview in the Boardroom of Tom's company, Thales International. There were five of us interviewed. Laurie had thrown his hat into the ring and was selected as a finalist, as was Bill Morton who had already been a Chief Executive with SE in Forth Valley based in Stirling. Some months prior to the interviews, Bill had taken a high profile secondment from SE and was never off TV as Chief Executive of the Scottish Qualifications Authority when they experienced a crisis, and their then Minister,

Jack McConnell, secured the resignation of the existing CEO. Bob Downes, the Scottish Director of BT was also in the frame but I'd been earlier guided by Gordon and Stuart that he'd probably pull out at the last minute and they were accurate in their appraisal. One other external candidate from the private sector made up the final five.

The interview lasted an hour and was robust. I'd prepared thoroughly and thought I'd done well. I was confident and hit every question I was asked over the boundary wall.

A week later, I received a letter saying I'd made it to the final interview, again at Thales but that this time the panel would be added to by the new CEO of Scottish Enterprise, Robert Crawford.

Again I prepared, and the interview lasted substantially over an hour, so it was just as well. I'd been warned in advance by Gordon that Robert would be aggressive and forceful in interview. He was but he was also pretty unsophisticated.

"If I gave you £10 million, would you want to spend it on businesses developing new technology or on the shipyards?"

"The days of commercial shipbuilding are over. We have to focus upon future markets, not sunset ones."

The fact that I actually believed in investment in both industries was neither here nor there but it seemed a ham-fisted attempt to 'out' me as a Luddite. Again my performance gathered strength as I grew in confidence. And again I felt that it would be difficult for the panel not to score me very highly indeed. But higher than the other candidate, Bill Morton?

Worryingly, some three weeks passed before I heard anything from Scottish Enterprise Glasgow. Eventually Tom phoned me.

"We have a wee problem, Ron."

"Really?"

"For the second time, you were given the unanimous vote at the interview, including Robert Crawford, but Robert has had further thoughts. He's aware that he has the power of veto over the appointment of all CEOs and he's used it. I've now come to an agreement that I will interview three other candidates of his choosing and if one of them is better than you, I'll recommend his appointment. I'm seeing them over the next week and I'll call you after that."

I was rather put out. Changing the rules mid-way through the process? However, I was not uncomfortable continuing my work at Govan and thought I hadn't let anyone down.

Tom phoned back a week later as he had promised.

"Well, now", he said. "I have to tell you that one of the candidates was, in my view, a more experienced, better, more rounded candidate than you. I recommended him to Robert who was, I have to tell you, delighted as I imagined that he anticipated that I would try to stitch him up."

"Ach well, Tom, it looks like I hit the woodwork," I said.

"Not really. The guy was earning more in the private sector than Robert Crawford (who was then the UK's highest paid public servant) and he baulked at paying someone more than he earned himself. He wouldn't agree my recommendation so you seem to be the best we've got. Congratulations! You're the new Chief Executive."

I was delighted and realised that Tom had merely taken his time to out-manoeuvre Robert in a way that I would see him do many times again in the future. Tom was delighted at the appointment and I was told to await contact from SEG.

A further period of a couple of weeks passed and I received a phone call from Jim McGowan, Head of HR, who asked me to meet him and Debbie in a dark and gloomy corner of an Italian restaurant, Fratelli Sarti's in Wellington Street. They both congratulated me and Jim took some pleasure in telling me that he'd been delighted at how Robert Crawford had been out-manoeuvred. They went through all of the procedures and everything was fine other than the fact that the contract which had been prepared by Robert Crawford's HR people showed me as being appointed as Chief Executive of Scottish Enterprise *Grampian*; not Glasgow .... I had some fun at Jim's expense suggesting that perhaps Robert still hadn't given up on his objective of not appointing me to Glasgow. We fixed the detail and on Monday 18th of September, in the year of our lord 2000, I came up in the lift from the basement car park at 6.45 am and took my seat at my desk before anyone else arrived. I turned on my computer and began my work as the new CEO of Scottish Enterprise Glasgow by writing a brief note to Robert Crawford announcing my arrival and intimating my hope that we'd work well together.

12. Prudence And Adventure

Do not fear the winds of adversity. Remember; a kite rises against the wind rather than with it.
Chinese Proverb.

In St Enoch's Square in Glasgow, two statues, beautifully carved in granite, stand tall above the entrance to a building that once housed a branch of Royal Bank of Scotland. Called Prudence and Adventure, I didn't know it at the time but they would characterise my term of office in Scottish Enterprise under Robert Crawford.

In the beginning Robert, to my face at least, was very encouraging but that didn't last long. He had been planning a Business Transformation exercise on which he spent many millions of pounds, largely in consultants' contracts with his previous firm, Ernst and Young, and he and I found ourselves early at odds with one another in respect of most of the implications of this initiative.

My office, on the fourth floor, of Atrium Court, 50 Waterloo Street, was very swish. It was substantial and kitted out in very trendy furnishing with subtle lighting and modern art on the walls. I set to work but I noticed that the pictures were rather unsettling. The wife of my predecessor, Stuart Gulliver, was an artist and the pictures hanging on the wall were all black and white etchings of distressed women... all very depressing. The only things I changed in the office were those pictures which I replaced with large and interesting photographs of Glasgow, the city I loved.

Everyone was very nice to me when they arrived at 9.00, all equally impressed, if unsettled, that I was in so early, some two hours before them. Out of devilment, the first information I asked for was a list of companies that had received a MAP (Manufacturing Assistance Programme) grant which was much sought after because it was just that … a grant of considerable substance which, it was alleged, was only being given out to 'trendy' companies. I discovered that the funds had been expended for the next four years in advance. This proved a problem as companies that had received a letter of confirmation from us that they would receive a sum of, say £150,000 three years in the future, had gone straight to the bank and cashed it in immediately against this promissory note. I stopped the practice immediately and instigated an appraisal of the efficacy of the scheme.

The other question I asked was for a note of all foreign travel over the past four years. One finding was that there was not one single example of any of my colleagues going abroad to undertake business or to attend a conference on their own. I wrote an e-mail asking whether this was so the second person was travelling *'just to haud the ladder?'* and informed my new colleagues that in the future I would sign off all requests myself and there had better be good reason for more than one person to attend. It reduced foreign trips substantially and increasing numbers of staff discovered that they didn't need an escort in order to learn.

After a few days of meeting and greeting my new colleagues, I made a surprisingly confident speech to all of the staff and received an equally surprising thunderous applause in response. I spoke of my values, my style of leadership; the *servant leader* whose job is to serve the staff, not the other way around; I killed rumours that I'd heard … I was a hard man; I ate babies; I was going to fire all the senior staff and bring in my own people … I told them that we could achieve great things but that we'd do this together … there would be no night of the long knives.

That said, I'd decided early on that one of my most senior staff had to go. I brought him into my office a few days after I started and told him that he'd be leaving with immediate effect. He left on the Friday and I received huge plaudits (unexpectedly) from senior colleagues at Scottish Enterprise National who, over several years it turned out, hadn't managed to find a way to say goodbye to him.

But I stood by my other senior colleagues whom I decided were more than capable of supporting me in my change agenda. Gordon Kennedy, my Deputy, was an intellectual powerhouse, a career economic development professional who knew where all the bodies were buried; Stuart Patrick, my friend and *compadre* who was just the best strategist on the planet; Peter Reilly, who was possessed of the cynical eyes of a man informed by earlier bitter experience but whose conservatism was useful in counterbalancing my exuberance; Debbie Mackie, a wonderfully talented young lady, then of Human Resources (Jim McGowan having retired) but soon promoted to support Stuart and Stephanie Young who was a most able skills and learning professional.

I loved working in Scottish Enterprise Glasgow. I really felt we were making a difference to the city's economic performance. Soon we built a great camaraderie within the senior staff team. However, my relationship with Robert Crawford was souring. I was most unimpressed by the style of leadership he displayed … *'do as I say'*… and felt completely alienated from his policies. But fortunately pretty much the entire Executive Team, many of the Glasgow Board and most of our staff all felt the same way so over the six years of my tenure there tended to be a 'Fortress Glasgow' mentality as we sought (with decent success) to out-manoeuvre headquarters.

Robert was besotted by the notion of 'Business Transformation', in itself a completely sound idea. The idea of modernising the organisation, of doing things faster, more intelligently, was a no-brainer. However,

Robert was a centraliser and from the outset fashioned the notion that Business Transformation was essential or we'd be closed down by the powers that be. "I know things you don't know", he'd say, menacingly. "We have no friends out there. We deliver on this or they'll close us."

Well, I happened to know *exactly* what they thought of Scottish Enterprise out there and it wasn't much. Not that they'd close us or bruise us …. they just didn't think much *about* us. Politically, the big hitters were Health, Education and the criminal justice system. I'd seen the '*they're all out to get us*' approach done by a professional, Alex Ferguson, and Robert just irritated me when he started these rants. Politically, enterprise and the economy were essentially factors more likely to be influenced by the levers pulled in Westminster by Gordon Brown as the then Chancellor of the Exchequer.

Robert compounded the felony in my book by instilling an atmosphere of, '*if you're not with me; you're against me*'. Perhaps unsurprisingly, almost to a man and to a woman, his staff at headquarters bought the line he was promoting. There was no dissent. There were no alternatives. There was no pause for thought. The organisation became one in which relatively inexperienced people at Scottish Enterprise National, because they bought the party line, found themselves in positions of real authority as Robert had tasked them with something or other. Meetings of headquarters' staff became feeding frenzies of self interest as people sought to out-do one another in advancing the latest cause.

That approach worked to consolidate Robert's grip on the organisation but it failed dismally in the last outpost; Glasgow.

Robert recognised this fact by trying ever harder both simultaneously to charm me and bully me. Once when I was on a ten day period of study at Harvard University in Boston, Robert phoned me and threatened to fire me because I should have known that one of his own Board meetings fell on a Friday of my stay and that he might have wanted to call on me to attend. The fact that he didn't, and the fact that I was able to deal with his bluster, left me studying in Harvard. I spoke with him upon my return and pointed out that there had been no requests *ever* made of me to attend his Board. Nothing in writing suggesting that I should do so. No protocols ... no custom and practice …. nothing. I told him I'd failed my 'O' Level telepathy and so couldn't have read his mind on this one. Robert took great umbrage at my 'insolent' approach but said he'd not take the matter further. He'd make a personal note of my actions …. It still confuses me objectively that he'd make such a song and dance about this. However, I figured that the judo principle; using his own power against him, might actually work in my favour. If matters ever required to come to a legal resolution, his own notes might well count against him.

Shortly after the commencement of my tenure, I appointed my Senior Director of Business Growth, the estimable Gordon Maclennan who, at that time, was Chief Executive of Business Ventures in Glasgow. Gordon was a worldly-wise businessman with a background in HR and engineering. What attracted me to him first of all, however, was his outgoing personality. He was great fun and wasn't slow to express his point of view on things, no matter how controversial.

Shortly after his arrival he attended a formal dinner representing the company and vouchsafed to his dinner companions his opinion that while the new headquarters of Scottish Enterprise National on Atlantic Quay were very modern and most salubrious, he nevertheless viewed the glazed lifts as ill-advised as they demonstrated to any departing visitors that 'the place was like the *Marie Celeste* after four o'clock', clearly implying that the staff at HQ weren't exactly working under excessive pressure.

The following morning, I received an early call from Robert Crawford who, true to form, advised me that he'd heard a report of this conversation and, if true, he intended to fire Gordon Maclennan for betraying the good name of SEN. I listened to his outburst and said, "Like you say, Robert...*if it's true*. Let me raise this directly with Gordon and I'll call you right back."

I pondered the situation for a moment and went downstairs to Gordon's office where, true to form, he was already hard at work.

"Morning, Ron," said Gordon.

"Never mind, 'good morning', Gordon. I'm going to ask you a question and before you say anything, your reply is that *if* HQ was empty at close of play it would look like the *Marie Celeste* because the lifts are glazed and permit an open view of each floor as they descend."

"Eh?" said Gordon.

I explained Crawford's intemperate phone call and asked who had been his dinner companions the previous evening. One, directly across from him had been a personal friend of Crawford, an ex-colleague and key business leader in the telecoms industry. I told Gordon to leave it with me.

I returned to my office, phoned Robert's secretary and arranged to see him straight away. He sat at his open-plan desk anticipating, I'm sure, an act of revenge upon a disbeliever. I reported my conversation with Gordon, making sure I emphasised the important word *if*!

"Looks like a simple misunderstanding, Robert. What with all the general hubbub at the dinner table. An easy mistake to make."

Clearly angry, his face closed and his hands made small fists before he grudgingly acknowledged the inherent fairness in letting the matter drop. I enjoyed that transaction.

He also threatened to fire me when I was in Manchester on holiday visiting my son Campbell, who had just moved flat as he was working down there for a period. While I was 200 miles away being shown round Campbell's new home, David Whitton, my hugely experienced media adviser (now elected to the Scottish Parliament) had penned an excellent short article for the *Evening Times* in my name but without my knowledge; a common event, such was the mutual level of trust and empathy we enjoyed. It spoke of the transformation we intended seeing in our ability to recruit Glaswegians to help build the city of the future by investing in construction skills. It was a great piece. Robert took huge exception to the article and phoned me up and told me that he'd just found out that the words had been written by David .... but if it *had* been me who'd written them, he'd have fired me. I laughed out loud at his nonsense and made banter with him along the lines of 'Aye, if it had been me who'd shot JFK, you could have probably have had me jailed ... if it had been me who'd .... etc etc. He was furious at my laughter and I had to listen to a homily about how I may not respect him but I should respect the office he represented. It was all just such a waste of energy. I wanted to get on with things in Glasgow.

And get on, we did. Each year we turned in the best results in the Network ... training programmes completed, jobs created, new business grown from scratch, shipyard jobs safeguarded, excellence programmes imbued within larger organisations, new physical developments undertaken; all performances Robert found hard to swallow, so he banned publication of all results that showed the relative performances of Local Enterprise Companies as we were invariably top of the pops.

But somehow these results still found their way into the press. We brought in our budget each year within 1%

of resources made available to us. We set up the biggest construction skills training scheme in the United Kingdom. I'd been asked by the Minister, Wendy Alexander, to chair a Task Force on Shipbuilding on the River Clyde. Stuart Patrick did all the heavy lifting but we brought forth a strategy that saw an increase in employment in the yards an an order book that shipbuilding giants like Jimmy Reid could only have dreamed of in his heyday. We started to look at the development of the Clyde Waterfront as the largest regeneration project ever undertaken by Glasgow, building the Squinty Bridge in the process. We brought the OECD (the Organisation for Economic Co-operation and Development) to Glasgow for a world conference on city regeneration. They were so impressed about what was going on that we had great press coverage and received a terrific double whammy when the subsequent book they published on the Glasgow success story, *Urban Renaissance: Glasgow*, hit the bookshops.

One aspect of the development of the River Clyde of which I'm quietly proud was the successful 're-titling' of The Clyde Arc as it was christened, to the more familiar 'Squinty Bridge'. When initially we presented our plans for public comment, we received an objection from the Royal Incorporation of Architects in Scotland who argued that the bridge should cross the River Clyde at right angles rather than fit with the roads configuration as we'd planned it. We began to describe it internally as 'squinty' and I took to using thus appellation as frequently as possible calculating that affectionate nicknames might bring public support much in the way Dubliners had taken to their works of public art by referring to them variously as 'The Stiletto in the Ghetto' (The Spire on O'Connell Street), 'The Tart with the Cart' (Molly Malone in Grafton Street), and 'The Dick with the Stick', (James Joyce, Earl Street).

In 2004 we entered Glasgow in the New York hosted 'Intelligent Community Award' along with over 200 city regions throughout the world. Nova Scotia, the State of Victoria in Australia, a Japanese city, a Korean city, Spokane in the US of A and ourselves competed for the final accolade and we won it. My Deputy, Gordon Kennedy, travelled to New York to collect the trophy as testimony to the hard work we'd all put in to make Glasgow a really smart city.

We took the seventeen organisations serving Glasgow's businesses and, working alongside them, reduced this to one single point of contact, doubled the number of companies being started each year in the city and halved the costs of doing this. The lesson about how change programmes might be undertaken collaboratively and without massive expenditure seemed lost on Robert Crawford.

Initially, Robert had a right-hand man, Alan Sim, the Director of Operations who was responsible for the twelve Local Enterprise Companies. I thought he was an okay guy but he was a major purveyor of the SE jargon that I came to despise, as it merely served to limit communication rather than clarify its transmission. I first met him at a black tie do at the Hilton Hotel on the Friday evening prior to my Monday start with SEG. We chatted amiably enough and he asked me what my priorities were when I took office on the following Monday. I wandered through a few matters I wanted to deal with early on and then mentioned my passion for excellence.

"I'm intent upon taking SEG on an excellence journey, Alan", I said. "I've been impressed by the way in which results improve if only an organisation focuses upon notions of continuous improvement, Lean Management Thinking… that kind of thing."

Alan was less enthusiastic. "I'd park that, Ron. We had a look at it a while back but couldn't see the value."

"Well, I'm convinced of the merits of continuous improvement and we'll be investing in it big time come Monday," I responded.

I didn't realise it at the time but this figment of our conversation, was subsequently relayed to Robert Crawford as, "I think Culley's going to be trouble" and, in my view was occasioned by two characteristics of SE life that subsequently shaped my relationship with the organisation. The first was my direct challenge. Over the piece, I found that the organisation did not know how to deal with a direct challenge ... someone just saying, "No". The second, perhaps more a manifestation of the first, was that they used jargon to conceal rather than to reveal the meaning of their communication. I may well have thought twice about my response if Alan had simply said, "I don't want you to do that"... (but then again?) ... but because he used the much lighter expression, "park it", I was able to respond more innocently, more authentically and more directly.

At a meeting, of which there were many, wherever I or anyone else for that matter raised a matter that was awkward but necessary to discuss, it could be guaranteed that someone would smile conspiratorially and say; "Don't let's *go* there" with the emphasis on the word "go". Its meaning was ... "*We all agree that this is an uncomfortable issue but let's not deal with it right now.*"

Alan Sim seemed to find dealing with myself and Glasgow hard work but never revealed his concerns, at least to me. At a meeting of Local Enterprise Company Board Chairmen (for they were all men at the time), Alan somewhat dramatically produced a piece of paper and insisted that he needed the Chairs to sign it demonstrating that he had authority over the Chief Executives of their Local Enterprise Companies. My own Chairman, Tom O'Neill, who was in attendance, told me afterwards that as far as he was concerned, the fact that Alan had felt that he had to take this step was enough to convince him that he wasn't up to the job and told Robert this.

Whether under instruction from his boss, Robert Crawford, or whether it was an approach he'd decided upon himself, Alan Sim clearly decided to bring Glasgow in general and me in particular to heel. To be honest, his imprecations were never close to being troublesome and I could sense his frustrations in never being close to landing a blow. His last telephone conversation with me was designed to break up my management team by removing my deputy. Foot and mouth disease had gripped the nation, no stocks were being moved and tons of cattle were being burned in funeral pyres, the smoke reaching skywards like so many rural, funereal smokestacks.

"Sorry about this, Ron, but I need to take Gordon Kennedy away from you and move him to Dumfries, to put him in charge of the business loans and grants schemes we're putting in place for the farming community in Dumfries and Galloway. Needs must, I'm afraid."

I could hear the smugness in his voice as he calculated that I wouldn't be able to resist the high profile request, due to its obvious reasonableness and practicality.

I could also hear the grating of his teeth when I drew his attention to the fact that Gordon didn't have a driving licence (He did, but hadn't been behind a wheel since he passed in his teens). "I *suppose* he could walk ... but then again, I suppose we'd look pretty stupid if a farmer was delayed in securing a payment because Gordon had developed blisters."

Some weeks later it was announced that Alan would be moving on. He was to be replaced by *three* people, each of whom would deal with four of the twelve LECs in Scotland. They would answer directly to Robert and

285

would be referred to as Senior Operational Directors. Too late they saw the acronym and changed it to Senior Directors (Operations). Too late. They were *SODs* and that was that.

After a meeting one day, John Phillips, the organisation's Head of Human Resources and the guy who acted for Robert in terms of appointments and discipline (although in my six years at Scottish Enterprise, I was never told of anyone who had been fired!) spoke to me and told me that because of the excellent results we'd been experiencing, Robert had asked him to speak to me and have me apply for one of the three SOD vacancies then available. I immediately figured that this was a crass attempt to lure me away from my fiefdom in Glasgow, where not only my passions lay, but also where I had the protection of my Board, and told John rather intemperately to tell Robert to 'stick the job up his arse!' I still blush in retrospect at the way I behaved sometimes and muse only that it was a reflection of the stresses I felt under over that period. Also, I accept that I can be a really pugnacious individual at times. I fully expect that John would have quoted me directly in his feedback to Robert and in a manner that would not have been designed to improve relationships between us.

The SOD eventually appointed in the west was big Ed Gillespie. Ed was approaching sixty years of age, at least six feet four inches tall and about the same wide. An enormous, bearded, bear of a man. He previously performed my CEO role in the Grampian Local Enterprise Company (LEC) based in Aberdeen but I didn't really know him. As a gesture of goodwill, I phoned him up, congratulated him and invited him for lunch …. Ed never refused a bite to eat.

We met at Est Est Est, a restaurant in Bothwell Street and Ed had a pizza. I've never seen a messier eater in all my life. He'd have been as well taking the dish in his hands and just wiping the contents on his tie before shovelling it into his mouth. More than once I reflected that were he to boil his tie in a pot it would have made a tasty bowl of soup. But he was a convivial soul and was, at least on this occasion, direct.

With a smile on his face and a quarter slice of pizza in his mouth he said, "Obbas senmi heerti putihemmms onya mmmcunahg"

"Eh?" I said.

Ed finished chewing. "Robert's sent me here to put the hems on you, Mr Culley. I believe he views you as something of a subversive!"

I smiled back, leaned over the table and placed my hand on Ed's bear-like forearm. "Just you give it your best shot, Ed."

He laughed uproariously and proceeded to tell me how Robert couldn't stand me … that Glasgow was the last outpost of dissent …. that I had to be cut down to size …. that Robert was pissed off at my political connections, my blind allegiance to Glasgow, but that none of these would save me … Robert was determined etc. etc.

Ed made it clear that Robert had it in for me and that he, Ed, was to be the author of my downfall. That said, he also made it clear that he (Ed) agreed with my overall dissent, told me that I was the only light relief he found at Network meetings and that he was thoroughly impressed by the results that I and Glasgow were producing.

"Sounds to me like you're the one who's subversive, Ed!"

Over the years, Ed and I got on surprisingly well although he was the champion of champions when it came to the use of jargon. Problems were always *'challenges'* and *'don't go theres'* and *'park its'* fell from his lips like pieces of pizza. Each year, although he grumbled as if to prepare his ground for the inevitable subsequent conversation with Robert as to why he was celebrating my successes rather than bringing me down, he gave me either "Very Good" or "Exceptional" gradings (the very top gradings) and invariably took my side of the argument. He left the organisation a couple of years later. I was sad to see him go but again got on well with his replacement, Bill Morton, who was a more experienced operator, more sophisticated, and the man I'd beaten in the final interview for the Glasgow job. He too, continued the practise of giving me top notch appraisals and the gradings and performance related pay increments to match, a not inconsiderable sum at my salary.

During Robert's tenure, I noticed on his electronic diary that he'd meet regularly with senior figures from the SNP, the political party with whom as a young man he'd been a full-time researcher. He insisted he'd no current political affiliations but his diary didn't show meetings with politicians from any other party; just the SNP. (Much later, in 2008, Robert was revealed as the prospective Westminster parliamentary candidate for Cunninghame South for the SNP, a candidacy from which he withdrew after a year and before any election took place.)

Around this time, relationships between Scottish Enterprise Glasgow and Scottish Enterprise National deteriorated. A lot of water has flown under the bridge since then but the stupendous errors of judgement being made in the name of progress, the payments of many millions of pounds being doled out to Crawford's erstwhile employers, Ernst and Young, the impact of cuts in frontline services, the foolishly ambitious projects that we knew the private sector felt were anti-competitive, all found their way onto the front pages of the Scottish broadsheets and were to be discussed regularly on television of an evening.

Within Scottish Enterprise, I was regarded with some significant suspicion. My general maverick, iconoclastic demeanour, my smart-arsed comments during Scottish Enterprise National meetings, my presumed relationship with Scottish Labour Cabinet members (always presumed much more substantial than in reality, although I never bothered to correct that impression) all gave rise to the view that I was the one responsible for the grief being suffered by SE in the media. That said, no one ever said it to my face or sought disambiguation perhaps because I was still one of the big beasts within the company and people still had a sense of hierarchy but the feedback from other friends within the organisation left me in no doubt that there was very much a collective view that I was a burr under the saddle. Even the media speculated on my role here, imagining that the Chief Executive of Scottish Enterprise Glasgow had quietly slipped a horseshoe into his boxing glove.

That said, many others made it clear that they were delighted that these various nonsenses were being given the oxygen of publicity but no one else in Robert's national leadership team was taking any responsibility for airing the views that I was during meetings, or in opposing the reprioritisation of projects away from the ordinary people and businesses of Scotland to the larger multinationals that I and others felt were better able to look after their own economic destiny.

Politically, Robert Crawford made a bad error after about three years in post. He enjoyed a really good relationship with the Minister for Enterprise, Transport and Lifelong Learning, Wendy Alexander MSP. They spoke regularly each day by telephone and their mutual admiration was palpable. However, I also enjoyed a good relationship with Wendy, and sometimes when we spoke together she'd utter the wish that Robert and I could get on better. I'd recite the impacts of his policies in Glasgow and she'd agree politically, but tended to square the circle by asking me to get involved in matters such as shipbuilding about which Robert knew little and cared not at all. His political downfall, however was that he invested all of his political capital in Wendy and when one day she resigned dramatically from the Cabinet with immediate effect, Robert was shell-shocked. He had no other close political relationships, at least within the Labour/Liberal coalition.

Anyway, Iain Gray MSP took over as Minister and didn't phone Robert for the first two weeks. He was a quiet defender of Robert over the piece, as the newspaper columns continued to pound him but eventually had to bring Robert and his Chairman in to give them both a very public dressing down when it became evident that Scottish Enterprise had failed to secure European monies, had failed to deliver on a host of projects, had spent astonishing monies on controversial projects and was generally being taken apart by an essentially misanthropic press, especially the *Scotsman* newspaper, which would normally have been expected to have been a keen supporter of the work of Scottish Enterprise. *Reporting Scotland* on BBC news also ran a series of stories where big Bob Wylie fronted the piece.

"I'm standing here outside this façade of steel and glass"… Bob Wylie would say in introduction, with the SE Headquarters building in shot behind him before going on to reveal the latest controversy being perpetrated by SE.

Eventually, Audit Scotland was called in to have a look at all of the allegations in the press and when the resulting document damned Scottish Enterprise on various levels, it was evident that a death knell had been sounded.

There were a number of television interviews where the Minister announced his support for the Chief

Executive and Chairman of Scottish Enterprise but these carried little conviction and after a few months, Crawford announced that he intended seeking fame and fortune elsewhere. His Chairman, Sir Ian Robinson, also announced that he wouldn't be seeking re-election. Crawford, branded *'the best business brain of his generation'*, took some months to move on and, it was whispered, was likely to take over at the helm of one of Scotland's banks just like some of his predecessors.

After a period, he announced that he was joining the Wood Group in Aberdeen following an invitation from Sir Ian Wood, a previous Chairman of Scottish Enterprise who had appointed Robert as CEO in the first place. He left after a year following a warm statement from Sir Ian saying that while Robert had considerable talents, he nevertheless didn't have the technical expertise to continue to serve the needs of the Wood Group. It was announced that he'd be returning to duty with the World Bank from whence he came, this time responsible for improving the economies of the Balkan states, then ravaged after years of internecine warfare. I found this a rich irony as he'd have to deal with those aspects of economic engagement which he'd previously treated with such disdain in Glasgow; community economic development, small business growth, regeneration and skills development…he'd have hated it.

After only a matter of some weeks it was then announced that he would take over as Chief Executive of the Mersey Partnership in Liverpool, a *bijou* organisation with a budget and staff compliment much smaller than the Govan Initiative I'd left some four years earlier. A year later, in 2006, he was announced as joining Glasgow Caledonian University in order to oversee their ambition to raise financial support from international sources. In 2008, despite being appointed Chairman of Clyde Gateway and despite his political ambitions in Ayrshire, he accepted the post of Chief Operating Officer of an enterprise agency in the south east of England – to which he told a disbelieving press he intended to commute from West Kilbride in Ayrshire! A year later he announced that he no longer intended contesting the seat in North Ayrshire.

Oh, how the mighty are fallen. I couldn't find it in myself to feel sorry for Robert. He'd decided for his own reasons to confront me. In terms of our personal and professional relationship, he spent more time taking umbrage than taking pains. It could all have been so different.

Robert once wrote to me telling me how much he admired Marcus Aurelius, the Roman General. I figured that Robert should have paid more attention to one of the sayings of the Roman philosopher, Seneca. *"You can kill as many of your enemies as you like, but your successor with be among the survivors."*

Now there was a vacancy. I was a survivor and myself and a few of my senior colleagues within SEG set to filling it with a vengeance. Culley for Chief Executive and Tom O'Neill for Chairman. Press stories heaped speculation upon speculation. *'Glasgow twosome to rescue Scottish Enterprise'*..... Scottish Enterprise National contracted the Hay Group, one of the world's top HR consultancies, and contracted them to support my future development within the organisation but I reworked their remit to ensure that they assisted me in making my CV state of the art. We undertook mock interviews. I was even provided with a session with a 'colourist' who spent time calculating which colours would make me look more presidential and businesslike (dark blue suit; black, highly polished shoes, white shirt, and strong coloured tie. No gold *accoutrements,* just silver watch, cufflinks etc. to match my silver *(sic)* hair .... hardly rocket science but interesting all the same).

We rehearsed new solutions to Scottish economic problems and ensured that our manifesto for change was sound as well as hitting all of the buttons we felt would appeal to the political and media worlds. Of course it wasn't they, but the outgoing Chairman and his fellow Board Members who would decide the next Chief Executive and it was clear that I was still regarded as an anathema. I was fully of the view that their attitude would have been *'you can't negotiate with terrorists'* but felt that there were important policy and organisational issues to be raised. From the outset I was clear that there was no real prospect that I might be found to be an acceptable candidate who could heal the wounds, but we pressed on.

Newspaper articles started to appear in the Sunday newspapers nominating Jack Perry, Chairman of the Scottish CBI (Confederation of British Industry) as the new man. It was evident that these carried some authority and we surmised that Jack McConnell, the First Minister, was leaking his preferences to a wider public to test the acceptability of his candidate.

I sent my polished and buffed CV to the head-hunters appointed to find a saviour and prepared to present the interview of my life in my attempt to secure the throne, but the call never came. Newspaper headlines screamed that the world-wide search was over and that a field of international candidates had been considered. Journalist Terry Murden, writing in *Scotland on Sunday*, had throughout been the sole recipient of leaked information but on 7th December 2003, he reported erroneously that the final short leet had comprised Ian Crawford, Vice President of IBM, Damien McDonald of the Defence Procurement Agency, Jack Perry, Ed Gillespie and Ron Culley.

Jack was appointed and after the fact, I was ushered into see the Chairman, Sir Ian, who, to be fair, was human and engaging. I expected a triumphant *'that'll learn you'* routine but was told that the Board had decided contrary to press leaks not to interview any internal candidates in order to bring fresh blood to the organisation.

He was much more affable and affirming that I had any right to expect and told me that despite all of the difficulties in which we'd been engaged, he could see my talent. He was almost avuncular when he told me that in his opinion I would be the *next* Chief Executive of Scottish Enterprise if I continued to demonstrate the same set of excellent performances and asked me to work in support of the new guy. I agreed, full in the knowledge that words are cheap and that he would have absolutely no say in any further appointments but it was a nice move. I responded in similar vein, but took the view that we were both being a bit disingenuous. It was as if he'd decided that there was no point in us fighting any further. We could have had an argument in private but Sir Ian had obviously chosen not to settler matters in that way. Now we had a new boss: Jack Perry.

13. Wrestling With Enterprise.

I don't know the key to success, but the key to failure is trying to please
everybody.
Bill Cosby.

In 2005, not only did Scottish Enterprise then have
a new head honcho in Jack Perry but his appointment
also coincided with the retirement of Tom O'Neill as our
Chairman in SE Glasgow. Tom had reached his sixtieth
birthday and had promised Maureen, his lovely wife,
that he'd step back from work commitments at that age
and enjoy the bounty that a long and successful career
had brought him. This took him from SEG as well but he
agreed to stay on as long as it took to see a new Chairman
appointed … as long as it didn't take too long. Tom
hankered after the golf course and the race course.

Some time earlier, Tom and I had together set our
sights on Willie Haughey, Executive Chairman of the
City Group. Based just over the Glasgow border in
Rutherglen, Willie's businesses then employed over ten
thousand people in facilities management across the UK
and he was one of Glasgow's most prominent citizens,
certainly one of the most successful business leaders ever
to have graced the city. He was also without doubt, one
of the best networked individuals within corporate life in
Scotland, and the UK for that matter.

Tom was anxious that Willie take the offer of board
membership on the basis that he would become Chairman
at Tom's retiral some six months later. Willie was up for
the challenge but was much more circumspect about
the presumption of Chairman. He was insistent that the
Board had to be given their place, as he knew of several
current board members of real quality that he respected
and who might see themselves as candidates. Tom agreed

but his own powers of persuasion, Willie's reputation and abilities combined so that at the point of his departure, the Board agreed his succession as Chairman unanimously.

In retrospect, it was an act of real serendipity that this transition took place. Tom was a superb Chairman, but the subsequent actions of Jack Perry and Sir John Ward, the Chairman of Scottish Enterprise National, could not have been addressed effectively had someone of the political weight and business acumen of Willie not held the Chair in Glasgow.

I was anxious not to have the same relationship with Jack Perry as I had had with Robert Crawford. Jean and I attended another New Year, black tie, dinner at the Kilmacolm home of Colin McClatchie, MD of News International. Jack Perry was present with his wife.

We enjoyed the Champagne available to guests and engaged in the most enjoyable discussions with the recently retired Controller of BBC Scotland, John McCormick, and his recently appointed successor Kenny McQuarrie. I enjoyed a good relationship with both men and knew John through our joint membership of the Board of the Glasgow Science Centre. John, a teacher in an earlier life before becoming involved in broadcasting, was most touching in his felicitous support of my wife Jean who had just completed her professional teaching qualification at Strathclyde's University's Jordanhill campus and was about to enter the world of pedagogy.

Kenny and I had hit it off some months earlier when I met him in his office for a chat. He was a *teuchter* as were most of the high heid yins at that time in BBC Scotland. We had allocated an hour for our discussion at BBC Scotland late one afternoon but ended up chatting for almost two.

However, at the dinner party, Jack Perry introduced himself after the two of us had circled each other for an hour. "I gather that you're someone I should make sure I get on with," he said, smiling at me.

"I'm sure that goes for both of us," I said, shaking his hand.

Jack Perry had been appointed by this time but would not take up office for several weeks. We found ourselves in deep conversation in the door jamb of a large room wherein an opera singer was performing before the remainder of the other sixty guests ... it was that size of a house. We were interrupted by First Minister, Jack McConnell who was exiting the operatic proceedings. Clearly implying the significance of the pair of us laughing and smiling at each other, he nodded in our direction.

"Glad to see you two are getting on. I hope this continues!"

We both smiled our assent and fell back into conversation. Perry was most convivial and was agreeing all of the sentiments I was expressing when we were approached by a Tory Grandee who was an elegant entrepreneur and who was involved on more Boards in corporate Scotland than you could shake a stick at.

Acknowledging the pair of us, he nevertheless only had eyes for Jack.

"Jack! Congratulations on the job. Great news, old chap."

After the niceties were taken care of, he started to enter some points of commentary.

"You know, Jack, in your new post, you really must do fewer things and do them better. Scottish Enterprise has far too wide a remit and you risk being sucked into too many difficult areas and suffering the fate of poor Robert. For example, I have no idea why you people are involved in skills training. Leave that stuff to the colleges."

I smiled, as Jack and I had just been discussing and agreeing the importance of this area of work, when Jack replied.

"Absolutely. I mean, I can make a good case for Scottish Enterprise running the schools, but that's not to say we're best placed to do it. And why in heaven's name we're engaged in regeneration work in some of the more poorly functioning parts of Scotland, I don't know."

The conversation continued in similar vein, completely contradicting all of the comments he'd been making to me moments earlier. Jack went on to say among other things that he'd no idea why careers advice was now a function of Scottish Enterprise. Eventually I lost patience and turned to the only aspect of the work of Scottish Enterprise that had not been traded in conversation; business support, and said, "Dear God, Jack! Why not invite the local authorities to undertake our responsibilities in business matters and we can turn the key in the lock, shut the place down entirely and save the taxpayer a few quid."

"Fair challenge, Ron. You make a good point."

Over the next couple of years I would come to understand that Jack had perfected the ability to 'fog' by agreeing with the essential essence of any argument put to him so as not to have to deal with the issue in question. I found him a man incapable of having an argument. He'd brush off points he didn't agree with using expressions of apparent agreement. I also didn't realise how perspicacious my point might become about redefining the responsibilities Scottish Enterprise could share with local authorities.

Initially, Willie was a cautious Chairman. But he was just learning. At meetings he was always keen to listen to every point of view. I wasn't slow at pointing out to him in private what I felt were the various inadequacies or unfairnesses being perpetrated on Glasgow by Scottish Enterprise National under the new direction of Jack Perry.

I was most troubled by the approach taken by Scottish Enterprise National to budgetary matters. Jack Perry, an accountant to trade, was concerned about the 'hockey stick' spend profile that beleaguered public sector organisations every year where there was a rush to spend money in the last quarter of the financial year; often in the last month, as not to spend would see the money returned to the Exchequer. Using this methodology, budgets were usually spent. "But", mused Jack not unreasonably, "Might not we even out this spend pattern and get better value for money?"

Jack's previous solution to this was to change the approach of the organisation whereby in that financial year, any element of the organisation which had failed to spend within ten percent of its profiled spend in any given month had that proportion of its budget taken back into the centre. Under Jack's new plan, in the ensuing financial year, there was to be no budget whatsoever allocated to business units within Scottish Enterprise. "Instead," proposed Jack, "we at the centre will approve an Operating Plan from each unit across Scotland which meets the ambitions of each Local Enterprise Company. You come up with the projects and we will fund them all from the centre. This provides a raft of new projects, new ideas and releases new energy into Scotland's economy."

Our Board had pointed out the financial madness of this approach and had responded that we in Glasgow would just rob the till and take advantage of the freedom to promote new ideas and secure funding for the pipeline of projects that had been gathering dust due to insufficient funding. We also predicted that so too would every other Chairman of Local Enterprise Companies and wrote, asking Jack how he'd be able to afford his new policy.

His response was that it would be a good problem to have. Perry reckoned that he expected Sir John and himself to meet with the First Minister and invite him to invest in the new initiatives they were undertaking on behalf of the Scottish economy.

Our Board had never heard such a crazy idea before and calculated that this would end in tears as it would bankrupt the organisation. How right they were. Our estimation of the lunacy of these spending plans were proved more accurate than anyone could have imagined. Compounding the felony was the absence that financial year (April through March) of any approach to mitigate spending until a somewhat belated e-mail was received by myself and colleague Local Enterprise Company Chief Executives all over Scotland which began with the words; "Let me begin by wishing you a Happy New Year….", and went on to explain, in perhaps more felicitous terms, that the financial mechanisms put in place to control spending had been so lax that no one at HQ had seen fit to put the brakes on until the last financial quarter at which point the organisation had found itself heading towards a £60 million overspend. Furious action to curb this resulted in a final figure of some £34 million being overspent and the subsequent year's budget being robbed of that amount to break even. Unfortunately, legal agreements within the overspend, and therefore already committed in Jack's new three year financial planning, meant that the *following* year's budget of some £500 million had already been overspent by some £30 million resulting in a £64 million cash shortfall in that year, 2006/7. Everyone realised that this would mean draconian cuts across all budgets to permit ends to meet.

There was significant political fall out as a consequence of this emerging financial crisis. The Enterprise Minister, Nicol Steven MSP was in no mood to find additional resources. Cabinet Members were up in arms at what they perceived to be either Perry's incompetence or his arrogance. The Enterprise Committee, chaired by SNP MSP Alex Neil, got its teeth into the issues and daily there would be new revelations. Daily, projects on every high street in cities, towns and villages across Scotland were announced as being abandoned as a consequence of the cuts and regularly, Jack Perry squirmed on television, before Parliament and in the press as he tried to wriggle free from the pernicious petard upon which he had hoist himself.

It became evident through discussions with friendly Ministers that Perry had only had one supporter in Cabinet, First Minister Jack McConnell, who at a Cabinet meeting where the issue took up more than half the time available and having heard Scottish Enterprise roundly condemned by each and every coalition Cabinet Member, summarised by agreeing to Nicol Stephen's proposal that an independent audit of Scottish Enterprise be undertaken by KPMG but that he'd back the Chairman and Chief Executive on the basis that he didn't want any problems through the run-in to the next Parliamentary elections some twelve months away. He didn't want to run the risk of further high visibility resignations given the resignation of Professor Alan Alexander as Chairman of Scottish Water only weeks previously.

Borrowing consent was made available to Scottish Enterprise on the basis that they had to agree to live within their means. They were also told to leave well alone further restructuring proposals whereby the ability of Local Enterprise Companies to *exist* never mind act with discretion was being proposed. The *coup de gras* came in late 2005 when Parliament's Enterprise Committee, having interviewed all associated with the delinquent overspend pronounced that the cash crisis was caused by Scottish Enterprise National engaging in "incomprehensible" and "wholly dissatisfactory" decision making.

As the crisis reached its zenith, Councillor Steven Purcell, then Leader of Glasgow City Council, announced in the press that he proposed the establishment of a 'Pathfinder' project in Glasgow whereby key organisations such as the Council, Scottish Enterprise Glasgow, elements of the Health Board such as community health and aspects of policing be co-located in premises to be developed at High Street and Duke Street. Steven proposed that there be a Board established comprising the Chairman and Chief Executive of each constituent organisation to seek harmonisation and efficiencies of scale.

It was as if a hand grenade had been thrown into the mix. Scottish Enterprise were flustered at having been out-manoeuvred by Steven. Surely it was *they* that were promoters of efficiencies? Surely *they* were the organisation that was associated with thrift and good business sense? As it was, the press fell on Steven's proposals as manna from Heaven, contrasting Steven's motherhood and apple-pie proposition with Jack Perry's calamitous, cack-handed financial management as proof that there were alternatives to the continued domination of Scottish Enterprise in matters both of enterprise and of modernising government.

Jean had an in-service day at school and had asked me to take the boys to school that day. Accordingly, I drove into the city that sunny morning later than my usual seven o'clock start when I took a call in my car from Gordon Kennedy, my Deputy Chief Executive.

"Hi, Ron. It's Gordon. "

"Hi, Gordon."

"Ron, I've got Bill Morton, Brian Jamieson and Caroline Stewart in your office…" His voice trailed off. They each held respectively the office of Senior Operations Director (SOD), Scottish Enterprise Company Secretary and Deputy Head of Human Resources.

In the background I could hear Bill shouting. "I said, *now!*"

"Don't raise your voice to me"… replied Gordon," and the line went dead.

I drove with greater urgency and arrived to find the four of them encamped in a small meeting room next to my office.

"Gentlemen … Caroline, I gather you were looking for me?"

Bill was by now mollified, Brian looked discomfited and Caroline was writing furiously everything that was said between us.

"Jack told us to meet with you urgently this morning to ask you what you know about the article that appeared this morning in the *Herald* suggesting that Scottish Enterprise Glasgow be incorporated within a joint venture with other Glasgow organisations."

"Seems a great idea to me."

"Hmmm. Jack wants to know the role you played in setting this up."

Brian interjected. "He takes the view that these proposals contravene the Operating Plan you've signed and may place you in breach of your contract of employment."

I had given thought to my general approach prior to arrival and had decided that I may have to fall back on controlled belligerence but found myself laughing.

"Dear God, Brian. If I had helped shape that approach and signed up to it, I'd expect to be fired …. but of course I didn't. I merely had discussions about a general direction of travel that was consistent with the Government's 'Modernising Government' agenda."

"So the article is inaccurate?"

"Insofar as it might suggest that I placed myself outwith the Operating Contract by signing up for a formal arrangement." I wasn't about to be cornered.

Eventually I relented. "Look guys. What you're dealing with here is politics for grown-ups. Steven is an aspiring, creative, modernising politician. In one leap he has captured all of the headlines with a bold initiative designed to advance service provision in the city, but also to put Scottish Enterprise behind the eight-ball. As far as I can see, it's worked!"

"So you didn't have meetings ...."

"Ah! ... You must be referring to that night I met with Steven Purcell in a smoke filled room to plot the downfall of Scottish Enterprise ..."

Bill had the good grace to smile.

Caroline looked shocked and proceeded to write furiously, her face screwed up as if forced to swallow unpalatable medicine. Bill placed his hand on her arm. "I think you can take it that Ron's joking."

Our banter continued for a further half hour but the atmosphere had changed, Caroline had stopped writing and we discussed what lay behind the article sensibly and without rancour.

I explained that myself and some other colleagues had been in dialogue with colleagues from Glasgow City Council about the possible co-location of our staff in one campus at the confluence of High Street and Duke Street which would host those of all regeneration agencies in the city and that Jack, inadvertently or not, had agreed that I should explore my ambitions in an e-mail a year previously following an exchange where he was considering 'folding' Scottish Enterprise Glasgow staff into Atlantic Quay and terminating our lease on Atrium Court. He may not have remembered, but I still had his agreement on paper.

I went on to explain that it seemed to be common sense to consider the prospect of savings and to reflect on opportunities that a move of this nature presented for more efficient ways of collaborating in the interests of the businesses and residents of Glasgow. The fact that Steven had decided to go public on these conversations must be embarrassing to Scottish Enterprise. I finished, confident that there was no real prospect of action against any of us. I turned to Caroline. "Did you get all that?"

No more was said by Scottish Enterprise National but Steven took up the cudgels and the notion of stronger collaboration grew with the passing months, eventually resulting, in 2007, in the establishment of a Pathfinder Board to bring city organisations together, to pool resources and to ensure a more integrated approach to social and economic regeneration and Scottish Enterprise couldn't do a thing about it. However, as the years elapsed, so too did the Pathfinder project due to Scottish Enterprise substantially reorienting their structure and functions making more than a hundred posts redundant in the process. Sometimes you win, sometimes you lose.

One of the mechanisms introduced by myself but dreamt up by Vice Chairman Reverend John Matthews some years earlier was the idea of 'Convivial Dinners' whereat the political and administrative leadership of the city from time to time broke bread in one another's company and dealt with a particular issue of significance to Glasgow. They were universally successful, enjoyable and effective in achieving their goal; to advance our shared agenda for Glasgow. Typically, the Chief Constable, Willie Rae, myself, Willie Haughey, John Matthews, Council Leader Steven Purcell or his predecessor Charlie Gordon, Sir John Arbuthnott, Chairman of the Greater Glasgow Health Board or his Chief Executive Tom Divers, Jim McColl, Chairman of Glasgow Works and perhaps John Gallagher, Chairman of the Glasgow Economic Forum, Lesley Sawers, Chief Executive of the Glasgow Chamber of Commerce would attend depending upon the matter at hand. These meetings were held under Chatham House Rules (frequently misunderstood to mean that the contents of the meeting required to remain confidential to those who attended so that people could be candid in their remarks. However, there is only *one* Chatham House Rule which is that the *identity* of anyone expressing an idea must remain confidential – the idea or proposition can be made public.)

At one of these dinners, in January 2006, the matter of the overspent Scottish Enterprise budget and the likely implications was discussed in the presence of a senior Cabinet Minister and it would be fair to say that there was presented a pretty powerful political endorsement of the collaborative work of those seated round the table. It was clear that the Glasgow leadership had the confidence of the Scottish Parliament and of the Labour/Liberal coalition Cabinet. That reassurance was not particularly in evidence in respect of Scottish Enterprise National.

Indeed, a friendly Cabinet Minister told me subsequently that at a further meeting of the Cabinet the following week, within the context of a debate about the *travails* of Scottish Enterprise, an exchange took place between Andy Kerr, Minister of Health and Malcolm Chisholm, Minister for Communities (and former Minister of Health whom Andy had displaced) where both spoke passionately of 'the need to support Scottish Enterprise Glasgow which was much more aligned with the ambitions of the Scottish Executive than their parent body, Scottish Enterprise National'. This brought gales of laughter as it was pointed out that this might just be the first occasion on which these two Cabinet heavyweights had been in agreement on anything. Indeed, there was unanimous support for our approach and unanimous opposition to the approach taken by Scottish Enterprise National, again with the single exception of First Minister Jack McConnell who still sided with Scottish Enterprise National, despite their obvious and admitted incompetence. Still, it was nice to know that our efforts in the city had been recognised.

However, the success of these convivial dinners was largely attributable to the energies of those who attended but the inspiration and organisation was down to one man; the Reverend John Matthews. As the Parish Minister for Ruchill, he tended his flock in one of the poorest communities in Glasgow but in a similar analysis to my own, he also determined that 'sorting people's heids one at a time' was an insufficient response.

I first met John at a meeting of the Glasgow Community Planning Board in 2001 when he spoke in support of a housing project in the company of residents from Ruchill. I was much taken by his passion and articulacy and scribbled notes in the margin of my pad that I must make an effort to meet this man. We had just advertised a vacancy on my own Board and thought that John would be the very man to bring expertise on areas like regeneration and employment. I met him at his home shortly thereafter and was tremendously impressed, recommending his application for appointment to my then Chairman, Tom O'Neill.

Not only had John the attributes I'd anticipated but prior to taking cloth in his forties, had built a very successful business career until 1981 when he left General Electric of USA having been CEO of Carboloy, the tungsten carbide businesses of GE's Man Made Materials Group. There he reported directly to the legendary Jack Welsh. He'd mentored many small businesses in Scotland and I realised that I'd be able to make a very effective case for his participation on our Board as membership had to be ratified by the parent Scottish Enterprise Board but I now realised that they could not easily reject John's candidacy. Nor did they.

Over the years, I came to respect John's gifts and was always keen to hear his views and enjoy his humour. He became adept at the politics of networking and following the election of the first SNP government in 2007, it came as no surprise over lunch one day when he revealed the meetings he'd already set up with the First Minister and his senior colleagues, always leaving with a promise of action or further meetings.

Over my time at SEG, I dealt with Tom O'Neill, John Thorburn, Willie Haughey, John Matthews and Vic Emery in their capacity as Chairs and Vice Chairs. I respected, admired and was very fond of all of them all in various proportions. They were each hugely successful and each was very different from the others in personality and outlook. One might occasionally be tetchy where another was affirming. One might 'take a view' on matters where another was more laid back. But all of them had huge experience, a great sense of humour and all of them sought to serve the City of Glasgow first and foremost, even if this meant taking issue with Scottish Enterprise at a national level.

Towards the end of my tenure at Scottish Enterprise Glasgow, I met with Jeane Freeman who had been a senior civil servant looking after the education portfolio and had been brought in by Jack McConnell, the First Minister, to become his *Special Adviser* or '*Spad*', as those who held these positions were known. I'd met Jeane some many years earlier when she was running Apex Scotland, the first agency to work with employers on recruiting people with a criminal record and I was running Govan Initiative. We'd got on well but had lost touch.

Jeane had recently parted company with the First Minister and had reinvented herself as an independent adviser on any number of matters. We got on famously and although I was already well served on most issues, I asked Jeane to assist me in a few areas such as regeneration where Scottish Enterprise in general and

Robert Crawford in particular clearly had no intention of delivering within Glasgow. I formed the view that only if they were *required* to undertake their responsibilities in respect of regeneration would they be likely to engage and I took huge delight listening to my colleagues at Scottish Enterprise Headquarters tell me that they were manoeuvring to step back from all responsibilities to do with regeneration at the same time that Jeane [at my behest] was quietly making the case for there to be two major national regeneration imperatives; on the River Clyde and in the East End of Glasgow. I was able to suggest ways of ensuring that Scottish Enterprise National had no option but to deploy their budget in these two areas and took great satisfaction when in 2006, the Government's Policy Statement, *People and Place* was issued forcing Scottish Enterprise National to fund and develop the regeneration of the Clyde as well as the east end of Glasgow. Jeane had been hard at work and I couldn't have written it better myself. Over the years she became a most valued friend and colleague with an unsurpassed knowledge of the Scottish political scene.

I actually met Jeane's partner, Susan Stewart, first as she'd been appointed as Jack McConnell's first 'Scottish Ambassador' to Washington. I'd met her in the British Embassy when I'd been asked to say a few words in Georgetown University about the Scottish Enterprise Glasgow approach to developing leadership via our 'Tomorrow's Leaders' programme. Susan was, and remains great value. Opinionated, witty and effervescent, she was not what one might expect of a seasoned diplomat but she was also shrewd and well connected. Interestingly, she was as much a committed supporter of the SNP as Jeane was Labour. Over the years, as the SNP became more of a force in the land, Susan and Jeane's contacts within each party paid substantial dividends.

In 2008, Scottish Enterprise had undergone a further period of review and rebuke under Jack Perry's leadership. The incoming SNP Government had determined that it wished to see more focus placed upon skills and under the chairmanship of Willie Roe, established a new Scottish Skills Agency, Skills Development Scotland and appointed Damien Yeates, my erstwhile friend and Assistant Chief Executive of Govan Initiative as its first Chief Executive. The new organisation was formed as an assemblage from the Careers Scotland element of Scottish Enterprise, Learn Direct and the skills and training wing of Scottish Enterprise. At a stroke, Scottish Enterprise lost about 50% of its annual budget but Jack Perry played it as if it were a positive benefit as now Scottish Enterprise was 'lean and fit for purpose' and could focus upon the real needs of the Scottish economy.

The fact that world-wide, observers envied the integrated approach taken by Scottish Enterprise to economic development was to be forgotten as Jack managed to shed those aspects of economic life about which he knew little and cared less. It was a matter of considerable regret that eventually he rid the organisation of most regeneration responsibilities, small business development, careers development, skills and training, all of those areas where there was market failure and where the economy was screaming for intervention as the private sector couldn't or wouldn't engage effectively. That he chose to retain only the business growth and investment portfolio, emulating the role of banks and financial institutions where there was no [long term] market failure, and got away with it, must rank as one of the most serious oversights that the civil service and its various Ministers must stand accused.

14. Lions And Donkeys.

You can fool all of the people some of the time and some of the people all of the time… and in the Scottish Labour Party, those are the ones you need to focus on".
Ron Culley…paraphrasing Abraham Lincoln

Over the years, political relationships had proved invaluable in achieving the ends of any particular organisation with which I was involved. I enjoyed my first limited exposure to senior Regional politicians when employed within the Chief Executive's Department of Strathclyde Regional Council. Many of the most able of them had gone on to build a political career in Westminster.

At Govan, my key political relationships remained pretty local. The Regional and District Councils had been disbanded under the Local Government (Scotland) Act 1994 and were replaced by a City Council (in the case of Glasgow) which took on all of the responsibilities previously undertaken by the two separate authorities. There was a real schism between the two associated elements of the Council. The new Provost (the civic persona and Queen's representative), Councillor Pat Lally, was previously a District Councillor and the new Leader (the political leader of the council) was Councillor Bob Gould. Pat had previously been Leader of Glasgow District Council and Bob had previously been Leader of the Regional Council.

Pat was famed for allegedly refusing ever to use the name 'Strathclyde Regional Council' in any of his utterances, preferring instead to refer more descriptively to 'a large authority in the West of Scotland'. Relationships between the factions were pretty sour and the entire *imbroglio* washed up in the press after Bob Gould exclaimed in a passing comment that Group discipline had deteriorated to the extent that he was required to buy the votes of his colleagues by promising them trips abroad on study visits. There was uproar. Litigation followed upon litigation. The Labour Party was in turmoil.

The General Secretary of the Labour Party in Scotland at that time was Jack McConnell, who attended a meeting of the Labour Group convened in order to secure the expulsion of Councillors Alex Mosson and Pat Lally among others. The action against Alex was comical in the extreme. Newspaper reports at the time claimed that Councillor Tommy Dingwall had alleged that Alex had secreted a pie in his Councillor's dooket in an attempt to intimidate him as it had a ticket pinned to the crust saying 'We're coming to get you'.

I got to know Bob Gould when he was Leader of Strathclyde Regional Council and I have to admit, I couldn't see much talent. His predecessors in office, Geoff Shaw, Dick Stewart and Charlie Gray were political giants compared with him. Bob was taciturn and slow. It was rumoured that he changed the times of some meetings so he could watch the horse racing on television in his office some afternoons. Horse racing was his passion and the rumours continued when he became Leader of the new City Council when it was established after the reform of local government.

That said, a number of elected members enjoyed a flutter – and no harm in that. However, one Saturday afternoon I'd been invited along with then Councillor Bill Miller (before he was elected to the European Parliament) to attend the Gold Cup at Ayr Racecourse. Bill and I stepped out to collect our modest winnings when we saw a Glasgow Councillor leaving the queue having obviously having had a refreshment. His fist held a wad of notes. He must have been clutching several hundred pounds.

"Bill", he exclaimed, recognising him and proffering his winnings. "Ya beauty!"

He and Bill exchanged pleasantries. I watched disinterestedly until I noticed the odds on the screen relating to the last race... evens. Presuming he was picking up winnings on this race, to win his bundle of notes, he must have had to bet a fortune, at least to me who normally in those days bet only a couple of quid on a race. Still do, as a matter of fact.

Over the years Bob Gould seemed to lurch from problem to problem. Politics towards the end of his time in power couldn't have been a pleasant experience. The last time I saw him he had been retired for some years and was getting into a lift in the Council Chambers with me. I didn't recognise him. He was bloated and yellow. He spoke slowly and quietly as ever.

"Ron, how're you doing? Long time no see."

"Not bad, Bob." I could hardly recognise the man before me and we exchanged a few words in the lift before he stepped out. I never saw him again.

Pat Lally was leader of the Council from 1986 to 1992 and again from 1994 to 1996. On both occasions he was succeeded by his bitter rival Jean McFadden. He was also Provost from 1996 until 1999 and dominated Glasgow politics at a city level throughout the 80's and 90's. I tended to deal with him only sporadically. He was largely given credit for the Glasgow Garden Festival in 1998, the city winning the 1990 European Year of Culture, the European City of Architecture in 1991 and for the building of the Royal Concert Hall; known colloquially as 'Lally's *Pallais*'.

To be fair, Pat was Glasgow through and through. He was suspended from the party on two occasions; once in 1977 over a housing row and again in 1997 when he and Alex Mosson were both suspended by the party, caught up in Bob Gould's 'Votes for Trips' scandal although both were reinstated by the Court of Session. No wonder he was called '*Lazarus*' as a consequence of his political come-backs.

I was invited to a dinner in his private chambers in 1998 when he and I had jointly welcomed a delegation from France who had wished to see more of Glasgow's approach to local economic development. Pat sat top centre with two long tables running away from him on either side of the top table. Everyone was very jolly and I was getting on famously with my French guests at the far end of the room. I had supposed that the evening would be characterised by a speech from Pat outlining the virtues of the city and by a response from the leader of the delegation thanking the city for its hospitality. That would be the usual protocol.

However, on this occasion, after the meal, Pat decided to open up the conversation and I was asked to say a few spontaneous words. To be honest, far from expecting this task to be asked of me, I'd treated the evening as a night off after a long day speaking with the French delegation and they were not backwards in coming forwards on the refreshment side. The result was their perception that I had just delivered a most loquacious and witty speech which received a thunderous applause; at least that's how I read it. I suspect that Pat, who'd been sipping gingerly all night, had decided that I should have observed the same conservative approach to the wine as he had done and took the opportunity of having me perform in a way which most assuredly would have shown me up, had our French guests not have wanted to have a knees-up, and they responded to each of my words as if I'd just uttered the most hilarious or brilliant statement ever. Lally glowered at me but honour was satisfied as I hadn't been too far gone to make a fool of myself, and was saved by the French reaction, but it was a close call. It made me realise that when politicians achieve power as did Lally, they can take the office they hold very seriously indeed and would - not unreasonably - see themselves as the final arbiter on whether the event should be more or less formal. I'd second-guessed Pat wrong on that occasion.

I had much more to do with Alex Mosson, Lally's successor as Lord Provost. Alex was a great wee guy. Standing about five feet five, if that, he'd been round the block a few times and was one of life's natural entertainers. He loved telling stories, was a great singer, and after an earlier life where he'd allegedly enjoyed a glass, now contained his imbibing to cokes and water.

When I presented my credentials to Alex in 2001, we spent an hour and a half in his magnificent suite in the City Chambers. Wendy Alexander MSP had just asked me to take charge of a Task Force to deal with an impending crisis on the Clyde where the prospect of 1,000 jobs were at risk as a consequence of an order not being allocated to BAE Systems Marine, the large defence conglomerate that owned the shipyards on the river.

I knew that Alex had been employed in the yards in the old days and almost as an afterthought, decided to use this as an opening gambit for my wanting to meet with him. It was a throwaway line, as I intended speaking with people with more seniority in the maritime world ,but Alex took my 'consultation' as a real compliment and we spent a great time in his rooms exchanging stories and discussing the economic performance of the city. So much so that he insisted I join a delegation he was hosting to Havana in the company of twelve Glasgow Businesses. I told him that these days, Robert Crawford, the Chief Executive of Scottish Enterprise national wanted to call all these shots and I speculated that Cuba wouldn't even appear on his radar screen… only Japan, the Pacific Rim,

North America and the main conurbations of France and Germany, to a lesser extent, interested him.

In those days, one of the repeated arguments I had with Robert was his blissful disregard for the 'Accession Countries'... those ten Eastern European nations such as Poland and Lithuania that had sought to become members of the European Community. I fell out with him and his side-kick Martin Togneri over this on a number of occasions as they laughed off my opinions as uninformed, left wing, bullshit. Their disregard for ambitious economies on the way up was total. On more than one occasion, Laurie Russell and I would shake our heads in astonishment at the short-sighted arrogance of Scottish Enterprise National. Only *they* were entitled to have a view on the impact on the Scottish economy of geo-political, socio-economic movements. They were completely blindsided by their own comfort zones.

The German word, *'schadenfreude'*... taking pleasure in the misfortunes of others... might not unreasonably have applied to some when not long afterwards, the dot-com bubble burst world-wide leaving many of Robert's Silicon Valley ambitions in tatters around the same time as Poles and other nationalities began flooding into Glasgow and asserting their impact upon our economy - just as Laurie and I had predicted.

It's funny how timing is everything – and not just in comedy. Only a few years ago, the American economy dominated everything - as yet it still does, if not from the dizzying heights as was the case then. Nowadays, all eyes are on the BRIC economies of Brazil, Russia, India and China – all countries that didn't then feature at all much on the investment horizon of Scottish Enterprise.

Anyway, Alex Mosson shook his head.... "Robert Crawford...?" He almost spat the words out in distaste. "Do you know who my best pal in politics is? Wendy

Alexander... his *Minister!*" And before I could stop him he'd asked his secretary to get Wendy on the phone. She took the call and I left his office with the Minister's assurance, via Alex, that while she didn't want to interfere in Robert's operational decisions, she nonetheless thoroughly approved of me attaching myself to the delegation as 'we have to play the long game too'. Not long afterwards, Robert phoned me and said he was somewhat perplexed at a request he'd had from Alex Mosson for me to visit Cuba with a delegation of Glasgow businesses. Normally, he said, he'd reject the overture as there was nothing in it for the Scottish economy in his opinion... but on reflection, he told me, there must be occasions when 'we have to play the long game' so I could go. I thanked him and made no mention of the telephone conversation I'd overheard only a couple of days before in which the same phraseology was used.

I'd organised Trade Missions before and was very familiar with all of the hard work that really goes in at the front end. Once the delegation arrives, all of the businesspeople go off on their visits and meet their appointments. They don't want organisers hanging around them so our tasks tended to be around issues such as trouble-shooting but in Cuba, I also took the opportunity to follow up some aspects of Cuban life that intrigued me.

Because of the work I was doing back on the Clyde, I asked if I might be taken to see the Cuban shipyards. I was allocated an interpreter by the Embassy, a Russian woman called Svetlana who had been dispatched to Havana some many years before, married an East German who was serving out there and who had stayed on when Gorbachev's '*Glasnost*' had kicked in. She was paid $50 for the morning, an astonishing amount when you consider that at the time, Cubans were living in a Peso economy

- the equivalent of about $8 *a month,* although all of their wider needs were taken care of by the state. There were evidently two classes of citizens in Cuba; those who lived in the local, peso economy, for whom life could be tough, and those who lived in the dollar economy who could enjoy living in the crumbling grandeur of Havana, rightly at the time being nominated as a city deserving of a World Heritage accolade.

Svetlana took me to what were little more than boatyards where fishing boats were being built but the yard owner obviously saw my visit as being something approaching a state occasion. He was very proud of his operation. I was shown round by him, speaking ten to the dozen in Spanish, with my interpreter translating into my other ear. We crossed the road before we left as he wanted to show me another part of his yard. On entering the building I spotted what looked like a mini-submarine sitting against a wall. It might have held two men.

"Is that a submarine?" I asked of Svetlana.

She asked and listened to the man, asking supplementary questions of him as he explained in ever greater explosions of raised eyebrows and wildly gesticulating hand gestures.

"Yes, he tells me that it was bought some six months ago by a man from Ireland. He came in here and bought it with a suitcase full of dollars. He has never returned to collect it. The money is being held in the bank until he takes it away."

I was astonished at the openness of Svetlana's explanation. Upon bidding her farewell, I asked our Liaison Officer from the Embassy if I could speak with their head of security. At first she was concerned lest I was about to complain about her.

"Have I done something wrong?"

"No. Not at all. I just need to see your security guy."

"What about?"

"If I told you, I'd need to shoot you", I joked.

Some minutes later a world weary man descended the staircase looking for all the world, I have to say, like what I would have imagined a head of security would look like. Six foot something, hard-man face, lean and fit. Almost James Bondish. He looked like he'd seen and done it all. He shook my hand.

"You asked to see me?"

I recounted the story told me by Svetlana expecting to be patted on the back and sent on my way. I couldn't have been more wrong. He listened to me with increasing interest and took me by my elbow into an anti-room where he took out a notebook and pen.

"Of course!" he exclaimed. "You reckon he said about six months ago?"

That was when it became clear to me also. Three Irishmen, Niall Connolly, Martin McCauley and James Monaghan had been sentenced by a Colombian court to seventeen years in jail for training the indigenous Marxist rebels in explosives and terrorism techniques. There was a lot of news coverage at the time when Colombia's most senior general blamed the improved fighting of rebels on their alleged training by instructors linked to the IRA. Prior to his arrest, Neil Connolly was resident in Cuba where the Cuban authorities claimed he was the Latin America representative for *Sinn Féin*. It had been reported in the papers that the deployment of a new model of home-made mortar and the more effective use of snipers by the guerrillas of FARC (the Revolutionary Armed Forces of Colombia) both owed a considerable debt to tactics honed in Northern Ireland.

News reports at the time stated, "What we are now seeing with the FARC is the direct result of IRA training," said Colombia's armed forces chief, Gen Carlos Alberto

Ospina. The FARC had started adding stabilising fins and new detonation methods to mortars. They then resembled the "barrack-busters" used by the IRA against the British Army.

Whether James Bond was humouring me or whether, as he seemed, very interested in what I told him, we'll never know. In retrospect, the notion of the IRA sailing a submarine up the River Laggan for an attack on the RUC seems rather far fetched. I can't see it ... just report what actually happened. That said, I did feel rather shame-faced when some years later, I reported the event to my great pal, Tadhg Dennehy who looked rather disapproving at my apparent attempt to assist the Brits in their war against Republican forces, even though the Good Friday Agreement was then in force.

Our delegation to Havana was actually combined with a more formal political one headed by Alan Johnson MP, Minister of State for Industry; a thoroughly nice guy. He handled himself with a measure of reserve but you could see in those moments when he was alone in the company of the Brits that he was good company and a very pleasant man. Some years later when he was a popular candidate for the leadership of the Labour Party, it was easy to see why, given his mix of real ability and down-to-earth blokishness.

He invited Alex Mosson, Steve Inch and I to attend a meeting he had arranged with the Head of the Cuban Treasury in order to negotiate the repayment of some significant millions owed to then Chancellor Gordon Brown by the Cubans. We met in the Board room of the Bank of Cuba where their first Chancellor after Castro's revolution, Ernesto Che Guevara, had held office. I was overwhelmed by the history of the place.

Negotiations were strained as it was evident that the Cubans either wouldn't or couldn't repay the money they owed Great Britain. Alan held his patience and after a half hour of fruitless discussion invited the Cubans to consider taking the matter to arbitration in front of an independent person of international stature.

Before anyone could say anything, Alex Mosson pulled himself up to his full height... "If I might be of any assistance?"

The thought of Glasgow's Lord Provost arbitrating had me biting my lip. Alan rejected his offer courteously. As a matter of fact, had Alex been asked to undertake this task, there would be no way that Cuba would have had to put their hand in its pocket as Alex was completely devoted to the people, their city, their country and the political regime that, frankly, controlled them. As we left, our Cuban hosts gave me a mounted collection of 1962 pesos in various paper denominations showing their Chancellor, Che Guevara on the back of the bills. It was an inexpensive but wonderful gift. My son Ron was studying politics at the time and I gave him the Pesos collection as a *memoir*. Over the years it was lost. I still live in hope of it resurfacing one day.

One evening, our delegation was invited to a reception at the British Embassy. Around six o'clock as I dressed in preparation, I had the television on and Fidel Castro was sitting behind a desk haranguing his audience, wagging his finger and blethering away in Spanish. Upon arrival at the Embassy, drink was offered and we had a grand time. Towards the end of the evening the tall frame of a bearded Fidel Castro hove into view and lots of photographs were being taken. With all the boldness endowed by a glass of wine, I excused my way to the front of the knot of people surrounding him and shook his hand. I started talking at him in English wishing him all the best from the Scottish people whilst all the time punctuating my comments with appeals to our crowd for someone to take a picture of us.

A smiling Castro clearly hadn't a clue what I was saying and presumed my meanderings were merely a passionate greeting. I must have hung on for thirty seconds or more, a long time in hand shaking terms, when finally one of the guys managed to get a photograph. I was delighted … although this quickly dissipated when the disc I was given was lost back in Glasgow.

Imagine my surprise when I returned to my hotel to see Castro on TV still sitting behind his desk, leafing through a large book from time to time as if advancing age had required that he now use a prompt for his imprecations. Either it was a re-run, or the Castro we met at the Embassy was one of the many *doppelgangers* he was reputed to have in his service. Me? I believe of course that I shook the hands of the real man. I mean would the *real* Castro have wanted to attend a reception with guests at the British Embassy or speak with his own people on television?

Alex proved himself on that trip to be the model Lord Provost. His speeches were all apposite, appropriately brief and towards the end of each, spontaneously witty. He was a great ambassador for the city. That said, I still tell the story of how Alex made great play of presenting any senior Cuban dignitary he met with a bottle of Lord Provost's Special Reserve Whisky. All *others* in the room were given what Alex normally gave to people he met in the course of his duties, a box containing a beautiful pair of gold leaf cufflinks with the coat of arms of Glasgow embossed on them. I had a pair myself and wore them with pride. However, I must admit to a measure of surprise when I saw Alex handing them out to the lesser mortals in the room. I touched his arm.

"Alex, are these cufflinks?"

Alex looked perturbed at the question. "Aye."

"Alex, this is Cuba. No one here even *owns* a long sleeved shirt. We're on a tropical island."

Realisation gradually crept across his face and he looked at me as if to say, *what do we do?*

I smiled and offered a suggestion. "Just tell them they're *Euros!*"

Alex laughed and went about his duties, handing out the cufflinks as if they were the crown jewels. It was a great experience, a tremendous country and a wonderful city. *Viva la Cuba libre'.*

Some years later *en route* to meet with Bill Miller MEP and the European Chairman of the Parliaments' Transport and Tourism Committee in the European Parliament in Brussels in order to discuss high speed rail between Glasgow and Edinburgh, I had elected to go by Eurostar, the high speed train which connects London with Brussels by means of the Channel Tunnel. I was in jaunty spirits as I prepared to board the train at Waterloo and hadn't realised that border controls were in place at the station. My jacket lapel carried a small metal pin portraying the Cuban flag, a souvenir of my trip to Havana. Turning a corner in the station, I found myself facing three gentlemen from Customs and Excise. They beckoned me over and while they had a look at my passport, one asked whether my trip to Brussels was for purposes of business or pleasure. The most elderly of the group noticed my badge and asked me conversationally what it was. Instead of replying 'the British Legion' or 'the county badge of East Renfrewshire' or something non-controversial, I ventured, "It's the Cuban flag."

Misreading his closer inspection as a general interest in world affairs, I went on to offer my usual mantra when asked about the badge...."*Viva la Cuba Libre*", I said, compounding it by clenching my fist shoulder high, smiling, "*Viva la revolucion*". Well, I just about avoided a strip search! These guys were bored and I was clearly an *agent provocateur*. I reminded myself not to be so smart-arsed at customs control in the future and walked to the train, chastened.

Scotland's first, First Minister was Donald Dewar. I met him initially when he was but a lowly MP down in Westminster. John McManus at that time was Director of the Drumchapel Community Organisations Council and had performed in a blisteringly successful way by establishing a collaborative grouping of all of the informal community organisations in Drumchapel and housing them all in a majestic new development called Merkat House in the centre of the community. He went on to acquire all of the properties in the Town Centre, dilapidated after years and years of neglect, and raise the cash necessary to develop them into something more appropriate for the needs and expectations of the people of Drumchapel. John's work was regarded as sufficiently ground-breaking that Glasgow University financed the writing of a book, to which I contributed elements of a chapter, entitled *Merkat Forces*. Not a best seller, but an excellent account, in my view, of how community development can change lives and the fortunes of a community.

Inevitably this brought John into sharp contact with the political elite of the area and the local MP for Garscadden, Donald Dewar towered above them all. In 1993 I had arranged to take a trade mission of some 29 Govan companies to Paris. Each company was permitted to travel only on the basis that they had formal agreements to meet three French businesses each day in order to sell their goods into the French market. While I was negotiating arrangements, I also took the opportunity to sign up John to accompany me to Paris for a four day holiday during which we'd also speak with one or two people in the British Embassy and generally check out the lie of the land ... but at our own pace and at our own expense.

John and I had a great time. We walked the streets of the French capital. We had a few drinks and enjoyed one another's company. Upon hearing of our venture, Donald Dewar asked us to pop in to see him in the Houses of Parliament on our return when we had to make a scheduled evening stop in Heathrow. He offered us dinner and wanted to discuss John's ambitious plans for his constituency. We agreed with alacrity.

Donald had a reputation as a glutton. He ate everything that was put in front of him and much of what was intended for others' *repas* but was the skinniest man imaginable. Tall and gangly, Donald - everyone knew him as Donald - sat us down in the Strangers' Bar in the House of Commons and over the duration of the conversation bought us a couple of pints, which we tended carefully so as not to imbibe too much, but also to ensure that we'd leave space for the grand dinner which I'd been building up in John's mind having dined out on a similar basis before with Tommy Graham MP.

During our chat, Donald simply demolished the bowls of dried peanuts that the waiter continued to replenish time after time. It was a *bravura* performance. He must have put away a couple of pounds of salted nuts. As our conversation drew to its *dénouement*, Donald asked if we were still hungry. Given that not a morsel of food had passed our lips - we'd steadfastly refused the peanuts lest they diminished our appetite - we nodded excitedly at the prospect at last of dining in grand fashion at tables where once would have sat political greats such as Winston Churchill, Nye Bevin, Tony Benn or Hugh Gaitskill.

"I actually forgot to book anything," said Donald in a tone that had our hearts sink. "It can be quite difficult at this time of night. Everything's usually all booked up. Let's see what we can organise."

What Donald was eventually able to organise was three rounds of bacon and beans on toast in a forlorn and empty cafeteria which was probably used by staff. Donald had obviously recovered his appetite after his fifteen minutes of abstinence and continued to demolish a further couple of re-fills of this stuff regaling us throughout with stories and anecdotes which had both of us in fits of laughter. Truly he was a man with no evident conceit of himself. He was a wonderful host and a man of great charm and wit. It almost compensated for the grand *repas* that we had anticipated, but missed.

Under the leadership of Tony Blair, Donald was variously Chief Whip and Secretary of State for Scotland. Inevitably he was brilliant at each task, singled out by Blair from time to time as the one man in his Cabinet upon whom he could rely completely. However, it was the personal urging of his predecessor, John Smith that ultimately drove Blair along the path towards a political settlement for Scotland, the *"settled will of Scotland"* as it was then described by the best Labour Prime Minister we never had.

Blair gave Donald the task of fashioning the Scotland Bill which began famously with the words. "There shall be a Scottish Parliament" and he worked hard along with others like Wendy Alexander to produce this flagship legislation which was laid before the Westminster Parliament on 22 March 1999.

When the Bill had become an Act and I had become a candidate for the Parliament, Donald, as I mentioned earlier, had announced that he wanted to visit Govan to meet with me, Iain White, the Headteacher of Govan High School and David Murray, Chairman of Rangers FC in front of the final year students. He wanted each of us to say a few words and to answer questions from the students. I was excited. Perhaps here I could speak in such a brilliant fashion that Donald would simply stop the proceedings and instruct his aides to do what must be done to find me a seat so that I might grace his Cabinet table after the election.

As ever, matters were rather more prosaic on the day. Donald's principle media adviser was David Whitton, an 'old school' media man who had cut his teeth on television, at the *Scotsman* and the *Daily Record* and was now Donald's closest advisor. I caught David's attention when the entourage arrived and asked whether it might be possible to have a few words with Donald after the meeting.

"No problem, Ron", said David and he was as good as his word. I had spoken well; passionate and humorous, my stock in trade, but I could see that Donald merely wanted the floor for himself and David Murray. It became evident that Iain and I were only the beards for Donald's ability innocently to meet informally with one of the business community's biggest beasts. Still, he was most encouraging. I should have really listened to his advice, though, if I was determined upon a political career, as he guided me not to place all of my political eggs in the Govan basket. "There are many other seats out there you'd have a chance of winning, Ron." There weren't, actually.

It wouldn't be until months later that I'd become aware of the political deal done between Donald and local MP Mohammad Sarwar to bring Gordon Jackson into Parliament in order to guarantee Donald of having at least one QC on board so he could fill the post of Attorney General. However, the very big upside of all of this was that it brought me into contact with his lieutenant, David Whitton and when he left government in October 2000 after Donald's untimely death, he became for some years, my own media adviser in Scottish Enterprise Glasgow until Robert Crawford attempted to sabotage our relationship by moving David to Paisley in order to break what he saw as Glasgow's Labour fiefdom!

I can still remember David on national television making the announcement of Donald's death following a slip where he cracked his head on the pavement and died of internal bleeding after a period of hospitalisation. David was quite obviously emotional as if he was announcing the demise of his own father and in a sense, he was. Donald Dewar was the father of the Scottish Parliament. He oversaw the 'Yes, Yes' Referendum. He wrote the Act. He selected the controversial site for the Parliament building. He selected the controversial Catalonian architect, Enrique Miralles. He was the first, First Minister and, in my and many others' view, he was the best by a distance. Over the years I'd got to know Donald well enough to be acknowledged if our paths crossed. I saw him from time to time walking in his stilted, limping, six feet five inches of dishevelledness to meetings in the City Chambers. He always brought out feelings of affection in me - not a usual reaction to seeing a politician cross George Square. Politicians could be respected, they might be reviled, they might be met warmly, but few were held in affection by the public. Donald was one of the few.

For some years, Laurie and Pam Russell lived above Donald, a single man, in a rambling semi-villa in Glasgow's Hyndland. Laurie spoke of a number of occasions when he would leave for work in the morning only to find Donald's brief case, doubtless full of state secrets outside his door where, absent-mindedly, he'd left it the night before, probably balancing a fish supper and some files while he tried to turn the key in his lock.

After Lally, Glasgow politics had descended into chaos. In 1996 the Party acted stutteringly, but eventually there was, in their terms, or more precisely in *media* terms, a clean out. A new, young Leader, Frank McAveety, was elected, much to his astonishment as he told me later.

Frank moved quickly to make his mark and instituted an Ethics Committee that was populated not by Elected Members but by senior people in the city including an editor of one of the papers critical of the previous regime.

I first met Frank when I was asked to act as Chief Executive of Glasgow North Ltd on an interim basis. Frank was Chairman. The previous Chief Executive had been accused of using money inappropriately, if legally, and had left the organisation. To get it back on its feet, I was asked to stand in. I agreed on the basis that there was a £10,000 fee paid to Govan Initiative and that I'd only spend half a day there until I made arrangements for a new Chief Executive to be appointed.

Having spent a week there and having reviewed the reasons for my predecessor's departure, I asked to see Frank. One of the main uses to which the money in question, set aside in a trust, was to be put was the re-housing of the company from its existing dilapidated accommodation. A substantial proportion of it, unwisely rather than illegally, had been used to finance a study tour of North America and Frank had been one of the entourage.

Frank explained that Paul Martin, the son of the local MP, Michael Martin - who rose eventually to become the Speaker of the House of Commons but who resigned dramatically in 2009 after a scandal involving the payment of expenses to MPs - saw him as a political threat. He reckoned that it was the intention of the Martin family that Paul should replace his father at Westminster. Frank figured that some might use this situation to bring bad publicity to the company as long as he was involved and I found myself making my first recommendation to my new Chairman that he resign his position forthwith. He duly did.

Frank went on to become Leader of Glasgow City Council and subsequently won the Shettleston seat in the

Scottish Parliament. He then served as Deputy Minister of Communities and Minister of Sport before returning to the back benches, after failing to win the support of the First Minister following a Parliamentary exchange which had embarrassed him. Over the piece, I enjoyed his company enormously. Over the early years we dined together fairly frequently. He was a very bright, hugely articulate, well read - he was an English Teacher until taking up politics full time - a really witty man, who used these gifts well in debate. Unfortunately, his main preoccupation was Frank McAveety. He spoke passionately about the poor and disadvantaged but essentially his ego prevailed. If he was chocolate, he would have eaten himself.

He was appointed Minister for Culture and Sport after the demise of Lord Mike Watson and had obviously determined that he wouldn't be caught out as was his predecessor, who was asked upon leaving Bute House, "What post have you been offered?" Mike, very proud, faced the cameras and said, "I'm proud to have been offered and have accepted the position of Minister for Culture and Sport."

The supplementary question – obviously well prepared by an on-the-ball journalist was, "What's your favourite opera?"

Mike was flustered and dumbstruck … and guess what interview was shown that evening on the television news?

Frank had learned well. A big Celtic fan, prior to his appointment to the same post, he'd recently returned from Seville where Celtic had just crowned a glorious season by contending the EUFA Cup Final against Porto. When after his appointment he stepped from Bute House and was asked the same operatic question by a journalist confident of another flustered reply, he replied without missing a beat, "The Barber of Seville". Witnessing this on television, I wrote to him to congratulate him on his new ministerial position and declared myself puzzled as in the interests of ecumenism, I'd presumed that his favourite opera was 'The Magic Flute!'

The last time I was with him in public was when I was in Washington DC giving a speech at Georgetown University to an audience of Scottish businessmen and women as well as a group of third year students from Glasgow universities whom we had placed with large American Corporations on the East Coast, all of which were owned or managed by Scots.

Frank was attending an event on the Mall in front of Capitol Hill on behalf of the Scottish Parliament. The heat and humidity in the large marquee was quite incredible but Frank, dressed in full Highland dress, stood at the podium and delivered a fine speech. We dined that night in the company of his aides and Susan Stewart, the first Scottish Ambassador to the USA, who was based in the British Embassy, and had a great time in the air conditioned atmosphere of a Georgetown restaurant. Frank was still wearing the kilt.

When 'Frankie went to Hollyrood' as we punned, referring to the Liverpool rock band, 'Frankie Goes To Hollywood', he was replaced as Leader of Glasgow City Council by his then Deputy, Councillor Charlie Gordon. Charlie had been a Board Member of Govan Initiative when I was Chief Executive but had been moved on from his Gorbals seat, to a Drumchapel seat to his final Ward in Knightswood.

Charlie and I never really got on. I found him a cold fish and he found me too friendly with people who weren't in his group. He was always polite enough to my face but I was always aware that he would do me no favours. The only time he ever said anything complimentary about me was once when he and I were addressing a gathering of major players in the banking industry at a dinner in the Stock Exchange in London.

London had ground to a halt that night because President George W. Bush was visiting the Queen for dinner in Buckingham Palace and security was unbelievably tight. Any protesters, and there were thousands upon thousands, were shepherded together in groups and completely surrounded by a ring of policemen from the Met and elsewhere. Travel in the centre of London that night was almost impossible.

I had delivered a light hearted speech. In my speech, prior to my passionate conclusion about the virtues of Glasgow - the main point of me getting to my feet - I had tapped into the undercurrent of frustration felt by the audience over the inconvenience the Presidential visit was causing and made a few jokes about Bush, never my favourite politician, and quipped that he was so lacking in intelligence, he was the first President ever to buy a corner table for the Oval Office. My speech went down very well. Charlie followed me and said how much he'd enjoyed my speech making reference *en passant* that I was well known as a 'Glasgow Nationalist'. However, it may have been designed as a back-handed compliment. While I was very proud of that accolade, I was also well aware that it would offend and upset many of my colleagues from Scottish Enterprise National who were dotted throughout the audience that night, who took the view that we were all involved in serving the *Scottish* cause and should stand ready to be moved at a moment's notice to serve only the greater interests of the *nation's* economy. Not me! I belonged to Glasgow.

During the period of Charlie's leadership, he presented a dour, combative face to the world. The front pages of the *Evening Times* would frequently see Charlie take a swipe at Parliamentary politicians of his own party. Not for him the background negotiations of other politicians.

When I was called to explain this phenomena to colleagues within Scottish Enterprise, I had to remind my inquisitor that politics in Glasgow had the potential to be a bit rough and that they had to realise that every time Charlie appeared defiant on the front page, he bolstered his own appeal within the *city* Labour group, probably to the same extent that he diminished his influence within the Scottish Executive as the Scottish Government was then called; but then, *they* didn't elect him.

Another example of Charlie's *modus operandi* was occasioned by a visit of Robert Crawford and Professor Neil Hood, the Vice Chair of Scottish Enterprise, to meet him in his office. Normally it would have been protocol for me to have attended with Robert but he chose his Vice Chairman and didn't bother informing me of his visit. I had to find out from a council source.

Robert could be unbelievably confident in his own abilities. Charlie was viewed as a 'bogie man' within Scottish Enterprise National and was certainly presented by me to them as an able man who was not easy to deal with. In my mind, I could hear Robert acting against the counsel of his advisers and saying, 'Ach, I'll just away down there myself and sort him out'.

In the event, Robert and Neil met with him for an hour and left his office feeling that they had had a good meeting that would lead to further areas of collaboration. Charlie shook their hand and without having informed them, went next door for a meeting with the press that he'd set up earlier and in which he went on to criticise Scottish Enterprise vociferously for the next day's press. Robert was shocked to the core.

My Chairman, Tom O'Neill didn't miss a trick and raised with Robert on a number of occasions the wisdom of trying to operate without an understanding of the local personalities and local circumstances. To be fair to

Robert, he phoned me and apologised, saying it wouldn't happen again... before launching into a tirade about Charlie. Well, he was telt!

Charlie was also a machine politician from the old school. He trusted no other organisation to contribute to the growth in fortunes of the city. Later on, my Deputy Chairman, John Matthews, asked him that very question and Charlie grudgingly accepted that perhaps the Health Board had a contribution to make but that there was little else that the Council could not run itself. Charlie wasn't one of nature's collaborators.

The story was told that following the dramatic and dreadfully sad death of Donald Dewar some of the more senior party officials and elected members found themselves together at a dinner in Glasgow's Art Galleries and an opportunity was taken to resolve the inevitable but thorny question about who would replace him. Despite newspaper talk of Donnie Munro, the lead singer of Scot-rock band Runrig, standing, an offer was allegedly made unconditionally to Charlie. His ward was within Donald's constituency of Anniesland, he was a senior politician - Charlie apparently took the view that as Leader of Glasgow City Council, he was the second most senior politician in Scotland after the First Minister - and he had the support of the local political big-wigs. Allegedly, Charlie agreed but made conditions so the offer went instead to Bill Butler who has since distinguished himself as a left-leaning backbencher of principle and purpose.

Some years later, Charlie had been deposed as leader and he announced to the press that he had achieved all he sought to achieve for Glasgow. His ambition now was to go to Parliament. An opportunity presented itself shortly thereafter when Lord Mike Watson, who had been accused of the unbelievable act of attempting to set fire to the curtains at the Prestonfield House Hotel during the November 2004 annual Politician of the Year Award, appeared at court for sentence. It had been the first of these Award dinners that I'd missed and given that I was friendly with Mike, it would not have been outwith the bounds of possibility that I could have been in his company when this brainstorm led to his arrest and sixteen months imprisonment.

Immediately upon leaving the courthouse in handcuffs, a statement was issued on his behalf which among other things stated his intention to resign the Glasgow Cathcart seat immediately.

First off the blocks was First Minister Jack McConnell who nominated millionaire Charan Gil, a very successful Indian entrepreneur, who had served on the Board of Scottish Enterprise Glasgow for four years during which I was Chief Executive. I always got on pretty well with Charan and there's little doubt he'd have been a great catch for the party, but I've never been a fan of candidates being parachuted into an alien constituency. After a local backlash it became evident that Charan wasn't even a party member and that his nomination wasn't competent. His demise came swiftly.

Shortly afterwards, I attended a table at one of his annual 'Hottest Night of the Year' dinners, always a great success and an opportunity for Charan to show off his great singing voice, tell a few jokes and raise money for charity. He was the butt of much of the humour that night. His business partner spoke warmly of Charan's abilities in what appeared at first to be a haranguing of the politicians present for their lack of foresightedness in not choosing Charan as the candidate.

"Charan's always been interested in helping the poor and disadvantaged ... he's always been keen to take his entrepreneurial skills into another context ... he's always

felt that he would eventually follow a political career ...."
He paused for effect. "The only thing he forgot to do was
to join a political *party!*"

Charan, always a witty and engaging public speaker,
got to his feet and went into his own speech that evening.
As ever it was peppered with jokes. In front of a more
political audience than he was perhaps used to, some of
them fell as flat as pancakes.

Charan's special guest that night was First Minister
Jack McConnell. Bob Wylie was at the table beyond
Charan's during this rendition. He got to his feet and
squeezing the First Minister on the shoulder as he passed,
asked rhetorically of him in mock horror, "So that's your
candidate?" and walked on serenely to the toilet ... or the
bar ... probably the bar!

The local front runner was Bill Miller. Indeed, Bill
was to have been a guest on the evening of Charan Gil's
Hottest Night of the Year but demurred on the basis that
Charan might find his attendance embarrassing given
the election. Bill and I had known one another for years
and had become friendly, meeting one another for a pint
regularly. Bill had been elected as the Member of the
European Parliament and served the interests of Glasgow
exceptionally well. He enjoyed a lot of political support
locally and in many other constituencies as he was
unstinting in helping others out in by-elections. Bill had
been cruelly robbed of his political career when the party
settled on the principle of gender balance and agreed that
in every election there should be an outcome which was
referred to as 'boy/girl; boy/girl' in terms of listing. Bill
should have been second on the list to David Martin, the
Senior Vice President of the European Parliament. Martin
wanted to stand for Strathkelvin & Bearsden but did not
even make the shortleet. Perhaps that was just as well for
him as in 2003, Labour lost Strathkelvin & Bearsden to

hospital campaigner Dr Jean Turner. So David Martin stood again for the 2004 European Elections and as a consequence of this act and the fact that interposed between he and Bill was a woman, Catherine Stihler, Bill came third, only a few hundred votes short of what was needed. A simply magnificent achievement but he was out of the European Parliament.

It was generally understood that if Bill made the short-leet for Holyrood in Cathcart, he'd win the party's nomination and the election in a canter. No one could stop him. The party in its wisdom therefore decided that the short-leet would be decided centrally and, unsurprisingly, Bill was not selected.

Charlie and a couple of others were selected for interview and it became evident that a political deal had been done. The eventual and inevitable winner of the charade was Charlie Gordon who went on to success in the election to follow. His political career will doubtless prosper as he as a most able and intelligent man ... If only his new comrades find him a warmer person than I did.

His political fortunes took a turn for the worse at the end of 2007 when he was involved in arranging a donation for the leadership campaign of Wendy Alexander from Paul Green, a businessman of Charlie's acquaintance who was a resident of the Channel Islands. It was subsequently exposed as an illegal donation and after a few twists and turns, led to the resignation of the leader of the party in Scotland, Wendy Alexander.

In the early 90's, I remember Laurie Russell telling me of a constituency meeting in the west end of Glasgow the previous night. It had been true to form in those days with members being barred, walkouts and general mayhem. "A new guy turned up", said Laurie. "This guy called Steven Purcell took the chair and handled the meeting like an old hand. He can't be twenty yet!"

Over the years, Steven's name was to become familiar to me although we had not then met. In November 1999, Sir Alex Ferguson was honoured by his city and he was made a Freeman of the City of Glasgow at a dinner I attended with Jean in the City Chambers. Steven was pointed out to me and I introduced myself to him.

"Of course, of course," said Steven as I told him who I was. "I've heard all about your work down in Govan." Steven was charming; a most engaging conversationalist. Warm and witty, he was everything that Charlie Gordon was not in his style of personal communication. From that evening, Steven appeared in my firmament and co-incidentally, when I joined Scottish Enterprise Glasgow as Chief Executive, he was appointed to my Board as he then occupied the post of Convenor of the Department of Regeneration Services.

'By the way', as we're wont to say in Glasgow when we seek a diversion in the conversation, the incorporation of Sir Alex as a Freeman of the City was memorable beyond meeting Steven Purcell for the first time. When introduced by the Chief Executive, who read from a heraldic scroll full of formality and pomp, Alex took the stage in the City Chambers to huge applause and picked up the microphone. He eyed the serried ranks of dignitaries all gathered to witness this great occasion and cleared his throat before breaking into song. *"Moooon River... wider than a mile, I'm crossing you in style some day...Oh, dream maker, you heart breaker...wherever you're going I'm going your way ..."* He finished with a huge smile on his face and received a big laugh and tumultuous applause. He waited until the room had settled ... "I've always wanted to do that," he said. "I thought it was traditional at Glasgow gatherings ..."

Some time afterwards, I had occasion to be in Westminster in order to meet the estimable John

Robertson MP about the shipbuilding crisis then brewing on the Clyde. I was aware that Steven was his election agent and that he was also in London that day working with John. I was in the company of the aforementioned Ken Wainwright; a political consultant and backroom figure who worked for the Labour Party and who fiercely avoided any personal publicity. As we entered the chambers to hear Prime Minister's Questions, we all four agreed to meet that evening for dinner.

In the event, John was delayed in Parliament. On that basis, we three went for a beer and after the first glass, the talk turned to politics and more precisely to the future that Steven saw for himself. There was little doubt that he was a politician of note and one with a very bright future. Both Ken and I questioned him sociably on where he thought he'd end up … the Council? … Westminster? … Holyrood? … Europe? Steven certainly had the ability to attain whatever political office he sought for himself.

The three of us got on famously and Ken and I were most affirming of Steven's ambitions. Ken was better placed than I was to assist Steven achieve any goal he sought but by the end of the evening we had settled upon the fact that politics can be as much about timing, being in the right place at the right time, as about ability. Steven's initial thought was that he'd consider challenging for the leadership of the Council when the time was right.

At the time, Steven was aware that there were many in the Glasgow Labour Group unhappy with the demeanour and political approach of Charlie Gordon but felt that he was unbeatable. We went through an analysis of this and agreed Steven's assessment but also agreed that this was something we should keep an eye on as Glasgow deserved better than finding itself at odds with every organisation internal to the city as well as externally in Parliament.

Over the next few years, Steven grew effortlessly in political stature. He refashioned the Department of Regeneration Services, bringing the planning function within the embrace of other forces for development and making it more action-orientated rather than merely regulatory; he was made Convenor of Education and completely rebuilt the city's crumbling school network by commissioning investment of some £220 million in 29 Secondary Schools throughout the city as well as a healthy smattering of Primary Schools. During this time he also saw off a dispute by Nursery staff who had a national pay grievance although Glasgow was the focus of media attentions if only because of its size.

Steven was always regarded as a nice guy and we all thought that his political credibility shot skywards as a consequence of the tough line he took over a political situation that might have seen another politician bend. After the Nursery dispute, he was viewed as a tough negotiator. It earned him a lot of political respect in the 'hard man' school of politics in the West of Scotland.

Ken, Steven and I kept in touch over his political ambitions, usually over dinner although there was one night when Ken and I were out having a pint and putting the world to rights. Both of us having discussed Steven's political prospects in his absence, Ken decided that the time was right for a face-to-face in order to move things along. I phoned Steven on his mobile and discovered as we'd anticipated that he'd be having a quiet pint in his local, the Station Bar, in his native Yoker.

Ken hailed a taxi and we were alongside him in the bar in no time. It was reassuring seeing Steven on his home turf. He was acknowledged by everyone in the pub - a Rangers' Bar, no less - and he was quite obviously comfortable in his own skin. Not someone you felt was edgy, always looking over your shoulder for the next conversation. Ken pressed him on his ambitions and we had a useful, if inebriated conversation about how Steven saw things going.

Steven increasingly reported to us that he was developing his band of supporters within the Council but that their numbers were too soft to permit a successful challenge to Charlie. One of the characteristics of Steven's support was that it was comprised by politicians that Ken and I felt were really decent people. Councillors like George Ryan, Irene Graham, Bob Winters and Aileen Colleran were all rounded, fully paid up members of the human race. His supporters were singularly devoid of the starey-eyed, fundamentalist politicians that often cling to the coat-tails of a promising new Leader. This was also most reassuring as it would be they, not any of Steven's informal advisers, who would ultimately put him in power and who would ultimately determine the success or otherwise of his tenure in office.

As the Council's 2005 AGM approached, one of whose tasks was to elect a Leader, Ken, Steven and I had more frequent meetings. Steven also met more regularly with his political supporters and great reams of paper were used up calculating and recalculating support for Steven *vis-a-vis* Charlie.

To an interested onlooker like me it was exciting; great fun. But to a serious politician like Steven, it was of fundamental importance. If he miscalculated, if he challenged a year too soon, it could set him back dramatically. We hummed and we hawed. We were confident then conservative. We usually had a glass of wine to assist our powers of analysis and then agree we shouldn't drink when taking a view on a matter of this importance and agreed to meet the following week where we had a glass of wine.....

Steven played a masterful game in rounding up his supporters. Advances were being made to opposition councillors. The *status quo* was being proposed by Steven. No politician would lose their job or their responsibility allowance. There was to be no *'Night of the Long Knives'*. Steven would be more collegiate and most importantly, he was recognised as the Leader with the most sophisticated understanding about what had to be done politically to secure the best result for the party in 2007, the year in which proportional representation was set to supplant 'first past the post' as the electoral system for local government in Scotland.

My re-reading this book saw me delete much of my account of how Steven actually went about challenging the leadership. Owing to my close involvement at the time I was able to see at first hand how a text-book operation like this should be organised. However, I decided that (a) this is Steven's story to tell and (b) writing what I know would change the nature of this book and give it a media value I do not seek. So I must report merely that Steven decided to compete for the office of Leader of the Labour Group with Charlie.

Charlie Gordon eventually bowed to the inevitable and asked to meet with Steven. He agreed not to put his name forward and instead to support that of Steven's so that the city Labour Group would continue on a path which presented unanimity to the world. He set out a few conditions which were all too easy for the 32-year-old Steven Purcell to agree and on the twenty-fourth of May, 2005, Glasgow found itself with the youngest Labour Leader in living memory.

One year later, Steven had been making a great success of his term of office. He was being name-checked by Tony Blair as an excellent example of the new leadership of the party and was enjoying great press. I was attending a seminar on public administration with Cisco Systems when a text from Steven arrived on my mobile stating that in view of media speculation, he was announcing the break up of his marriage to Katrina and cited his homosexuality as the cause.

It had been a very brave decision by Steven. I'd been aware of the earlier conversations regarding this. One wing of his advisers argued that he should wait until after the next election, then four months away, and have the matter drowned in the wash of a nation-wide poll that would see local issues like this overlooked. The other view, and that of my own, was that this kind of story would surface inevitably as a political enemy would not be able to resist the chance to seize the opportunity and that Steven may as well deal with it immediately so he was in charge of events.

In the event, Steven took the latter approach and was treated with great sympathy by the press and by his political colleagues. He went on over the next period to have tremendous success as Leader and was constantly being mentioned in dispatches, even as an emergency call-up when Labour Leader Wendy Alexander was being out-debated by Alex Salmond in the Scottish Parliament. There was an undercurrent suggesting that the party was bound to lose the next election unless it did something dramatic and a strong line in many newspapers was the elevation and election of Steven as head of the party in Scotland. This didn't happen but the future of Steven Purcell as a major Labour figure in Scottish and UK politics was, to all intents and purposes, assured.

However, 'a week is a long time in politics' as Harold Wilson once said, and Steven found himself embroiled in controversy in March 2010 when he resigned abruptly from the council citing 'stress and exhaustion'. The press offered quotes from 'senior figures' within the council to the effect that he was suffering from a 'chemical dependency' but Steven went on record to intimate that while he'd dabbled with illegal substances over a year previously, his frailty was that of many in the west of Scotland; alcohol.

Press interest was all consuming. Steven went to ground in an effort to seek treatment and support and admitted himself to Castle Craig Hospital, a drug and alcohol addictions facility in the Scottish Borders. After a short stay, Steven disappeared and went for some rest and relaxation, first to a relative's in Australia then to another in Ireland before returning to his family in Glasgow. Six weeks after coming back to his city and leading a relatively normal life in his community, a tabloid newspaper ran an 'exclusive', "Purcell Back!" headline ... perhaps testimony to the local protective arm placed around him by those who knew him best.

Steven has polarised opinion in the political world. There are those who take the view that a politician who allegedly breaks the law should be banished from public life. Others regret the fact of his all too human frailties and prefer to forgive an enormously talented politician who might yet defy his critics and return to serve at some point in the future once he has tholed his assize. I'm firmly in the latter camp.

Over the years I've thoroughly enjoyed working with politicians. I've seen them at their best and I've seen them at their worst. Often I've found them self-serving and insecure. Sometimes I've found them noble and many serve without ever achieving high office or of being associated with great works. Some manage to carry their original motivations throughout their political career; to serve those more vulnerable than themselves. Well, I have been fortunate to have seen many up close and have formed the assessment that ... some have been lions ... and some have been donkeys. All have been interesting.

15. Convivial Temulence And The *Craic*

Count your life by smiles, not tears. Count your age by friends, not years.
Jewish Proverb.

Following my appointment as Chief Executive of the Glasgow Development Agency / Scottish Enterprise Glasgow in September 2000, a letter arrived asking me to complete a questionnaire in order that I might have my personal details included in that year's edition of *Who's Who Scotland*. Close on its heels arrived another letter asking the same of me in relation to its big brother, the UK edition of *Who's Who*. Whilst appreciating that it was the office I held that had secured their interest in me rather than any personal achievements, I was flattered. I completed them both with a backwards glance at the earlier entries of the lustrous, the great and the inconsequential which all held to a pretty tight format as prescribed by *Who's Who*. I followed the rules as requested whilst looking for something to demonstrate my own personality. My only real opportunity came when asked to reveal my hobbies at the end of the entry. Most others had offered 'polo', 'horse riding', 'rugby football' or somesuch. After much thought and having accurately entered, 'watching Manchester United', I also ventured, 'laughing out loud', 'irreverence' and 'convivial temulence'. To my surprise they were accepted – as was my choice of Club – my local pub, the Redhurst instead of Groucho's, the Athenaeum or the Reform Club as favoured by others.

The previous Christmas I'd received a stocking-filler gift of a book of large words, presumably due to my interest in speech, grammar and communication. I loved the word *temulence*; 'the act of becoming inebriated' and given my enthusiasm for having a pint and a laugh with pals, began to tell others that one of my favourite hobbies was convivial temulence. I found this a useful way of responding to questions of my interests because at first breath it gave the impression of an interest that clearly required practice. No one has ever known the meaning of temulence when I have used the expression and have invariably smiled at it having been defined. The only occasion on which I was caused problems was when the *Evening Times* did a feature on me for their '*My Life*' column one Friday. I was asked to provide a few hundred words in response to the same several questions they asked of a prominent Glaswegian each week … describe your family … how do you earn a living … describe your home … what are your hobbies?

Presumably because I wasn't there to reassure the journalist that there really *was* a word called 'temulence', my hobby was presented to the great unwashed of Glasgow as 'convivial *temperance*'. The reaction of friends and family was, not unreasonably, one of astonished disbelief coupled with a wry supposition that what I was really about was trying to spin a new persona for media purposes!

However, over the years, having a refreshment with friends has been a great joy whether enjoying a glass of chilled white wine, a beer with a pal one-on-one, a formal, black tie dinner or a more substantial session.

I suspect because of my father's untimely death owing in part at least to over indulgence in alcohol, I didn't really take much in the way of a drink until I was about twenty-five. Prior to that I'd taken a sociable shandy and worked my way up to a glass of sweet white wine, usually *Liebfraumilch* - or sugarolly watter, to my pals with a more discerning palate - into which I'd stir a couple of spoonfuls of sugar to make it more drinkable. I just didn't enjoy the taste of any alcohol. My first adolescent engagement with the demon drink came when as a member of the *Ryat*

Lynn folk group, we decided aged sixteen, to attempt entry to the Malletsheugh Pub in rural Newton Mearns as we had been practising in the Gorbals Waterworks just a mile away. Les Carson claimed the most experience in this area of activity, having once having had a pint with his father, and explained in great detail what probably lay behind the forbidding doors of the pub. We none of us had had any insight into the drinkers' world, as in those days pubs were pretty dismal, closed and smoky places with all of the windows frosted over as if actually seeing topers downing a pint would have led to frenzied abandon on behalf of otherwise God-fearing people.

Upon entering, Carson ordered for the three of us. I'd earlier agreed that he should buy me a neat vodka as I'd been told it had neither smell nor taste. What could be more acceptable? Standing on tip-toe and deepening his voice to something resembling the sonorous rumblings of Robert Mitchum in *Build My Gallows High*, he ordered a round. Much to our astonishment the barman merely nodded and proceeded to pour our drinks whilst continuing his conversation with another customer. Everything went according to plan until following our retreat to the snug, we toasted our success and I immediately and athletically coughed back up a spray of the fiery poison that had just sand-papered my larynx, covering everyone within reach in my vodka.

However, over the years I've managed a more civilised relationship with drink. Like many in the west of Scotland, I've a sweet tooth and in my case, still struggle to enjoy a pint of Guinness preferring the more refreshing lager. I've enjoyed brandy for decades when taken on its own or more frequently accompanied by a diet coke, again in deference to my sweet palate. The one surprising, to me, exception has been the enjoyment I now find in dry white wine. No more spoonfuls of sugar.

I've also been fortunate in two other ways. First, I've always been a 'happy imbiber'. If this has caused me problems over the years it has been as a consequence of my laughter and general giddiness when having taken perhaps one too many.

Second, my body tells me when I should give it a rest…not *during* a drinking session, but over the few days afterwards when I just don't feel like a drink. In consequence Magnetic Resonance Imaging [MRI] scans have shown my liver to be in pretty good nick despite the intermittent traumas I put it through. I've never really suffered from hangovers but after a heavy session have usually felt tired the following day. The only exception to this is when I drink beer, brandy and wine during the same session. I do tend to suffer 'the wrath of grapes' after that.

On foreign holidays when *en famille*, I've justified Jean's description of the period as a 'drying out fortnight for Ron' as almost invariably I hire a car upon arrival and chauffeur the family around every day, a practice which forbids alcohol consumption. However, when away with pals, or on holiday with them, the consumption of bevy features centre-stage but I can honestly say that after a heavy night, I don't look forward to yet another round of drinking. In those circumstances, with one or two honourable exceptions, I usually drink more moderately so I can maintain pace with some of my friends who are far less judicious than me in this regard!

Danny Brennan, when he shared an office with Laurie, David Asquith and me was perhaps my pal who most seriously seemed headed towards alcoholism. His regular tipple was a *triple* spiced rum and my recollection of those days was of his ability to find an argument in the least promising situations. Back in the eighties and nineties, we all used to drink in the Ritz Bar at Charing Cross and one night Danny and Damien Yeates got into a furious row that threatened to come to blows over which nation had the most planes in the sky that day over Bosnia, the United States or European air forces of NATO!

Danny married a girl from Nottingham, settled down in England and when last I visited him down there, he'd taken a far more moderate line on his drinking.

Over a few decades a drinking club was established and met once a month on its last Friday. Its membership remained pretty constant over that time. Core membership included John McManus who always had a measured approach to drink, usually holding to a few bottles of beer or, when gathered in company, a few pints. His sole delinquency when drunk was to slur his words and to decide against the last train, paying a fortune to get a taxi back to Kilmarnock from Glasgow.

Neil Graham is of Irish stock and was therefore programmed by God to enjoy Guinness by the gallon. His appetite for the black stuff is impressive but it only affects him insofar as his modest persona will break into a rendition of *The Ould Triangle* if someone mentioned geometry never mind Dublin. His ancestry was never very far below the surface and he'd take any excuse to discuss the fortunes of his beloved Glasgow Celtic.

Equally modest was David Asquith, a long-standing member of our wee drinking club, if one who seldom involved himself in its various sub-committees established over the years - music appreciation, football, golfing, horse racing. David was our only English member and was a cricket *aficionado*. Cricket was never discussed so David tended to tend his pint of warm beer, quietly awaiting an opportunity to start a trend. He was also our Club Secretary and without his dedicated stewardship the group would not have survived the years in such fine fettle.

Bill Miller was elected European Member of Parliament in 2004 but as I've mentioned earlier, was cruelly removed from office by the Labour Party's decision to interpose a women candidate between all of the male candidates. Following Charlie Gordon's election as MSP for Cathcart, Bill took a job as the west of Scotland's 'man in Europe', set up office in Brussels and was therefore usually only able to attend on Fridays. Bill was notable for his ability to match everyone in the lager stakes before suggesting 'one for the pavement' and taking (usually) Neil and myself to The Pot Still in Hope Street for some quality malt whiskies before heading for a taxi or train.

Our most specialised drinker was Laurie who, like the rest of my pals, could sink a few. Unlike the others though, Laurie could take quite a few pints and could continue articulately to converse into the evening without any apparent effect. His metabolism however, appeared to hold back his drunkenness until a moment chosen by his central nervous system when at a precise, single sip of his pint he was reduced instantaneously to drunken mumblings. No hint of his gradual descent into oblivion. It happened in the blink of an eye and remains most impressive, even today.

Gary Hamilton was much younger than the rest of us and had an enormous appetite for lager tops. He attended meetings of the Friday evening club and contributed markedly to the general gaiety but when the rest of us groped our way to the door, he would leave us in his wake as he headed towards the city centre to meet up with younger friends for a real session!

Over the years we moved from the Ritz to the Universal Bar in Sauchiehall Lane. We'd been regular drinkers in the Ritz for years but it became evident that the bar was losing custom. One evening as we gathered, a large sound system was erected on the pub floor as we supped our pints and had a chat. Perhaps only a dozen people were in the bar. Around six o'clock it started to emit the most earsplitting cacophony in an attempt to lure customers. We protested to no avail and eventually left (to the applause of the new bar staff, I might say!) for the Bon Accord next door which was absolutely jammed with people having a drink and a conversation. We never returned to the Ritz which seemed unable to make its new formula work.

When my son, Ron first found gainful employment with COSLA after completing his Doctorate, he would attend the Universal on occasion. He'd known most of my pals over the years and enjoyed their company. He was usually a one pint man before heading for his home, then near Bathgate. A couple of pints usually signified that his wife Lisa was *en route* to collect him. Over the years the Universal served us well and Ron held one of his stag-nights there - the other was in Belfast - before marrying Lisa as a way of ensuring his lift home. In August 2009, Ron and Lisa bought a house in Busby, just up the road so I look forward to enjoying Ron's company over a beer rather more frequently that was ever possible in the past. In 2008, we moved lock, stock and barrel to the Griffin Bar, opposite the Kings Theatre, as it was more of a working man's pub and had been taken over by Bobbsie, the previous owner of the Universal and who imported all of the excellent customer care for which it rightly had become noted.

Occasionally we'd have visiting guests. Sometimes we'd have politicians come and spend some time with us and everyone there was pretty much Labour, or at least left of centre in their political beliefs. Fraser Kelly was a frequent imbiber and a good laugh. Jim Tait came along for a period and would sit regally sipping at a glass of dry white wine which he'd pour himself from a bottle he'd order upon arrival. Bob Wylie would attend after work from time to time but was never comfortable in the Universal as he always preferred to stand while drinking and the Universal encouraged a seated arrangement.

Many people who enjoy socialising like to enjoy a drink. In Glasgow, there are those who might best be described as taking a *terrible* drink. Others, who enjoyed a refreshment even more, might be described as being capable of taking a *fierce* drink. Bob was one of life's great topers and now and again would plead guilty to enjoying a *terrible fierce* drink. If he was out for a session he'd drink Guinness but if behaving himself would restrict himself to an equal number of pints of Tennents' Lager; 'council lager' in Bob's parlance. How *that* worked I'll never know but Bob swears by its efficacy.

Our social club activities were invariably successful. There was almost always a trip or event on the planning horizon. Concerts (always with our wives), sporadic football matches, golf matches and horse racing usually at Ayr or Hamilton, but sometimes at Musselburgh, were always popular with our small fraternity.

Typically, Neil, Laurie and Bill were knowledgeable punters who would back their hunches with £40 or £50 bets. John McManus, who for years owned a couple of racehorses, *Sir Mulberry Hawk* and *Merchant of Dubai* as part of a syndicate with his brothers, Alistair and David, was an enthusiastic but more modest gambler. I'd go along and put a tenner on the second favourite so as to get higher odds. Usually I lost, but never too much. Earlier in my youth I'd read a quote from an American source where a dedicated punter's prayer to his lord was, *"Dear God, help me break even today. I sure could use the money."* I was always cautious.

I'd worked out a theory I figured was foolproof. (Subsequently I found that it dated back centuries and was called 'the Martingale Theory') which involved always backing the second favourite as it was inevitable that at some point a second favourite would win. My calculation was that if you lost, you just kept doubling your bet until you won, which at some point you must. My fellow gamblers ridiculed this approach, so at a meeting at Hamilton also attended by our wives, I put my theory to the test but instead of starting at £1, I started with £5 so escalating the cost of my test substantially. I then proceeded to go on a real losing streak and bet £5, £10, £20, £40 and £80 at which point Jean stopped my research before I became penniless. I bet a fiver on the next two races and lost so I should have been laying some £640 on the first race at the next meeting which I won at 3/1 and so should have pocketed £2560 against total bets of £1275. If only I'd had the balls and deep enough pockets. Of course, if I'd only won at evens my return of £1280 would only have won me a fiver. Hmmm.

I'd also attend the races as a guest of others. Once, Jean and I were invited to the Saints and Sinners evening at Hamilton. The table was situated in a large marquee and our table was populated by a very posh mob. Initially I wasn't bothered as over the years I'd developed a talent for getting on with anyone but as the Champagne was quaffed in ever greater quantities, the women became a bunch of braying Veronicas who took great pleasure in ridiculing the young ladies who had also dressed up in their finery as if guests at a wedding and who did rather stagger around on high heels.

Jean and I excused ourselves and went out to the paddock where we met Jamie McGrattan, one of my board members at Scottish Enterprise Glasgow. Jamie ran a piling company and had sponsored the first race, We chatted and he talked me through the rest of the card, even though he was there only to place a large bet on the fifth race which he 'was certain' would win; now there's a professional for you. Jamie had once been a bookmaker, had put two bookies out of business and was then taking weekly payments from a bookie in Glasgow to pay off a large bet he'd won, so this man was no mug.

Having received the sum of his wisdom, we returned to the table where I shared our new knowledge with my now well-inebriated fellow punters. Our host was excited at this information as he was also aware of Jamie's reputation. That evening I sat and watched in amusement as the toffs placed ever more substantial bets on Jamie's prophesies. Unbelievably, each of Jamie's predictions won until the last race by which time they thought him unbeatable. Astonishing bets were laid … and the horse was beaten by a nose! I found this hilarious, particularly as Jean and I couldn't believe that he'd forecast every race and we'd been picky, winning a few bob but not losing everything on the last chase. I enjoyed with some measure of *schadenfreude*, the discomfort of my fellow guests. That'll teach them to look down upon the *lumpenproletariat* enjoying themselves!

A more recent drinking buddy has been the wonderful Bob Baldry. He it was who took the reins at the Braehead Retail Centre, saw it built and made it profitable. Bob has a beautiful eight berth yacht berthed in Inverkip and is a keen sailor. From time to time he invites me and others for a day's sailing and although Bob stays off the hard stuff, his guests don't.

In the summer of 2006, I was sitting, glass in hand, in Ocean Blue – Bob's thirty foot yacht sailing in the Firth of Clyde with Bob's business partner Anne Ledgerwood, Jim Tait, John Smith, Head of Security at NASA and George Abbey – until some months previously the Director of NASA at the Johnson Space Centre who had become friendly with Jim and I. George was a senior Democrat from Texas and spoke slowly and ponderously but with feeling about how Bush had stolen the 2000 election from Al Gore, how the American people were equally horrified by President George W Bush's actions and how they were resolved to ensure that the evangelical right wing would not again represent the will of the American people. I was reminded that Bush was not representative of the great mass of Americans and that there was an America I could still love and respect – as well as Elvis.

I first met George when I visited Houston, Texas to visit a group of Glasgow teenage students who had taken part in a project organised by Scottish Enterprise Glasgow. Essentially we'd sought to encourage the take-up of science in schools so as to provide a conveyor belt of talented young Scots for these industries of the future and supporting Danny Logue from Careers Scotland, fashioned the Scottish Space School. Fifteen bright - actually, very bright - young Glaswegians travelled to Houston, to NASA's Johnson Space Centre each summer and spent ten days working with real live astronauts. Each year, eight or so astronauts travelled in the other direction and spent a week visiting schools in the West of Scotland telling pupils stories of space travel and trying to inspire a love of science in young minds. The reason this unusually generous facility was made available was due to the munificence of Dr. George Abbey, Director of NASA.

George and I were introduced by Danny Logue at a reception in Houston hosted by the British Ambassador and quickly got on like a house on fire. He was a real Scotophile. I spent four days in and around the Space Centre and we really hit it off. Once George discovered that I could play guitar and that I could knock out a few jigs and reels, he pestered me continuously to perform. I always desisted but one night in a local Italian restaurant in which a relative of his had an owning interest, he produced a guitar from behind the bar. As ever, I resisted his blandishments but eventually gave in and took the only device I could think of – my plastic debit card – to use as a guitar pick. This completely impressed George and after a few Scottish jigs he was completely won over.

George had resigned his Air Force commission in 1967, and distinguished himself at the Johnson Space Centre through increasingly responsible positions where he served as the Director of Flight Operations. There, he was responsible for the early operational flights of the Space Shuttle, and became the Director of Flight Crew Operations, responsible for management of flight crews as well as centre aircraft. As Director, he oversaw all of the centre's many activities, including the International Space Station and he had complete control over the selection of astronaut crews. Unofficially he was known as "King George," and sometimes "Darth Vader," for what newspapers at the time called his mysterious and imposing style. George also held senior level positions at NASA Headquarters before his JSC post. In 1991, he was appointed to the Executive Office of the President as Senior Director, Civil Space Policy, National Space Council.

The respect shown towards George was amazing. When in Houston we walked into a room full of astronauts, everyone stood up. He took me into top secret establishments around Houston like Lockheed Douglas and their top brass stood as he approached and treated him like royalty – he made it clear that I was a trusted compadre and as such, I was accorded similar status.

George could reasonably be described as lugubrious. He didn't say much but it became evident that people around him saw him as the saviour of space flight in the USA. On January 26 1986, when space shuttle Challenger - a reusable winged spaceship - exploded, there was a press outcry demanding the cancellation of future flight as they were too expensive and too risky. There had been nine previous space shuttle flights – all successful - but booster failure on this flight resulted in the death of all seven astronauts aboard. I noticed that in every board room or CEO's office I entered while in Houston one wall would be adorned with a photograph of the crew. Anyway, immediately after the Challenger disaster, George took a flight to Washington and persuaded Vice-President George Bush Snr to continue the programme.

Ever since Kennedy had caused NASA to exist, responsibility for it had passed to the Vice-President - Lincoln Baines Johnson, in the first case. Unsurprisingly, LBJ took the decision to locate one of its main operating locations in Houston – and called it Johnson Space Centre just to remind the electorate who had been responsible for the decision.

George had been responsible for selecting the astronauts and also for choosing which of them would fly on which missions. This might have rendered him a negative image as people might have feared him and the power he had – but it was obvious that he was held in great affection within the space community.

Perhaps the most poignant moment I had with George was when he brought space flight home to us in a very personal way in Glasgow. On February 1, 2003, Space Shuttle Columbia broke up on re-entry to the earth's atmosphere and all of the astronauts were killed. One of them, Lauren Clark, was a mission specialist and flight surgeon who had served in Scotland on the Holy Loch where she'd met her husband, Jonathan. B. Clark – also a flight surgeon. During their time in Scotland, both had fallen in love with the place, fallen in love with each other, had become great admirers of our music and had a particularly soft spot for Runrig – especially their rendition of Loch Lomond, which Lauren used as her wake up alarm call each morning on Space Shuttle Columbia.

One year after Columbia perished, in 2004, George led one of his trips to the Scottish Space School with eight astronauts and brought Lauren's husband Jonathan and their young baby with him. At a ceremony in the City Chambers to mark the space party's arrival, Jonathan said a few words about the importance of science – the objective of the mission to Scotland. Seated at a table in front of him were members of Runrig who had been invited along because of Lauren's enthusiasm for their music. You could have heard a pin drop as Jonathan spoke of his feelings for his wife and for the enjoyment they'd shared together of their time in Scotland, their love of life – and of Scottish music. He then bent down and picking up an item from below the podium, asked Runrig to join him on stage where he presented them with a framed copy of their Loch Lomond CD that had been recovered from the desert in Arizona after pieces of the shuttle had fallen to earth. He told the assembled company that the CD Lauren listened to every morning had returned to earth undamaged and that he wanted to present it to Runrig as a measure of the affection in which he and Lauren had held the work of the band. There wasn't a dry eye in the house.

Although George had a reputation for a dour calmness, his Head of Security, John Smith – a Dundonian – told me how when George was Deputy Head of Space Operations, he once set up his Director whose job he would assume some years later. Only hours before a launch, George's boss was testing count-down procedures and was watching the missile sit, steaming on the launch pad. Several times he counted down, ten … nine … eight … seven … until aborting on the final call. George arranged for him to take a phone call and inserted a recorded video shot of a previous launch on his monitor. Upon retaking his seat at launch command, you could imagine his reaction when he reached three … two … one … zero – only to see the spacecraft launch skywards! John Smith shook with laughter as he recounted the story telling me that George had been fired and re-hired five times that day by a shaken Director.

George was ultimately removed from his post rather unceremoniously. Over the years, George had run NASA in a particularly stern way with fines being doled out to contractors who failed to meet deadlines or standards. Over the forty years, he had risen through the ranks to the most senior position and had been responsible for imposing the most severe financial punishments upon one of the largest delinquent contractors – Halliburton, whose CEO was Dick Cheney. As I mentioned, the space business in the USA is controlled by the Vice-President and when Cheney took office as Veep under George W Bush, his first act was to remove George Abbey from office.

Bob Baldry invited George, some friends and I to sail the Firth of Clyde in his yacht to view the scenery that George championed so much back in America. As ever with Bob, he was a most convivial host but there had been a torrential downpour throughout the West of Scotland the day previously; all of the drains had overflowed into the firth. Given George's love of Scotland, it was therefore rather embarrassing when *Ocean Blue* found itself carrying the recently retired Head of NASA towards Rothesay surrounded by a sea of shite!

However, over the years, as I entered my fifties, Bob became my most regular drinking companion. He lived for a while with his beautiful Romanian wife Lida in the Battlefield area of Glasgow and phoned me one night to ask my advice about schooling. Bob had been the top man in the left-wing Militant movement in Scotland and was concerned about the quality of schooling available locally for his daughter, Kathryn. He was wrestling with the prospect of sending her privately to Hutcheson's Grammar School and was clearly uncomfortable at the prospect. I figured that he'd get a hard time from those he still called friends within the movement.

I'd earlier calculated with another friend his own interest in making similar educational provision and worked out that it would cost him something in the region of a quarter of a million pounds to send his two daughters to private education from aged five until university and it was evident to me that the wise approach to take was to invest money in your home and take advantage of the extremely high standard of state schooling to be found in East Renfrewshire where Jean and I lived.

I advised accordingly and some months later, having negotiated a price with my old economics professor, Dr Doug Strachan, who lived in Eastwoodmains Road, Clarkston before selling up and moving upon retirement to Ayrshire, Bob moved *en famille* into his house just round the corner and conveniently placed for the odd 'tea-time pint' with me in the bar of the Redhurst Hotel.

I must have attended well over a hundred functions over the years, mostly in Glasgow but also Edinburgh or London. I suppose the dinners at the Houses of Parliament in Westminster were the most impressive to someone like me who enjoyed the political world, but the large hotels of Glasgow were the most frequented by me and most of my friends and colleagues over the years.

I had some great times at formal dinners. Once I was asked to speak at short notice to a large audience in the Glasgow Hilton. Donald Dewar had just died, and that night's speaker, Henry McLeish, had been called to take care of responsibilities associated with his own elevation as Leader of the party. I was told by the civil servants that I should play it straight with no jokes but I always liked to start with a couple of informalities to ease my way into my main theme. However, that night I'd steeled myself to keep to the script I'd been given but as I climbed the stage to the podium I noticed that every one of the sixty or so tables had, as their table's centrepiece, a large cluster of helium filled balloons reaching to the ceiling. I turned to my audience and announced, "I haven't seen this many balloons since the last time I was in the main stand at Ibrox."

It went down well, but not as well as that night's humorous speaker - whose name I forget. He'd been brought up from England and had been billed as something special. He was seated between me and Jackie Bird, the BBC newsreader who was MC that evening. Throughout dinner he was most solicitous and asked all sorts of questions about me, evincing a genuine interest in my background. Of course when it was his turn to speak, he used this knowledge to present me as the butt of all of his jokes to the great amusement of all.

However, what were more impressive were his skills as a motivational speaker and illusionist! At one point he asked me up on to the stage and asked me to point to any table in the hall and having done so, to select a man seated at the table. I did this and he wrote something on a piece of paper, placed it in a sealed envelope and asked me to put it in my pocket. He then asked me to select another five men from different tables and when they were all standing he asked each of them to count the change they had in their pockets. They did so and he added up the amounts as each was revealed. The final amount was something like £11.57 and of course when I opened the envelope, *that* was the amount he'd written down. Astonishing!

Some years later I was a guest at a table in the Radisson Hotel and I saw that he was speaking again. Excitedly, I informed the table that the guy was really impressive and that they could look forward to an amazing number of jokes, tricks and illusions. At the comfort break I noticed him wandering around the tables saying hello to people and told myself that he was also obviously just as solicitous as he was when he dined with me some years earlier.

I was most disappointed when he constrained himself to an inspirational speech with a complete absence of tricks and jokes. I resigned myself to accusations of exaggeration at the conclusion of his peroration when, in closing, he said he wanted to say goodbye and in doing so, he named every person sitting in the hall in his farewell! His half-time wander had been designed to memorise all of the name-place toblerones at each place setting. Most impressive.

Not infrequently I'd have a speaking part at these dinners and would behave myself until my task had been completed. I was always very professional about that. Even if I was only required to stand and hand over an award of some nature, I'd restrict myself to a single glass of wine while the rest of the table would pour wine down their throats with gay abandon. However, when I attended as a guest I was able to relax and enjoy the company and the *craic*.

I learned my lesson the hard way in this regard as in 1997 when my company, Govan Initiative had been voted one of the top five performing businesses in Europe against private sector opposition. We held a Christmas party for all staff in Ibrox Stadium. I'd made it known that I was now officially off-duty and was having a whale of a time at our table drinking in the Christmas spirit, so to speak, when one of our colleagues who was organising the event approached me and asked if I'd mind taking the microphone and reading out a list of those among the staff who'd achieved some sort of recognition that year … a degree, a Higher National Diploma, promotion or whatever. I agreed on the basis that I was among friends and anyway, how hard could *that* task be.

Accordingly I took to the stage and started to make my way through the list. In doing so, my eyes fell on one of those who was to have their success celebrated; my wife Jean. Jean and I always made use of her maiden name at work, Jean Pollock, so as not to make it quite so evident that she was married to the boss. Jean was also tremendously popular with our colleagues so when I saw an opportunity to make a joke at her expense, I should have reflected further.

I kept her name until last and then said, "Of course, I was delighted earlier in the year when I was informed that Jean had successfully achieved the advanced Apple Macintosh Certificate. Indeed, I was so delighted that I went out and bought her a dozen long stemmed roses to congratulate her. She looked at the roses and exclaimed, "I suppose you'll expect me on my back with my legs in the air for this?" And I responded, "Why, have you not got a vase?"

Big laugh... and I forgot all about it until we reassembled after the New Year on our first day back after the holidays and were all getting on board one of several buses to take all of the staff to the City Chambers where we were to be given a Civic Reception for our success in Europe. The audience in the packed Grand Banqueting Suite was composed of the great and the good as well as all of the staff. Just as we were settling down, Jim Carruth, one of my Assistant Chief Executives, approached me and said, "Ron, we may have a problem. As we were standing around waiting on the buses, a number of staff told me they were upset that you told that joke about Jean. I suspect it might spoil the day if we don't deal with it."

I listened to him and took the course of action I was taught to follow whenever a mistake was made ... admit it, apologise, reassure, explain what we were going to do to fix it and move on. Slightly embarrassed, I took to the microphone to begin a short speech setting the scene and introducing the then Leader of the Council, Frank McAveety to start the proceedings. However I now said, "Ladies and gentlemen, before we start, let me step aside briefly from my prepared notes this afternoon to make an apology to those staff who were offended by a joke I made in reference to my wife, Jean, at our Christmas party. I know some colleagues were upset at the nature of the joke and I was wrong to make fun as I did, even at a social event like that ... And for those who didn't hear the joke, I won't be recounting it. Now let's get back to the ceremony..."

Once the ceremony was over, I wondered how this had been received. Jim came over to my table and told me that my words had gone down very well with the staff who had complained to him and that the matter was finished. Indeed, they were impressed that I'd taken such immediate action. The reaction of the great and the good was a different matter. Bruce Millan MP, ex- Secretary of State for Scotland and a European Commissioner was in the audience and he was known as a Calvinistic, dour individual. Others, equally senior were also seated in the serried ranks. I needn't have worried. Frank McAveety MSP set the trend. "What was the joke?"

I spent the first half hour of the reception explaining to all whom I half expected to shake their head at my exploits that I would stick to my guns but after a few Champagnes, I started to tell the joke to gales of laughter all round. Even Bruce Millan laughed, which must be an all time first!

As I became more sought after as a speaker at dinners and because my style of oratory included an easy ability to introduce a few light-hearted comments as part of a speech, I was asked increasingly to undertake after-dinner speaking whose main purpose was entertainment.

I almost always found a ready response to my

contributions but an important skill was having the ability to read the audience to whom I was speaking. In 2006, just before I left Scottish Enterprise Glasgow, I was asked by the estimable Vic Emery, Managing Director of BAE Systems Marine, the owners of the shipbuilding yards in Govan and Scotstoun, if I'd say a few words of welcome to a large international shipbuilding and naval conference that was to be held in the Forte Crest Hotel on the banks of the Clyde. I researched it well, recounting the traditions of Red Clydeside, its shipbuilding heritage and did a real humorous, tub-thumper of a speech that resulted in a tumultuous standing ovation from an audience that included the First Sea Lord, Admirals of the Fleet, Cabinet Ministers, industrialists and trades union officials. I was lauded that night and was asked to come and speak all over the UK at other events.

The following week, I had been asked to speak at a black-tie dinner in Trades House in Glassford Street at invitation of the Incorporation of Hammermen. Fuelled by my new celebrity, I asked my eldest sons, Ron and Campbell to come along as well as my friend John McManus in order to let them witness the immense talent I'd discovered I had as an after dinner speaker of some note. The guy organising the event had heard me speak previously and wanted me to deliver the same kind of speech he'd then experienced but as I entered the hall, I noticed that there were a goodly number of senior citizens - the blue rinse brigade, in attendance. I asked him for reassurance that my contribution was to be as he'd earlier described and was encouraged that I should feel free to speak unrestrained.

My instincts were to stick to the softer jokes and I'd devised a system whereby I'd colour the text in my speeches so denoting passages that I felt might be somewhat *outré* and which could be skipped if the audience wasn't responding to my line of travel. However, bolstered by the sure knowledge that material similar to that which I held in my hands had gone down so well the week previously, I started to say a few words and initially all went well. Not long into the speech, however I told a joke that went down like lead and never recovered my rather conservative audience. I died on my arse. So much for impressing Ron and Campbell!

Burns week has always been a big favourite of mine. I really enjoy the work of the Bard and frequently read his verse, not just each January. I've done many Toasts to the Lassies and Responses from the Guests but have always rejected invitations to do the Immortal Memory as I believe that task should fall to a scholar of Burns... someone who can offer insight into his work rather than merely provide light entertainment. The Glasgow Lord Provost's Burns Supper is one of the most prestigious in the world and over a couple of decades from the early nineties and into the new millennium, I regularly took two or three tables, inviting Cabinet Ministers, major industrialists, partners and stakeholders to this great event. Strathclyde Police also do a smashing Burns Supper as do British Transport Police...lots of in-jokes and much teasing of senior officers but always very funny.

Jean's birthday is January 24th, the day before Burns' birthday and when she was forty she organised a *Jean Armour* Supper where she invited only women. Burns Suppers were usually dominated by males present and in some cases - the Bridgeton Burns Supper comes to mind - women were strictly forbidden. Jean Armour was Burns' long suffering wife and Jean's full name is Jean Linda *Armour* Culley (*née* Pollock) hence the connection with Jean Armour. Jim Tait was permitted to attend to provide some musical entertainment and Laurie was also permitted to say a few words, as was I. Other than that, it was strictly women only and was a great success. Jean delivered a great speech and took the piss out of me comprehensively!

I always looked forward to the big set piece dinners in the city. Over the years I came to know and befriend many Glasgow stalwarts and it was an unusual event where I didn't know a great number of people there attending. Being a social animal and having 'convivial temulence' as my hobby, these events were ideal.

My most memorable event was a lunch in the Thistle Hotel in Cambridge Street attended by President Bill Clinton in 2006. I'd heard Colin Powell speak, Tony Blair, Al Gore, Caspar Weinberger, Jimmy Carter, Kofi Anan, Gordon Brown and most of the great British Politicians but Clinton was in a class of his own. After lunch, which went on until the evening as a consequence of the security song and dance that went on around Clinton, I was invited to meet him and have my photograph taken with him. When I viewed it afterwards it was easy to see which of the two of us was the more excited at meeting the other.

I also met Blair in 2007 for breakfast in the Boardroom of the Chamber of Commerce in George Square. I'd vehemently opposed his decision, his madness, his colossal miscalculation, to invade Iraq in March 2003 and when invited to be photographed with him, I determined to do so with a fixed, grim look on my face conveying my opposition for posterity. Unfortunately, Willie Haughey was next in line for a shot and as I turned to face the camera, he made a witty comment. I smiled at Willie, shaking hands with Blair just as the flash lit up the room.

I suspect that in retirement, the invitations will slow up if not dry up, as they do, in my experience, and that I'll have to make other arrangements to pursue my interests in the *Craic* but I'm sure that my predilection for convivial temulence and the *Craic* will find an outlet.

16. Salt in my Porridge.

*For that is the mark of the Scot of all classes: that he stands in an attitude
towards the past unthinkable to Englishmen, and remembers and cherishes
the memory of his forebears, good or bad; and there burns alive in him a
sense of identity with the dead even to the twentieth generation.*
Robert Louis Stevenson.

Much as I've made a fuss about my love of cities in general and Glasgow in particular, there's no denying my love of my own homeland, Scotland. Its personality has infused my soul and directed my life although I have to confess to elements that as I grew older, were judged less worthy by social commentators. I belonged to the old school and took the position that I supported two teams, Scotland...and ABE; anyone but England. My attitude was tempered only by accepting that I genuinely had no problems with the English people *per se*, I support Manchester United and thought their English players magnificent, was personally friendly with many people from south of the border and could enjoy and admire their entertainers, cities and produce. But when it came to team sports it was a different matter. I invariably not only wanted Ireland or Israel or Iran to beat England at tiddlywinks but also Racing Club de Paris or Racing Club de Timbuktu to beat Racing Club de Bradford.

I found it easy to dislike those English people such as defender Nobby Styles - at least a temporary dislike shared by a focussed Denis Law who allegedly responded to the invitation to shake the hand of his Manchester United team mate (while they awaited the referee's signal to take the field in a Scotland-England game at Wembley) by saying, "Fuck off ya specky wee bowley bastard".

Alan Ball and Jackie Charlton were also rather unpopular in a boring but all-conquering English Team. Other essentially English figures of dislike included

Jimmy Saville, Jimmy Hill, Mick Channon and then along came Margaret Thatcher. She carried the mantle for years. One of my most joyous occasions was when she foolishly accepted an invitation to attend as Prime Minister and present the cup at the Scottish Cup Final of 1988. Some 80,000 Scots booed their disdain and made their feelings for her known by whistling and showing her a red card, specially printed for the occasion.

This *lacuna* in an otherwise positive absorption of the culture of my homeland I find easy to forgive in myself. I don't beat myself up about it but permit it to surface only when in the company of like minded souls or at least where no one from England is present so I can only surmise that I'm not particularly proud of these feelings. But other than this rather shameful weakness, which I bury deeply when in the company of dear English friends like Kate McAlpine or David Asquith, I am of the view that my Scottishness has endowed me with nothing but advantage.

Once, when studying at Jordanhill College, myself and fellow students were presented with an exercise whereby a sheet of A4 paper was placed in front of us. Written in the left hand margin were listed perhaps thirty nationalities including Italians, Chinese, English and Americans. On the right hand side of the page were listed a schedule of adjectives; inscrutable, passionate, reserved, loud, etc... and we were asked to pair them up, the subsequent discussion revealing the obvious point that you cannot ascribe general characteristics to untold millions of people who happen to enjoy the same nationality. We could all point to examples like President Jimmy Carter, an American who wasn't loud; we figured that there had to be depressive, uncommunicative Italians and expressive Chinese. Lord knows, we saw little reserved about Englishman Oliver Reed. There were also those who would even stratify Scotland itself in this way...people from Edinburgh are tight, Glaswegians are aggressive, Aberdonians are mean, Teuchters are either alcoholics or Calvinists.

How might it be possible to define the Scottish character when the country has produced influences as diverse as Robert Burns and John Knox; Donald Dewar MSP and Tommy Graham MP; Robert Louis Stevenson and Irvine Welsh?

So there were many among us in the lecture theatre that day who understood the truism that we who were working class Scots had more in common with a Durham miner than with the Duke of Argyll and that the argument was more about class than about nationality.

In 2007, I was a serving member of the Board of the Wise Group under the exemplary leadership of Laurie Russell who had moved there from his previous role as Chief Executive of Strathclyde European Partnership. One of our fellow Board Members was the famous Guardian journalist Polly Toynbee who took issue with me for speaking warmly and optimistically about the influx of Eastern European residents, especially Poles, who had come to Glasgow to find work.

Polly couldn't understand my point of view. "But surely they'll take work from the less able Glaswegians, Ron?"

"Sure they might. But we'll just have to work harder to accommodate all of our citizens, old and new. We have a saying here in Scotland, Polly, 'We're a' Jock Tamson's bairns'. It tries to convey the notion that we're all the same under the sun."

I pointed out that over the centuries Glasgow, pretty successfully, had assimilated Jewish, Italian, Irish, Polish, Indian, Pakistani, Chinese - to a lesser extent - Lithuanian and English immigrants and that we'd somehow managed to make them part of the great Glasgow family.

The new economic migrants were equally welcome; particularly because of research of which I was aware that the more able, first generation children of newly arrived immigrants tended to become entrepreneurs rather than professionals and that the Glasgow economy required a boost in this area.

She didn't seem to get it and neither apparently did our fellow Board Member, Will Hutton, the equally famous intellectual and author of the best selling book, *"The State We're In"*, who sought time to reflect and take the argument on board. Each of them flew up quarterly from London to attend Wise Group Board meetings but both seemed estranged, or at least unacquainted with the notion of 'a man's a man' that seems to characterise the Scottish culture in a way that seems is not quite the case south of the border, or at least in the Home Counties.

But I sense that these sayings *do* reflect an attitude that's Scottish. It *does* capture something about our national sentiment. So I did feel that there were cultural influences that looking back, shaped me. But I suppose that I'd listen to an argument that it wasn't any individual characteristic but the blend, the melange of prevailing influences upon my life and that of those around me. Hard work, thrift, a pride in my country, a preference for the underdog and honesty were all traits I could relate to. But as a young man, there were others; the love of a fight, respect for education and deference which were all alien to me. So the Scottish 'fingerprint'; its DNA, wasn't 100% ubiquitous in all of my circumstances. I was more a product of working class Glasgow, of my family and of my community.

And while I was horrified by the circumstances of too many of my fellow Scots, sufficient to commit my working life to the alleviation of the causes of their predicament, I was always inordinately proud of most other aspects of my nation. For a while in my teenage years this was reflected in my three year membership of the SNP until I was persuaded by a class-based analysis of social improvement and became subsequently a life-long member of the Labour Party in Scotland.

I stood for the SNP in a school election and won, largely because I pointed up some economic advantages I'd read about in a nationalist pamphlet about Scotland's oil but mostly because I was able to engender outrage as I quoted the omitted lines from the British National Anthem which includes the stanza;

Lord grant that Marshal Wade
May by thy mighty aid
Victory bring.
May he sedition hush,
And like a torrent rush,
Rebellious Scots to crush.
God save the Queen.

As a youth, I refused to stand for the National Anthem in the local cinema where it was played to a largely deferential audience at the end of every evening's performance as it was when the television programmes ceased at night. Even today I hold it in some contempt and where I am required socially to toast the health of the monarch, I deal with it by quietly toasting the memory of my departed parents and grandparents, a solution which causes no embarrassment to my guests or hosts and which genuinely permits me to remember my antecedents. In some way it appeals to my sentimentality too as it is analogous to the approach taken by some Highland clans and regiments who passed their drink over a glass of water during the Loyal Toast, a secret device intended to conceal their opposition to the throne and to assert their support of the 'King over the water'; Bonnie Prince Charlie, who represented Jacobitism, the political movement dedicated to the restoration of the Stuart kings to the thrones of England and Scotland but which was outlawed for many years.

That said, I always described myself as a Scottish social democrat and am comfortable on that cusp of the Labour Party that was keen on the prospect of maximum devolution of governance. If Scottish Independence was to be the preference of a majority of Scots, I could live with that too, but as long as the resultant government was left of centre.

But beyond politics, I developed a real love of wilderness Scotland in my teenage years. A combination of my scouting experience and school-based Duke of Edinburgh Award Scheme activities resulted in me learning camping and outdoor skills in my teenage years. Regularly at weekends my Mum would take us to youth hostels around Scotland where I developed an early, healthy respect for the tyrannical midge.

Since that time, I've been fortunate in having been able to visit most of Scotland's towns and villages. Oban was an early favourite and has stayed the course in my affections over my adult years. If the sun was out, I always got a real feeling of peacefulness whenever I turned into Gallanach Road and viewed the harbour. Fishing boats are less numerous now. They've reduced in number over the years in every port in Scotland but there were always a hardy few who made a living from the sea. However, the main activity always surrounded the arrival and departure of the Caledonian MacBrayne ferries taking islanders and tourists to Mull, Barra and Uist and other craft setting sail for destinations all over the Inner and Outer Hebrides. Gently bobbing at the quay wall, the ships would await their next adventure and gangplanks were always busy with people loading and unloading or cleaning and hosing.

And so too it was in Stornoway, Ullapool, St Andrews, Girvan and Berwick among others. Great wee towns; all thriving, if in a different way to how they'd earned a living in the past. The sea and the climate determined everything about these ports. They lived by the sea and they lived off the sea and I love them all.

Another grand passion I have had in regard to my homeland is its music. Growing up not just with the folk tunes of the Corries but also with the Scottish schmaltz of such as Andy Stewart and Calum Kennedy who tended towards the tartan shortbread tin dimension of Scottish music. But I loved the sweep of Scottish music then and I love it now. I loved the waltzes of Jimmy Shand, whose Bluebell Polka was drummed into me at dance classes at primary school; the pipes and drums of the Scottish regiments, the fiddle orchestras, the songs of Burns and the reels of Aly Bain and Phil Cunningham as well as their more sombre slip-jigs and slow-air strathspeys.

One disappointment over the years was the fact that Jean didn't share my musical enthusiasms and retired after the bells at Hogmanay to the kitchen TV where she preferred to watch whatever channel was showing the Top 50 whatevers, muttering her distaste for '*hoochter choochter music*'. As a result, over the years, Hogmanay lost some of its familial characteristic for me. We'll see how the boys fare but while it's a bit of a cliché to say that Scottish music tugs at my heartstrings, it certainly has the ability to puncture my tear ducts, swell my chest and set my feet tapping. I can get emotional about Scottish music in all its forms in a way that is denied me in other types of music.

This passion also showed up in my enthusiasm to dance. I was never a dancer and felt silly dancing to the music of the day unless I had the contents of a wee glass inside me. Even then, I tended to stand and shuffle ungainly. The one dance in which I was confident I could pass muster was the Gay Gordons. On certain occasions in later life when *more* than the one wee glass had been consumed, it wasn't at all rare for me to be seen clearing the floor for my version of the Gay Gordons to the music of the Rolling Stones or Bruce Springsteen.

The geography of Scotland also suits me fine. Whilst in Scottish Enterprise, I was acutely aware that Scotland didn't sit in a position that made for the easy import and export of goods. Once, when we organised a conference on the regeneration of Glasgow with some real big intellectuals from the OECD, Josef Konvitz, the leader of their delegation, dined with me and in discussion, drew a sketch map of Europe on his napkin. He connected Dublin, Glasgow/Edinburgh, Oslo, Stockholm and Helsinki and became quite excited as he conjured up the concept of 'the Celtic Arc' until we pointed out that there were major Nordic influences in there as well. And his proposition, that nations on the extremities of Europe have had to look to innovations in the new technologies to survive, didn't wash either as *all* countries were attempting to secure advantage in this field.

But what we lack in being at the centre of everything like Berlin or Paris also has its compensation. When I drive north from England and witness not only the glorious scenery but the distance between Carlisle and the first Scottish city, Glasgow, I realise that the Scottish culture won't easily be assimilated into the English. When I fly north from London and see the rolling hills of the borders spread below me like a large unmade bed, I marvel of the amount of wilderness we have up here. We are possessed of space and room to accommodate our population. We have great scenery and wonderful opportunities in developing renewable energies and will be inoculated against the future perils of having poor access to clean water. And with a coastline greater than that of France (largely due to our 790 islands) we are well placed to take advantage of all that the sea has to offer.

And our nation's history has come to mean a lot to me. I suppose I was one of the last schoolchildren almost exclusively to have been taught British history; The Battle of Hastings, The Empire, Ethelred the Unready and Henry the Eighth. All important, but not to the semi-exclusion of Scottish history like the Clearances, Bruce and Wallace, Culloden, or the Darien Scheme. I came late to all of this and were it not for an elderly history teacher in my final years of secondary schooling who we all thought was crazy because it was rumoured she was a Nationalist and thought to be a militant, Stone of Destiny-stealing, anarchistic, starey-eyed nutcase, I'd have found out very little of our distant past while at school. All I'd have left with would have been a map of the world imprinted on my mind with large swathes of pink denoting the - by then rapidly diminishing - power of the British Empire.

I was and remain so very proud of those Scots whose contributions have shaped the world; John Logie Baird's television, Sir Alexander Fleming's penicillin, Alexander Graham Bell's telephone, James Watt's steam engine that made possible the industrial revolution, Adam Smith's seminal economic thoughts which led to an understanding of Capitalism, Robert Burns' poetry, David Hume's philosophy and his leadership of the Scottish Enlightenment and Adam Ferguson, the father of sociology. I am still chided by my Irish friend, Tadhg Dennehy who frequently asks me if the Scots invented the tea-towel, so often have I proudly visited the innovations of my countrymen on him by drawing his attention to the ubiquitous drying towel that displays the major Scottish inventions over the ages.

I very much agree with Churchill's statement that, "Of all the small nations on earth, perhaps only the ancient Greeks surpass the Scots in their contribution to mankind." Back in the 18th Century Voltaire recorded, "We look to Scotland for all our ideas of civilisation". And in a response to the Thomas Paine tome, *The Rights of Man*" published in 1791 just after the French Revolution, Burns wrote in his poem, *"The Rights of Woman"*;

"Amid this mighty fuss just let me mention,
The rights of women merit some attention."

And, in doing do, so became the first women's libber!

Even in modern Scotland, I've taken great pride whenever a Scot has proved himself or herself able to stand out from the crowd, Jim Baxter, Kenny Dalglish, Jock Stein and Sir Alex Ferguson from football; in politics, Ramsay MacDonald, Jimmy Reid, John McLean and James Connolly; in entertainment, Billy Connolly, Sean Connery, Ewan McGregor and Lulu! The list goes on.

And as for the magnificent Tartan Army, what great ambassadors for Scotland they've been! I read of the Mayor of Cordoba whose city had played host to the Scots during the 1978 Argentina World Cup telling a civic reception many years later that they had good cause to remember the friendly raucousness of the Scottish football fans.

"We remember 1978 for three things," he said. "First, it would be good if St. Martin could have his sword back," as he pointed to a weaponless soldier on a horse, bereft of his thirty-foot sword. "I believe it's in a place called Paisley."

"Secondly, during the World Cup, we regularly had to send to Parana for more beer supplies as the Scots drank the city dry. And finally, we have an extraordinary number of red-headed graduates leaving our university this year."

On Christmas morning, 1989, I still remember the delight expressed by Ron. Campbell had taken delivery of a number of large parcels from Santa and I could see Ron beginning to calculate that his presents were materially smaller and less expensive until he opened a wrapping which contained the board game, Travel Scrabble.

Opening it, he could see that across the middle of the board was pinned the anagram, *'dodagrltphthnwigtoewdcoiu'*. It took him a few minutes but with a bit of help he worked out that it spelled, 'Going to the World Cup with Dad'. I don't recall seeing him with a wider smile.

And so it was that in 1990, John McManus, myself and our two eldest boys, Ron and Paul, took off for the World Cup in Italy. I'd always loved France and the French and could never understand the negative English attitude towards such an interesting nation, its columnists jeering at Johnny Foreigner, especially when the English retire there in their droves and head for its beaches in their millions each summer. So we stayed in France, travelling over the border to Turin to see the games against Brazil and Costa Rica both of which we lost. We stayed in our posh French campsite near Port Grimaud and St. Tropez in the French Riviera for the game in Genoa against Sweden which we won. That match was also memorable for the party atmosphere inside the bar which was filled with Scots and Irish. Outside around the pool, a larger crowd sat silent as Bobby Robson's England played Holland and drew 0-0 in what seemed to be a comprehensively boring match. The difference between the two sets of fans at the end of the evening was telling and perhaps also reflects something of the personality of all three nationalities.

We had wanted to keep the boys away from the crowds and any problems associated with a large travelling support but we needn't have bothered. Since the Tartan Army was established as a counterpoint to the then terrible violence of the English supporters, they have won Fair Play awards, Best Supporters trophies and have been acclaimed across the globe as the best fans in the world. They police themselves, and have demonstrated a collective sense of humour that invariably won the hearts of those who lived in the countries they visited.

I find Scotland thrilling. I love Para Handy and the Kailyard school of writing. I stir at the sound of the pipes and can shed a tear at a pibroch or a lament. I still laugh at re-runs of Ricky Fulton. I love my urban heartland but also appreciate the sheer beauty of the highlands and islands that can provide a wonderful, still silence that is somehow more than just the absence of sound. Yet I understand in my bones that I'm an internationalist as well as a nationalist, that I'm a social person as well as a Scottish person. Still, after all of these qualifications are accounted for, I'm a Scot and I'm very, very proud so to be.

17. Trains And Boats And Planes.

Only those who risk going too far can possibly find out how far they can
go.
T. S. Eliot.

In December 2005, I was settling in to face a winter of discontent. Scottish Enterprise National had a budget that was shredded and in tatters. Daily there were reports in the press that Jack Perry was refusing to resign despite this being demanded in various quarters. It was evident that there was going to be a very tough spending round that would adversely affect lots of favoured projects dear to the heart of us in Glasgow. I found it ironic. Perry was about to achieve, through his incompetence, that which he could not achieve by his out-manoeuvring us.

My PA, Susan, came in to see me with a list of calls that I'd missed and one of them was to arrange to pop over to the Chambers to see Council Leader Steven Purcell when I had a moment. This wasn't unusual and I asked her to arrange something that suited both our diaries. The only thing that set this meeting apart from others was that I'd no idea what the subject matter might be. Still, it was always a joy to see Steven so I headed over to the Chambers the following morning on an unseasonably sunny day and looked forward to a chat with him over a coffee.

The City Chambers can justifiably claim to be one of the most elegant and beautiful buildings in the UK. The Leader's office at the end of the Councillors' Corridor as it is called is no less impressive. Steven had changed the location of the furniture to suit his needs and had set up a computer station in one of the corners, demonstrating the fact yet again that he was a new type of political leader, one who was comfortable with the trappings of modern business practices. He was as ebullient as ever and we relaxed into shared reminiscences over an early morning coffee. After a while he came to the business he wanted to conduct.

"You know the importance we place upon 'Team Glasgow' here in the city?"

I sipped my coffee and nodded assent.

"I was wondering if you felt we might take steps to bring transport more in line with every other institution that's collaborating in support of the common good."

"Sure. What do you have in mind?"

"It seems to me," Steven went on, "that the one area that has consistently eluded us and which is fundamental to us achieving our goal of social inclusion, is bringing SPTA (Strathclyde Passenger Transport Authority) on board. We've the prospect of the Commonwealth Games coming to Glasgow in 2014 and we'll need to be able to demonstrate to the Commissioners before then that we can move people around the city quickly and safely. We need to bring jobs to the people and people to the jobs. To do this, SPTA has to play its part."

I was surprised at his comments. "I've not dealt with them much."

"Well", said Steven. "So what do you think about you throwing your hat into the ring for the Chief Executive's job? It's about to be advertised because Dr. Malcolm Reed [the previous Director General] has moved to head up Transport Scotland. There will be strong internal applicants but we need change."

I was flabbergasted. "Me? I'm sure I'd be of more use to you in my present role or in the Community Planning role."

"You and I both know that there are people out there who could continue the work you're doing but I can think of no one else who could transform transport. You've built a reputation as someone who can change organisations for the better. If you could do to SPT what you've done for SEG, what a difference it would mean not just for the city but for the West of Scotland. The post is to be advertised shortly but you might want to read it and see what you think."

I was still unsure. "You'll need to let me think this through, Steven. It's a big leap."

I went back to my office and spent some time looking at the SPT web site. It was evident that big changes were on the way. The Scottish Parliament had brought in a new act, the Transport [Scotland] Act 2005, due to be implemented four months later, in April 2006. It created transport functions in each of seven geographies within Scotland. By far the largest was SPT, the biggest transport authority outside London. Based in Glasgow above Queen Street Station, it employed almost 800 staff and looked after the Glasgow Subway, new rail initiatives, bus stations, bus subsidies, school buses, freight, sustainable development, new roads and ferries. Some staff were to be transferred to Transport Scotland in support of rail duties that would fall to them in April 2006 when SPT would then become an acronym for Strathclyde Partnership for Transport, underlining the collaborative role the Executive saw it playing in the future. I was intrigued.

I discussed it with Jean and as previously, she counselled me to do what I felt best. It was another big leap in salary, the equivalent of the Chief Executive's job in larger Councils across Scotland. When I reviewed the prospect of a dispiriting future with Scottish Enterprise, I decided to take Steven up on his suggestion and throw my hat into the ring. Again, newspaper speculation connected me with the job but the public sector works differently to the private sector where 'strategic hiring' is the order of the day and recruiters can employ pretty much whomsoever they please. In the public sector the interviews are always conducted scrupulously fairly, advertised widely and interviews require to be open handed. The entire process would be managed by South Lanarkshire Council as a surrogate for SPT.

I also spoke with my Chairman at Scottish Enterprise Glasgow, Willie Haughey who initially asked me not to apply, arguing that I'd be far better staying on or running the Glasgow Housing Agency if a vacancy occurred at CEO level. I demurred on the basis that there wasn't a vacancy there although I acknowledged that it would probably only be a matter of time due to what was viewed as the political obstinacy of the then incumbent, Michael Lennon, a Scottish ex-pat from the Antipodes who was an academic and who was possessed of a handlebar moustache that screamed vanity.

Eventually Willie's concerns were assuaged and I moved into a period of study. I knew little about transport and I figured I'd need to be on top form if I were to land this catch. I phoned Steven and told him I'd consulted Jean and Willie and that I'd decided to apply. He reminded me that I was rather going out on a limb as he would not be on the panel and that there would be those who would wish to see continuity rather than change.

In the event, my studied approach was entirely necessary. The formal interview took the traditional form of a collection of six councillors seated as if they were dining at the Last Supper. My presentation went well but I was asked to hurry it along as I approached the last slide and managed what I thought was a pretty seamless segue into my conclusions. Again I performed well and dealt with all of the questions articulately and easily. It became obvious that there were at least two camps on the panel and I could tell from the line of questioning that one particular Councillor was not in mine. He asked me how I'd deal with the problem of transporting home, the

40,000 inebriated Glaswegians who exited the city's clubs at 3.00am every Friday and Saturday morning.

As luck would have it I'd taken a tour of the city at precisely that time along with senior police officers, the Procurator Fiscal and Steven Purcell only two months earlier and having thought through that precise situation, was able to reply, "Well, I'd increase the number of taxi ranks from midnight until 4.00, I'd place temporary bus stops on the major routes, I'd ask the clubs to provide coffee for those leaving their establishment to dissipate the departure of their clientele and would ask the Council to stagger the hours of closing so that not everyone comes on to the street at once. I'd open the Subway but would only make use of one of the tracks so that maintenance could be continued on the free one and would only open key stations like Byres Road, Govan and Buchanan Street. I'd also allow private hire taxis to collect from the side of the road from midnight to 4.00am to ease the pressure on black cabs."

It was evident that the Councillor hadn't expected such a comprehensive answer.

"Anything else you'd do?" he asked. Heads turned to look at him as if choreographed by a higher power. It was evident that others felt that the answer had been sufficiently rounded.

I was obviously seen as the external candidate where others were seen as continuing the steady state. I had been first to be interviewed that morning but it wasn't until 6.00 p.m. that the Chairman, Councillor Alistair Watson phoned me. "Congratulations, Ron. You're the new heid bummer."

I started on 1st April 2006 and my first three months proved very difficult as even those elected members who sought change weren't quite so comfortable with the proposals I was making. I was frequently assailed by members who - politely, it has to be said - argued the retention of their version of the status quo. However, I prevailed and the Partnership agreed a Chief Executive's Review which saw John Halliday and Valerie Davidson promoted to Assistant Chief Executive and a third person, Gordon Maclennan (my Senior Director of Business Growth in SEG) appointed as my Deputy. With the exception of Valerie and John, both of whom I promoted (and who were strongly supported by senior politicians), many other senior staff were bid farewell. Gordon was a crucial appointment. When I'd appointed him to the SEG post of Senior Director of Business Growth in 2001, I'd done so because I needed his buccaneering spirit within SPT. I was guided by my political masters that SPT needed to change and do things differently and while I normally and naturally engage in consultative mode, I was very aware of the Henry Ford quote, "If I'd asked my customers what they wanted, they'd have said a faster horse," so I figured that I'd be the one to set what became my four 'big ticket items' so I could bring change that was transformational. 'Change Management' had loomed large in interview and was prominent in the job description so I brought forward a paper to the Authority which set out the areas of improvement that I felt were necessary.

First, I intimated that we had to do something to improve internal and external relationships. A stakeholder survey I commissioned before I arrived told us that our partners felt we were very sound technically but that we should work at improving our partnership working. I also spoke openly to an all staff meeting in The Royal Concert Hall about the feedback that had been received from our customers and asked their assistance in changing perceptions.

Second, we needed to provide more focus. I was astonished to find out that we had over one thousand projects out there. One thousand expectations that a station would be developed or that there would be a Park and Ride facility established in an area or whatever. We needed a much more strategic approach with priorities, deadlines and accountable officers.

Third, I wanted to bring about a change in culture with a much greater focus upon delivery and customer primacy. I decided to fall back on the processes that had stood me in such good stead in Govan and SE Glasgow and determined that we'd go on an Excellence Journey using a raft of quality mechanisms like EFQM, IIP and various ISO accreditations. I confess that in bringing about this goal, I was frustrated that in certain aspects of private and public life, strategic hiring was the norm. Tony Blair didn't advertise for a Chief of Staff; he appointed Jonathan Powell. The BBC didn't advertise for someone to front their flagship Saturday evening football programme; they approached Gary Lineker. And of course in the private sector a substantial number of appointments are made without any advertising. However, this approach wasn't available to me although I could encourage applications and then hope that the system of public administration under which we worked would bring the candidate I admired into the fold. I was therefore subsequently delighted that Julie Riley would lead the continuous improvement exercise. She'd masterminded the Govan experience and there just wasn't anyone better in Scotland.

Finally, I decided that I'd put the organisation through a Business Transformation exercise. I'd reorganise and realign elements of the business, grow some areas and shrink or abandon others. No one had looked under the bonnet for ten years and it was long overdue. Gordon's early appointment was crucial as I knew his entrepreneurial abilities and his drive and was convinced that he'd be the missing ingredient that would help transform the organisation as well as give me the emotional support and encouragement I'd need on this journey as he would be as determined as I'd be in wanting to improve things.

I then set out a five stage Chief Executive's Review incorporating the first element of the Senior Staff Review as the initial stage. Inter alia, as stage three of the Review, I asked an independent law firm, Levy and McRae, to undertake an audit of the legal team. SPT employed ten solicitors and I couldn't believe that it was necessary to employ lawyers in that number. I'd known law firms that didn't employ that number of solicitors. I also took the same approach to the Information Technology Department.

I was delighted that the appointments system was beginning to introduce people whom I knew to be real experts in their field. Donny Macleod (ex Superintendent with Strathclyde Police) as Head of Security, Julie Riley (who twice took Govan Initiative to the European finals of the European Quality Awards) as Head of Organisational Development, Bob Wylie (BBC Senior Investigative correspondent and BAFTA Award nominee) as Director of Communications, Pamela Miller (ex of Govan Initiative and the Red Cross) who was a superb HR professional, Eric Stewart (previously the top man in First Bus in Scotland) as Director of Bus Operations, Alan Murray to drive Community Planning, Gordon Maclennan as Assistant Chief Executive and Anne-Marie Waugh as my Executive Officer to work with me on key matters I needed to drive through but where I didn't have the time to deal with the detailed increments of change.

A year later the top team was strengthened yet again with the dual appointments of Bruce Kiloh and Ian Catterson as Senior Transport Advisors to ensure a more robust internal challenge and to follow through on all of the many initiatives that we wanted to pursue. The Human Resources Directorate also set out a process that saw the appointment of the multi-talented Debbie Mackie (previously Director of Operational Development in Scottish Enterprise Glasgow before she was promoted to Senior Director of Growing Business) as Head of Leadership Development and finally, David Christie, then the Police Divisional Commander of 'A' Division (Glasgow City) who was appointed as the Operations Manager for the Subway.

But Gordon was a star. Most mornings he'd come into my office saying, "I had an idea last night," and would proceed to let me know of his thoughts on how to improve aspects of our organisational or operational performance and I still have to struggle to think of one which didn't make sense and which we didn't move to implement. He was completely brilliant. The fact that he was also great fun was an additional benefit.

As the senior team assembled it was quite apparent that not only were they effecting the kind of changes I wanted to see culturally as well as operationally but that their impact was being recognised externally. I received a lot of great feedback from Local Authorities, Local Enterprise Companies, Health Boards and Police and Fire Boards and our own staff who told the Hay Group, the Consultants I had brought in to assist me, that the key appointments I'd brought in were all 'whirlwinds'. It was also fun to have these new appointments around as they were very much simpatico with my own approach. It became great coming into work knowing that there were now more of my kindred spirits than existed in those parts of the organisation where my influence was still to be felt. As Christmas 2007 approached, my working life wasn't quite so much of a lonely struggle.

My Chairman, Alistair Watson brought twenty-five years in the rail industry to his role as Chair. He was usually the best informed person in the room when we discussed rail routes or rail development opportunities and over the years he'd amassed a substantial body of knowledge in relation to other modes of transport. The problem with this knowledge base, however, was that in 2006, on the same day as I joined the re-cast SPT, Parliament determined that Transport Scotland should be the rail authority; a very sensible decision as you can't run a railroad on a regional basis as was previously the case with SPTA in its earlier role. This came as a profound cultural shock to the system of SPT in general and Alistair in particular as it meant that we'd have to carve out a new, wider role but with much less emphasis on rail matters. Alistair wrestled with this for years, his natural inclination as a railway man, determining priorities that weren't always aligned with the new realities.

He was articulate in the way that Glasgow politicians arc and loved few things more than saying a few words in generous explanation of his views on matters at hand. He had a passion to communicate. Over the first year we grew in each other's affections and he accepted affably my informalities in his office as long as no other outsider was in attendance. Alistair was passionate about transport and saw the need to reform the organisation, a task we took on enthusiastically.

One of my Vice Chairmen was Davie McLachlan. Formerly a bus driver and now an experienced long distance lorry driver as well as a motor cyclist, Davie understood and was also passionate about transport yet was always eager to learn more. He was a busy elected member, represented the organisation eloquently and well in a number of important areas of concern and could be formidable in debate. My second Vice Chair was David Fagan, a councillor from North Lanarkshire. David was a very talented politician who had not unreasonable ambitions of future preferment within the party. Unfortunately he was a councillor in the benighted Monklands Constituency which alone among others seemed to attract the attentions of the Labour Party centrally. After the service of Jimmy Dempsey and Tom Clark (both local residents of the area) the party foisted successively John Smith, Helen Liddell, John Reid and most recently a twenty-five year old researcher, Pamela Nash (one of sitting MP John Reid's research team), on the area, thereby limiting its capacity to nourish a generation of talented politicians like David who lived within the constituency.

David wasn't just an articulate and polished political operator; he was also a graduate of the Arts School and had a wide range of interests such as music, arts and design – talents that would serve SPT well in the redesigning of its Subway stations and rolling stock. He was also a really nice guy.

I was always ambitious to over-achieve on any objectives I was set on any job I undertook and set to my task with SPT in this light. I was fortunate in the sense that we were required by the Minster for Transport to submit a Regional Transport Strategy one year after our incorporation. So in addition to using that period to undertake the Chief Executive's Review and deal with the four 'Big Ticket Items' I'd identified, I also faced the valuable prospect of setting out an operational agenda that could be as ambitious as possible.

We consulted over a period of twelve months from April 2006 until April 2007 and spoke with some 250 different organisations, received and reviewed some 240 written pieces of evidence and sent out information on our ambitions to around 1.3 million people. And our strategy boys didn't let us down. I had told them that if we didn't get a raised eyebrows reaction from the Transport Civil Servants signalling their apprehension at the scale of our ambitions and that there was no way our ambitions could be funded, we'd have failed. Well, we got that reaction in spades. Variously we set out a raft of proposals that we saw as being of fundamental importance to the needs of the travelling public in the west of Scotland.

We argued for the comprehensive redevelopment of the existing Subway and plotted a new route that took it on a second loop towards the east end with a station at Parkhead. We listed the significant number of trunk roads that required upgrading such as the A77 where it takes traffic to the port of Cairnryan near Stranraer and encouraged a tunnel solution to the gridlock at the Raith Interchange just south of East Kilbride. We brought forward proposals to develop Maglev as the preferred mode of high speed ground transport between Edinburgh and Glasgow as well as south to London and sought the support of the Scottish Executive to introduce legislation to re-regulate aspects of the bus industry. In the background were a host of rail, road, freight, parking and health access projects, all of which amounted to a considerable sum of money if they were all implemented. The only thing we were concerned to take out of the Regional Transport Strategy was road-pricing (charging the motorist to use a particular stretch of road so as to encourage them to make use of other modes of transport) arguing that the political proposition was that road pricing was meant to replace car tax not supplement it and that because neither we nor indeed the Scottish Government could remove car tax as this was a reserved function of the Westminster Parliament, we would have to await their initiative at a national level.

Improving delivery was of great importance and I also introduced the principle of Key Personal Performance

Indicators. This wasn't rocket science. Everyone from me down had to fill in a sheet stating what they expected to achieve by the year end. In aggregate this should amount to the Annual Operating Plan. We'd review this with individuals twice a year and hold people to account for delivery. Unlike the Scottish Enterprise approach, I'd set my face against attaching financial reward to outcomes as I found this approach to be incredibly divisive. Most tasks are accomplished by a team and to use an approach whereby one member was singled out for payment and one (using the principle of the Bell Curve… as no organisation has a bottomless pit of money) had to be described as 'unsatisfactory' was not an approach designed to bring group harmony. My approach gave me the discipline I sought without the need for energy being used to deal with staff disillusionment.

In May 2007 we were all on tenterhooks as the Scottish Election approached. I was relatively sanguine at the prospect of an SNP victory at national level but I couldn't see the numbers adding up. They might win more seats than anyone else, indeed possibly a larger share of the vote, but who would form a coalition with them? Like most others, I was predicting another Labour/Lib Dem coalition. I was more anxious about local elections for Councils as that would more immediately determine the political shape of the Partnership Board and therefore the tone of my administration.

After a shambles of a count, abandoned all over Scotland, as a consequence of the high number of spoiled papers occasioned by asking two questions on one sheet of paper and stating at the top of the paper, "You have two votes", meaning one vote for each election but interpreted widely in the voting booths as two votes for each candidate list. The outcome was close with the SNP securing one more seat than Labour and forming a minority administration. At local level in the West of Scotland, Labour hung on … just! Our Partnership was controlled by twenty elected members, sent as delegates from each of the twelve local authorities in the west. The Labour numbers were cut from seventeen members to fifteen out of twenty so political stability was assured but we had to face up to a new administration at Holyrood.

After the election Bob Wylie took journalists (Brian Currie of the *Evening Times*, Brian Lironi of the *Sunday Mail*, Ken Symon of *Scotland on Sunday* and Louise Batchelor of the BBC) over to Shanghai and demonstrated the capacities of Maglev. Their enthusiastic coverage in their media outlets made it an issue that the new government couldn't avoid addressing even if the powerful forces of Transport Scotland and civil servants wished the issue hadn't arisen.

At the same time, I sent a two page summary of Maglev to Steven Purcell for onward transmission to the new First Minister, Alex Salmond MSP. The SNP policy was to kill a bill seeking to link Edinburgh Airport with its city as they didn't like the route or the cost. Maglev would sweep past the airport en route to Edinburgh and would solve his political problem by providing a cost effective, four minute link. I was interested in his reaction to this solution.

There were many, including within SPT, who saw Maglev as too ambitious for a wee country like Scotland. Invariably, I'd contradict them and, as in November 2008 when I gave evidence on High Speed Rail to the Scottish Parliament's Transport Committee, I used the analogy of the time when a 'man once stood on a beach at Panama and, looking at the towering mountain range in front of him exclaimed, "I've got a great idea, why don't we build a canal here?" He would have had his idea derided too. Without that kind of vision and ambition, I argued that Scotland would always linger in the backwater. Glasgow to Edinburgh in thirteen minutes? Glasgow to London travelling at 500 kilometres an hour and taking only two hours thirty-five minutes? I took the view that this was a debate that had to take place. It would rebalance the economic geography of the UK. This was, and is, of fundamental importance, as during my stint as Chief Executive of Scottish Enterprise Glasgow, research had demonstrated that fully 80% of those businesses deciding not to locate within Scotland gave 'poor transport connectedness' as their number one reason for investing elsewhere. Maglev would solve that – but not if plans to build it from London to a northern English city were to come to fruition. That would only exacerbate Scotland's isolation.

One latent benefit of my time at SPT was the opportunity it afforded me to involve myself again in police work. I took office at a time when there were understandable and immediate concerns about the safety of the travelling public. I moved early on to create a post of Head of Security, reporting directly to me and dealing also with Health and Safety. We appointed British Transport Police to improve security on the Subway and I commissioned two external reports (one involving John Smith, ex-Head of Security with NASA), each of which set out an Action Plan which would tighten security and target harden stations, rolling stock and bus depots as well.

Just over a year after my appointment, in June 2007, terrorists attempted to drive a Landrover loaded with a deadly cocktail of petrol, calor gas and explosives into the concourse at Glasgow Airport. I was on the M8 motorway just outside the airport when the incident happened although I was unaware of the nature of the event. I did realise that whatever had happened, it had brought both sides of the motorway to a complete halt and phoned my wife Jean whom I calculated accurately would just be leaving the cinema at Springfield Quay with my sons Conor and Ciaran at that time.

"There must've been an accident. Choose a route home that uses the back roads. Everywhere else is gridlocked."

Only later did we all discover that Glasgow had had a lucky escape as the vehicle only went on fire but did not explode and the General Manager of the airport, Gordon Dewar, was able proudly to reopen the facility 23 hours and 59 minutes after the attack. No one was injured and the name of John Smeaton came to be a byword for heroism under fire when he booted and punched the terrorists, later going on television to announce that "These terrorists better no' come back here. This is Glasgow. We'll jist set about them!"

After about a year in post I wrote to the British Transport Police Authority and asked that they advise me if any vacancy arose on the board of the Authority. Some months later I received a letter inviting me to submit my CV and shortly afterwards a second letter inviting me to interview. I thought I performed pretty well but found the Chairman, Sir Alistair Graham to be distant and uninterested in my answers. I was disappointed but pretty phlegmatic about my subsequent rejection. The vacancy advertised was for someone with a railway background and I comforted myself that the running of the Glasgow Subway clearly didn't wholly meet that requirement.

Some months later I received an e-mail from BTPA intimating that a second vacancy had arisen again for someone with a railway background, asking me to reapply. I sent off the same documentation as previously with the dates changed and headed off to London figuring that they wouldn't have asked me back if they didn't view my credentials as competent. This time the interview went well enough but Sir Alistair seemed to be even more disinterested in my answers and ostentatiously marked down variously a score of 2, 3 or 4 in the pro-forma against the question he'd just asked. I began to become irked at his performance and my answers became more direct. I also hoped that the other two independent panellists found my answers more worthy but towards the end of the interview, I didn't care if I ruffled feathers. I just responded as I saw fit with little regard for advancing my candidature.

Afterwards I just hoped that he was marking me out of five and not out of ten ... or a hundred, but reported back to Jean and colleagues at SPT that I'd blown it again. It was therefore with some considerable surprise a few days later that I opened a letter offering me a remunerated, non-executive position on the Authority and when I subsequently met Sir Alistair along with Chief Executive Richard Hemmings for an introductory dinner in a very posh restaurant in Saville Row in London, I was delighted to find them both hospitable, receptive and engaging. I'd anticipated a very dusty dinner that evening.

The following morning at an induction meeting, Richard asked me to serve on both the Personnel and Remuneration and the Performance and Standards Committees. He also asked if I'd take responsibility for monitoring the police activity in the north-west of England; Carlisle down to Stoke including Manchester and Liverpool. Finally, he told me that Members accepted a functional responsibility and asked that I become the Authority's point man on matters to do with counter-terrorism. I was delighted to accept all requests and turned my mind to how the hell I might choreograph my available time to fit in these new responsibilities. That said, I rather complicated matters further when I enrolled at St Andrews University to undertake a period of study to learn more about counter-terrorism – the same course being undertaken by serving police officers. Using on-line pedagogy, I completed the Certificate in Terrorist Studies in regulation time and achieving straight As.

One of the great delights of serving on the BTPA over the years – quite apart from the professional satisfaction of dealing with my allocated policing responsibilities, was the journey down to London. Previously when travelling to London, I'd automatically have headed for the airport but now I was charged with modal shift and of encouraging green transport and so was pointed in the direction of rail travel. Granted it was First Class rail travel, but it really was a more civilised way to get from A to B. It took more than five hours to get to or from London whether I went via the east coast or the west but, particularly on the west route, it provided a quite glorious scenic treat.

I'd always ask my treasured colleague Shona Young to book me a solo seat and typically I'd sit with my laptop computer on the table in front of me and my iPod playing some selected music in my ears while (if on the east coast route) I watched the clear blue waters of the sea at Berwick upon Tweed flow under the stout, ancient and muscular bridges that span that beautiful town as the train trundled from the station south into England. For some reason the sun was always shining as I made my way to London and it reminded me if ever it was necessary that Scotland is blessed, truly blessed, with some of the most magnificent scenery in the world.

English scenery *en route* was ok.

One of my more frequent travelling companions on the journey south was the Conservative Peer, Lord James Douglas Hamilton, who had been Thatcher's Parliamentary Under-Secretary of State in the Scottish Office towards the end of her term in office. I tutted at my own indulgences, listening to music and reading from a book, as from the moment he'd get on at Waverley he'd pour over Parliamentary papers, marking important paragraphs in an orange highlighter. On each occasion that the refreshment trolley passed he'd forsake the *paté de fois gras* and ask instead for a bag of Whatsits, which left his fingers glowing in a toxic orange colour, giving the impression that he'd worked his fingers to the bone. He'd work diligently until just before arrival at Kings Cross in London whereupon he'd don his heavy Crombie coat and sit bolt upright for the last ten minutes prior to departure.

The one facet of rail travel I couldn't get used to was the new-fangled toilets. I couldn't see much wrong with the old style train lavatories which had a bowl, a sink and a towel rack inside and a regular door that closed and locked. In the early part of the new millennium during which period I am now writing, the rail operators have introduced a rounded door that opens with a sci-fi hiss but which, if not locked properly once inside, re-opens with a hushed pssshhhh, parading the occupant in mid-flow to the rest of the coach as if revealing the latest gadget on one of those advertising channels. A further disadvantage of course is that the old toilets had approximately the same floor space as the old red phone boxes whereas the new version provides generous amounts of circulation space so that rather than the controlled stream that was possible previously, now I stagger around like a drunk man, copiously spraying the floor and my shoes. Progress?

One evening in January 2008 while in my car *en route* to collecting Conor from his brass band rehearsals, my mobile phone rang. It was Stewart Stevenson MSP, Minister for Transport, who had called to talk to me about taking the implementation of the Glasgow Airport Rail Link [GARL] into the capable hands of Transport Scotland as they were the new rail authority and had been established for just that purpose. I agreed with him completely as we had successfully completed the development phase but knew that it would go down poorly back at SPT, which would see it as a loss in terms of prestige.

I took all of the paperwork home and after reading the Master Agreement between ourselves and BAA, took the view that Transport Scotland would be better placed to implement the plans we'd completed. As I'd anticipated, our politicians were concerned but reluctantly agreed my assessment that this merely reflected the shift in task that had been legislated previously in Parliament. We'd still retain the right to advance rail proposals but wouldn't build out the more substantial projects.

Some time later, the SNP Government, reeling after the Treasury cut budgets in real terms by their calculations of some half a billion pounds, decided to cancel the Glasgow Airport Rail Link in the face of furious opposition. So much effort had gone into the project. It was both a blow and a real disappointment that Glasgow Airport couldn't enjoy a rail link to its city in the way that most of its competitor cities could... and after all that fuss! Only time will tell if political and financial circumstances change sufficiently for the decision to be reversed.

Gordon remained very strong in respect of the reform agenda and spoke to me about the need to change comprehensively the way in which we dealt with our Trades Unions and the terms and conditions they'd enjoyed for years.

We set about creating expectations of change by developing a 'Customer Focus' strategy that gave us elbow room to challenge conditions that worked against customer primacy or where we felt efficiencies might be found. I met with Donald Martin, then the editor of both the *Evening Times* and *The Herald* as he had just taken his staff through just the process that Gordon and I intended to utilise within SPT. We sought best practice from other local authorities and set out a schedule that would see us work with the unions in order to modernise and to bring about efficiencies.

We made pretty decent progress in reviewing the terms and conditions of employment of all staff, particularly those of the Subway. The two representatives of Unison were upbeat, aware and supportive of the need for change but the reps on the Unite side were more suspicious and moved immediately to involve their full-time officials. We engaged the services of Alan Irwin, an academic from Ruskin College (the Trades Union College at Oxford University) who won the respect of the Convenors and Shop Stewards and who worked with us to bring about the flexibilities that we saw as being absolutely necessary if we were to modernise practices and meet the challenges of the reduced budgets we face as a consequence of the 2008 world recession.

However, the four 'Big Ticket Items' were dealt with expeditiously. We improved Partner and Stakeholder relationships quite dramatically, from 45% approval ratings in 2006, through 75% the following year to 92% in subsequent years where it's hovered ever since. We introduced Transport Outcome Reports that we negotiated with our local authorities that set an agreed six or seven annual initiatives, allocated resources around them and identified responsible individuals and time frames, thereby consigning the 1008 projects to the dustbin and creating a more reasonable and deliverable annual set of tasks that numbered around 80. We worked hard at developing our continuous improvement programme under Julie Riley, scored an astonishing 320 points first time out and were 'Recognised for Excellence' by Quality Scotland. The Chief Executive's Review was implemented across the organisation but might usefully have gone further in Subway Operations so Gordon brought in a small number of new senior managers and initiated a further review, telling those involved that they'd be expected to come up with radical efficiencies.

Each week I wrote a Weekly Note to all staff in which I set out all of the key issues facing the organisation and during 2009 I relentlessly reminded staff of the realities of the recession, pointing out that there's always a lag between the private sector entering and leaving a downward economic cycle and the public sector doing the same. We were in for a squeeze, the likes of which no one at work would have seen in their working life. SPT would face a substantial cut in both capital and revenue budgets and would have to face up to decisions to cut deeply into ferry and bus services, subway operations and back office staff functions. Some considerable time previously, I saw the need to prepare staff for the inevitability of cuts and we offered voluntary severance packages to reduce the numbers on the payroll. Our task was to balance the budget as it appeared probable that the final period of my time in public life would be focussed upon the diminution of many services rather than their enhancement. How ironic and how sad ... but markets and vicious economic realities don't spare anyone and people and institutions throughout the world have had to address the wounding effects of flawed banking systems in America and Europe.

In early December 2009, I was seated comfortably on the early morning West Coast Mainline train to London *en route* to attending a meeting with the senior officer responsible for counter-terrorism within British Transport Police as part of my Board responsibilities. The entire nation had been covered in a blanket of snow for days and everything was being delayed, cancelled, or postponed. Few planes flew. The train journey of four and a half hours took seven. Outside the scenery was a winter wonderland but I was in no mood to appreciate it.

For a couple of weeks previously, I hadn't been able to shake off a headache. Self-administered medication hadn't worked but I dismissed my symptoms as a tension headache. Everything would be ok once I managed to get a few days' rest over Christmas which was just round the corner. On the train, the discomfort became more intense and my heart started thumping as if it was attempting to burst out of my chest. I tried to fall asleep to calm things down but even having taken some tablets as a soporific, I couldn't command drowsiness. The meetings in London passed in a daze and I headed northwards feeling just as discomfited as I had been on the way south. Matters were compounded when the train arrived three and a half hours late after an eight hour journey and a disembodied voice informed everyone that it couldn't progress beyond Motherwell due to the weather. A freezing taxi journey onwards to Giffnock didn't help my mood or my condition.

I decided that I'd better check things out and secured a next-day appointment with Norrie Gaw, my doctor. It turned out that my blood pressure was sky-high and I was suffering from cardiac dysrhythmia – dangerous but controllable if treated and if I rested. Truth be told, I was heading for a fall. My lifestyle of many years had been characterised by burning the candle at both ends. Early morning starts, full-on meetings, no lunch but often getting home to ruffle the kids' hair before setting off for another evening meeting with a politician, media man, transport professional or adviser. No exercise, coupled with a lax approach to my diet, saw me put on some unneeded poundage, and it became clear that my body was beginning to protest. The headaches were a signal that my blood pressure was beginning to spin out of control. I needed to rest, and my doctor insisted that I take my medication, take time off work, to deal with what might otherwise become very serious indeed. I wasn't to appreciate it at the time, but my condition was sufficiently worrying and would require such rest and convalescence as would culminate in the Strathclyde Pension Fund eventually agreeing that I should be retired on the grounds of ill-health, on the basis that I would not be able to hold down my responsibilities over the foreseeable future. I certainly wouldn't be able to work at the level I had been used to.

Some months earlier, an enquiry had been made under the Freedom of Information Act whereby we had been asked to provide details of any foreign visits made by myself and senior colleagues in the previous three years. I was phlegmatic about this as it wasn't unusual to receive requests of this nature. Indeed, every time the Partnership approved a visit abroad it was contained within the Authority's papers which were routinely sent to all media outlets. Invariably there would be some column inches informing their readership of the visit and its purpose and these reports were invariably positive, highlighting the improvements we sought to implement as a consequence of the trip.

What I hadn't anticipated was that I was about to be swept up in a 'perfect storm'.

In May 2009, the *Daily Telegraph* newspaper began to issue daily bulletins which set out the expenses, often unreceipted, claimed by the country's Members of Parliament. As details emerged, the public mood changed from shock to outrage to anger. MPs were claiming famously to have a moat cleaned, they paid money to their own companies, they avoided capital gains tax on their second homes, claimed pornographic movies on expenses, continued to claim for mortgages that had been redeemed or had not existed and in one celebrated case, sought public money to have a duck house built on a lake in their rural idyll.

Taking, not unreasonably, a commercial line as well as a sensationalist one, the *Daily Telegraph* eked out the stories day by day, week by week. It caused all other arms of the media to await the revelations that sped from the *Daily Telegraph*'s presses each morning before they too could comment and join the siren call for retribution. After gorging themselves on Westminster, enquiries turned to Holyrood ... to local councils ... to Quangos and then to SPT. Still ill-abed, I was being sheltered from the intensity of the enquiry by well-meaning colleagues – and to be honest, I wasn't in a fit state to assist much anyway.

The London *Times*, once regarded as a 'newspaper of record' was first off the blocks and reported the trips taken by senior staff but presented it in such a way that the time span was conflated, allowing a reader to presume that these trips were all taken one after the other as opposed to over a period of four years, monies spent were agglomerated to sensationalise the article and a measure of ambiguation was introduced to permit a reader to assume that I had taken part in every trip. No copy presented the benefits that were accrued, the ambitions we had ... everything was thrown on to a bonfire of accusation and faux outrage.

Understandably, the local broadsheets followed – but the tone had been set. It became an 'expenses row'. Set now against the banking collapse and a new frugality, it provided a dripping roast for the media.

Steven Purcell's top media man, Colin Edgar, phoned me at home and asked after my health. He went on to ask whether I felt well enough to see him and Steven. I recognised the request for what it was, an opportunity for Steven to ask my thoughts about my own situation. In the event, Steven and Colin were most hospitable and friendly. Prior to his arrival I had in any event contemplated my own thoughts about what I wanted to do and was well aware that the sensible approach to take was to advise everyone that as I was off work on long-term sick leave, that I was quite content to await the findings of Audit Scotland and base any decision regarding my future on their verdict. I was entirely confident that they would have no grounds to criticise me as all of the trips abroad which had caused so much controversy had been predicated upon a business need, reflected the ambitious goals we sought to achieve for the travelling public of the west of Scotland, had been approved in advance by a full Partnership meeting (unanimously and across party boundaries) and had been positively reported each time by the media during a time when economic conditions were much more propitious.

However, I felt dreadfully ill, tired and melancholic and decided that it made sense to seek early retirement on the grounds of ill-health. My personal digital photograph library had been hacked into, digital information from other personal files turned up in the columns of newspapers and my home was besieged by journalists looking for comment. However, the entire *imbroglio* had also taken place on my watch so I did also feel a sense of maintaining my honour as well as my health in electing to retire.

That said, I also felt a real sense of frustration as I was well aware of the political agenda being pursued by the London *Times*; 'present all you can as redolent of Labour sleaze'. The 2010 Parliamentary elections were a couple of months away and Gordon Brown was trailing David Cameron in the polls – but not so distantly that a Tory administration could be considered as taken for granted... so all hands to the pump. Equally, the nationalist press saw political advantage in seeing regular criticism of a Labour administration and the story fitted this strategy perfectly given their lead in the polls falling dramatically along with the upcoming requirement to hold a Scottish election only twelve months later. So I decided to be as phlegmatic and as philosophical as possible and get on with my life. My health, my family and friends were more important.

The doctor selected by the Strathclyde Pension Fund to assess health capacity is an independent person whose sole concern is to consider the ability of someone to continue in employment. He determined that my health had deteriorated to the point where I was not capable of returning to work and I was encouraged to retire from all other Board appointments, including the Wise Group and the British Transport Police Authority on grounds of ill-health. On 26 March 2010, exactly four years after I had started as Chief Executive of SPT, I retired. I had my bus pass. I was now a pensioner.

In May 2010, only some weeks after I had retired, Audit Scotland produced a report that listed the nine complaints made by various elements of the media and, as I'd anticipated, did not find against me, but I did feel a measure of frustration about the way in which the press dealt with matters such as this. News is now available 24 hours a day on satellite television as well as on-line. In order to find a role for themselves, newspapers today have to rely upon breaking a local story that won't initially interest the big boys. To sell papers this story has to be dramatic and conflictual and to ensure that this is the case, information has to be brought to the attention of a real or imagined adversary who has to intimate their outrage at the event. Increasingly, the media 'sells' a story rather than 'tells' a story.

Sometimes information has to be concealed to make a story worthy of inclusion. One year I had attended the Politician of the Year Award in Edinburgh sponsored by the *Herald* newspaper which encouraged my attendance. After it finished, around 1.00 am, I took a taxi back to

Glasgow in the company of three others, thereby saving the cost of four bed-nights in an Edinburgh hotel. No other transport alternative was available. The journalist writing the piece knew all of this but merely reported that I had taken a taxi from Edinburgh to Glasgow, thereby permitting the notion that I did this casually during the day on my own rather than take the train – which I always did – but then, there's no story in that. Increasingly, it seems that the venerable broadsheets of old have adopted some tabloid tendencies to meet the new commercial and political objectives they face.

Again, timing is everything in respect of public opinion. When the media supports your endeavours, comments are benign. Any slip is merely a mis-step on the way to a wider and much desired objective. However, *per contra*, when the mood changes, situations are magnified and previous convictions recalled and reinterpreted in a way that suits the new attitude. Motives can be misrepresented and your sincerity and ethics can be derided. But it is perhaps the apparent blanket of cynicism that troubles me most. Scotland can ill-afford to be a nation with little ambition. It must rise to great challenges and will fail in some but a media and body-politic which seem to take a delight in berating attempts to achieve these heights do not serve the nation well. I cannot stress enough the crucial importance of high speed ground transport, mobile inward investment, the digitalisation of the economy, large scale regeneration, business sector re-engineering. And in the case of certain of these, you just can't deliver without an appreciation of how the world's best are addressing the matter. If high speed rail eventually connects London to Leeds or Manchester but no further, it's going to be a wounding blow to the Scottish economy. Make no mistake. But to make the case for a £32 billion investment, you don't draft a business case on the back of an envelope or research it on the internet; you do it properly and if that means meeting those in other countries who have already implemented that which we would see in our own country, then so be it.

18. I Hope You Dance.

There's no hurry any more, when all is said and done.
Abba

I trust that I'm not tempting fate when I remind myself of the quote of Captain Edwin. J. Smith who said, "In all my experience I've never been in an accident, or any worth speaking about. I've seen but one vessel in distress in all my days at sea. Nor was I ever in any predicament that threatened to end in disaster of any sort." This was the last diary entry of Captain Smith before he edged the *RMS Titanic* out of port on its maiden voyage in 1907. He planned to retire after the voyage.

Well, as I begin to edge out of port, I guess I've been very fortunate in my life. I've enjoyed my time on earth. My family and I have avoided war, plague and pestilence and I've been loved by those I've loved. I've coped with a couple of recessions and weathered a couple of pandemic alerts. I've been educated. I've developed great friendships and I've laughed A lot.

Those of my Grandfather's generation got something of a raw deal. Hector was of an age to have lived through the First World War, a global recession, the Second World War, the Suez Crisis, the Korean War and then lived in some significant level of fear over the prospect of a nuclear bomb coming down his chimney during the Cuba crisis. Born in 1901 and died in 1981. Uncertainty and apprehension must have dogged him. Me? I missed strife almost in its entirety. I was a very fortunate man who witnessed and participated in the most transformational and rapid technological changes ever known. Wars were always distant and when they involved British troops, only required enlisted men. Medical breakthroughs were commonplace and European integration brought not only greater understanding but regulations that made my world safer if more homogenised.

My five senses have been used to great effect. With my eyes, I've seen the birth of my four children, sunset over Iona, the inside of a Space Shuttle, the Grand Canyon, and the proud smile on the face of each of my boys as they've achieved something important to them. I've watched a man walk on the surface of the moon. I've plumbed the depths of the Mediterranean Sea in a submarine and flown over Vietnam just as did the American bombers against which I protested in the 60's and 70's. With my ears I've listened to the soundtrack of my life played by Eric Clapton, Willie Nelson, Ry Cooder, Abba (oft derided but great melodies and harmonies) and most of all The Beatles. Daily, I've listened to those around me laughing. I've kissed the nape of my wife's neck, kissed the Blarney Stone, shaken the hand of President Bill Clinton and had dinner and breakfast the following morning with Tony Blair. I've scented the wonderful, beery smell of dank, spit and sawdust Glasgow pubs, caught the smell of wood-smoke on the wind, Johnson's baby-powder on my kids' bums and the addictive scent of burned toast. With my lips, I've helped people agree, made people laugh and *usually* with regret, made people cry.

In the process of living, I've been able to identify those values that inspire me and have had an opportunity to try to live up to them. The icing on the cake has been the opportunity that fate has dealt me to serve the city I love; the City of Glasgow. I've also been inspired by my friends and many of my acquaintances over the years.

I was inspired by Michael Carroll whose teachings helped John McManus and I so much in our thirties. A man of religion reaching John and I - me at least, a heathen; despite the odds. I was inspired by John himself who, aged fourteen, was condemned by a crap educational system to a future as a farm labourer, but

410

who became a highly successful consultant, despite the odds. I recently came across another inspirational man called Bill Winning, an erstwhile 'toerag' in his own words, whose young life growing up in Parkhead was punctuated by run-ins with the law but who found Jesus and raised a wonderful family. He is a real working-class hero, who sees his job these days as simply, 'just loving people' and holding to his socialist convictions, despite the odds.

I was inspired by John Matthews who took cloth after fashioning a very successful career with Union Carbide and became the *Reverend* John Matthews who still today serves Ruchill, one of the poorest communities in Glasgow and somehow maintains the drive and passion to care for his flock, despite the odds that he'd be wedded to big business for the rest of his life. John Matthews is a force of nature, supporting the poor in Ruchill as opposed to chasing the mighty dollar… despite the odds.

And I was inspired by those with whom I've genuinely been privileged to have worked with over the years; all of whom I hold in great affection and many of whom I count as friends…Gordon Maclennan, Ann-marie Waugh, Pamela Millar, Julie Riley, David Christie, Donnie McLeod, Tom Hughes, Bruce Kiloh, Rodney Mortimer, Alan Murray, Debbie Mackie, Alistair Mitchell, Stuart Patrick, Gordon Kennedy, David Whitton, John Crawford, Peter Reilly, Raymond Hendry, Alison Sinclair, Tommy Docherty, Richie Cameron, George Burns, Allan Thomson, Jim Carruth, Steve Inch, Simon Clark, Bob Baldry, Kevin Doran, Colin Edgar, Sandy Forrest, Jeane Freeman, Jim Tait, Steven Purcell, Sohan Singh Randhawa, George Thomson, Calum Graham, Ian and Kate McAlpine, Gary Hamilton, Danny and Marj Logue, Colin Keenan, Fraser Kelly, Ian Manson, John Matthews, Lindsay McGarvie, Jamie McGrattan, Stewart McIlwraith, Kevin McKenna, Alastair McManus, Betty Cunningham, Alistair Watson,

Davie McLachlan, Davie Fagan, Eddie Phillips, Bill Perry, Professor Tom Carbery, John McLaughlin, Sharon Ward, Jim McPhie, Maggie Morrison, Ian Patterson, Sir Willie Rae, Sir Alex Ferguson, Neil Rankin, Ed Crozier, Lorne Crerar, Ken Symon, George Redmond, Tom O'Neill, Vic Emery, Eleanor Walker, Craig Gardner, Oli Norman, Robert Gall, Billy Barnes and many, many others. Yet more are celebrated throughout the pages of this book.

Since my first appointment as a Chief Executive, some twenty-three years ago, I've been fortunate in that my work-life has been guided by a posse of wonderful personal assistants; PAs as they're known. Variously, Jean Pollock, Anne McFadden, Susan Dumigan and Shona Young have all looked after me superbly well, have structured my day for me, made all of my arrangements and generally allowed me the space to run whatever business in which I was engaged at the time. I was so taken by my first PA that I married her!

Some time ago, I remember reflecting on the question, *who would I rather have been if not myself,* and after considering a raft of contenders, friends as well as the famous, I couldn't think of anyone whose life or lifestyle tempted me more than my own. It kind of suggests I've been contented with my lot and I suppose I have. For a while I imagined I'd like to acquire the wit and erudition of a younger Stephen Fry but over the years I find that inadvertently I have developed only his girth and general lumpiness. Perhaps the effortless sincerity and charm of Michael Palin? I might have preferred to have been as accomplished as John McManus or Gordon Maclennan in the DIY field or as astute a punter as Laurie Russell… perhaps even as *fit* as Laurie or as intellectual as Stuart Patrick or my two oldest sons Ron or Campbell. But overall, I wouldn't trade my personality and makeup for anyone else.

I've been fortunate in having lived during a period when the world opened up to permit witness of its wonders like never before. Author Clive James points out in his book, 'Cultural Amnesia' that Mozart never heard most of the works of Bach. Manet never saw all of his own works in the one place, but my generation could. Transport miracles have permitted me to see more of the world than the greatest explorers. Over my life, as Cristiano Ronaldo dazzled the crowds at Old Trafford and the Bernabéu the next Cristiano Ronaldo could watch and emulate him, in real time, from the comfort of his home in Rio de Janeiro, Mogadishu or Beijing. The world got smaller and more interdependent. More than ever before it became possible to understand the auld Scots' saying, "We're a' Jock Tamson's bairns". It was perhaps put best by President John Fitzgerald Kennedy who, in a speech at a university in Washington in 1963, said pretty much the same thing if more poetically. "We all inhabit this small planet. We all breathe the same air. We all cherish our children's future. And we are all mortal."

I guess that happiness is a relative term as well as an absolute but on both counts I've been a happy man, if one who has endured the normal sadnesses of life when relationships have ended or when those close to me have died or become ill. I've never been religious since my enforced, pre-teens attendance at church when the Reverend Campbell, Minister of Priesthill Parish Church, used to stand in the pulpit of a Sunday morning and fulminate against Roman Catholics. It sat awkwardly with me then and it instilled in me a life-long cynicism about organised religion which I'm yet confident is little more than superstition. War after war has been fought in the name of religion and while it would be comforting to permit the notion that we'll all meet again in the wide blue yonder, I guess by my take on life, it's not to be. I'll have to say goodbye and be done with it. In some small way, I suspect that this book is my way of compensating for the absence of belief. I don't anticipate being able to have these conversations when I'm gone so I'd better share them while I can.

Also, second time round I was an 'older father'. I was 48 when Ciaran was born so I'm not sure whether I'll see his great grandchildren graduate sometime around 2110. If not, I hope that these memoirs might provide some context, some family history.

I've had a great time. A really wonderful time. It's been a blast. What really matters to me as I finish this autumnal life-chapter is the ongoing health and happiness of friends and family. My life task going forward as I see it is to further enable that prospect. I've had my fair share.

Although I have dedicated my future life to taking my foot off the work/sleep accelerator, I expect that there will be some unexpected twists and turns in the way I spend my waking hours. Given the pace of technological changes and the fact that change must now be measured intra-generationally rather than inter-generationally, I'm really looking forward to the gadgets and medicaments of tomorrow which, I'm certain will transform our lives in ways we probably can't even imagine. I still want to visit Iceland before it melts, witness the *aurora borealis* in a winter sky from the Outer Hebrides, see new cities, meet new people, watch the new Scottish Parliament flourish, write more stuff, see the Pyramids, traverse the globe, continue my hobby of convivial temulence, write a travel book and a novel set in Glasgow, laugh at new jokes, visit Australia, serve the city I love in some way and provide for and enjoy the ongoing health and success of friends and family.

I anticipate the prospect of retirement with mixed feelings. There are mornings when the thought of just pottering about my home office has a certain appeal, especially if I'm feeling tired. That said, when on holiday and expected to relax, I have to confess that it's not something at which I'm particularly good. I actually experience mild feelings of stress if I don't have some sort of programme, a project, a book, a task to occupy me. Without some sort of work compass, I'm adrift in a sea of boredom so in consequence I find myself creating things to do just to be doing something … an issue I suspect I'll now have to master.

My hypochondriacal tendencies increase slightly as the aches and pains of ageing kick in. My lower back, always a reminder that I'm no longer the football playing athlete of my youth, is continually problematic. Gout pains my big toe and I can feel the early onset of arthritis in my fingers, making the playing of the chord of 'F' on guitar painful and difficult. Presently, prescription medicines and very little exercise are keeping immobility at bay but I do have a sense that this is a problem I have to make go away before it begins to limit my ability to walk round to the pub.

I also find myself becoming more irascible as I head towards my sixties. Perhaps this too, comes with old age. I suspect it's a 'Grumpy Old Man' thing, however. A real sense of irritation whenever I come across thoughtlessness or selfishness. I find it hard not to sigh inwardly even where this misdemeanour is minor … like the person who packs all of their groceries at the check-out, smiles beatifically at the attendant before remembering that they require to pay for their goods, and then, and only then, start to fumble around in their bag for means to settle their debt.

So, who knows? My autumnal years might see me become a hirpling, crabbit, social isolate grumping away at all and sundry or perhaps I might find a fulfilling life seeing more interesting parts of the world and enjoying the company of friends and family. I hope, and expect, that it'll be the latter. But let me know if you see me slipping.

I conclude these pages in the autumn of 2010 having been retired now for some eight months. And as I turn my attention to proof-reading the text I earlier committed to my memory-sticks, I reflect that upon commencement of this tome some years ago, I would have actually committed my bletherings to paper. A memory-stick the size of my middle finger is now more powerful than my first home computer, such is the pace of change we have experienced.

And in deciding to stop writing and publish, I do so in the knowledge that I leave incomplete so many unanswered questions. What events are yet to unfold involving my family in terms of their health, relationships, new members, achievements and disappointments?

In respect of Glasgow, how will my efforts to modernise the workforce of SPT pan out in the longer run? Will Glasgow's economy prosper? What about ambitions such as building a mass-transit system for Glasgow and its conurbation? How will our peripheral estates fare under the new economic vicissitudes that we all face? Modernising the Subway? How about high speed rail from London to Glasgow and from Glasgow to Edinburgh, whether Maglev or conventional? Can inward mobile investment to the city continue in the face of our economic *travails*? Politically will Scotland continue to shape and reshape its constitution? Are there more coalitions in prospect or might we return to one-party government such as I was used to for most of my life?

I've worked hard successfully to bring many operational ideas to the attention of decision makers in both Parliaments but will any one of the political parties have the ability to address any of them? Will the sum of my efforts provide for a greener Glasgow; one where technological advances demonstrate the obvious truth stated earlier, that it's easier to move electrons than atoms? Will the present recession limit any ability to do anything but reduce the quality of public services that I and so many others have devoted our working lives to improving? How will my friends and family fare as they face the same challenges I do and more besides?

In 2008, I invited a 'motivational speaker' to address a gathering of staff. As part of his routine, he teased listeners with a promise that not only had he worked out the secret of life but that he'd reveal it at the end of his speech. He eventually went on to tell us that he'd figured out that this was, "Build a strong family and love them, develop great friendships and nurture them and make a positive contribution to society". Perhaps more the *purpose* of life, but not bad, not bad. It comes pretty close to my own thoughts and in this regard, I hope that the love and respect I have for my family and friends shines from every page of these, my recollections. It is to them (or *you*, dear reader if you're one of them) that I owe my greatest debts of gratitude.

I mentioned earlier that I was attracted to the musical simplicity of the Country and Western *genre* as well as the homespun philosophy it embraces....*Three Chords and the Truth...* Hell, yeah! One song, written by Tia Sillers, seems to me to sum up my approach to life if not, ironically, to the dance-floor, suggesting as it does that taking the initiative, just *doing* it, taking the path less travelled, surprising people... provides a richer, more fulfilling life experience. A lovely melody adds lustre to these lyrics which end each verse;

And if you get the chance,
to sit it out or dance....
I hope you dance.

Well, I hope you dance.

I did.

My four Boys. (Top left to right, clockwise)
Campbell, Conor, Ron and Ciaran Culley.

With my wife Jean.

*Consummate politicians all…and Margaret Thatcher. (Top left to right, clockwise)
With Bill Clinton, with Tony Blair, with Donald Dewar, Thatcher, Fidel Castro,
with George Abbey, with Sir Alex Ferguson.*

421

Extended family. (Top left to right, top to bottom.) All Culleys unless noted.
Alastair, Holly, Sean, Ronnie Pollok, my dad Ronnie, Francesca, Campbell, mum May, Arran,
Lisa, Ron, Raymond, Anne, Claire, Matthew Pollok, Margaret, grandmother Madge McLeod, Bobbi
Pollok, Bobby Pollok, Jack Pollok, Alastair, grandfather Hector McLeod, Campbell, Hannah.

Friends and colleagues. (Top left to right, top to bottom.)
Gordon Maclennan, Sohan Singh, Irene Graham, Neil Graham, Tom O'Neil, Stuart Patrick,
Bob Wylie, Tadhg Dennehy, Alan Blackie, Rev. John Matthews, Mary Dennehy, Colin Keenan,
Gary Hamilton, Ian McAlpine, John McManus, David Christie, Steven Purcell, Kate McAlpine,
Laurie Russell, Eleanor Walker, Danny Logue, Bill Miller, Pamela Millar, David Asquith,
Ann-marie Waugh, Debbie Mackie, Julie Riley, Bob Baldry, Jim Tait, Shona Young,
Alan McCreath, Billy Barnes, Fraser Kelly, Ed Crozier, Vic Emery, Alan Murray,
Jim Carruth, Jeane Freeman, John McLaughlin.

The seven ages of man. (Top left to right, top to bottom.)
Aged 2. Thinking of joining the IRA apparently. Aged 12, school photograph. Aged 22. A hippy working in America. Aged 32 on holiday in Glasgow. Aged 42 on holiday in Cyprus. Aged 52 at Scottish Enterprise. Aged 60. Driving Route 66 in America with John McManus and Laurie Russell. It was Westminster election results night and I thought the Native American owned hotel guests should be made privy to my political views.

The author in his prime.

Index

Broomloan Road 196
Bruce, Sue *see* Sue Angus
Brussels 5, 166, 259, 323, 350
Buchanan Street 239, 384
Buggins' turn 191, 241
Bundy 76, 101
Burnbrae Folk Club 77, 78, 100
Burns, Robert 22, 85, 224, 366, 370, 374, 376, 377, 411
Business of the Year in Scotland 213
Business Transformation 275, 277, 278, 386
Butchard, Robert 85
Butler, Bill MSP 334
Byres Road 108, 198, 384

C

Cairnbaan 51
Calderwood, Sir Robert 167, 168, 176, 182, 186
Calvert, Rev Robert 224
Cameron, Richie 193, 248, 411
Canavan, Denis MP 245
Candren Oval 117
Caprington 130, 133, 141
Carbery, Prof Tom 27, 412
Cardonald College 68, 127, 187, 191
Careers Scotland 310, 355
Carroll, Michael 135, 136, 158, 410
Carruth, Jim 192, 259, 363, 411
Carson, Les 33, 34, 38, 39, 50, 52, 58, 59, 61, 74, 347
Castlemilk 94, 185
Castro, Fidel 320, 321, 322
Catterson, Ian 387
Celtic FC 21, 87, 89, 90, 177, 178, 181, 186, 264, 330, 349, 375

Chancellor Bar 198, 199, 200, 255, 278, 320, 321
Charing Cross 9, 239, 348
Chatham House Rules 305
Chief Executive's Department 150, 167, 174, 252, 311
Children's Hearings 96
Chisholm , Malcolm MSP 306
Christie, David 194, 388, 411
Clark, Jonathon 357, 390, 411
Clinton , President Bill 367, 410
Closs, Davie 77
Clyde Arc, The (Squinty Bridge) 282
Clyde FC 86
Coliseum Cinema 72
Community Council, Riccarton 133, 134, 138, 139, 249
Community Development 126, 134, 157, 160
Community Education Service 175
Connolly, Billy 80, 120, 319, 377
Coodham 135, 138, 139, 141, 142, 158, 230
Cordoba 377
Corkerhill 12
Corries, The 73, 79, 374
Coutts, Big Davie 259, 260
Craigbank 7, 18, 19, 28, 75, 85
Crampsey, Bob 181
Crawford, Robert 18, 268, 271-277, 280-296, 309, 315, 316, 327, 333, 411
Crème de Bull 107
Crerar, Lorne 412
Crew, The 76, 101, 356
Croftfoot 127, 128, 130
Crofthouse Road 127
Crossflat Crescent 126
Crossroads Youth and Community Association 175

McMurtrie, Ian 141, 145, 150
McPhie, Jim 412
McQuarrie, Rev Stuart 251, 253, 296

M

Mackie, Debbie 271, 277, 388, 411
Maine 110
Malletsheugh Pub 347
Manchester United viii, 188, 204, 229, 345, 368
Manpower Services Commission 134
Manson, Ian 411
Manufacturing Assistance Programme 275
Marie Celeste 279, 280
Martin, Michael MP 160
Martin, Paul MSP 329
Martin, David MEP 336, 337
Martin, Donald 399
Maryhill 200, 229
Matthews, Rev John 305, 307, 308, 334, 411
May, Terry 109, 114,
Militant Tendency 94, 95, 122, 156, 359
Millan, Bruce 249, 250, 364
Millar, Joan 141
Miller, Bill MEP 155, 176, 312, 323, 336, 349, 411
Miller, Pamela 387
Moray House College of Education 114, 115, 126
Morrison, Maggie 412
Mortimer , Rodney 411
Morton, Bill 271, 272, 288, 302
Mosson , Alex 312, 313, 315, 316, 317, 320, 321
MSF 248
Mullen, Jim 193, 196, 223

Murden, Terry 293
Murphy, Jim MP 250
Murray, Alan 85, 107, 248, 326, 327, 387, 411

N

Newton, Pop 53, 58, 80, 181, 203, 347
Nil Sine Labore 206
Nitshill 28, 44, 47, 85
Noble, Mr 37

O

Oldrey, Brian 165
Old Trafford 206, 207, 208, 227, 413
One Devonshire Gardens 106
O'Neill, Tom 262, 263, 267, 284, 292, 295, 307, 308, 333, 412
Orchard Park Folk Club 33, 77, 78, 79, 8, 100
Organisation for Economic Co-operation and Development (OECD) 282, 375

P

Paisley 12, 73, 74, 98, 116, 121, 122, 124, 126, 127, 160, 164, 171, 172, 202, 217, 327, 377
Palace Theatre 147
Paris 221, 222, 324, 368, 375
Parkhead 89, 177, 391, 411
Partick, Stuart 158, 193, 201, 268, 271, 272, 275, 277, 282, 373, 411, 412
Patrick, Brother 158
Patterson, Ian 412
Perry, Bill 177, 178, 261, 293, 294, 295, 296, 297, 298, 299, 300, 301, 302, 310, 380, 412

`,... also ...

get it right

up ye!

R

xxx

Lightning Source UK Ltd.
Milton Keynes UK
10 January 2011

165434UK00005B/9/P

9 781845 301002